THE BRITISH GENERAL STAFF

CASS SERIES: MILITARY HISTORY AND POLICY
Series Editors: John Gooch and Brian Holden Reid
ISSN: 1465-8488

This series will publish studies on historical and contemporary aspects of land power, spanning the period from the eighteenth century to the present day, and will include national, international and comparative studies. From time to time, the series will publish edited collections of essays and 'classics'.

THE BRITISH GENERAL STAFF
Reform and Innovation
*c.*1890–1939

Edited by

DAVID FRENCH
University College London

and

BRIAN HOLDEN REID
King's College London

FRANK CASS
LONDON • PORTLAND, OR

First published in 2002 in Great Britain by
FRANK CASS PUBLISHERS
Chase House, 47 Chase Side, Southgate
London N14 5BP

and in the United States of America by
FRANK CASS PUBLISHERS
c/o ISBS, 5824 N.E. Hassalo Street
Portland, Oregon, 97213-3644

Website: www.frankcass.com

British Library Cataloguing in Publication Data

The British General Staff: reform and innovation,
c.1890–1939. – (Cass series. Military history and policy;
10)
1. Great Britain, Army, General Staff – History 2. Great
Britain – History, Military – 19th century 3. Great Britain
– History, Military – 20th century
I. French, David, 1954– II. Reid, Brian Holden
355.3'3042'0941'09034

ISBN 0-7146-5325-X (cloth)
ISSN 1465-8488

Library of Congress Cataloging-in-Publication Data

The British General Staff: reform and innovation, c. 1890–1939 / edited by David French
and Brian Holden Reid.
    p.   cm. – (Cass series–military history and policy; no. 10)
Includes bibliographical references and index.
ISBN 0-7146-5325-X (cloth)
  1. Great Britain. Army. General Staff–History–19th century. 2. Great Britain. Army.
General Staff–History–20th century. I. French, David, 1954– II. Reid, Brian Holden.
III. Series.

UA649.3 .B75 2002
355.3'3'09410904–dc21   2002026782

Typeset in Sabon, 10.5 on 12pt by Vitaset, Paddock Wood, Kent
Printed in Great Britain by
MPG Books Ltd, Victoria Square, Bodmin, Cornwall

Contents

Acknowledgements

The editors and authors are grateful to the following people and institutions for permission to quote from material to which they own the copyright: Australian War Memorial (Bean mss); the British Library Board (Arnold-Forster); the Director of the Royal United Services Institute for Defence Studies; the Foundation Nationale des Sciences Politiques; the Trustees of the Liddell Hart Centre for Military Archives, King's College London (Alanbrooke mss; Bartholomew mss; Hamilton mss; Howell mss; Liddell Hart mss; Montgomery-Massingberd mss; O'Connor mss); the Masters and Fellows of Churchill College, Cambridge University (Bonham-Carter mss; Cavan mss; Esher mss; Hore-Belisha mss); the Mitchell Library, State Library of New South Wales (G. B. Hughes mss; J. T. Hutton mss); the National Army Museum (Roberts mss; Wilkinson mss); National Library of Scotland (Haig mss); the Piggott family (papers of Major-General F. S. G. Piggott); Queen Mary and Westfield College (Lyttelton mss); the Service Historique de l'Armée de Terre; the Librarian at the University of Sheffield (Malcolm Kennedy papers); the Trustees of the Imperial War Museum (Pender–Cudlip papers, Wilson mss). Dr Towle's efforts to contact the members of the Wards family through the Imperial War Museum have failed, but he hopes that they would feel he has made appropriate and sensitive use of the papers in the Wards collection.

Crown copyright material appears by kind permission of the Public Record Office, Kew. Quotations from the Royal Archives appear by gracious permission of Her Majesty the Queen.

An earlier version of Dr Harris's chapter was first published in the *Bulletin of the Institute of Historical Research*.

The editors and authors wish to apologise to anyone whose copyrights they have inadvertently infringed. All of the individual authors owe a myriad of personal debts to friends and colleagues who have assisted them in so many ways. We hope that they will forgive us if we do not mention each of them by name, but our gratitude is none the less very real.

Abbreviations

AHQ	Army Headquarters
AIF	Australian Imperial Force
AWM	Australian War Memorial
BEF	British Expeditionary Force
BGGS	Brigadier-General, General Staff
BL	British Library
CAB	Cabinet
CAC	Churchill Archives Centre, Cambridge
CGS	Chief of the General Staff
CGSI	Chief of the General Staff in India
CID	Committee of Imperial Defence
CIGS	Chief of the Imperial General Staff
C-in-C	Commander-in-Chief
CO	Colonial Office
DBFP	*Documents on British Foreign Policy*
DDSD	Deputy Director of Staff Duties
DMI	Director of Military Intelligence
DMO	Director of Military Operations
DMO&I	Director of Military Operations and Intelligence
DMT	Director of Military Training
DPR	Defence Policy and Requirements Sub-Committee
DRC	Defence Requirements Committee
DSD	Director of Staff Duties
FBI	Federation of British Industries
FO	Foreign Office
GHQ	General Headquarters
GOC	General Officer Commanding
GOC-in-C	General Officer Commanding-in-Chief
GSO	General Staff Officer
IGS	Imperial General Staff
IWM	Imperial War Museum
JAWM	*Journal of the Australian War Memorial*

ABBREVIATIONS

LHCMA	Liddell Hart Centre for Military Archives, King's College, London
MGGS	Major-General, General Staff
MLS	Mitchell Library, Sydney
NAM	National Army Museum
NCO	non-commissioned officer
NLS	National Library of Scotland
OIOC	Oriental and India Office Collection
PP	Parliamentary Papers
PRO	Public Record Office
psc	passed Staff College
QMG	Quartermaster-General
QMWC	Queen Mary and Westfield College, University of London
RA	Royal Archives
RAF	Royal Air Force
RAMC	Royal Army Medical Corps
RASC	Royal Army Service Corps
RFC	Royal Flying Corps
RNAS	Royal Naval Air Service
RE	Royal Engineers
RTC	Royal Tank Corps
SHAT	Service Historique de l'Armée de Terre
WO	War Office

Works written or edited by Brian Bond

Victorian Military Campaigns, ed.
  (London: Hutchinson, 1967).
The Victorian Army and the Staff College, 1854–1914
  (London: Eyre Methuen, 1972).
Chief of Staff: The Diaries of Lieutenant-General Sir Henry Pownall, 1933–44, ed.
  (London: Leo Cooper, 2 vols, 1972–74).
France and Belgium 1939–1940
  (London: Davis-Poynter, 1975).
War and Society, ed. with Ian Roy
  (London: Croom Helm, 1976–77).
Liddell Hart: A Study of his Military Thought
  (London: Cassell, 1977).
British Military Policy between the Two World Wars
  (Oxford: Clarendon, 1980).
War and Society in Europe, 1870–1970
  (London: Fontana, 1984).
Staff Officer: The Diaries of Lord Moyne 1914–1918,
  ed. with Simon Robbins
  (London: Leo Cooper, 1987).
Fallen Stars: Eleven Studies of Twentieth Century Military Disasters, ed.
  (London: Brassey's, 1991).
The First World War and British Military History, ed.
  (Oxford: Clarendon Press, 1991).
The Pursuit of Victory: From Napoleon to Saddam Hussein
  (Oxford: Oxford University Press, 1996).
'Look to your Front': Studies in the First World War by the British Commission for Military History, ed.
  (Staplehurst, Kent: Spellmount, 1999).
Haig: A Reappraisal 70 Years On, ed. with Nigel Cave
  (Barnsley, South Yorkshire: Leo Cooper, 1999).
The Battle for France and Flanders 1940: Sixty Years On, ed. with Michael Taylor
  (London: Leo Cooper, 2001).

Introduction:
Brian Bond, Military Historian

Brian Holden Reid

Among historians engaged in the military realm from about 1960 onwards, Brian Bond has been outstanding both in the range and also in the scholarly quality of his work. Bond has had many pupils and has had a profound influence on the development of his profession. Working in the Department of War Studies, King's College, London, for 35 years, he has taught a large proportion of the military historians writing in Britain today. The present volume is a tribute paid by his friends, pupils and those whose doctoral theses he has examined.

Brian Bond was born in Medmenham, a small village near Marlow, Buckinghamshire, in 1936. He attended the Sir William Borlase's Grammar School in Marlow before going up to Worcester College, Oxford, in 1956, having gained a National Service Commission in the Royal Artillery (1954–56). A countryman born and bred, he still lives in his parents' house. At Worcester College he was an enthusiastic games player (College 1st XI in soccer and cricket; 1st XV rugby), and a future academic career was not mooted. His tutor, the late H. G. Pitt, enjoyed a close relationship with many of his pupils, but Bond was not admitted to this inner circle. Pitt had come to the conclusion that Bond was a games-playing grammar school master and he strongly discouraged Bond's ambitions to undertake postgraduate research.

Consequently, Bond felt rather rejected by his College, though he remains devoted to Oxford. Pitt could be rather indulgent when the mood took him. One of his favourites shrugged off a superficial essay with the frank admission that 'If I read more than one book I get confused'. But in December 1958 chance was to play a major part in overcoming this early setback when Captain (later Sir) Basil Liddell Hart moved to States House, Medmenham, from Wolverton Park, also in Buckinghamshire. He lived in Medmenham until his death in January 1970. Bond makes clear his profound, personal debt to Liddell Hart in his later work, *Liddell Hart:*

1

A Study of his Military Thought (1977). Liddell Hart read his under-graduate essays, allowed Bond to use his huge library and gave him signed copies of his works. But this was not all. His most important legacy 'was that he encouraged me to believe that I was good enough to make a career as a military historian'. Bond became an 'unofficial research assistant' and protégé of Liddell Hart. 'He went to a lot of trouble in persuading me to "stick it out" and in helping me to take the all-important first step on the academic ladder.'[1]

As Bond emphasised in his Inaugural Lecture, he only had two teachers, Liddell Hart and Michael Howard. The former put Bond in touch with the latter, then a lecturer in the History Department at King's College, London. Although Bond might have felt rejected by his principal college tutor, he was singularly fortunate in his teachers – the two most important influences on the writing of military history in Britain during the last half of the twentieth century.[2]

The attitudes that Liddell Hart and Howard inculcated in Bond were broadly similar. Both emphasised literary skills – Liddell Hart was very fussy about grammar and punctuation and the presentation of literary work. He was also strict about the employment of sources, and in estab-lishing who did what and when.[3] Much of Liddell Hart's philosophy of history was determined by his belief in great men; Bond was influenced by this view although he was not persuaded by it to the same extent. None the less, he shared his mentor's fascination with the life and career of T. E. Lawrence (the historical figure he would most like to have met). But Liddell Hart's approach to history was more journalistic than academic. He was casual, for instance, in his prejudice against footnotes on the frivolous grounds that they clutter up a page and distract readers. More seriously, Liddell Hart was so intent on deriving relevant 'lessons' from the past that he seldom wrote about it for its own intrinsic interest. Never-theless, Liddell Hart's patronage was enormously beneficial. Bond was given the opportunity to meet the likes of Bernard Levin, Sir Reginald (later Lord) Paget QC, and Lord Chalfont. It was an intimidating assign-ment for a shy and nervous young man to be sent out into the grounds of States House to 'chat' for an hour with the severe, unyielding (and equally shy) Major-General J. F. C. Fuller. The latter did not make conversation easy. Asked whether he still regarded gas as a humane weapon, he simply replied 'yes'.

Michael Howard's major legacy was to impart the most rigorous academic standards. A student, Howard held, should aim at ever higher levels of expression and discussion. Bond greatly admired – and admires – Howard's lucidity both as a speaker and a writer. When they first met in 1959, Michael Howard was only 37 and had yet to publish much (his *Franco–Prussian War*, which Liddell Hart greatly esteemed, followed in 1961). Indeed in the days before hasty and sometimes premature publication was urged on young dons by bureaucratic fiat, Howard encouraged Bond *not* to publish too soon. Bond has attempted (in my view successfully), in his turn, to impart these values to his pupils. Certainly, he openly acknowledges the tremendous influence of Howard in making his students think about producing good writing.

After a spell of four years at the University of Liverpool, in 1966 Bond returned to King's College, London, to take his place in the newly created Department of War Studies. Howard had founded the department the year before when he was awarded the Chair. Bond joined Wolf Mendl (1926–99), a future Head of Department (1978–82), and helped to create an academic department dedicated to the study of conflict which rested on the vital combination of contemporary affairs and military history. Out of this conjunction arose a creative tension that many have attempted to imitate but none has quite replicated. In 1968 Howard moved to All Souls College, Oxford, and was succeeded by Professor (now Sir) Laurence Martin. Two further members joined the department, M. L. Dockrill in 1970 and Barrie Paskins a year later. Also at this time Professor Bryan McL. Ranft (1917–2001), having just retired from the Royal Naval College, Greenwich, became a Senior Research Fellow, and taught naval history. Bond forged an enduring partnership with Dockrill and between them (despite, or perhaps because of very differing styles) they would have a profound influence on British postgraduate education in military history. Bond still continues to co-chair the graduate seminar in Military History at the Institute of Historical Research (he has been a member of the seminar since 1959). Bond's achievements were rather belatedly recognised by King's College, London, by the award of a Readership in 1978, and eventually the established Chair in Military History in 1986, which he held until his retirement in 2001.

This Introduction is not designed as a detailed biographical sketch. It attempts to survey Bond's views on the nature of historical study, and focus on the subject of this volume – the evolution of the British General Staff.

Brian Bond has never been enthusiastic about free-floating 'theories' in history. He believes passionately (like the present author) that the study of the past cannot be moulded like plasticine to fit the pattern set by the preconceptions of the present. Liddell Hart's attempt to find a 'key' to military successes in past wars through a consistent application of a 'strategy of indirect approach' illustrates the dangers of imposing a theory on complex events. Such efforts give the impression (at least to the historian) of being a passing fad. Bond is openly contemptuous of initiatives that require the imposition of 'methodology' on military history. He argues that the true credo of the historian is simpler: whatever period he or she selects for study and analysis, the historian must attempt to empathise with it; this process should not necessarily imply sympathy, but understanding the values of the period and how they were estimated at the time should be a high priority of the scholar, not the degree to which they accord with contemporary preoccupations.

Personally, Bond is not indifferent to theory; he is particularly interested in the influence of theorists in history, but he has never attempted to place it within an integrated historical structure. As a scholar he does not deem this either necessary or desirable. Bond has always been very interested in literature and he has sometimes taken an interest in literary theory, but he has become very suspicious of its influence on the writing of history. It might offer insights but these can never be a substitute for rigorous analysis of evidence. For instance, historians can benefit from a book like Paul Fussell's *The Great War and Modern Memory* (1975), the work of a distinguished literary scholar, and agree that it offers a stimulating way of thinking about the First World War. But if his approach was accepted uncritically it can lead to the writing of bad history – because it imposes literary values which are unrepresentative and cannot provide answers to most of the questions that interest historians.

Bond is certainly prepared to accept the importance of *ideas* in history, but these are not identical to theory. Their working out must depend on the individual historian and his or her area of expertise. But the evolution of ideas about a subject should be placed within a broad perspective of ideas in the period under study. Bond's most ambitious treatment of a grand theme is *The Pursuit of Victory: From Napoleon to Saddam Hussein* (1996). Here he sought to apply clear definitions as to what the term 'victory' actually means, and by extension what the implications are of a phrase like 'decisive battle'. Visions of 'decisive battles' have hypnotised military historians (especially in the Anglo-Saxon world) since the appearance of Sir Edward Creasy's *Fifteen Decisive Battles of the World* (1851). The result is one of Bond's most stimulating and challenging works.

One aspect of historiography that has engaged Bond's attention over the last decade is the symbolic or mythic importance enjoyed by the First World War as an expression of the futility of war. He gave the annual Liddell Hart Lecture on this theme in 1997 with the title 'A Victory Worse than Defeat? British Interpretations of the First World War'. Bond developed this theme in his 2000 Lees Knowles Lectures at Trinity College, Cambridge. Non-historical sources, including memoirs, poetry, plays and film, Bond argues, have exerted excessive influence in forming a negative image of the First World War – or more precisely, of the Western Front. Bond has argued persuasively that brilliant, individual accounts of experience at the front used indiscriminately cannot possibly convey a balanced assessment of a war in its full social and political context. He is disturbed by the increasing gap between the reading public (who in so far as they consult historians remain steeped in Liddell Hart's critical views), and professional historians, who have spent more than a decade revising the hyper-critical judgements of Liddell Hart and his disciples. Yet the influence of the works of scholarly historians in this field (as in many others) appears to have been too easily submerged by the popular impact of films such as *Oh, What a Lovely War!* and the television series *Blackadder Goes Forth*.

Brian Bond has made a notable contribution to various aspects of mainly British and European military history (although one should not overlook his keen interest in the military history of the American Civil War, another legacy of Liddell Hart).[4] He has none the less made the subject of the British General Staff peculiarly his own. Bond has never completed an overarching history of the General Staff, but he has made a signal contribution to its study. He considers himself fortunate in having come to the subject via his interest in the late Victorian army and the Cardwell Reforms, in particular. The impact of the Prussian General Staff reforms on European armies in the later nineteenth century was evident (as it was in the United States), but it remained a very neglected theme in British military history.

As the British Army developed in the nineteenth century with the regimental system dominant, it assumed the form of a small, colonial (and in some ways archaic) constabulary, which was slow to appreciate the import of the General Staff revolution. Some progress was made with the establishment of the Staff College after the Crimean War, but the real breakthrough came in the 1890s when the Staff College, Camberley, became a 'school of thought' associated first with Colonel G. F. R. Henderson as chief instructor, and then after 1906–10 with Sir Henry Wilson as Commandant. Bond's *The Victorian Army and the Staff College, 1854–1914* (1972) is an exemplary institutional history. It not only recreates vividly the Camberley system and ethos (which, as the present author can testify from personal experience and observation, survived in a modified form for another century), but demonstrates how the Staff College refracted debates going on around it in the army at large; the Staff College then influenced the future direction of these discussions as its graduates assumed the highest commands in the army.

Bond's interests shifted from the late Victorian army to the interwar years mainly because of his absorption with Liddell Hart and his work. His editing of the diaries of two distinguished staff officers also provided an important catalyst on his outlook. The most important undoubtedly was *Chief of Staff: The Diaries of Lieutenant General Sir Henry Pownall, 1933–44* (2 vols, 1972–74). The shrewdness and quality of Pownall's diary underlined in Bond's mind the enormous contribution made to British military history by highly talented staff officers who were either self-effacing or overshadowed by the fame of field commanders. Early efforts at joint or combined approaches or liaison, first with the Dominions, and eventually with the United States, raised Bond's awareness of and respect for staff work (exemplified by Sir Maurice Hankey and Sir Hastings 'Pug' Ismay, as well as Pownall) as a servant of government. Thus in *France and Belgium, 1939–1940* (1975), Bond could see how well the staff at General Headquarters (GHQ) of the British Expeditionary Force (BEF), operated at a higher level. Despite the strain and frustrations of a long retreat, GHQ flourished and made a major contribution to the extrication of the BEF at Dunkirk.[5]

The other edited diary of more modest compass was *Staff Officer: The Diaries of Walter Guinness, First Lord Moyne, 1914–1918* (1987). Moyne was a highly capable, Territorial Army officer who thought he could never rise above the level of a general staff officer grade 2 (GSO2), a major. But despite this career limitation, Bond soon grasped how vital Moyne's duties were on the Western Front in terms of logistics, the movement of small units and ensuring liaison at the front with adjoining battalions and brigades.

There exist, in short, a number of linking themes that bind together his writings on the General Staff. One important aspect is a revision of Liddell Hart's depiction of the British Army, notably in his *Memoirs* (2 vols, 1965), as obscurantist. For many years, Liddell Hart's *Memoirs* rendered him the ultimate authority on the interwar years. Yet brilliantly written though these volumes are, Liddell Hart essentially caricatured the British Army, and its officer corps in particular. He was certainly unfair to the army as a whole, the General Staff and the wisdom of its strategic policy. Indeed Liddell Hart's opposition to a continental role for the army in the 1930s actually added to the General Staff's problems. Bond believes that the solution to the conundrums facing decision-makers, as expounded in his *British Military Policy Between the Two World Wars* (1980), lay not so much in operational methods or issues but in the higher realm of politics and grand strategy: in short the reluctance of successive governments to accept that Britain must prepare for all-out war with Germany.

Brian Bond is not only one of the most distinguished military historians of his generation, but an outstanding teacher. His list of doctoral pupils is truly impressive. His qualities as a historian are manifest. Both in his writings and in his teaching at King's College, London, he has dedicated himself to the belief that military theory is meaningless in a vacuum. Theorists must always be placed in a broad context. In the strength of this conviction, he has attempted to carry on the traditions founded by Michael Howard. Bond believes that not only do we need to understand the strengths and limitations of theorists, but to understand what they actually wrote (rather than what they claimed they wrote, or what devotees claim on their behalf). Pursuing theories in isolation from their broader context leads only to myth-making and intellectual confusion.

Bond has provided his own pupils and those whose theses he has examined (and both of these categories are represented in this volume) with an example of scholarly dedication and patience. He is a conservative and cautious historian, pre-eminently a scholar of finely weighed and sensible judgement. Yet despite his diffident nature, his work has not been lacking in strong and forcefully expressed views. On the contrary, Bond is by nature a revisionist and seems to react against any notion of received wisdom. Despite this predilection, Bond has never attempted himself to create a school of thought and impose a particular point of view on his pupils. This will become clear after a reading of this book, as many of the contributors disagree on points of detail and interpretation. Nevertheless, all of his pupils are happy to acknowledge his enormous contribution to their subject, and dedicate this volume in his honour with respect, affection and admiration.

1

Planning for War in the Final Years of *Pax Britannica*, 1889–1903

Halik Kochanski

The aim of this chapter is to examine how Britain planned for war in the last years of the nineteenth century and why no Chief of Staff was created in the British Army. During this period the army underwent a series of reforms designed to improve its capability to wage war: the so-called Cardwell Reforms. Yet, until the publication of the second part of the report of the Royal Commission under the presidency of Lord Hartington, little serious consideration was given to the desirability of establishing a Chief of Staff. The historical background to the Hartington Commission will be covered briefly, but the main focus of this chapter is to examine who opposed the recommendations of the commissioners and why. The sheer strength of this opposition reveals a great deal about the state of civil–military relations and the links between the Crown, Parliament and the army. The chapter will then analyse the effect of the 1895 Order in Council, which paid some lip-service to the Hartington Commission, but, arguably, damaged the War Office's ability to plan for war. The consequences were felt on the outbreak of the South African War in 1899. The Royal Commission, under Lord Elgin, examined the issues and highlighted many failures of military planning. It was not, however, until the Esher Committee on the Reconstitution of the War Office reported in 1904 that the political will existed to institute a thorough alteration to the composition of the military side of the War Office and accept the need for a General Staff.

The victories of the German army, first over Austria in 1866 and then over France in 1870, impelled the war departments of the European countries to reconsider their army systems. Britain, under the Secretary of State for War Edward Cardwell, followed suit. Various reforms were introduced following the German model, of which short service, the creation of an Army Reserve and the reorganisation and linking of battalions were the most important. But little thought was given to the adoption of the German system for war planning: the General

9

Staff. Cardwell did suggest the appointment of a Chief of Staff to the Commander-in-Chief (C-in-C), the Duke of Cambridge, but the duke could see little value in such an appointment during peacetime: the Chief of Staff would be 'a fifth wheel to the coach'.[1] Cardwell was unwilling to pursue the subject further. He was aware that the War Office Act, which made the C-in-C subordinate to the Secretary of State, had offended the duke, particularly as he was forced to move his office from Horse Guards to the War Office. Furthermore Cardwell, who had already encountered political difficulties with his reforms, particularly the abolition of the purchase of commissions, was unsure whether he would have the support of the Liberal Party for a Chief of Staff. To many Liberals the army was seen as a threat to freedom and there was a belief that planning for war led to war.

The 1870 War Office Act also set the trend for the administration of the War Office for virtually the remainder of the century. The C-in-C was to be the Secretary of State's principal adviser on all questions of military policy, including the organisation and the preparation of the army for war. In 1873 an Intelligence Branch was established to collect and collate information on foreign powers. These developments appeared to negate the need for a Chief of Staff. However, the C-in-C also bore heavy administrative duties, with overall responsibility for recruitment, promotion, discipline, training and education as well as command and inspection duties for the home army. In 1888 the abolition of the post of Surveyor-General of the Ordnance meant that the C-in-C now assumed responsibility for the supervision of supply and transport.[2] Clearly overburdened by administrative duties, it was apparent that the C-in-C could not devote attention to all areas equally, and consequently some, like the planning for war, suffered.

The weaknesses in the system of planning for war were concealed by Britain's record in colonial warfare. There were many victories in Britain's colonial campaigns, and the few defeats, normally soon reversed, could be blamed on the general in command. Planning for war was an *ad hoc* arrangement. When a crisis arose a general would be appointed to command the field force. He would make his own plans of campaign and discuss his military requirements with the C-in-C and the Secretary of State. This system worked well when responsibility for such campaigns was given to highly skilled individualistic commanders such as Sir Garnet Wolseley and Sir Frederick Roberts but it was not professional. It was assumed that the troops would be found from somewhere and that the navy would be able to transport them to the seat of the war. No system existed to ensure army–navy co-operation. The Egyptian campaign in 1882 highlighted many problems. For example, troops had to be gathered from the United Kingdom, Mediterranean stations and India and, although the navy found the required transport, it did not take any steps to ensure that its policy was in tune with War Office plans. Consequently the bombardment of Alexandria took place when there were no troops in the area to seize control from the Egyptian nationalists.

In 1888 the Adjutant-General, Wolseley, was so alarmed at the small size of the army in relation to its worldwide responsibilities that he publicised Britain's vulnerability to invasion by France. The consequences of the ensuing parliamentary debates were far-reaching. On the one hand, the Secretary of State, Edward Stanhope, urged Wolseley to supervise plans for defence against invasion. These plans also led to the drawing up of the first workable system of mobilisation. On the other hand, the debates in Parliament revealed a total difference in opinion on the subject of invasion between the War Office and the Admiralty. The latter department was adamant that no invasion force could be gathered and despatched without the Royal Navy becoming aware of the danger and making the required dispositions to defeat the enterprise. The War Office argued that sufficient shipping existed in French Channel ports for an invasion and the lack of warning meant that the army would form an essential force to defeat a landing.

The Prime Minister, Lord Salisbury, was so horrified by the differences of opinion between the Admiralty and the War Office that he set up a Royal Commission to examine the issues. The Hartington Commission should have been a powerful body with three former Secretaries of State for War on it along with Randolph Churchill, who had recently completed a long committee on the War Office estimates. Hearings began in 1888 and the report was issued in two parts: in July 1889 and February 1890. The evidence was considered so damning and revealing of the existing systems that it was never published.

The first part of the report covered Admiralty–War Office communication. It recommended the establishment of a committee comprised of Cabinet ministers, soldiers and sailors to consider the estimates of the two services together. It was not clear whether the politicians and the professional advisers would have equal status. Churchill wrote a strident dissent to this part of the report. He argued that professional issues were too complex for a civilian minister to understand. Therefore the Secretary of State for War and the First Lord of the Admiralty should be a professional soldier and sailor, above party politics and directly responsible to Parliament. Furthermore, to facilitate inter-service communication, the two offices should be combined into one Minister of Defence.[3] His proposal was not taken seriously by the politicians who believed that a single minister responsible for both services would be hopelessly overworked to the detriment of national defence, and the idea of a non-party professional at the head of the services would contravene the principle of parliamentary responsibility.

The second report of the Hartington Commission proved far more controversial. It outlined the general lines on which it thought War Office administration should be based 'at the occurrence of a vacancy in the office of C-in-C, or at any favourable opportunity'.[4] Principal among its recommendations was the abolition of the post of C-in-C. In its place a War Office Council of the Adjutant-General, Quartermaster-General and other senior officers, on an equal footing, would meet the Secretary of State to discuss issues of military administration. Responsibility for the planning for war would be given to a new office: that of Chief of Staff. His functions would be: to advise the Secretary of State on all matters of general military policy and all questions regarding the distribution and mobilisation of the army; to collect and co-ordinate military intelligence; to prepare and revise plans for action in certain contingencies; to com- municate directly with the First Naval Lord on all matters of inter-service policy; to liaise with other state departments and communicate with General Officers Commanding abroad; and to produce an annual report for the Secretary of State on the military requirements of the empire. The commissioners hoped that the creation of such a post would ensure that 'the military defence of the Empire would be considered as a whole, and its requirements dealt with in accordance with a definite and harmonious plan'.[5]

Sir Henry Campbell-Bannerman was the Commission's principal dissenter on this subject. He believed that the creation of a post of Chief of Staff was unnecessary in Britain. Home defence had been recently planned for by the Adjutant-General's department, and Indian defence was best left to the authorities on the spot and the India Office. Campbell- Bannerman was content to leave the planning for small wars on its exist- ing *ad hoc* basis. He felt that the adoption of the European model for the planning for war was potentially dangerous for Britain. Because Britain had no designs on her European neighbours and since all other areas were already being covered, the Chief of Staff might be tempted to create a role for himself and encourage an aggressive military policy in Europe.[6] Campbell-Bannerman also disagreed with the functions to be assigned to the Chief of Staff. He wrote to the chairman, 'What I fear is that your new Chief of Staff will be virtually a new Pope: and therefore I am against him.' He argued that the new post was perpetuating the worst anomalies of the present C-in-C system. The Chief of Staff would have so much knowledge of the workings of all departments and the ear of the Secretary of State that he would dominate the new War Office Council and the members would not have the equal ranking hoped for by the Commission.[7]

The proposal to abolish the post of C-in-C and to create a Chief of Staff was greeted with outrage in many quarters. The Cabinet felt the recommendations were too drastic and approached the subject with caution. The War Office's attitude is summed up by Wolseley's reaction:

'We sorely want a doctor, I admit, but Brackenbury and Co. have sent us an executioner'.[8] The Duke of Cambridge immediately began a campaign to save his position, and the Queen, his cousin, was not slow to commit herself in his support. Those outside official military, court and political circles also gave their opinions.

Wolseley's approach to the Hartington Commission revealed a great deal about his opinions on military policy and his own ambitions. His term of office as Adjutant-General was a success: cohesive workable defence plans for the United Kingdom and mobilisation plans had been drawn up and he had successfully pressed Stanhope to set out the purposes of the army in the so-called Stanhope Memorandum. Wolseley was ambitious and wanted to succeed the duke as C-in-C. In his evidence to the Hartington Commission he made clear his support for the idea of a single professional Minister of Defence and that he believed that the creation of a post of Chief of Staff was essential:

> I think we require it more than any nation abroad for many reasons, particularly on account of the peculiar constitution of our army, and the fact of its being stationed all over the world, and of the numerous responsibilities which devolve upon it, and consequently the numerous phases of war for which it should be always prepared.[9]

Britain needed to constantly revise and update its plans as imperial requirements dictated, whereas the European powers knew their likely enemies and only had to make slight alterations to their plans as manpower provisions changed or new technology became available.

Yet Wolseley was strongly hostile to the Commission's proposals on two grounds: the first was that he believed that the Chief of Staff should be an additional post, responsible to the C-in-C; and secondly, he feared for his own future position. His ideal of a Chief of Staff would be a man who would take the responsibility for the mobilisation plans and defence plans away from the Adjutant-General's office and receive the services of a greatly expanded Intelligence Department. The Chief of Staff would then be able to concentrate on planning for war without the distractions of administrative duties which plagued the offices of C-in-C and Adjutant-General. Wolseley himself would have been interested in taking such a position but the abolition of the post of C-in-C and the creation of the Chief of Staff as envisaged by the Hartington Commission would leave him no future at the War Office. His protégé, Sir Henry Brackenbury, with great experience of intelligence work, would be better suited.[10]

The Duke of Cambridge required no assistance from anyone in making his opposition to the recommendations of the Commission clear to the Queen. Her private secretary, Sir Henry Ponsonby, hastened to reassure the duke that the Queen would not approve any great change he opposed. The Queen's reasoning was that she wished to preserve the unique link between the army and the Crown embodied in having a member of the royal family holding the post of C-in-C. Until her son, the Duke of Connaught, was experienced and senior enough to be appointed, the Duke of Cambridge had to remain in office. She made her opinions clear to Salisbury and was pleased to hear that the C-in-C was not to be abolished and that the Adjutant-General would be replaced that autumn at the end of Wolseley's tenure without the intervention of a Chief of Staff. The Queen was not totally satisfied, writing to Salisbury of her 'desire that the changes now made shall be *permanent*, and *not depending* on the tenure of office of the *present* C-in-C'. Salisbury could offer no such assurance because he could not dictate the policy of any future government. The new appointee to the post of Adjutant-General, Redvers Buller, was disappointed not to be gazetted Adjutant-General and Chief of Staff but the government was not prepared to adopt such a drastically opposite policy to that recommended by the Commission by appointing a Chief of Staff to the C-in-C.[11]

Outside these circles informed commentators like Sir George Chesney, Sir Charles Dilke and H. Spenser Wilkinson added their opinions. Chesney wrote an article which highlighted the weaknesses of the proposed Chief of Staff. His sole function was to prepare the country for war but he would have no executive responsibilities and therefore no means to ensure that his proposals were carried out. Furthermore it was clear that the Chief of Staff would need a staff to gather and collate the material for his recommendations. Chesney wrote to Roberts in India to seek his support and Roberts agreed that a Chief of Staff with purely consultative functions was out of place in the British Army. Dilke and Wilkinson had frequently published the fact that the country was not prepared for war but felt that the proposed Chief of Staff would not be empowered to rectify this. He needed a department to provide support and backing: this should not be an administrative office but more a 'school of generalship' where staff officers would learn more of the practicalities of preparing for war than the Staff College gave them.[12]

Two recommendations of the Hartington Commission were accepted and a War Office Council was established in May 1890. But its constitution was not in accordance with the ideal of the commissioners. The Secretary of State's dominance was preserved, as no item could be raised for discussion without his prior approval and only his decisions were recorded. Meetings were called only sporadically. Stanhope called eleven in 1891 but his successor, Campbell-Bannerman, perhaps realising that the Council did not fulfil the hopes of his fellow commissioners, called them less frequently during each term of office and not at all in 1895 before the Liberal government fell from office.[13] In 1891 a Joint Naval and Military Committee was set up to facilitate discussion on issues involving both departments.

In 1895 an opportunity arose to revise the organisation of the War Office because the Duke of Cambridge's health was failing and his retirement appeared imminent. The Secretary of State for War, Campbell-Bannerman, had been a member of the Hartington Commission which had suggested timing the implementation of its recommendations to coincide with the duke's retirement. Campbell-Bannerman was keen to reduce the overwhelming power of the C-in-C but, as he had made clear in his dissent from the Commission's report, not to establish a Chief of Staff. The Order in Council he presented to the House of Commons on 21 June 1895 sought to reduce the power of the C-in-C and to invest some of that power in a new Army Board. The C-in-C would still be the 'principal adviser of the Secretary of State', but associated with him were to be four other military heads of department, each 'directly responsible to the Secretary of State'. Instead of a Chief of Staff, some of the C-in-C's responsibilities, such as for discipline, were to pass to the Adjutant-General, and the C-in-C should be freer to concentrate on preparing plans of defence and offence.[14]

It is conceivable that Campbell-Bannerman's plan might have worked had his first choice to replace the Duke of Cambridge, Buller, been appointed. However, the Liberal government fell from office before the Order in Council had been sanctioned and Buller's appointment confirmed. The new Unionist government, with Lord Lansdowne as Secretary of State, pressed ahead with the Order in Council and announced its terms in the House of Lords on 26 August 1895.[15] Instead of the amenable Buller, Wolseley was appointed C-in-C. Wolseley had already made his opinions on the role of the C-in-C known after the Hartington Commission. He resented all attempts to tamper with the role now that he had reached the highest position in the army. Wolseley's resistance to the Order in Council soured relations between him and Lansdowne, making the new system virtually unworkable, limiting army reform, damaging civil–military relations and, ultimately, harming Britain's ability to prepare for war.

Wolseley was quite correct to doubt the workability of the new Order in Council. In a series of letters to Lansdowne he made clear his belief that the public would hold him, as C-in-C, responsible for the efficiency of the army, not realising that this responsibility had been devolved to the Army Board. He was adamant that the C-in-C should be responsible for the discipline of the army because, if he was not, then 'it is impossible he could be in any way responsible for that fighting efficiency'. Wolseley produced his own draft Order in Council 'as a sort of compromise between the extremely civilian views embodied in the Hartington Commission Report, and the purely military view of the armymen who have experience in army administration'.[16] Despite the Queen's disquiet at rumours of dissatisfaction emanating from the War Office, Lansdowne was determined to give the new system a trial.

A full analysis of the problems caused by the dispute over the Order in Council lies outside the scope of this chapter. What is important, however, is the damage it caused to the ability to plan for war. The Order in Council charged the C-in-C with 'the preparation of schemes of offensive and defensive operations'. The Director of Military Intelligence, Sir John Ardagh, was not made a member of the Army Board and reported directly to the C-in-C. It has been argued that Wolseley could have made his role approximate to that of a Chief of Staff had he been temperamentally inclined to do so.[17] Yet it is apparent that Wolseley was not suited to such a role. His career at the War Office had been focused on reforming the army to turn it into a professional, efficient and effective body of fighting men. His interventions in the field of imperial strategy had been by-products of his campaign to persuade politicians of the need to increase the establishment of the army. As C-in-C he continued this campaign and won Lansdowne's acquiescence in a substantial increase in the number of infantry regiments, limited only by Treasury parsimony.[18] It should be remembered when considering Wolseley's role in the preparation of war plans that the Order in Council had not succeeded in reducing his administrative and executive burdens significantly. The C-in-C was not as free to concentrate on the wider strategic issues as the politicians thought.

The Hartington Commission had revealed a lack of communication and co-operation between the army and navy. This fault was largely rectified by the establishment of the Joint Military and Naval Committee. Salisbury identified a need for complementary political co-operation. He felt that

> the distribution of our strength has been rather a matter of hazard than of design, and often rather represents the relative force of importunity from the Colonial Office, the India Office, and the Foreign Office than any large scheme of Imperial defence.[19]

To rectify this, in 1895 he established a Committee of the Cabinet on Defence under Lord Hartington, now Duke of Devonshire. Arnold-Forster described it as 'a joke, and a very bad one'.[20] The committee met only occasionally, kept no minutes and rarely summoned either the C-in-C or the First Sea Lord to give professional advice. This was in accordance with Salisbury's opinion that: 'I have the greatest respect for the advice of soldiers as regards the conduct of war, none whatever for their opinions as to the policy which dictates war.'[21] As a result, the Cabinet Defence Committee served as little more than a forerunner to the Committee of Imperial Defence, established in 1902, when the politicians had belatedly realised that war was a serious business.

At no point did the weaknesses of the British system for planning for war become clearer than in the years preceding the outbreak of the

Second South African War in October 1899. Political resistance to military encroachments into the realm of imperial strategy is apparent when considering Salisbury's reaction to a memorandum produced by Ardagh in 1896. Wolseley was alarmed by the evidence that, following the Jameson Raid, the Boers were amassing vast stockpiles of rifles and ammunition including modern artillery guns. At his instigation Ardagh prepared a memorandum on the military status of the Boer republics. This memorandum, issued as *Military Notes on the Dutch Republics*, carefully analysed the numbers of burghers liable for military duty in the Transvaal and Orange Free State and estimated the number of foreign sympathisers. He concluded that Britain might have to face an army of 48,000 men.[22]

Ardagh also commented on strategy, both offensive and defensive. Wolseley passed this memorandum to Lansdowne who showed it to Salisbury. Salisbury confessed to Lansdowne on 21 April 1897 that 'I am astonished at reading the recommendations of Sir J. Ardagh'.[23] It was not Ardagh's place to comment on government policy. Salisbury's strongest objection was to the request that a decision be taken on the possibility of blockading the Portuguese port of Lourenço Marques, through which most of the Boer imports of armaments were made. Both military men were prepared to risk a war with Portugal, which had negligible military resources, in order to stop the imports. Salisbury clearly did not welcome military advice on what he believed to be diplomatic issues and, consequently, when war seemed imminent in South Africa, military plans had to be forged in ignorance of the state of diplomacy. Lansdowne could have acted as a conduit between the Cabinet and the military planners but was not the man to fill the role: Wolseley complained that 'I have to deal in Lansdowne with a man of the smallest mind and who is surprisingly ignorant on every point connected with soldiers and with war'.[24]

The existing system for the creation of plans for offence and defence might have worked with reference to South Africa had the right man been in place there. Responsibility for planning was split between two people: the General Officer Commanding in South Africa and the C-in-C in London. Wolseley encouraged the military authorities in South Africa to draw up defensive plans. This was in accordance with current practice: the War Office believed that the man on the spot was best able to make detailed plans which he would then forward to the War Office for approval. For example, in 1896 the General Officer Commanding (GOC) in South Africa, Lieutenant-General Goodenough, sent plans for the defence of Natal and an estimate of the numbers needed for the defence of the British colonies. His plans were approved by Lansdowne in September 1897. The system broke down at the end of 1898 when Wolseley asked Goodenough's successor, Sir William Butler, to answer a list of questions on the state of South African defences. Butler had his own agenda. Convinced that some politicians and soldiers were trying 'to bring about a war at an early date', he delayed sending a reply until June 1899. This was soon followed by his resignation and replacement by Sir William Penn Symons.[25]

The argument that had a General Staff existed in 1899 the British Army would have been better prepared for war than it was rests on the assumption that the Cabinet would have been more willing to accept advice from a professional body than from an individual, the C-in-C. Certainly abundant evidence exists that there was poor communication between the Cabinet and the War Office and, indeed, between Wolseley and Lansdowne. The Elgin Commission accepted without question Lansdowne's statement that 'I cannot call to mind any proposal on the part of the C-in-C for a large strengthening of the army in South Africa as an antidote to the Boer preparations'. The commissioners' report believed that Wolseley had not prepared schemes for offensive and defensive operations 'on this occasion in any systematic fashion'.[26] Yet the government had made it impossible for Wolseley to do so by keeping him in ignorance of the state of diplomacy, failing to seek his advice, and dismissing it when it was proffered unasked. In short, the government appeared totally incapable of understanding the complexities of waging war in South Africa.

Even before the Bloemfontein Conference opened on 31 May 1899 to discuss the franchise question, the High Commissioner in South Africa, Sir Alfred Milner, had been sending requests to London for an increase in the size of the British garrison. Wolseley had responded favourably to these requests but his advice was dismissed by the government. Milner was not hopeful of a satisfactory outcome from the conference and requested reinforcements of some 10–30,000 men to defend Natal. Lansdowne later summed up the government's reaction: 'I have never heard of sending out reinforcements to a country which might become a theatre of war merely in order that the reinforcements might successfully defend themselves against attack.'[27] When the conference broke up after a few days, Wolseley immediately prepared a memorandum on the military strength of South Africa. He did not want a war. Indeed his suggestion to mobilise the First Army Corps on Salisbury Plain was designed to avert one by waking 'up the Transvaal to the fact that England was at last serious'. Even if reinforcements were not to be sent out then at least the purchase and collection of supplies and mules should begin.[28] The Cabinet ignored his advice. The only sign it gave of having read his memorandum was to discuss the possibility of despatching a brigade from India to Natal.

In July Wolseley established a committee at the War Office, with a similar composition to the Army Board, to discuss questions specifically relating to operations in South Africa. He probably had two reasons for this act: firstly, to convince Lansdowne that his proposals had the backing of the entire military side of the War Office and, secondly, to have a committee in place when preparations were finally sanctioned.[29]

Strategy could not be planned adequately because not only was Wolseley left in ignorance of the state of diplomacy, but also the Cabinet refused to make a decision on whether or not the Orange Free State should be considered hostile. The attitude of the Orange Free State was a vital factor. If the Orange Free State was to be neutral, as it had been in 1881, then the bulk of British forces would be despatched to Natal and cross the mountainous Drakensburg range into the Transvaal. Small detachments would be left in Cape Colony to guard the bridges over the Orange River against sabotage. But if, however, the Orange Free State was hostile then the First Army Corps could use the most favourable line of advance along the railway to the Boer capitals. Troops could not be switched easily between the two British colonies as no railway existed linking them. Wolseley repeatedly pressed Lansdowne to make a decision on this issue but even when, in July, Buller was appointed commander of the First Army Corps, the Cabinet had not reached a decision. Wolseley was merely given the unhelpful advice by Lansdowne 'to be in *utrumque parantus*', with a plan for each contingency.[30]

In August Wolseley informed Lansdowne that there would be a gap of three or four months between the date when the Army Corps was mobilised and when it could start its campaign in South Africa.[31] The Cabinet appeared to disregard the possible consequences and in September Wolseley wrote to Lansdowne:

> The Government are acting without complete knowledge of what the military can do, while the military authorities on their side are equally without full knowledge of what the Government expects them to do; nor are they given authority to make such antecedent preparations as will enable them to act with the least possible delay.[32]

He went on to urge a delay in the break of relations between the Transvaal and Britain for at least five or six weeks to collect a substantial force in Natal. The government responded by ordering the Viceroy of India to despatch troops to Natal. Only at the end of September was Wolseley given permission to spend £64,000 on specified items.

On 25 September Lansdowne informed the Cabinet that the Orange Free State would most likely be hostile and, indeed, two days later the Orange Free State concluded an alliance with the Transvaal.[33] Two days later the Transvaal commandos were called out, but it was not until 7 October that the First Army Corps was mobilised and the Army Reserve called out. On 9 October Kruger issued an ultimatum demanding the withdrawal of British reinforcements sent to South Africa and the recall of those still on the high seas. Two days later this ultimatum expired and the Boers crossed into Natal heading for Ladysmith, Pietermaritzburg and the coast. Buller and the First Army Corps did not reach the Cape until the end of the month.

The lack of an adequate machinery for the planning for war made an immediate impact. Before the First Army Corps reached South Africa the Boers outnumbered the British by four to one and made full use of their advantage. As Leo Amery pointed out in *The Times History of the War in South Africa*, 'the keystone to the whole scheme was the assumption that Sir G. White could hold his own in Natal for an indefinite length of time. That assumption gave way at the very outset.'[34] The Boers besieged the Indian brigade in Ladysmith and mounted sieges of Mafeking in Bechuana-land and Kimberley in Cape Colony. On his arrival in Cape Town Buller was forced to split the Army Corps: he himself took command of the force to relieve Ladysmith, sending Lord Methuen and Lieutenant-General Gatacre to relieve Kimberley and Mafeking. British strategy had been ruined at the outset by the Boers' rapid advance. Now, instead of advancing into Boer territory, the British were forced to repair the damage caused by the tardy despatch of the First Army Corps and White's error in not withdrawing his forces behind the Tugela river.

Before the end of the year another serious consequence of Britain's unprofessional approach to the planning for war emerged. The mobilisation scheme had worked smoothly for the despatch of the First Army Corps, but thereafter troops were sent out by divisions. This was less than what Wolseley recommended. On 3 November, once it had become clear that the First Army Corps had to be divided, he urged the mobilisation of the entire Second Army Corps. The government demurred, partly because it did not see the necessity, but also because of the difficulties already encountered in supplying troops with uniforms and equipment. Brackenbury had been requested to undertake a thorough survey of the state of British armaments early in 1899 and produced a detailed memorandum on 15 September explaining the existing stores and what the ordnance factories and trade could produce. The picture he painted showed the extent to which the provision of modern armaments had been neglected over the years. Brackenbury concluded: 'the above is, I submit, sufficient to prove that we are attempting to maintain the largest Empire the world has ever seen with armaments and reserves that would be sufficient for a third class military Power'. The result was that many orders were immediately placed with the ordnance factories, trade and foreign firms but the orders could not be filled for some time.[35]

Once hostilities had been opened, the War Office, in deference to tradition, delegated all military decisions on strategy and tactics to the commanders on the spot. The military authorities in London and the public could only watch with frustration as serious basic errors were made. These culminated in three defeats – Colenso, Magersfontein and Stormberg – between 10 and 15 December which came to be known as Black Week.[36] Lansdowne lost patience with Buller after he recommended the abandonment of Ladysmith and the troops in it. Roberts was appointed to supersede him, with Kitchener as his Chief of Staff. The C-in-C, Wolseley, was not consulted prior to the announcement of these appointments.[37]

On 30 November 1900 Wolseley retired as C-in-C and was replaced by Roberts, who left South Africa believing the war there was over. The Queen encouraged Wolseley to write a memorandum highlighting the weaknesses of the C-in-C under the 1895 Order in Council. In it Wolseley argued that the C-in-C

> has neither the supreme control exercised by the Secretary of State, nor the administrative functions now conferred on those below him. Between the Ministerial Head on the one hand and the Departmental Heads on the other, he has been crushed out, and the Secretary of State has become the actual C-in-C of the army.

He concluded that either the Order in Council of 1895 should be rescinded and 'the army again placed under a military Commander, who shall be responsible for its discipline and military training and efficiency', or the post should be abolished since 'it is now merely a high sounding title, with no real responsibility attached to it, and answers no useful military purpose'.[38] Wolseley did not specifically refer to the possibility of appointing a Chief of Staff.

Lansdowne retaliated with a strongly worded memorandum in which he listed the functions the Order in Council had placed on the C-in-C. He noted that:

> It is remarkable that in his account of the duties which he has been performing during the last five years, the C-in-C has omitted all reference to mobilisation, to the preparation of schemes of offensive and defensive operations, as well as to the important duties to the Department of the Director of Military Intelligence, who, with the Military Secretary, is placed in direct subordination to the C-in-C.[39]

Lansdowne's argument was that, had Wolseley performed all the functions of the C-in-C, his time would have been so filled that it would have been impossible for him to do more.

In March 1901 the question of army administration and the state of civil–military relations became public with a series of debates in the House of Lords. Whereas Wolseley made a calm and measured criticism of the main features of the 1895 Order in Council, Lansdowne stunned the House by making a personal attack on him. Lord Northbrook voiced the sentiments of the majority of the House when he deplored Lansdowne's conduct: it is 'more extraordinary that the noble Marquess should have departed from the course he had prescribed for himself and endeavoured to shelter himself behind the C-in-C in respect to the advice given with reference to the war in South Africa'. By placing all the blame for the government's errors onto Wolseley, Lansdowne was damaging the functioning of a parliamentary democracy.[40]

The military appeared to have gained the upper hand during the debates in the House of Lords. This was confirmed by further events. Brackenbury had forewarned Roberts that he would not find the 'position of C-in-C very satisfactory' as matters stood. Roberts was appalled when he learnt of his duties: he had had much greater powers as C-in-C in India and less political interference. Roberts wrote a memorandum which outlined how red tape and responsibility for minor details should be removed from the duties of the C-in-C. Furthermore, he suggested that responsibility for mobilisation and intelligence should be returned to the Adjutant-General. The C-in-C should alone be responsible to the Secretary of State and the Adjutant-General should be his chief staff officer. The new Secretary of State, William St John Brodrick, saw this memorandum as an attempt to revert to the pre-1895 system without taking into account the recommendations of the Hartington Commission. He suggested the creation of a new officer, higher in status than the present Director of Military Intelligence, to undertake the work of intelligence and mobilisation, to be named the Chief of Staff.[41] No agreement seemed possible between the military and civil authorities at the War Office and the government appointed the Dawkins Committee to arbitrate.

In May 1901 the Dawkins Committee reported. It found that the War Office suffered from confusion in administration between the civil and military side, and that there was an absence of clearly defined individual responsibility. It supported Wolseley by recommending that the C-in-C should be given more responsibility, but criticised him for having failed to produce adequate offensive and defensive plans. The bulk of the recommendations of the Dawkins Committee were incorporated in the Order in Council of 4 November 1901.[42] This gave the C-in-C responsibility for discipline, training and staff planning, and the Adjutant-General was placed under him. The Director of Military Intelligence was renamed the Director-General of Military Intelligence and had a seat at the War Office Council.[43] He was responsible for:

> the preparation and maintenance of detailed plans for the military defence of the Empire and for the organisation and mobilisation of the regular and auxiliary forces, the preparation and maintenance of schemes of offensive operations, and the collection and distribution of information relating to the military geography, resources and armed forces of foreign countries and of British colonies and possessions.[44]

The South African War had taught the War Office that intelligence needed greater resources and responsibility.

It had taken 256,340 officers and men of the regular army, 109,048 auxiliaries, 30,633 men from the colonies and 50–60,000 men raised in South Africa to bring the Boers to the negotiating table in May 1902.[45] The length of the war and the performance of the British Army led to the appointment of a Royal Commission to investigate all matters pertaining to the war, the Elgin Commission. The Commission took evidence for 51 days and heard 114 witnesses. Lord Esher, a member, provided the new King, Edward VII, with a daily commentary of the Commission's proceedings. Eventually he reported that 'the Commission have unanimously come to the sad conclusion, that the responsibility for most of the early failures must rest upon the shoulders of the late C-in-C'.[46] This reversed the trend of blaming Lansdowne and the Cabinet for not having acted upon Wolseley's advice. By placing the blame for the early defeats suffered by the British Army in South Africa on Wolseley, the Commission concealed the real issue at stake: the failure of the system to ensure that military intelligence was passed from the military authorities to the politicians who were ultimately responsible for deciding when mobilisation should be declared. The Commission primarily concentrated on past events and what had gone wrong rather than on the future.

The Commission ignored the evidence of witnesses who were in favour of the establishment of a Chief of Staff. For example, the former Head of the Intelligence Department, Ardagh, stated:

> The leading impression in my mind as regards the Intelligence Department is that it should be brought as far as possible to resemble, and perform the functions of and to have that influence on the military policy of the country which is attributed very properly and correctly to, the body known in Germany as the Great General Staff.

He believed that his position and voice at the War Office had been undermined by the fact that he was only a major-general whereas the other senior officers held the rank of lieutenant-general or above. He was relieved to see that his successor, Sir William Nicholson, was a lieutenant-general and now had a seat at the War Office Council.[47] The former Adjutant-General, Evelyn Wood, lent his support to the idea of a Chief of Staff, wanting the powers of Adjutant-General increased to correspond with such a title.[48]

Lord Esher wrote a dissent to the Elgin Commission report. In it he made it clear that the whole system of army administration was at fault: the C-in-C no longer had any justifiable role, and should be abolished and replaced by an officer, called the Inspector-General of His Majesty's Forces, who would inspect the regular and auxiliary forces and report directly to the Secretary of State on their efficiency. At this stage Esher did not recommend the establishment of a Chief of the Staff, although he did recommend an increase in the size of the Intelligence Department.

Several factors influenced the decision to investigate further the system of army administration and to consider seriously the abolition of the post of C-in-C. The state of affairs revealed by the Elgin Commission created the will to make substantial reforms but the accession of a new king was, arguably, a more important factor. As Brian Bond has pointed out, 'no statesman dared to abolish the outdated title so long as Queen Victoria lived'.[49] The Queen had been determined to uphold the principle of having a member of the royal family as C-in-C. She had only sanctioned Wolseley's appointment because she accepted the Cabinet's argument that her son, the Duke of Connaught, had insufficient experience for the job, and agreed to Roberts because she saw the need to reward him for his conduct of the war in South Africa. Although Edward VII was no less determined to uphold royal status, he wisely declined the suggestion that he himself should become C-in-C. Esher was a close friend of the King and advised him on army, and indeed many naval, matters. He outlined an argument for the abolition of the post of C-in-C which the King accepted. The question remained of what new system should be created.

Esher's work on the Elgin Commission had impressed the Prime Minister, Balfour, and ensured that when a committee, the War Office Reconstitution Committee, was appointed in November 1903 to define a new system, Esher was appointed its chairman, with Admiral Sir John Fisher and George Clarke as the other two members. The committee worked with great speed and issued the three parts of its report when and as they were ready. The result was a somewhat confused document.

In the first part of the report of the Esher Committee, issued on 11 January 1904, it was noted that:

> the scientific study of Imperial resources, the co-ordination of the ever-varying facts upon which Imperial rule rests, the calculation of forces required, and the broad plans necessary to sustain the burden of Empire, have, until quite recently, found no place in our system of government.

Britain's defence problems were more complex than those of the European powers because Britain was a naval, Indian and colonial power. This necessitated the creation of a system of defence planning that could co-ordinate the political departments involved and ensure that the ministers received the professional advice essential for decisions. The system of War Office administration was to be completely reformed on the lines of the Board of the Admiralty. The aim was to divorce administrative from executive functions, prevent an overlapping of duties, clarify where responsibility lay, and increase professionalism and efficiency. The committee stressed that there should be a major change in personnel at the War Office so as to bring new minds to bear upon new measures.

The duties of the seven members of the Army Council – four military and three civil – were detailed. The post of C-in-C would be abolished and the first military member would be the newly created Chief of the General Staff. He would be responsible for overseeing military policy in all its branches: war staff duties; intelligence; mobilisation; plans of operation; training; military history; higher education and war regulations: in fact anything that came under the general heading of 'operations of war'. Other executive responsibilities, formerly the provenance of the C-in-C, would be shared out among the other senior officers, and his inspection duties given to a newly created post of Inspector-General of the Forces. The Chief of Staff would head a department which would devote 'its undivided attention to military problems in the widest sense'. The staff would concentrate in time of peace on the training of all ranks of the army and, in time of war, direct operations in the field.[50]

The government had already agreed to the principle of appointing a Chief of Staff before the Esher Committee completed its deliberations and provided the details of the post. On 4 February 1904 Sir Neville Lyttelton was appointed Chief of Staff and Sir James Grierson to the new role of Director of Military Operations. These two men were to serve as the professional advisers of the government on the Committee of Imperial Defence which had been created in December 1902. This committee of ministers with their professional advisers was established to consider the strategic needs of the empire. It had a permanent secretary and records of the discussions and decisions reached were kept. In January 1905 an army order was issued creating the General Staff. When the pay, conditions and duties of the appointed officers had been decided later in the year the General Staff came into a recognisable existence in 1906.[51]

Before 1899 Britain successfully waged war without a General Staff. Whilst it is true that on some occasions, particularly 1879–80 and 1885, the resources of the empire were stretched, nevertheless Britain's record in small wars was enviable. The tradition of *ad hoc* planning combined with the determination of the Queen to uphold her special link with the army, and joined with the desire on the part of some senior officers to preserve their career paths, proved forces too strong to permit the creation of a General Staff prior to 1899. The war in South Africa against a determined well-armed enemy of European origin provided the shock necessary to force politicians and soldiers alike to reconsider how Britain prepared for war. Two problems needed resolution: the first, how professional advice was collected and collated at the War Office, and the second, to whom this advice was passed. The solution to the first problem was the creation of a General Staff, and to the second the establishment of the CID. After 1904 all military advice submitted to the CID came from the General Staff.

2

Towards a Ministry of Defence: First Faltering Steps, 1890–1923

John Sweetman

AWAKENING

In November 1923, Lord Salisbury observed that 'since the War the most widely discussed proposal for overcoming our defects in co-ordination is a Ministry of Defence, which has been put forward repeatedly'. Nineteen years earlier, Lord Esher had observed that proposals for a Ministry of Defence had already been advanced 'from time to time'. In fact, the first salient attempt to create such a body may be traced more precisely to 1890.[1]

Self-evident deficiencies in operational planning and inter-service co-operation were by no means of recent origin. During the Napoleonic Wars, for example, in 1799 the navy independently planned to land only 3,000 of the 10,000 soldiers committed to invading the Helder peninsula in the Netherlands, and failed to provide sea transport for subsequent reinforcements or flat-bottomed boats for a military assault on Amsterdam via the canals once the force had gone ashore. The following year, Admiral Lord Keith and General Sir Ralph Abercromby contrived acrimoniously to abort an attack on Cádiz. Abercromby claimed to have secured Keith's agreement before embarking 22,000 men in 120 troopships at Gibraltar in September 1800. Once off Cádiz, Keith decided that he had only enough boats to off-load 4,000 and could not deploy sufficient warships to cover even that reduced number. Furthermore, owing to the inclement weather, he could not guarantee maintaining contact with any soldiers at all once they had landed.

The inherent danger of divided command in the field was further under-lined in the Crimea, where Lord Raglan, the army commander, could only request the 'active co-operation' of Vice-Admiral Sir James Dundas and his fleet in the bombardment of Sevastopol. Thus, on 17 October 1854, instead of taking part in a combined artillery assault at dawn as agreed, warships failed to open fire until 1.30 p.m., three hours after explosions in their ammunition magazines had silenced French guns ashore. Nor did Raglan have direct authority in Balaclava, where Rear-Admiral Edward Boxer exercised command over the army's sole supply base. Boxer's warrant of appointment made him answerable only to a superior naval officer, leaving the army commander frustrated in the face of mounting complaints about the port's disorganisation. No single executive authority at Westminster existed to overcome parochial departmentalism, and lack of central military or naval planning staffs was also of pivotal importance. When the expeditionary force to support Turkey against Russia gathered in February 1854, its staff officers had to glean information on an *ad hoc* basis about geographical features in the area of likely conflict, population and climate, availability of local transport and supplies, as well as intelligence concerning the strength and disposition of enemy forces.[2]

The political will to make fundamental change simply did not exist. Rather, politicians opted for departmental tinkering in a search for administrative improvement. In 1832, the Navy Board at Somerset House was merged with the Board of Admiralty; the civilian First Lord of the Admiralty clearly exercised undivided political control over the Royal Navy. The army had no similar framework until 10 June 1854, when a distinct Secretary of State for War was appointed to replace the over-lapping responsibilities of the Secretary of State for War and the Colonies and Secretary at War (a post finally abolished in 1863). None the less, military responsibility remained divided. The Master-General of the Ordnance commanded the Ordnance Corps of Royal Engineers, Corps of Royal Sappers and Miners and Royal Artillery entirely separately from the cavalry and infantry (which were under the Commander-in-Chief (C-in-C) at the Horse Guards) and civilian Ordnance Department, which undertook a wide miscellany of supply, financial and equipment duties for both the army and navy at home and abroad. The separate ordnance structure was dismantled by an Order in Council on 6 June 1855; the post of Master-General was discontinued. Further rationalisation took place with the abolition of the East India Company in 1861, its army being brought under the Horse Guards. But these changes still left the two armed services with powerful political heads of independent ministries, no planning staffs and an in-built system of annual competition for financial provision from the government.[3]

Meanwhile, technological advances had begun to transform warfare. At sea, sail gave way to steam with crucial implications for the swift transportation of troops and equipment, arousing fears that hostile forces might land at will on the British coastline irrespective of wind and tide. Echoing similar anxiety about an impending cross-Channel invasion two decades previously, a Royal Commission on national defences concluded in 1860, 'we can no longer rely upon being able to prevent the landing of a hostile force in the country'.[4] Artillery on land and at sea not only expanded in the calibre of shot, but acquired destructive shells and rifled gun barrels giving much greater velocity, penetration and range. Breach-loading small arms and cannon fundamentally altered military tactics. The Prussian army's impressive victories over Austria and France, signs that the United States and Japan were no longer willing to acquiesce in British domination of the seas and suspicion that the French and Russian navies were gaining strength presented added problems for the United Kingdom. Before the close of the nineteenth century, the internal combustion engine signalled the demise of the horse as a primary feature of the battlefield, and visual telegraph systems were doomed by the advent of wireless telegraphy. At sea, besides the advent of steam (which required secure fuelling bases), the evolution of mines, torpedoes, destroyers and submarines disturbed the equilibrium. Yet more inventive technology threatened even greater tactical and strategic uncertainty.

There was a further serious complication for Britain, revolving round the reluctance of self-governing colonies to commit themselves in terms of finance, soldiers or sailors to wider imperial defence, and tension between the navy and army authorities in Whitehall over precisely what did constitute imperial defence. An Admiralty minute of 24 January 1857 opposed creation of naval forces by individual colonies: 'It is perfectly impossible to localize naval defence'; the Royal Navy must protect the empire. Successive secretaries of state at the War Office, Major-General Jonathan Peel and Lord Herbert of Lea, 1859–60, argued that regular battalions of troops must not only defend the colonies but be prepared to quell local disorder. A Commons Select Committee on Colonial Military Expenditure, chaired by Arthur Mills, failed to resolve the differences, and this unsatisfactory state of affairs remained; essentially there was confusion both over the definition of imperial defence and whether any sort of strategic view of it were even needed.[5]

The Balkans crisis of 1877–79, when Russia threatened to overrun European Turkey and gain unimpeded naval access from the Black Sea into the Mediterranean, caused a furore of activity including irrational fears about danger to the colonies. In Canada, rumours were rife of 'a Russian ship crammed with guns and men cruising off the east coast ... ready to bombard Canadian ports'; Sir Michael Hicks Beach, the British Colonial Secretary, voiced alarm that valuable coaling stations might be seized further afield. He therefore initiated a Colonial Defence Committee, charged with considering 'what steps could be taken at short notice to provide some measure of security for Colonial Ports'. It comprised officials from the Admiralty, War Office, Colonial Office and Treasury but survived little more than a year. It had, though, established a valuable principle of co-operation and need to co-ordinate the work of the two services in the cause of the wider national interest. Recognising the importance of imperial defence, in 1879 Hicks Beach persuaded his predecessor as

Colonial Secretary (the Earl of Carnarvon) to head a Royal Commission tasked with studying the defence of trade routes and the colonies. Surviving the change of government in 1880, it sat for three years, came to no innovative conclusions and did not review the question of inter-service co-operation. However, it had undoubtedly examined aspects of imperial defence, an indirect legacy of the latest Balkan crisis.[6]

Involvement of Canadian and Australian contingents in the restoration of order in the Sudan, following the death of Major-General Charles Gordon, and perceived Russian threats to the North-West Frontier of India prompted the Colonial Office to resurrect the Colonial Defence Committee in a different form. With the Inspector-General of Fortifications in the chair, it convened on 22 April 1885 and within three months had acquired Major George Clarke RE as its secretary. By October 1891, the committee had met 58 times. Only a departmental advisory body, it did nevertheless provide a useful forum for the exchange of information with other authorities.[7]

INITIAL CALLS

Meanwhile, critical parliamentarians spearheaded by Lord Randolph Churchill, who pithily declared 'reform your system', used the presentation of the Army Estimates on 5 March 1888 to attack the government for not 'setting forth the general principles of defence which have determined the gross amount proposed to be allocated to naval and military purposes respectively, and indicating the main lines of the general plan or programme of British defence'. A fierce debate about 'protection of the Empire' ensued and carried over to a second day. Sir Edward Hamley, for instance, highlighted a provocative assertion by the French Minister of Marine referring to the evolution of iron-clad warships and 'the day when England's shores will be insulted and her ports burnt by the fleet of a victorious enemy'. The critics failed in their immediate aim. But they mustered 63 anti-government votes and their persistence led to the appointment of a Royal Commission under Spencer Cavendish, Marquis of Hartington, 'to inquire into the Civil and Professional Administration of the Naval and Military Departments, and the relation of each to the other and to the Treasury'. Clarke and Reginald Brett, Hartington's former Private Secretary, were made joint secretaries to the Commission, and Churchill was one of its members.[8]

In retrospect, the Hartington Commission was the first major step on a very long road. It discovered two service departments engaged in 'what is, or ought to be, one duty and one combined work, viz primarily the defence of the United Kingdom, its colonies and dependencies', noting that in time of war both were dependent on the other. Yet 'it has been stated in evidence before us that no combined plan of operations for the defence of the Empire in any given contingency had ever been worked out or decided upon by the two Departments'. In its report, the Commission concluded that 'there does not appear to us to exist sufficient provision for the consideration by either Service of the wants of the other. To remedy this unsatisfactory and dangerous condition of affairs', some witnesses had suggested that the Admiralty and War Office 'be placed in closer relation to each other ... by the creation of a Minister of Defence who would be the supreme and responsible head of both Services'. However, there was no unanimity about the structure of the proposed ministry. Lieutenant-General Henry Brackenbury believed that the two departments would not unite for 'one duty and one combined work unless they are ... controlled by one authority'. Lord Randolph Churchill argued in a comprehensive memorandum, printed as an appendix to the final report, that each service department should have a professional head with 'a civilian minister of high rank ... [providing] a channel of communication between them on all subjects of mutual importance'.

Hartington, whose final report appeared on 11 February 1890, pointed to the fact that no other European country had an overriding Minister of Defence and that the United States had abandoned the practice after a brief period. He therefore thought it 'inexpedient' to introduce a Ministry of Defence into the United Kingdom. Describing Churchill's memorandum as 'bold', he nevertheless pointed out that his proposed minister would not necessarily be in the Commons and acknowledged fears that he would become so powerful that he would acquire the status of the Minister of Defence which the Commission had rejected. Hartington suggested a compromise: 'There might be some advantage in the formation of a Naval and Military Council, which should probably be presided over by the Prime Minister and consist of the Parliamentary Heads of the two Services, and their principal professional advisers.' This body could be convened to examine the annual estimates and 'summoned from time to time to consider and authoritatively decide upon unsettled questions'. Since 1889, departmental officials had been part of a consultative Naval and Military Committee, and Hartington effectively proposed that this be elevated to ministerial level. The idea found scant immediate support.[9]

The Liberal politician Sir Charles Dilke was unwilling to drop the 'all important matter' of a defence ministry. In a book written jointly with the military historian Spenser Wilkinson, in 1892 he argued for the necessity of complete co-operation between the army and navy and one minister responsible for the two services. He carried his crusade into Whitehall. On 20 December 1893, Dilke discussed it in 'the tea room' with the leader of the Conservatives in the Commons, A. J. Balfour, and next day followed up with a letter which re-emphasised his position. He recorded, too, his intention of lobbying leaders of the major parties in both Houses of Parliament and 'confidentially' the Prince of Wales, 'it not being right' to approach the Queen directly. In his letter to Balfour, Dilke suggested that influential political figures, backed by Wilkinson 'as a civilian expert', should collectively write to the Prime Minister (W. E. Gladstone) to 'press for the joint consideration of the naval and military problem, and should point to creation of a Defence Ministry, of which the War Office and Admiralty would be branches'. If this was currently unattainable, an interim solution might be 'a more active control of the Secretary of State for War and the First Lord of the Admiralty by the Prime Minister personally'.[10]

Balfour claimed in his reply that 'I have always [sic] been in favour of a Defence Committee of the Cabinet with expert (military) advisers and permanent records carrying on the work from Government to Government ... Oddly enough', he had discussed this 'all-important subject ... last week' with the Home Secretary, H. H. Asquith, who judged that the Foreign Secretary, Lord Rosebery, would be in favour but 'not so the older members of the [Liberal] Cabinet'. Balfour recognised the 'real evils' of the present system, but foresaw 'serious' difficulties in changing 'traditional methods of dealing with the Admiralty and the War Office'. He would, however, discuss Dilke's letter with Salisbury, the Conservative Party leader. Balfour personally preferred a Cabinet committee rather than a new overarching ministry. So did Austen Chamberlain, who declared himself 'favourably inclined ... to the closer union between the two great departments of national defence, and the recognition of the responsibility of the professional advisers of the Cabinet on all questions of military and naval provision and administration'. After the Conservatives regained office in June 1895, a Defence Committee of the Cabinet met under the Duke of Devonshire (formerly Hartington and Lord President of the Council). The practice of not taking minutes later led Lord (formerly Lieutenant-Colonel M. P. A.) Hankey to dismiss this body, sometimes referred to as the Council or Committee of National Defence, as 'august but ineffective'. This may be strictly true. The committee concerned itself mainly with the annual estimates not strategic planning. Devonshire lacked political clout and, contrary to Dilke's proposal, the Prime Minister did not initially chair the committee.[11]

However, Salisbury did deal firmly with an attempt by Field Marshal Lord Wolseley, then holder of that post, to regain influence previously lost by the C-in-C. Wolseley submitted a memorandum to Salisbury and addressed the Lords at length on 4 March 1901. He claimed that further serious erosion of the C-in-C's powers beyond those laid down in 1870 (when the political supremacy of the Secretary of State had been established) took place through an Order in Council of 21 November 1895. Wolseley had given the new arrangement 'a fair trial of five years', but it had clearly produced 'military weakness and ... is likely to become a positive danger in times of war ... a Minister ... however able and conscientious, can of necessity have at best but a surface acquaintance with things military'. The following day Salisbury unequivocally buttressed ministerial supremacy: 'any attempt to take the opinion of the expert above the opinion of the politician must, in view of all the circumstances of our Constitution, inevitably fail'.[12]

AFTER THE BOER WAR

Parallel to pressure for more effective political direction through a Minister of Defence, ran demands for permanent planning staffs for the army and navy, with the needs of imperial defence a central platform. The Hartington Commission had rejected the concept of a Chief of the General Staff with his own dedicated group of uniformed planners. In 1890 and 1892, Dilke published proposals for such organisations to be linked with similar bodies in the self-governing colonies. At the Colonial Conference in London in 1897 agreement could not be reached on the commitment to imperial defence of naval or military forces from the self-governing colonies beyond their respective homelands. Despite strong support from the empire during the Boer War, another conference commencing in July 1902 encountered the same impasse. Perhaps even more disturbing was the transparent division between the two armed services. The First Lord of the Admiralty (Lord Selborne) and his professional advisers, while pressing for greater financial contribution from overseas, opposed localisation of maritime defence and emphasised that the Royal Navy's primary duty was to defeat an enemy at sea, not protect outlying territories. Receiving determined, but isolated, support from New Zealand, the Secretary of State for War (St John Brodrick) and his advisers wanted trained reserves in each colony liable for imperial mobilisation alongside continuing British garrisons and a field force in the United Kingdom. The navy seemed not to be closely concerned with defending the colonies, the army bent on retaining a significant physical presence there. Evidently alarmed at the inflexible views of their service chiefs, Selborne and St John Brodrick jointly pressed the Prime Minister (now Balfour) for more positive action in securing inter-service co-operation through the Cabinet Defence Committee. As a result, Balfour did more frequently take the chair himself and ensured that military officers were regularly in attendance. However, there was still no permanent secretariat.[13]

This particular deficiency was addressed on 9 September 1902, when the Elgin Royal Commission was tasked 'to enquire into the military preparations for the War in South Africa and into the supply of men, ammunition, equipment and transport by sea and land in connection with the campaign and into Military Operations up to the occupation of Pretoria'. Its report of 9 July 1903 concentrated on practical matters like provision of supplies and transport. A minority report by Lord Esher, however, focused on the administrative failings of the War Office and resulted in his heading a three-man War Office Reconstitution Committee with Colonel Sir George Clarke RE and the forthright, enigmatic Admiral Sir John Fisher. The Esher Committee widened its scope to consider establishment of a Ministry of Defence, rejecting it and concluding that Hartington's reasons for doing so had been 'unimpeachable'. None the less, it considered the Cabinet Defence Committee, with its *ad hoc*, occasional meetings and lack of secretariat, inadequate to achieve the required co-operation and co-ordination between the service ministries: 'There is no one charged with the duty of making a continuous study of (relevant) questions ... no means for co-ordinating defence problems or for dealing with them as a whole.' Esher produced three reports (11 January, 23 February and 9 March 1904), recommending reorganisation of the Cabinet Defence Committee, and the widening of its scope 'to survey as a whole the strategical military needs of the Empire'. In a covering letter to Balfour on 11 January 1904, Esher emphasised that in considering reconstruction of the Defence Committee, the commissioners wanted 'its invariable President the Prime Minister of the day', which was 'essential', and that he should have 'absolute discretion' over its membership.[14]

Action along the recommended lines came swiftly. Responding to Esher, on 5 March 1903 Balfour announced in the Commons that the reconstructed Defence Committee, which had met on 18 December 1902, would concern itself with 'as a whole the strategical military need of the Empire'. Renamed the Committee of Imperial Defence (CID), it formally received its new title and terms of reference on 4 May 1904. With the Prime Minister 'Chairman of the Committee and responsible for its proceedings', it now had a permanent secretariat. Much of its work would be delegated to specialist sub-committees like the permanent Ports Defence Committee and *ad hoc* ones dealing with such diverse subjects as aerial navigation, a Channel tunnel and invasion threats. Their meetings tended to replace formal ones of the CID, which occurred less frequently – sixteen times in 1906–08, roughly one-third the frequency of the previous three years. However, the CID (and its sub-committees) only advised the Prime Minister, who nominally determined its membership and indeed was its only permanent member. In Balfour's words, it had no power 'to give an order to the humblest soldier of His Majesty's Army or the most powerful sloop under the control of the Admiralty'. It therefore fell well short of being a Ministry of Defence, but, as Hankey (its secretary from 1912 till 1938) observed, 'we had in the CID the nucleus of a working system'. Its establishment theoretically formalised inter-service co-operation. However, as Hankey acknowledged, 'any system dealing with such immeasurable forces must depend upon good team-work', which soon appeared less than whole-hearted.[15]

Fisher, the First Sea Lord from 20 October 1904, opposed a central naval planning staff and, according to its secretary, Captain C. L. Ottley, kept the naval war plans from the CID for fear of compromise through exposure to such a wide circle. His forceful character may have dragged his own service into the twentieth century; it did nothing for inter-service co-ordination. He thus indirectly demonstrated that the CID lacked the teeth demanded by protagonists of a Ministry of Defence.[16]

In 1904, Esher proposed 'the creation of a trained (Army) General Staff', which came into being the following year; its head acquiring the title of Chief of the Imperial General Staff (CIGS) in 1909, though his staff lacked officers from forces of the self-governing colonies. In 1912, a Naval War Staff (comprising Operations, Mobilisation and Intelligence divisions) was created. It may be true that, under the influence of powerful ministers, Churchill at the Admiralty and R. B. (from 1911 Viscount) Haldane at the War Office, the new staffs to some extent undermined the influence of the CID, which proved unable to counteract the centrifugal tendencies of the two services. Nevertheless, however unsatisfactory in terms of strategic planning or operational direction, the CID did provide a forum for inter-departmental discussion and consideration of issues affecting both services.[17]

Once hostilities commenced, the CID became moribund. Direction of the British war effort was undertaken by a War Council (comprising political and military members), which gave way successively to the purely political Dardanelles Committee, the War Committee of the Cabinet and, after Lloyd George succeeded Asquith in December 1916, to a small War Cabinet. To these latter bodies, service chiefs were called when appropriate to proffer opinion and advice; they had lost their equality of status under the Prime Minister in the CID. As one politician, Sir Samuel Scott, recalled: 'I asked one of them one day why he said nothing, and he replied, "We are not there to talk, but sit and suffer, and, when required, answer questions".' Asquith disingenuously maintained that the service chiefs attended the War Council 'to give lay members the benefit of their advice'. Lord Crewe, the Lord Privy Seal, admitted that proceedings were conducted like a Cabinet meeting: 'The political members did too much of the talking, and the expert members too little.' The First Sea Lord believed it 'a mistake' to call the service chiefs 'members ... we are the experts there who were to open our mouths when told to'. Furthermore, appointment of a legendary soldier, Field Marshal Lord Kitchener, to be Secretary of State for War together with Churchill's recall of Fisher as First Sea Lord did not augur well for inter-service co-operation. The service staffs continued to advance quite separate plans to their responsible ministers and, in effect, many of the Boer War faults re-emerged. Lloyd George complained of 'no co-ordination of effort ... no connected plan of action'.[18]

Air power highlighted this syndrome. In practice, separation of the Military and Naval wings of the Royal Flying Corps already existed in

1914, but was confirmed in July 1915 when the Admiralty unilaterally declared the Royal Naval Air Service to be its dedicated air arm.[19] Attempts thereafter to rationalise use of manufacturing facilities, aeronautical research and development and indeed to produce a coherent national policy for the war in the air foundered on the intransigence of two distinct services intent on fighting their own administrative corner. A short-lived Joint War Air Committee and two Air Boards accentuated rather than eliminated differences. Asquith perversely dismissed the in-fighting as 'generous rivalry'. Friction between ministers and service chiefs further muddied the waters of co-operation. Fisher clashed spectacularly with Churchill over the Dardanelles venture and ostentatiously resigned. The naval historian N. A. M. Rodger later concluded that 'Churchill and Fisher fought each other as energetically as they fought the Germans, each claiming that the other acted without consulting him'. Admiral Lord Jellicoe, as First Sea Lord, lost the confidence of successive political masters Sir Edward Carson and Sir Eric Geddes.[20]

At the War Office in the opening phase of the war, Kitchener reputedly browbeat successive CIGSs and overawed civilian ministers. When Lloyd George became Prime Minister he had an uneasy relationship with the CIGS, General (later Field Marshal) Sir William Robertson, and the commander of the British Expeditionary Force, Sir Douglas Haig. Once the Allied Supreme War Council was created, the Prime Minister relied more upon the strategic opinions of the mercurial General Sir Henry Wilson, the British representative, which enraged Robertson and indirectly led to the CIGS being removed from office. None of this manoeuvring advanced the cause of inter-service co-ordination nor co-operation between senior officers and politicians.[21]

One major reason for creation of the independent Royal Air Force (RAF) on 1 April 1918 out of the Royal Flying Corps (RFC) and Royal Naval Air Service (RNAS) was the inability – even sheer unwillingness – of the two air arms to work together. The new service did not enjoy a smooth start. An Air Ministry had been established in January to make necessary administrative preparations and Major-General H. M. Trenchard appointed Chief of the Air Staff. Before the RAF formally came into being, Trenchard quarrelled with the Secretary of State, Lord Rothermere, and resigned. Scarcely had Trenchard's successor, Major-General F. H. Sykes, settled at his desk than the Vice-President of the Air Council (Sir David Henderson) departed 'on the grounds that he felt he would be unable to work with the new Chief of the Air Staff', and Rothermere left office 'for personal reasons'. Sykes and Rothermere's successor, Lord Weir, were acutely aware of danger ahead for their infant prodigy once hostilities ceased and, therefore, were essentially inward-looking and protective. Serious internecine spats across the tables of the Joint War Air Committee and two Air Boards had concerned the supply of aero-engines and availability of air frames. Future contretemps were likely to centre on the very existence of the RAF, with pressure for it to be dissolved once more into integral air arms of either the army or navy. Inter-service strategic planning was not, therefore, a high priority for the Air Staff.[22]

NEAR YET FAR

In July 1917, Lord Haldane chaired a committee appointed to recommend the structure of postwar organisation. In December 1918, it eschewed creating a Ministry of Defence, instead recommending resuscitation of the CID. Essentially, Haldane feared not only that the work would be beyond one man but, paradoxically, if the system did succeed the Defence Minister might exercise more power than the Prime Minister in a national emergency; shades of Hartington's similar reservation in 1890. None the less, shortly after the Armistice the concept of a Ministry of Defence again came under serious consideration. The emergence of the RAF brought the realisation that, in future, operationally at least two of the three armed forces must work together; co-ordinated strategic planning and direction made eminent sense. Moreover, one ministry instead of three would reduce financial overheads. To some extent, the hesitant reappearance of the CID, which in the immediate postwar period functioned again through its sub-committees rather than in full session, suggested that such a development might be in train. The appointment of Winston Churchill to be Secretary of State for both War and Air on 9 January 1919, was interpreted by enthusiasts as a positive step towards a Ministry of Defence. Three days after his appointment, he denied that this development was imminent without entirely ruling out its future implementation.[23]

In a memorandum to Lloyd George on 4 July, J. E. B. Seely, the Under Secretary of State for Air, reopened the debate. Referring to the present 'lop-sided' administrative system, whose 'inherent difficulties … are insurmountable', he favoured 'a Minister and Ministry of Defence with executive powers' over the three services. However, this may well have been a tactic to preserve the independent air force, for in conclusion he argued that if such a tri-service arrangement could not be achieved, political responsibility for War and Air should again be divided with 'the direction of the Air (placed) on a sound footing'.[24] Four days later the CIGS, Wilson, declared that he was 'all in favour' of a Ministry of Defence with an Under Secretary of State each for land, sea and air, in a 'long talk' with Churchill. Minister and general then pressed their case during a visit to Lloyd George at Criccieth, expanding the under secretaries to four by adding 'Supplies'. Hankey, who was present, recorded that Churchill seemed keen to head the proposed new ministry himself. Subsequently, Wilson told Lloyd George that he had a 'private and informal' talk with Admiral Sir David Beatty (soon to become First Sea Lord) and 'found him

36

almost as keen ... as I am' about a Defence Ministry. Meanwhile, Churchill had modified his proposal and wanted four parliamentary secretaries, but only three under secretaries of state (excluding Supplies). This would, he claimed, reduce by two the number of existing officials with a saving of £5,000 per year. On 16 July, Wilson alerted Lloyd George to another conversation with Beatty, who urged rapid action, and Wilson himself continued to lobby the Prime Minister. Lloyd George, though, was aware of strong Admiralty opposition, which may well explain why the First Sea Lord (Admiral Sir Rosslyn Wemyss) did not figure prominently in these discussions. On 4 August, Churchill once more pressed Lloyd George to create a Ministry of Defence on the grounds of financial saving and strategic efficiency. He added that, after initial reservations, Trenchard had come to support the concept. Churchill's pleas, which included emphasis on his father's advocacy of the combined ministry, fell increasingly on deaf ears. Wilson believed that 'Winston himself has killed the Ministry' by his persistence. The claim by George Riddell early in November, of Lloyd George being impressed by Churchill's arguments that a Ministry of Defence would bring greater tri-service co-operation, does not undermine this contention. Churchill had not yet lived down the reputation of a political maverick acquired for crossing the floor before the war and responsibility for the Dardanelles disaster during it. Having been First Lord of the Admiralty, currently Secretary of State for War and Air, he was too obviously placed (and, according to Hankey, enthusiastic) to head the new ministry and therefore open to the charge that personal ambition, not principle, fuelled his fervour.[25]

The issue of a Ministry of Defence did not long lay dormant. In December 1921, the first interim report of Sir Eric Geddes' Committee on National Expenditure (better remembered for the wielding of its celebrated 'axe' on defence spending) recommended creation of a Ministry of Defence in the cause of reducing overheads; 'the creation of a Co-ordinating authority or a Ministry of Defence responsible for seeing that each force plays its part and is allotted appropriate responsibility for carrying out various functions'. The Admiralty emphatically recorded its dissent. According to Salisbury, the Cabinet committee which reviewed Geddes's recommendations 'while admitting the creation of a Ministry of Defence may be the ultimate solution ... did not consider that the present time is appropriate for the fusion of the administration of the three Services under one Minister'.[26]

Nevertheless, calls for such a minister continued. On 21 March 1922, Churchill declared: 'I have formed the opinion that there is no final solution of a harmonious kind to be found ... except in a Ministry of Defence'. Josiah Wedgwood, the Labour politician, added flavour to the debate by emphasising the changing face of warfare: 'There will be more people who realise that the Navy is not our first line of defence but that the air service is.' As Colonial Secretary, Churchill appointed his own investigative committee firstly under Sir Alfred Mond, then Lord Weir, to examine whether any fusion of administrative arrangements common to the three services might be achieved. Weir reported that amalgamation 'would only be practicable if it formed part of a comprehensive scheme of reorganisation, which provided for a Ministry to control a defence force in which the identity of the Navy, the Army and Air Force had been merged' – a radical and totally unacceptable proposition.[27]

In the Commons, representing a wider spectrum of underlying concern, Lieutenant-Colonel W. Guinness called for a minister to head a body 'of professional representatives of the three fighting services' and Lieutenant-General Sir Aylmer Hunter-Weston sought 'a feeling of corporate responsibility for defence'. Mindful of the strength of support for it which persisted, on 27 June 1922 Lloyd George informed the Commons that creation of a defence ministry would receive active attention at an early date. Mr C. L. Malone conveniently asked him 'whether the question of the creation of a Ministry of Defence has yet been considered by the Committee of Imperial Defence'. The Prime Minister replied that it would be looked at by its Standing Defence Committee. Dissatisfied with this response, the naval air power protagonist Rear-Admiral Murray Sueter pressed for parliamentary time 'to discuss the whole question of the three fighting services, and the advisability of setting up without further delay a Ministry of Defence as advocated in the Geddes Report'. Lloyd George indicated that it would be 'impossible' to allocate the required time and reiterated that the matter was already under consideration by the CID.[28]

Early in 1923, further cross-service salvoes on the subject of naval aviation ensured that the subject could no longer be shelved. The Secretary of State for Air, Sir Samuel Hoare, complained: 'The naval controversy is breaking out with renewed fury ... the Admiralty have very big guns and they are bringing them to bear.' Beatty's threat of resignation was only averted, according to the First Lord (Leo Amery), by the promise of Bonar Law, Lloyd George's successor as Prime Minister, of an inquiry. Independently, Hoare noted that Hankey counselled against a swift decision, to allow time for 'the only real solution, the creation of a Ministry of National Defence to be brought into the field of practical politics'. At length, in May 1923 a sub-committee of the CID under Lord Salisbury, Lord President of the Council, was convened 'to enquire into the co-operation and correlation between the Navy, Army and Air Force from the point of view of National and Imperial Defence generally, including the question of establishing some co-ordinating authority, whether by a Ministry of Defence or otherwise'. Salisbury's body spawned its own sub-committee under Balfour specifically to examine 'the relation of the Navy and Air Force as regards control of Fleet air work', which in July 1923 ruled in favour of the RAF: 'The main reason for the creation of a national air service was to achieve unity of air development, policy and administration.'[29]

All three service chiefs gave evidence before the main Salisbury Committee, which defined 'National and Imperial Defence' as 'Defence of Territory and Defence of Communications'. Robertson, an erstwhile CIGS, in typically robust fashion, dismissed the idea of a Ministry of Defence as 'fantastical as well as dreadfully mischievous'. More reasonably, Salisbury admitted uncertainty as to what a Ministry of Defence entailed. Only two expert witnesses favoured the notion and they disagreed about its form; lack of a coherent campaign by its protagonists again being transparent. Sir Eric Geddes wanted a single secretary of state for 'Warfare' or 'Defence' with responsibility for all three services. Major-General Sir Frederick Sykes, a former Chief of the Air Staff, thought that 'the real solution lies in definite, unified supreme control by a Defence Ministry, with the Prime Minister as independent Chairman and a joint Staff which would really think out defence as a whole'. There was, too, alternative strong support for the CID from experienced figures like Haldane, who held that 'we have evolved this Committee to meet Dominion as well as Home necessities, and to meet the former it is far better adapted than any special Ministry of Defence could be'. This view was endorsed by the current CIGS, General Lord Cavan, Major-General Sir J. H. Davidson, Lieutenant-General Sir Aylmer Hunter-Wilson and the former Cabinet minister, Major-General J. E. B. Seely, who all 'advocated definite extensions of the CID organisation'. So the Salisbury Committee came out 'overwhelmingly' against 'setting up a Ministry of Defence or any Minister of Defence with authority overriding that of the Ministers at the Head of Service Departments'.[30]

While confirming Balfour's arguments for the independent RAF, in his final report of 15 November 1923, instead of a Ministry of Defence, Salisbury opted for a permanent sub-committee of the CID comprising the three service chiefs, soon generally known as the Chiefs of Staff Committee. It represented both a compromise and at the same time a giant leap forward. 'Each of the three Chiefs of Staff will have an individual and collective responsibility for advising on defence policy as a whole, the three constituting, as it were, a Super-Chief of a War Staff in Commission.' As a constituent part of the CID, the Chiefs of Staff Committee could be chaired by the Prime Minister and, in theory, reported to him.[31]

A full-blown Ministry of Defence lay far ahead. Yet, since 1890 the concept had not only been debated on numerous occasions, but arguably had become embedded in the political psyche. By 1923, hopes of its ultimate achievement remained remote but were no longer quite so far-fetched. Little realising that the goal would not be achieved until the year before his nonagenarian death, in 1922 Churchill declared:

No solution of a harmonious or symmetrical character will be achieved in the co-ordination of the Services except through the agency of a Ministry of Defence, but it is not possible to create such a body at the present time nor will it be possible for a considerable time.[32]

Effective though the Chiefs of Staff Committee might prove, its creation rested largely on reluctance to stomach the more extreme political alternative. However, its establishment did undoubtedly advance the cause of the sub-text apparent throughout these years to create permanent service planning staffs and to achieve better co-ordination between them in the pursuit of defence efficiency.

3

'Selection by Disparagement': Lord Esher, the General Staff and the Politics of Command, 1904–14

Ian F. W. Beckett

The disasters of the South African War (1899–1902), not least the perceived shortcomings of those who had commanded British forces at its outbreak, led to a series of major government inquiries into the British Army and its organisation between 1901 and 1903. In addition, the war led to radically different reform schemes from three successive Secretaries of State for War between 1902 and 1908.[1] Arguably, amid these changes, the greatest impact derived from what has been characterised by John Gooch as the resulting 'managerial revolution', the 'crowning achievement' of which was the work of the War Office (Reconstitution) Committee, chaired by Lord Esher, in February and March 1904.[2]

The principal recommendations of Esher and his colleagues are well known: the abolition of the post of Commander-in-Chief; the creation of that of Chief of the General Staff (CGS) and, in due course, the establishment of a General Staff; an Army Council; and a permanent secretariat for the existing Committee of Imperial Defence (CID). In reality, however, the construction and functioning of the new machine was less impressive in retrospect than it appeared. Above all, success or failure rested upon what Esher himself referred to as 'the officer question',[3] namely the capacity of those selected for appointment as members of the Army Council.

Previously, the army's promotion system had been one of 'seniority tempered by selection' followed, in theory, by one of selection by merit. In pursuit of its managerial revolution, the Esher Committee deliberately chose what one of its members, Admiral Sir John Fisher, proclaimed as 'selection by disparagement' in effecting what was frequently described as a 'clean sweep' of the War Office's leading soldiers in February 1904.[4] In practice, however, the politics of command in the Edwardian army was not very different from that of its Victorian predecessor. Esher and his colleagues had changed the personalities, but not the process, as a consideration of the appointment of Chief of the General Staff between 1904 and 1914 serves to illustrate.

Following the abolition of the purchase system in 1871, the army's patronage was vested in the Commander-in-Chief (C-in-C) acting through the Military Secretary at the War Office. There were those, including the long-serving C-in-C between 1855 and 1895, the Duke of Cambridge, who favoured seniority over selection. Equally, others like Lord Wolseley, championed selection. With the establishment of a Selection Board in 1889, selection by merit became a much more significant factor in promotion to the rank of major-general and above. When Wolseley finally succeeded Cambridge in 1895, promotion was vested in an Army Board (renamed the Selection Board once more in 1899), on which the C-in-C was theoretically only 'first among equals', with lists of candidates for its consideration drawn up by a separate Army Promotions Board. In practice, however, seniority remained of account while, on the outbreak of the South African War, Wolseley himself lamented the longevity of 'the old fashioned lot who were promoted by seniority before I came into office'.[5]

Promotion and appointment, however, were far from being simply a matter of either seniority or merit. Certain commands, for example, such as those at Edinburgh and Portsmouth, required a man of considerable private means, since the incumbent would be required to attend upon the monarch when the latter was resident at Balmoral or Osborne. The Cairo command had ceased to be of significance once the Sirdar of the reconstituted Egyptian army had effectively taken control of military affairs in Egypt and the Sudan. It was, therefore, largely a matter of finding a General Officer Commanding (GOC) whose wife would be equal to the social duties associated with Cairo. Similarly, the command at the Cape had become a backwater after the end of the Eighth Kaffir (Cape Frontier) War in 1853, the flurry of military activity between 1877 and 1881 represented by the Ninth Kaffir War, the Zulu War and the Transvaal War requiring only temporary arrangements for Natal. Even in the South African War, the GOC at the Cape had largely been required to administer lines of communication. Malta and Gibraltar were traditionally regarded as billets for those about to retire.

Even more significantly, the Victorian army had been bedevilled by the rivalry of the 'rings' such as that associated with Wolseley and variously known as the 'Wolseley Gang', the 'Ashanti Ring' and the 'Mutual Admiration Society'. The struggle between Wolseley and his rivals ranged widely over such policy issues as short service and imperial strategy as he sought to manoeuvre his adherents into campaign and administrative appointments in defiance of Cambridge, while simultaneously trying to outwit the rival machinations of Lord Roberts and his 'Indian' faction. Neither particular issues, nor the positions assumed by individuals with respect to them, were necessarily constant, but the contest was frequently poisonous. On occasions, the poison was applied by military wives rather than their husbands.

Military competence, of course, was not insignificant, though there was a somewhat alarming tendency to equate winning the Victoria Cross with suitability for future high command. Yet, intellect was increasingly likely to triumph over 'character', hence the increasing importance attached to attendance at the Staff College. Perceived public opinion and the concomitant intervention of politicians in the process of selection and appointment also played its role. The influence of the Crown, as exerted by both Queen Victoria and, later, King Edward VII, remained extremely significant.[6]

The South African War had seen the apparent eclipse of Wolseley's ring, Roberts superseding General Sir Redvers Buller as C-in-C in South Africa in December 1899 and then returning home to succeed Wolseley as C-in-C at the War Office in January 1901. Just as Wolseley had seen the retirement of Cambridge as the opportunity to effect major changes in the army, so Roberts, in the view of the Assistant Under Secretary at the War Office, Guy Fleetwood-Wilson, saw himself as being chosen by divine providence to cleanse an especially foul Augean stable. Roberts's command in South Africa had already been the occasion for the settling of old scores.[7]

The war, however, had also seen further evidence of the increasing importance of another leading military figure, who owed relatively little to either Wolseley or Roberts. This was Lord Kitchener, who had made his reputation as Sirdar since 1892, particularly in the reconquest of the Sudan between 1896 and 1898. Not only had Kitchener been suggested by some for the chief command in South Africa from the very beginning, but the Prime Minister, Lord Salisbury, had made his acceptance of Roberts in December 1899 largely conditional upon Kitchener's appointment as Roberts's chief of staff. Kitchener then succeeded Roberts in the South Africa command in January 1901. The result had been an uneasy mix of officers of different traditions, backgrounds and persuasions. Buller, indeed, when visiting Pretoria in July 1900, remarked that, 'I found Roberts sitting in one building with his Hindu staff, Kitchener in another with his Egyptian staff, and [Lieutenant-General Sir Thomas] Kelly-Kenny in a third with an English staff, all pulling against each other.'[8]

The legacy of this internal conflict was of too recent memory to be easily overridden by the Esher Committee. In any case, of course, rivalries and animosities were to be expected in any relatively small profession such as the army. Between 1885 and 1906, for example, a total of only 16,472 men were commissioned into the army and, in 1899, there were just 113 officers of major-general's rank or above on the active list.[9]

In many respects, the recommendations of the Esher Committee were not new. The Hartington Commission had advocated the replacement of the C-in-C with a Chief of Staff in 1890. As indicated earlier, the powers of the C-in-C had been curtailed in 1895. In 1900, the War Office Council, re-established in response to Hartington, absorbed the Army Board – set up to oversee mobilisation in 1899 – as a more efficient means of bringing soldiers and civilians together rather than allowing them to maintain a separate existence as antagonistic bodies preoccupied with keeping checks on one another. A new post of Director-General of Mobilisation and Military Intelligence had been created in November 1901 to provide the Secretary of State with better support and guidance on strategic questions. In the following year, the suggestion by the Secretary of State, St John Brodrick, for an improved defence committee of the Cabinet resulted in the establishment of the CID.[10]

The effect of Esher's recommendations, however, was to implement a new era of formalised 'defence by committee'. The Secretary of State was firmly set at the apex of an efficient bureaucratic structure and thus established as an authoritative voice within the Cabinet based on his much improved military guidance. The relationship between the Secretary of State and the permanent secretary of the CID, however, remained potentially difficult. Moreover, while the reorganisation had established a better machinery for discussion and debate, it could not guarantee that civil–military friction would cease. The success of the system would depend 'upon the qualities of mind and character of the men' chosen to administer it. In establishing its recommendations, Esher and his two colleagues, Fisher and Sir George Clarke, soon to be the first secretary of the CID, were adamant that the new system could not work while what Fisher variously described as the 'old lot' and the 'old gang' remained in post.[11]

The 'old lot' were Roberts and his circle, who now dominated the War Office. A former associate of Wolseley, General Sir Henry Brackenbury, remained Director-General of Ordnance, but Brackenbury's adherence to Wolseley had considerably lessened. Indeed, Brackenbury had been instrumental in persuading the Hartington Commission, on which he served, to recommend the creation of a Chief of Staff, most felt with the intention of filling the post himself. Kelly-Kenny, who had become Adjutant-General in October 1901, was of the British rather than the Indian establishment, but had served with Roberts in Abyssinia in 1867–68. The Quartermaster-General since April 1903 had been Lieutenant-General Sir

Ian Hamilton, previously Military Secretary at the War Office under Roberts and, most recently, Kitchener's chief of staff in South Africa. Another key figure and, like Hamilton, a long-term adherent of Roberts was Lieutenant-General Sir William Nicholson, as Director-General of Mobilisation and Military Intelligence.

It needs to be emphasised that, in carrying out the 'clean sweep' of Roberts and his colleagues, Esher, Fisher and Clarke were usurping all established procedures. As the committee's 80 witnesses were interviewed, itself an informal process by which the secretary, Lieutenant-Colonel Gerald Ellison, made notes that were not published as formal minutes of evidence, they were also being vetted for their suitability for future employment. Working with great speed and unprecedented authority largely deriving from the King's backing, the committee, which had only been announced on 7 November 1903, produced its first report on 1 February 1904. Since Esher was anxious to avoid parliamentary scrutiny before the measures were enacted, the reforms were introduced by Orders in Council. Subsequently, the new appointees to the Army Council were similarly approved by Letters Patent under the Great Seal. Indeed, the appointments were made before the duties of many of the offices had been finalised and the new appointees themselves were to assist in compiling the committee's second and third reports, published respectively on 25 February and 9 March 1904.[12]

Kelly-Kenny, Nicholson and Hamilton were made aware by letter from the Secretary of State for War, H. O. Arnold-Forster, on Sunday 31 January 1904 that their appointments were to be discontinued in their present form, but only received these letters at the same time as the newspaper accounts of the report on 1 February. They were not made aware, however, that they were not in contention for the new appointments though the names of the new Council had already been submitted to the King on 29 January. Esher and his colleagues had also decided who would occupy the various directorates responsible to the Army Council. Brigadier-General James Grierson, for example, accepted the new post of Director of Military Operations, with the rank of major-general, at a meeting attended by Fisher, Clarke and Ellison on 5 February.

On Sunday 7 February, the names of the new nominees were released to the press, again without the victims being informed. On 8 February, therefore, Major-General Sir Henry Hildyard, the Director-General of Military Education and Training, was surprised by Major-General Sir Frederick Stopford appearing at his door to announce that 'he had been appointed in his place and had come to take over his office' as the new Director of Military Training (DMT). Grierson similarly appeared at Nicholson's door three days later, at which point, according to Roberts, Nicholson's language was 'not altogether what it ought to have been!' The Deputy Adjutant-General, Major-General A. S. Wynne, appears to have been informed unofficially of his dismissal by the Permanent Under Secretary at the War Office, Sir Edward Ward.

Excluding Roberts, who had himself been surprised to learn of the abolition of the post of C-in-C and had fully expected to be consulted on the new appointments, eight general officers were replaced on 'Black Monday'. Other officers were subsequently removed such as Major-General Alfred Turner, the Inspector-General of Auxiliary Forces, who was replaced on 5 April 1904 by Major-General W. H. Mackinnon as the new Director of Auxiliary Forces.[13] Interestingly, there appears to have been much relief in some quarters at the removal of the 'female belongings' of Roberts and his circle.[14]

Understandably, there was great resentment at the way in which the appointments had been carried out and William Robertson, then serving under Nicholson in the Intelligence Division, believed his chief was 'never quite the same man again', his 'old military zeal' diminishing and his cynicism in manner becoming 'more pronounced than before'. Roberts complained to the Foreign Secretary and former Secretary of State for War, Lord Lansdowne, at the way Esher had been allowed to 'usurp all authority, settling appointments and ordering officers about as he liked'.[15]

Arnold-Forster found his own position at the War Office greatly undermined by Esher's influence over the Prime Minister, Arthur Balfour, and the King. He, too, resented appointments being made without being consulted. He was certainly not mollified by Clarke insisting that he had been consulted on the appointments of Stopford and Grierson by having the names put before him. Brodrick, who had resigned from the War Office in September 1903 after the failure of his own army reform scheme and had been switched to the India Office, similarly believed Esher's influence akin to power without responsibility. Indeed, Esher had declined the War Office when offered it after Brodrick's resignation. Brodrick therefore raised the matter in Cabinet, but Esher threatened that his committee would cease work if their nominees were not accepted *en bloc*.[16]

In the words of Fleetwood-Wilson, Esher 'satiated with Kings and Courts and Constitutions, sauntered into shady Pall Mall and, *pour passer le temps*, destroyed a Commander-in-Chief'.[17] Certainly, Roberts was the chief victim. He had not been in the best of health and, during the initial deliberations of the committee, it had seemed he might be induced to go quietly. Then, to Esher's dismay, Roberts had returned to the War Office in January 1904 seemingly invigorated and, as Esher reported to the King, 'no longer looks forward with the same degree of calmness to early retirement'.

A possible solution was to appoint Roberts to the new post of Inspector-General of Forces, intended as a voice independent of the Army Council, assuming the former duties of the C-in-C with respect to training and thus divorcing the executive and administrative powers of the former office. It was also intended that the Inspector-General be the president of the new Selection Board. There were fears in the Cabinet, however, not least on the part of Brodrick, that the committee was removing the C-in-C only to vest significant powers in the Inspector-General. Consequently, since Esher and his colleagues did not regard the issue as quite as vital as some other aspects of their recommendations, they were prepared to concede on the Inspector-General by giving him no formal executive powers.[18]

It was unlikely that Roberts would accept a post with less authority than originally intended since he believed only some executive power would induce the Army Council to listen to the Inspector-General's recommendations. In any case, there were fears that if Roberts became Inspector-General, Nicholson and the formidable Lady Roberts might induce him to stay beyond the temporary period envisaged, and that Roberts would appoint Nicholson as some kind of chief of staff to himself. Another factor was the desire of the King that his brother, the Duke of Connaught, should become Inspector-General. Thus, while the King expressed his concern to Roberts that he should not accept a 'derogatory' post, Roberts had little doubt that the King was working closely with Esher not only to oust him as C-in-C, but also to prevent him becoming Inspector-General. Indeed, he recalled that the King had enquired if he was likely to retire back in 1902 and now considered that 'when he found there was no chance of my doing so, he thought the best thing was to do away with the appointment'. Roberts turned down an offer to be Lord Warden of the Cinque Ports, but did accept the proffered seat on the CID.[19]

Roberts suspected that both the King and Esher intended that the King should become the C-in-C, the King himself remarking to Roberts on 16 February that a C-in-C was only necessary 'when the Sovereign happened to be a Queen'. Esher certainly frequently wrote of the King as *de jure* rather than simply *de facto* C-in-C in his correspondence with the King's private secretary, Lord Knollys, in a manner likely to encourage the King in such an interpretation. Pointedly, General Lord Grenfell, when offered the post of Inspector-General after Roberts, declined, saying he would 'not be a d–d Royal warming pan'. Connaught was duly appointed, but there was to be a subsequent controversy over the marginalisation of Connaught and his departure for a new Mediterranean command embracing Gibraltar, Malta, Cyprus and Egypt in 1907. Kitchener was to turn down the same peripheral post in 1909, Hamilton being induced to accept it.[20]

As suggested by the fear that Nicholson might become chief of staff to Roberts as Inspector-General, 'old Nick' was regarded with particular suspicion by Esher and his colleagues, especially as Nicholson was an obvious candidate for CGS. He supported a German model likely to recommend itself to Esher and was favoured for the appointment by the Prime Minister, Balfour, as well as by Roberts.[21] But, if Nicholson was able, he was also viewed as a dangerous intriguer.

Nicholson had certainly played a full role in the war of words between the Wolseley and Roberts factions. It might be added that Nicholson was generally resentful of the preference he detected so often shown to Connaught. Knowing Nicholson's opposition to many of their recommendations, Clarke and Fisher suspected Nicholson was feeding the defence journalist, Henry Spenser Wilkinson, who, in turn, was prompting Sir Charles Dilke to 'discredit our report in anticipation'. To Esher, Nicholson appeared 'grasping', but also altogether too critical and negative in his disposition and lacking an 'original mind'. The King believed Nicholson generally unpopular and, as predominantly an office soldier, unlikely to command the army's confidence in war. Even Roberts was on record as doubting Nicholson's ability to command in the field, a general assumption being that the CGS would become the C-in-C in the event of a war.[22]

An even more substantial objection to Nicholson was his antipathy to the Admiralty's strategic ideas. Nicholson took a much more realistic view than some soldiers in the past of the likelihood of invasion. While acknowledging the navy's primacy in home defence, however, Nicholson remained convinced that France or Germany might contemplate it on a far larger scale than the mere small raid anticipated by the Admiralty. Moreover, Nicholson believed that the Army Estimates would be cut if the navy was seen to be capable of defending Britain alone. Similarly, like most other leading soldiers, Nicholson doubted the effectiveness of the navy's preferred wartime maritime strategy of raiding French colonial possessions or the Russian coast.[23]

According to Fisher, Nicholson had made himself 'so hateful to the Admiralty (and such a thorough cad)' that it was only the forbearance of Lord Walter Kerr, the First Sea Lord, and Prince Louis of Battenberg, the Director of Naval Intelligence, that allowed co-operation between the War Office and Admiralty to continue at all. Indeed, Fisher believed Nicholson's continuation in office would limit the selection of Kerr's successor, ruling himself out of contention in such circumstances. Fisher believed Nicholson to have considerable influence over both Roberts and Kelly-Kenny and friends in the Cabinet such as the First Lord of the Admiralty, Selborne, anxious to retain his presence at least on the CID. This would be equally fatal to Clarke's prospects as Permanent Secretary, since Nicholson opposed a secretariat on the grounds that it would rival the service departments and was also personally hostile to Clarke.[24]

It thus became important to remove Nicholson, a point backed up by Esher's veiled threat to Balfour that he would resign from the committee if Nicholson remained. To leave Nicholson unemployed, however, was not regarded as safe. Gibraltar was one option and Fisher lamented that Nicholson had not been despatched to replace Clarke, who had been Governor of Victoria before being summoned to join Esher's committee. Another possibility was making Nicholson the Military Member on the Viceroy's Council in place of Major-General Sir Edmund Elles, who wished to come home, but it would depend on persuading the Viceroy, Lord Curzon, and it was also known that Nicholson actively disliked Kitchener, who had become C-in-C in India in October 1902. Indeed, such was the antipathy between them that, at Kitchener's memorial service in June 1916, Jean, Lady Hamilton, recorded the cynical presence of Nicholson openly 'rejoicing at the death of his life-long enemy'.[25]

Fortunately, a solution presented itself with the outbreak of the Russo-Japanese War in February 1904 and Nicholson was despatched as chief British military observer with the Japanese army. Hamilton, with whom Nicholson had a somewhat ambivalent relationship, was also despatched to Manchuria but, in any case, like Kelly-Kenny, he presented less of a problem than Nicholson since it was felt he was not restricted to office appointments. Indeed, Hamilton had acquired the reputation of being a bad administrator, though Esher for one did not entirely believe it. It was also the case that, in public, Hamilton supported the principles behind the reforms. This was misconstrued by Brodrick, who apparently wished to use Hamilton in Cabinet as an example of a 'discontented' general for his own purposes in scoring points off Arnold-Forster, and felt betrayed by Hamilton's apparent support for the changes.

In reality, Hamilton believed the changes the result of 'court and political intrigue' with any organisational benefit a purely secondary motive for those who had perpetuated them. Hamilton was not prepared to take the Cape command, and it was tacitly agreed that, on his return from Japan, Hamilton should get command of II Corps on Salisbury Plain when Field-Marshal Sir Evelyn Wood retired at the end of 1904. Hamilton, however, remained unsure that the promise made him by Arnold-Forster and Esher would be honoured and he was careful to ensure the support of the new Military Secretary, Major-General John Spencer Ewart, by asking him to be his chief of staff if he got a corps command. Additional uncertainty for Hamilton derived from his visit to Manchuria, though approved by Roberts and the King, being initially without official accreditation since Nicholson had suggested this might enable the War Office to prevent him going. When Nicholson subsequently became the official attaché to the Japanese army, Hamilton was seemingly left without any recognised post but, somewhat reluctantly, Kitchener was compelled to accept Hamilton as official representative of the Indian Army in Manchuria.[26]

Kelly-Kenny was a difficult individual at the best of times and had taken strong exception to Ellison, whom he felt held 'opinions' and who had become secretary to the Esher Committee without his consent, the second-ment having been agreed by Arnold-Forster and Nicholson in the Adjutant-General's absence.[27] One suggestion was that Kelly-Kenny could be offered the Irish command in place of Connaught, or perhaps York or Gibraltar. The King appears to have been well disposed towards Kelly-Kenny and apologised to him personally for the way he had been treated, but believed that he should have accepted the offer of the Cape command, which he had declined. Subsequently, the King opposed the early return of Hamilton from Manchuria because he wished Kelly-Kenny to receive command of II Corps. To complete what he described as the 'Golden Bridge' for the 'old gang', Fisher suggested Kelly-Kenny could command I Corps at Aldershot in place of Lieutenant-General Sir John French, whom he wished to see as CGS, and Grenfell could replace Connaught in the Irish command. Another victim, Major-General Ronald 'Rowdy' Lane, the Military Secretary, could be given the Portsmouth command.[28]

NEW MEN FOR NEW MEASURES

Having disposed of the former leadership of the War Office, Esher, Fisher and Clarke had to find suitable 'new men' for 'new measures'. Fisher's 'selection by disparagement' was intended to justify the choice of the new men by disparaging the claims of the old. Thus, the suggestion of each of his personal selections was accompanied by a quasi-political slogan, as in his support for French as CGS: 'Plump for French and Efficiency! Every vote given against French is a vote given to Kelly Kenny!' What made French acceptable to Fisher was his greater flexibility with regard to strategy and, particularly, amphibious operations. In reality, French showed little consistency in his strategic ideas, but Fisher was essentially correct in seeing French, who had begun his career as a midshipman in the Royal Navy before transferring to the army, as 'almost solitary amongst all the Generals, who all want to play at the German Army'.[29]

Esher recognised the mercurial French's intellectual limitations, writing to Knollys, 'I daresay that he is not the cleverest man, but he is the most successful soldier we could find. *He has never failed.*' This echoed almost exactly Fisher's sentiments in proposing French 'because he never failed in Africa (the grave of military reputations)' and, as already indicated, it was assumed that the CGS would become the C-in-C in the field in the event of war. French also scored for Fisher in being '*young* and *energetic*' and, while Esher felt it necessary to provide French with sound sub-ordinates, Fisher believed French at least had shown the knack in South Africa of choosing an efficient staff. It was important to Esher, too, that a CGS should have a clear idea of the direction in which he wished to lead the army and he was to write, after observing French presiding over the annual autumn manoeuvres as Inspector-General in 1907, that, 'It was generally remarked that it was a comfort to find a Leader, who, whether right or wrong, invariably knew his own mind, and possessed the force of character to stick to his opinions, and the force of intellect to defend them.'[30]

French, who took Esher's son on his military staff at Aldershot in the summer of 1904, remained the only soldier for whom Esher acknowledged a clear preference. Unfortunately from the committee's point of view, the King refused to accept French's nomination. On reflection, Esher expressed the view to French that it was probably too soon for him to be CGS and that 'you will find the post more to your taste in a few years time'. French, who had not wished to go to the War Office, remained at Aldershot, but became a member of the CID on the nomination of Esher in December 1905 with limitless tenure.[31]

With French ruled out, the choice of CGS next fell on the man originally considered by the committee as the Second Military Member (Adjutant-General), Lieutenant-General the Hon. Sir Neville Lyttelton, GOC at the Cape: Fisher preferred Lieutenant-General Sir Horace Smith-Dorrien, finding Lyttelton 'the dullest dog I'd ever met'. Lyttelton had successfully commanded a brigade in the Sudan and a division in South Africa, the switch in his personal allegiance from the Wolseley ring to that of Roberts being marked by some trenchant criticism of Buller's performance in Natal. He had then been considered in the summer of 1900 a 'safe pair of hands' to take over the South African command in succession to Roberts, the assumption being that the war was all but over. In the event, of course, the war was far from over, but Lyttelton duly succeeded Kitchener in command in June 1902, having been one of only three officers – the others were General Lord Methuen and French – to have served in South Africa throughout the war.[32]

Lyttelton, who would have preferred to stay in South Africa, was to prove a disastrous choice for CGS. He was certainly well connected, his brother, Alfred, who had urged him to accept, being Balfour's Colonial Secretary. He was, however, as one astute observer, the military correspondent of *The Times*, Charles à Court Repington, noted, a better judge of cricket than strategy. Indeed, Lyttelton knew 'nothing of great problems of Imperial defence and less than that about the problems which confront foreign strategists and military administrators, which we have, after all, to consider in our own arrangements'. Roberts, too, felt Lyttelton had 'neither the brains, energy, nor strength of character' to preside over the crucial areas of intelligence, mobilisation and training that would fall under his remit, but he might be suitable as Adjutant-General. Similarly, though a friend of Lyttelton, Hamilton considered that he 'has neither the force of character, industry or brains for such a billet and his straightness, kindness and good sense will not make up for this'.[33]

In many respects, it was Lyttelton's shortcomings which made him most attractive to Esher and Clarke since he would be likely to prove malleable and, therefore, not pose any challenge to the primacy of the CID. Yet, it soon became apparent that, while amiable, Lyttelton was incapable of taking a firm grip of his duties. Colonel Henry Wilson, who acted as Director of Staff Duties (DSD) until the arrival of Major-General H. D. Hutchinson from India, found Lyttelton interested only in cricket and 'run by his wife'. Memorably, Wilson was to comment in December 1906 that Lyttelton 'has been increasingly useless until he has reached an almost incredible degree of uselessness'. Even Lyttelton's wife remarked on her husband's 'non self-assertiveness'.

Within a few months, Esher was also lamenting that Lyttelton was 'vacillating and devoid of imagination' and the fact that he took 'far more interest in the County Championship than in the administration of the Army'. By December 1904 Esher wanted him ousted. That same month, indeed, Lyttelton made an extraordinary speech at Leicester, contravening the strict enjoinder to the Military Members not to make controversial public statements, in which he let slip that there was friction between himself and the Adjutant-General, Major-General Sir Charles 'Sunny Jim' Douglas, and that he himself did not understand the workings of the Army Council system. He explained himself to Arnold-Forster by writing that 'I began public speaking too late in life to become a safe speaker, and I blunder into things which a more experienced hand would avoid instinctively, and in future I shall do as little of it as I possibly can.'[34]

Arnold-Forster was equally determined to be rid of Lyttelton, who, with Douglas and the Fourth Military Member (Master-General of the Ordnance), Major-General Sir James Wolfe Murray, was proving immensely obstructive to his army reform scheme. The combination of Arnold-Forster's high-handedness on the one hand and the indecisiveness of the Military Members on the other proved one further nail in the coffin of a scheme already opposed by Clarke, Balfour, Brodrick and other Cabinet members. Lyttelton was too well-connected, however, to shift easily, resulting in a series of ploys to try to force his resignation. In May 1905, Arnold-Forster tried to get Lyttelton to accept the Gibraltar command and, when he refused, tried to force his resignation over the report of the Butler Committee into irregularities in the sale of army stores to contractors while Lyttelton had been GOC in South Africa. Arnold-Forster made another attempt to persuade Lyttelton to accept the Scottish command in November 1905, but he refused that as well. There was some hope, however, that Lyttelton might find Malta attractive. Remarkably for a man who had not wanted the job, regretted accepting it and looked forward to leaving it, Lyttelton proved highly attached to the office of CGS.[35]

The question remained, however, as to who would be the most suitable candidate to replace Lyttelton. French remained a possible alternative in the view of many, including Connaught and Arnold-Forster, but was not now prepared to go to the War Office. Repington, whose opinions were respected by Esher, was a strong advocate of Kitchener as CGS. Though believing Kitchener more important in India than at the War Office, Esher approached him in August 1905. Kitchener was promised promotion to field-marshal, but he declined to take the bait. Esher considered Grenfell too old and Methuen too fussy. Lieutenant-General Sir William Butler, now very close to retirement and whom Esher had seen as a possible Quartermaster-General in 1904, seemed a better candidate. Butler, indeed, chaired the committee examining the South African stores scandal, but he was totally unacceptable to the Cabinet as CGS: a result of his sympathies for the Boers, which had led to his removal from the Cape command in August 1899. Lieutenant-General Sir Archibald Hunter, commanding the Poona corps in India, who had impressed Esher as a witness during the Royal Commission on the War in South Africa, was another possibility, but was notoriously tactless. In some desperation, Esher even suggested Brackenbury or the former Quartermaster-General (QMG) under Wolseley, Sir Mansfield Clarke.[36]

Part of the difficulty, of course, was that Nicholson remained the best choice as CGS. Indeed, at the apparent suggestion of Hamilton, Arnold-Forster entered negotiations with Nicholson in July 1905, just after Nicholson had refused the Gibraltar command. Nicholson was offered the post of CGS if he was prepared to accept Arnold-Forster's army reform scheme. Nicholson indicated that he would be prepared to accept, but the King still opposed him. Arnold-Forster hoped that Esher, who had finally despaired of Lyttelton, could be pressed into service to persuade the King and Balfour to accept the change. They remained unconvinced while Douglas, who curiously had never apparently met Nicholson, assured Arnold-Forster that the army would have no confidence in his appointment. Clarke similarly continued to distrust Nicholson, believing he would not 'run straight', create friction, try to re-establish the office of C-in-C, while also still being too close to Spenser Wilkinson. Fisher, too, resolutely resisted any talk of Nicholson. As a result of the opposition, Esher came up with yet a further suggestion that Lyttelton be replaced by Hildyard, now languishing in the South African command.[37]

One other possible solution was to retain Lyttelton, but to replace Hutchinson in the key role of DSD since the post had become much more significant in terms of establishing the General Staff through the incapacity of the CGS. Major-General Douglas Haig, the Inspector-General of Cavalry in India, was the replacement most had in mind. It was a ploy urged by French, who cared for neither Lyttelton nor Hutchinson, and Esher, who now claimed the appointments in 1904 had been 'experimental'. It was also acceptable to the King, who believed Hutchinson 'not up to his duties'. One objection raised to this solution was that as Hutchinson was an officer of the Indian Army, he could not be readily considered for an alternative command in England such as Chatham, a paradox Esher found somewhat bizarre when Hutchinson was apparently qualified to be DSD at the War Office.

Arnold-Forster was reluctant to accept Haig, whom he felt was using his influence with the King to push for the post, Haig having recently married one of the Queen's ladies-in-waiting. In any case, Lyttelton was by no means anxious to accept Haig and, subsequently, Haig was brought to the War Office as DMT in August 1906 before succeeding Hutchinson as DSD in November 1907.[38]

On entering the War Office in December 1905 after the Unionist defeat in the general election, the new Secretary of State for War, R. B. Haldane, knew Nicholson to be the best candidate, describing him as 'one of the cleverest men I ever came across'. Apparently, however, Haldane feared to install him as CGS until he had established his own authority. Possibly influenced by his cousin, Colonel Aylmer Haldane, an old friend of Nicholson who had accompanied him to Manchuria, Haldane therefore conceived of offsetting Lyttelton's incompetence by bringing Nicholson on to the Army Council as Third Military Member (Quartermaster-General). Clarke believed that Nicholson had not changed and that he should certainly not be allowed on the CID and it was certainly the case that Nicholson believed that military considerations had been subordinated to the naval view on the CID since the changes in 1904. The King, however, was persuaded by Esher 'to bring in a great but difficult soldier' in place of Major-General Herbert Plumer and it was tacitly accepted that Nicholson would succeed Lyttelton in due course.

Having reluctantly accepted Gibraltar after his spell in Manchuria, largely because his wife wished to be addressed as 'Her Excellency', Nicholson was eager for more rewarding employment. Taking on board Haldane's lightly veiled promise for the future, he therefore accepted the offer of QMG even though feeling it 'was not one for which I was specially fitted or should myself have selected'. Esher recognised that Nicholson was 'generally an irritating personage' but found him now ready to act in accordance with the Esher Committee's principles. Moreover, bringing Nicholson on to the Army Council would accustom 'Generals who dislike Nick' to his presence amongst them.[39]

Plumer had been the only member of the Army Council to see merit in Arnold-Forster's reform proposals. Rather bitterly, Arnold-Forster remarked that, while Haldane justified Plumer's removal on the grounds that he had to have a brain on the Council, 'if he had wanted to get rid of empty heads, there were two on the Council [Lyttelton and Wolfe Murray] which simply rattle'. Douglas appears to have played a major role in the removal of Plumer, though Arnold-Forster believed he also detected Esher's hand. Repington had always believed Douglas would have considerable influence on the Army Council through having a far stronger personality than Lyttelton. The notoriously bad-tempered Douglas certainly had his own likes and dislikes. He shared Lyttelton's dislike of Hamilton, but, in turn, both Douglas and his wife disliked Lyttelton. Douglas also appears to have attempted to block Aylmer Haldane for a brigade command while James Edmonds, the future official historian of the Great War, believed Douglas to have 'done a lot of harm – he chose all the wrong men and penalised any who had ideas and originality'.[40]

Lyttelton offered his resignation to Haldane in August 1906 following the critical report of the Butler Committee. Haldane, however, considered that Lyttelton had not been personally to blame for the system in place in South Africa and declined to accept it. Moreover, the ineffectiveness of the Army Council as a collective body under Lyttelton also recommended his retention to a Secretary of State intent on introducing controversial reforms. Though a friend of Lyttelton and his wife, however, Haldane eventually resorted to Arnold-Forster's method of trying to persuade Lyttelton to go to a different command, offering Grenfell a Field-Marshal's baton to vacate the Irish command to make way for Lyttelton. Once again, Lyttelton declined to move. Consequently, Lyttelton saw out his four-year term of office and Nicholson finally succeeded him as CGS in April 1908, the King having accepted that this would be so in the previous year. One additional safeguard to reassure the King, however, was to give the post of Inspector-General more influence over training, and French succeeded Connaught despite Repington's attempt to talk up Kitchener as a candidate. Esher's assumption now was that the Inspector-General rather than the CGS should be the potential C-in-C in the field in the event of war. Haldane had also resolved that French would command in the event of a war.[41]

'OLD NICK' TRIUMPHANT

As CGS and, from 1909, as Chief of the Imperial General Staff (CIGS), Nicholson proved a success in establishing the General Staff. Once one of his greatest critics, Esher now came to regard Nicholson as much underrated: 'no one, I fear, will ever know what a large debt of gratitude is due to him for his hard work, patience and good sense in administering the Army'. Nicholson and French appear to have worked well together, despite French's dislike for Nicholson: he had once characterised Nicholson as 'born to be a damned nuisance to everyone'. In due course, and with no discernible controversy, French succeeded Nicholson as CIGS in March 1912, though Repington for one felt the efficiency of the War Office much reduced with the departure of both Haldane and Nicholson.[42]

In the event, French and Spencer Ewart, now Adjutant-General, were forced to resign over the Curragh incident in March 1914. Douglas, who was the choice of both French and Ewart, succeeded as CIGS. There was some horror at the prospect of Hamilton succeeding and, in some quarters, at the possibility that Nicholson might be recalled, though this was never seriously contemplated.[43]

By this time, Esher's influence had diminished, not least through the death of Edward VII in May 1910.[44] The organisation Esher had created, however, remained. Unfortunately, for all its potential, it was far from perfect. Moreover, through choosing 'selection by disparagement', Esher and his colleagues had only succeeded in exacerbating the tensions within the army's highly personalised command structure.

4

Lord Kitchener, the General Staff and the Army in India, 1902–14

Timothy Moreman

The army in India was the largest permanent overseas military commitment for the British armed forces between 1900 and 1914. In 1901, a force of 66,086 troops of the British Army and 142,831 British-officered, locally recruited troops of the Indian Army garrisoned the subcontinent.[1] The latter had a distinctive organisation, equipment and ethos of its own. It had three distinctive military commitments: maintaining internal security, guarding India's long and troubled land frontiers both from potential Russian or Afghan threats and more immediately the frontier tribes, and lastly, providing troops for overseas garrisons and expeditionary forces. The army in India was not a mere replica of the British Army at home in terms of higher organisation, staff and command arrangements. It was led by the C-in-C in India, who was, in turn, directly responsible to the Government of India, the Governor-General and ultimately the Secretary of State for India in London. The writ of the War Office only extended so far as the interior economy of British regiments on the Indian establishment, leaving questions of organisation, equipment and training in the hands of the local government. Perhaps surprisingly given the size of the army in India and its later role in the First World War, little attention has been paid to the development of the General Staff in the subcontinent. While Brian Bond has charted the development of higher military education and the General Staff in the United Kingdom in his ground-breaking study of the Staff College, India was only mentioned in passing. Similarly, in his *The Plans of War* John Gooch ignores British arms in India, focusing instead on the formation of the General Staff and its extension to the self-governing Dominions.[2] This chapter examines Lord Kitchener's efforts to improve the Indian staff system during the early 1900s, eventually culminating in the formation of the General Staff in India in April 1910. It concludes by briefly examining the work of the new Indian General Staff before the outbreak of the First World War, focusing on its efforts to improve the preparedness of the army in India.

The appointment of Lord Kitchener as C-in-C in India on 28 November 1902 began a period of far-reaching reform of the military in British India. Intent on passing on lessons learnt by the British Army during the Second Boer War, Kitchener tackled his new post with his customary drive and determination. It was quickly apparent that considerable remedial work, however, was needed to improve the preparedness of the army in India for war, with the objective of transforming it into a modern fighting force capable of holding in check a Russian invasion. As Kitchener noted in December 1902: 'I am not very deeply impressed with its efficiency for the field. In fact I fear that if the army were called upon to take part in war, it would come to considerable grief.'[3] In 1903–04, Kitchener submitted sweeping plans to improve the army in India, eventually involving the formation of nine divisions and three cavalry brigades during peacetime, each complete with its own integral staff and ancillary troops that would take the field in war. It required a major redistribution of units throughout the subcontinent and involved considerable changes in its organisation, equipment and training.[4]

The standard of training of staff officers at the Army Headquarters (AHQ) and the organisation of the staff immediately concerned the new C-in-C in India, who realised radical improvements were needed. In 1902 the staff of AHQ was organised on the same lines as that in the UK, with the Adjutant-General dealing with discipline, administration and training and the Quartermaster-General responsible for operations, intelligence, mobilisation and logistics.[5] No attempt had been made to organise a staff on the continental model. In many ways the Mobilisation Branch in the Quartermaster-General's Department was the closest thing the army in India had to a General Staff, being responsible for all of its duties with the exception of training and intelligence.[6] It was in the view of one officer, however, 'absurdly under-staffed'. In some respects the Intelligence Branch was more advanced, but it was little more than an office for recording information, with no system for turning knowledge into plans for war.[7] Both were considerably overworked, requiring further staff in 1903 to function effectively.[8] Under the Adjutant-General military training was largely limited to the regimental level, with only occasional camps of exercise held. No real division was made between day-to-day administration and the various duties involved in preparing the army in India for war, with the result that, like the British Army before the Second Boer War, it was ill-prepared for hostilities. The existing staff in India did not, moreover, enjoy a reputation for efficiency. As George MacMunn, a graduate of Camberley serving in the Mobilisation Branch during the 1900s, later recalled:

> It had long been a subject of bitter and contemptuous comment among the more instructed that India preferred to appoint to its Staff those who thought Frontier activity to be the be all and end all

of soldiering, or nice-looking young men with friends at court. Further, it was a matter of common comment that the Staff in India was pretty amateur and inefficient.[9]

Its many weaknesses had been exposed during the great frontier rising in 1897–98, when efforts to mobilise 59,000 troops and raise all the necessary transport had been chaotic.[10] Trained staff officers had been in short supply throughout the fighting, with only 28 out of 85 staff officers employed with field forces having received higher military education at the Staff College at Camberley in the UK.[11] Since so few Indian Army officers had attended this establishment, undue reliance was placed on the small number of British service officers with certificates for having passed Staff College ('pscs') serving in the subcontinent. Most appointments were filled in default by officers whose only qualification for staff duties was having passed the promotion examination for major and having a language qualification in Hindustani.[12]

The best means of improving the higher education and supply of qualified staff officers formed the first focus of Lord Kitchener's attention, as his redistribution scheme demanded a far greater number of staff officers than the existing system could provide. Moreover, as Kitchener explained to Lord Roberts in May 1903, a college was 'very much needed to enable us to have a sufficient number of trained staff officers in case of active operations'.[13] This was not a new problem. In 1875 the government of India had proposed establishing a college in India to instruct officers in staff duties.[14] Indeed, the output of the Staff College at Camberley – 32 a year – was barely sufficient for the British Army at home, let alone that for the army in India. This request had been refused, however, because of the fear that it would lack Camberley's prestige, the expense involved, shortages of suitably qualified staff, the absence of battlefields where modern warfare could be studied, an unsuitable climate and lastly fears that its graduates would not be treated equally with those of Camberley. Although the Staff College was opened in 1876 to six Indian service officers each year, the expense barred many attending. In any event, a 'psc' was not an essential qualification for staff employment in India and officers ran the risk of missing active service in a frontier campaign.[15] A further plea in 1889–90 to increase the number of Indian service officers attending Camberley also fell on deaf ears, leaving India badly deficient in staff officers.[16]

In October 1903 the government of India submitted, with the strong endorsement of the Viceroy, Lord Curzon and his Viceregal Council, its new proposal for an Indian Staff College to the Secretary of State for India.[17] It met strong opposition, however, from the Army Council. A committee appointed by the War Office to consider the proposal gave it short shrift, preferring instead to have the money spent on Camberley and encouraging a greater number of Indian service officers to attend.[18] The Army Council concurred with this conclusion, stressing the importance of ensuring that the staff organisation of all imperial forces follow the same line.[19] Despite this disparaging reception, Lord Kitchener persevered and won the agreement of the Secretary of State after accepting that it would have the same entrance examinations, graduates from Camberley would form its staff and it would follow the same curriculum and syllabus.[20]

The Indian Staff College finally opened its doors in temporary accommodation at Deolali in the Deccan on 1 June 1905 pending construction of a new building elsewhere. Under the command of Brigadier-General A. W. Bayly, it initially had vacancies for 24 students, 7 British and 17 Indian service officers. Its Commandant and three professors were graduates of Camberley, ensuring continuity of teaching between the two staff establishments upon whose syllabus the curriculum was based. Despite an ongoing debate in 1905 about the dangers of creating a 'school of thought' in India distinct from that in the UK, the new Staff College prospered. In March 1906 Colonel Thompson Capper became Commandant and oversaw the College's expansion to full strength and later supervised its move to a new permanent site, while a party of officers toured the battlefields of the Russo-Japanese War in Manchuria. The Indian Staff College opened at its permanent location at Quetta in Baluchistan in April 1907, where it began steadily turning out badly needed qualified staff officers to fill staff appointments in India.[21]

The reorganisation of staff duties offered the quickest alternative means of improving the preparation of the army in India for war, while the future of the Staff College was being decided. A considerable delay in improving military efficiency had been caused by having no distinct divide between routine administrative work and training for war at AHQ and elsewhere in India. As the Adjutant-General explained in July 1903:

> This routine work cannot be neglected, for on its careful and punctual performance the comfort and well-being of the troops in peace almost entirely depends, but ... to allow it to absorb all the energies of the staff is to lose sight of the fact that the army exists for war and that its training for war must take precedence of everything else.[22]

In India Army Order no. 246 of 1904, outlining various measures to improve training and military education, Kitchener acknowledged that assistance from a 'thoroughly trained and highly educated general staff' was required by senior officers 'to prepare them for all the changing phases and emergencies of war'. In Kitchener's words,

> This has never yet been fully realised in India, where no special staff training has up to the present been provided, and where, in fact, no facilities whatever exist for any higher military education than that necessary for promotion to the rank of major.[23]

Until the Indian Staff College could produce a 'thoroughly practical general staff', the C-in-C announced a new allotment of staff duties, for the first time separating routine administrative duties from those connected with preparation for war. Two divisions of the staff were formed. 'The Art of War' was concerned with studying 'higher problems of war' and based on such study the 'battle training of the personnel' and 'the preparation and development of material resources'. In turn this division of the staff was sub-divided into two sections: training and preparation for war and maintenance of movement. Both were intended to work in close co-operation with 'that combination of purpose and perfect smoothness of execution which is possessed by the twin screws of a ship … to drive the vessel of the army towards perfect efficiency'. A 'Routine' section of the staff was assigned responsibility for day-to-day administration of the army in both peace and war, dealing with the mundane but important duties of ensuring the efficiency of troops in barracks and in the field.[24]

This reorganisation was a significant step towards preparing the army in India for war. In several respects it foreshadowed and anticipated later proposals for the formation of a General Staff.[25] The titles given to the new divisions were, however, a source of considerable amusement. As one officer later wryly recalled both titles were 'singularly inappropriate', with 'little in staff duties being artistic'. Indeed, the term 'Routine', he went on, was enough to stifle enthusiasm and scare off the ambitious.[26] Other staff officers were more irreverent, dubbing the 'Art of War' Section as 'Bloodshed', while 'Routine' was known simply as 'Inkshed'.[27]

The staff at AHQ also underwent reorganisation to simplify administration and improve readiness for war, when a new Division of the Chief of Staff was established early in 1906 to act as the 'thinking staff' of the army in India. A new appointment of Chief of Staff, working directly under the C-in-C in India, was created as its head with responsibility for the 'Art of War' section and overseeing the other divisions of the staff.[28] This new division was given overall charge for policy affecting the army, its organisation and distribution for external war and internal security, preparation for war, intelligence, mobilisation, higher training and education, organisation, plans of operations and schemes for offence and defence, staff training and organisation and finally manoeuvres and the actual conduct of war. Under the command of Lieutenant-General Sir Beauchamp Duff it was divided into two sections: Military Operations, and Training and Staff Duties. The former, commanded by Colonel Herbert Mullaly, was split into three sub-divisions: intelligence, mobilisation (formerly the responsibility of the QMG) and a new strategical branch.[29] The latter made possible, for the first time, theoretical study of strategic problems, concentrating on the Russian threat, although it did not prepare detailed schemes for either external operations or internal security. It produced in 1909, for example, detailed strategical studies for operations across the North-West Frontier of India in Afghanistan.[30] Many serious gaps, however, still existed in terms of war plans.[31] The Training and Staff Duties Section, headed by Colonel Jack Cowan, dealt with higher training and the education of officers, co-operation between the three arms, manoeuvres, camps of exercise, learning lessons, reconnaissance, staff organisation, duties and training, the Staff College and the education of officers. While undoubtedly an important step forward, however, the Adjutant-General still retained control of regimental training, in addition to its many other time-consuming administrative duties. Following the abolition of the Military Department in March 1906, as a result of the acrimonious Kitchener–Curzon dispute over Indian military administration, the Division of the Chief of Staff also assumed many of its administrative duties.

The formation of the General Staff at the War Office in London in September 1906, based upon recommendations submitted two years before by the Esher Committee, did not escape attention in India. Lord Kitchener was kept closely informed of changes in progress at the War Office and in general was not opposed to a similar organisation in India. The hostile reception given to Beauchamp Duff before a sub-committee of the CID in January 1907, however, quickly made him highly critical of the 'miserable lot' in the General Staff at the War Office.[32] As Kitchener noted in March 1907: 'The General Staff at home are really too absurdly effete for words. I think we could do better here but it makes me doubt the advisability of creating a General Staff when one sees the fiasco at home.'[33] The resolutions of the Imperial Conference in April 1907, however, added further impetus to developing a similar organisation in India, emphasising the importance of a wider Imperial General Staff. In a memorandum dated 5 August 1907, Kitchener outlined his own proposals for a new staff system in India:

> The time has arrived when it becomes desirable to carry out the organisation of the Army in India another step further by commencing the development of a part of the existing staff into the higher form of a General Staff. Such a body as the latter cannot, however, be called into being, by the mere fiat of superior authority, but must be slowly evolved, and in order that this evolution might take the right direction, it is necessary that, from the very commencement, the end to be attained should be clearly understood.
>
> To think out plans in all their details when dealing with large and complex forces surpasses the power of the individual, not from want of ability but from lack of time to elaborate them. Another branch of the staff then becomes necessary to relieve the General of the labour of elaborating detail – and so set him free to work out the broad and essential features of his schemes. It is to this branch of the staff that

the name of 'General Staff' is applied. A General Staff is, therefore, primarily and essentially a war organisation, though it has important duties to perform in peace.[34]

This memorandum discussed at length the role and function of a general staff, envisaging it being primarily designed just to assist a commanding general. As he explained: 'The first duty of a General Staff is to think, but their thinking must be directed solely to furthering the intentions of their General. The idea aimed at is to enable him to use their brains as if they were extensions of his own.' Kitchener stressed that its task in peacetime lay in studying and preparing for war, upon which the preparation and training of the army as a whole would be based. It would deal with military policy, strategy, mobilisation, concentration and location of troops, training and manoeuvres and the collection and compilation of intelligence. Kitchener emphasised that such an organisation would take time to create and could not be found 'ready made', stressing the importance of careful selection and gradual training of suitable officers and that accordingly 'the evolution of a General Staff must always be a slow process'. Indeed, he was mindful of the dangers of creating a General Staff apart from the rest of the army, with close contacts being maintained instead by officers only serving periodic tours of duty with the staff and then returning to regimental service. Finally, Kitchener acknowledged that the demanding work of a General Staff officer justified reward in terms of accelerated promotion for meritorious service so that the very best officers would compete for admission to the General Staff, although he was mindful of creating professional jealousy within the rest of the army.[35] In a letter written at the same time Kitchener observed: 'I am only just starting the show & as you will see I think on rather better lines than the W.O. Our staff has now worked up & been organised up to this from the *bottom*. The W.O. seems always to work from top & never get very deep down.'[36]

These detailed proposals for a General Staff in India, working under the orders of the government of India, were formally submitted in a despatch to the Secretary of State for India in October 1907.[37] It enclosed a Draft India Army Order, incorporating Kitchener's memorandum, setting out in detail the organisation of a General Staff composed of 80 officers at AHQ and with the troops in divisions and independent brigades, terms of service for officers and rewards for meritorious service.[38] When he responded in March 1908 Lord Morley, the Secretary of State for India, expressed his full agreement, except regarding the proposed terms of service and rewards of staff officers, mindful that these would cause harmful divergence between India and the UK.[39] The Indian military authorities, however, strongly resisted any suggestion that each and every rule and regulation laid down by the Army Council should apply to India, especially those it feared would be detrimental to the efficiency of regimental officers by being overly generous to those in staff employ. As the government of India emphasised in its reply:

> We find ourselves unable to admit that this involves our accepting as applicable to the Indian Army any and every rule laid down by the Army Council whether suitable to Indian conditions or not and irrespective of whether we have not been consulted in regard to it.

Since the provisions about accelerated promotion laid down in the draft India Army Order were regarded as a central element of Kitchener's scheme, this was a major stumbling block causing the issue to be referred back to the India Office. Accordingly the despatch concluded: 'Until this very important question of promotion is decided we considered that it would not be wise to embark on the creation of a General staff in India which might be foredoomed to failure.'[40]

The question of the formation of a General Staff in India largely fell into abeyance until a detailed memorandum prepared by the War Office, proposing the formation of an Imperial General Staff (IGS), prompted further debate when it was forwarded in April 1909 to the C-in-C and the government of India for their observations.[41] Originally prepared by the General Staff in accordance with a resolution passed at the Imperial Defence Conference in April 1907, this detailed paper was submitted in December 1908, directed almost in its entirety towards the governments of South Africa, Canada, New Zealand and the Commonwealth of Australia. It stressed that the best means of ensuring that troops from throughout the empire could work in close combination, either for local defence or for wider imperial purposes, was by organising them all on the same general principles, especially regarding command and staff work. In its view:

> The ideal to be arrived at is that all divisions of military force should be capable of acting in war as parts of a whole. This ideal can only be fully realized when all the parts are organized and trained by one brain, and in the modern army that brain is the General Staff. The General Staff must therefore be an entity throughout the Empire, and to make it so, all its members ought to be uniformly trained in principles and practice in one school under one head.[42]

After discussing the duties of a General Staff in peace and war, it emphasised the importance of a central body in London – an Imperial General Staff – studying and formulating general principles and also in collecting and disseminating information of wider application to the rest of the British Empire. It envisaged the formation of local branches, each part of the Imperial General Staff, in each overseas regular garrison, Dominion and in India studying local problems and needs, as well as supervising the application of broad principles to local conditions. A

Chief of the Imperial General Staff (CIGS) in London would provide uniformity of method of purpose, co-ordinating the work of the local sections and supervising the central 'brain' of the British Empire at the War Office. It did recognise, however, that the control of these Chiefs of Local Sections might cause difficulties, since they would be advisers to their own governments as well as being under the CIGS.[43]

These new proposals received a mixed reaction in India. While Kitchener and the Viceregal Council completely agreed that every part of the British Empire should maintain sufficient military forces to defend itself and that an Imperial General Staff would have considerable value in 'federating the military forces of the Empire', they had serious misgivings about several key points. Indeed, the very fact that it had been drawn up without consultation with the government of India caused anger, but specific criticism was reserved for several recommendations it had made about India. In particular, the suggestion that the Indian staff would only constitute a 'Local Section' of the Imperial General Staff, responsible directly to the CIGS rather than to the government of India, aroused fierce opposition. As the government of India pointed out in June 1909: 'It must be remembered that, in all matters of military organisation, numerous questions of policy and finance must always be involved, in the decision of which, the Secretary of State and the Government of India must be left entirely untrammeled.' Two other concerns were raised. Its recommendation that only officers drawn from the central body would be employed on the staff of 'a supreme commander' in war, caused considerable misgivings, given the 'special circumstances' involved in campaigning in India and fears that Indian service officers would be excluded from senior staff appointments. The status of the Staff College at Quetta also caused concern, since it had been stated that Camberley was the 'Central School' of higher military education of the whole empire and that all higher educational appointments would only be filled by its graduates. Despite these important reservations the despatch concluded:

> The creation of such a General Staff in this country is … a matter of urgent importance, particularly as it will not be possible to proceed with the formation of any Local Section of the Imperial General Staff until a General Staff in India has been created; and we, therefore, strongly recommend that permission may now be given to proceed with its formation on the lines agreed upon.[44]

The Secretary of State for India, Lord Morley, acted quickly and, during the summer of 1909, successfully addressed most of the fears expressed by the government of India. Regarding the relationship between the Indian General Staff and Imperial General Staff and with the C-in-C and the government of India, the Army Council was reminded in August 1909:

In India the C-in-C is the sole military adviser of the Government. He performs, in addition to his other duties, those which the Chief of the Imperial General Staff performs in this country, in relation to the Secretary of State for War, and the Chief of the Staff is and must be subordinate to him. Although, therefore, in consideration of the burden of work imposed on the C-in-C in India, the Indian Chief of the General Staff may be placed in direct communication with the Chief of the Imperial General Staff, on the principle set forth in the War Office statement, such communication must be limited to matters of routine, such as operations, training and staff duties, and must be absolutely under the control, and subject to the approval, of the C-in-C. No direct communications between those officers on questions of policy or finance could be permitted, as such matters can, in India, only be dealt with by the C-in-C and the Government. The C-in-C would be responsible for the strict observance of these conditions.[45]

The War Office quickly acknowledged this point, as well as agreeing that it would be impossible to restrict staff appointments to Imperial General Staff officers in the event of a war involving the Indian Army.[46] In an official despatch dated 1 October, Lord Morley allayed the other fears expressed that summer and formally authorised the government of India to proceed finally with the establishment of a General Staff in India 'on the lines laid down by His Majesty's Government for an Imperial General Staff'.[47]

The drawn-out discussions about the organisation, duties and terms of service of the proposed General Staff scheme between 1907 and 1909 meant that Kitchener was not still in office when agreement was finally reached. In his place General Sir O'Moore Creagh VC, formerly Military Secretary at the India Office, was made C-in-C in India in September 1909 to the surprise of many observers, including his predecessor. As Kitchener had noted in February 1909 when news had leaked out:

It seems too absurd as he is hardly a second rate man and the whole of the Indian Army will roar with laughter if he is made C in C ... I pity the Head Quarter organisation as it now is if it is to be left to O'Moore Creagh he will wreck the whole show ... through ignorance and incapacity.[48]

While he had successfully led the Indian contingent during the Boxer Rebellion, O'Moore Creagh – an extrovert, happy-go-lucky Irishman quickly dubbed by his subordinates as 'No more K' – lacked his predecessor's drive and had little practical experience of high command. As one staff officer at AHQ later recorded: 'Grande Guerre and its preparations were strange subjects to him.'[49] This in part explains his choice of

Lieutenant-General Sir Douglas Haig as his new Chief of Staff. As Director of Military Training and later Director of Staff Duties at the War Office in 1906–09, Haig was well qualified for overseeing the establishment of an Indian General Staff, having been closely associated with the implementation of the General Staff scheme in the UK and preparation of *Field Service Regulations*. Indeed, as he admitted, one of the main reasons he had accepted the post was 'the importance of starting a Gen. Staff in India and weeding out Simla and developing the Imp General staff'.[50]

When Haig arrived in India the creation of the Indian General Staff, organised on the lines of papers on the organisation and working of an Imperial General Staff and agreed at the Imperial Conference in 1909, was immediately put in hand. Applying these principles, however, did not prove an easy task as financial restrictions prevented any additional staff appointments being made and the diversity of local conditions in India made the application of a uniform organisation difficult. Indeed, many senior officers were apprehensive of the proposed new organisation, fearing it would cause a rift between the General Staff and army as a whole and between the general and administrative branches of the staff.[51] In late 1909 a memorandum outlining the proposed scheme was drawn up by the new Chief of Staff and circulated to army, division and independent brigade commanders for comment to allay these fears. A revised scheme was prepared by the CGS, Adjutant-General and Quartermaster-General during the spring of 1910, incorporating various modifications based on these comments, that, following its approval by O'Moore Creagh, was circulated to explain the principles underlying the formation of a General Staff in India.[52]

The new General Staff organisation was finally announced in a Special India Army Order issued on 19 March 1910, covering the establishment of the General Staff and the consequent reorganisation of the administrative staff. In accordance with the Imperial General Staff scheme, the Indian General Staff was grouped into two principal divisions, the General Staff at AHQ and the General Staff in armies, divisions and independent brigades. Its functions at AHQ were to advise on the distribution of the army, to supervise the education of officers and the training and preparation of the army for war, to study offensive and defensive military schemes, to direct army policy and to secure continuity in the execution of that policy. The staff with the army was tasked with assisting commanders in promoting efficiency, especially regarding officer education and training, and aiding them in carrying out the policy laid down by the AHQ. In terms of internal organisation, AHQ closely followed that in force at the War Office, with the notable exception that 'Staff Duties' and 'Military Training' were amalgamated to form a single directorate. The new Military Operations Directorate was divided into three branches: Strategical, Organisation and Intelligence, while the Staff Duties and

Training Directorate was split into separate General Staff, Co-ordination and Military Training branches. In the consequent redistribution of duties, mobilisation was transferred to the Adjutant-General and concentration to the Quartermaster-General. Perhaps most importantly, responsibility for regimental training, previously assigned to the Adjutant-General, was given to the Chief of the General Staff.

The staff of armies underwent no change, as they had no administrative staffs following the earlier reorganisation of the army in India. Based on home war establishments each divisional HQ was assigned three General Staff Officers, as well as two administrative staff officers. The three independent frontier brigades and garrisons of the defended ports of Aden, Karachi, Bombay and Calcutta necessitated further modification of the IGS scheme, with each assigned an additional General Staff and an administrative staff officer to carry out their special duties in peace and war.[53]

The General Staff in India, with Lieutenant-General Sir Douglas Haig as its first Chief of the General Staff, faced a wide range of problems in preparing the army in India for war. Under the new organisation the General Staff Branch at AHQ, re-designated as such in July 1911, acted as a co-ordinating staff at AHQ, both supervising and working in close co-operation with the administrative staff headed by the Adjutant-General and Quartermaster-General.[54] A committee under Brigadier-General A. Hamilton Gordon assembled at AHQ in December 1910, for example, considered reorganising the branches of AHQ India on the principles obtaining at the War Office and co-ordinating the work of the various sections.[55] It also played an important part in compiling a War Book co-ordinating the action of the government of India and local governments in event of a major war.[56] Some efforts were made to co-ordinate work with the War Office in London, although the Indian CGS was restricted to discussing questions not affecting policy or finance. Any efforts at closer co-operation, however, met strong resistance from the government of India. When Haig sent a memorandum outlining the duties and responsibilities of the army in India direct to the War Office in 1911, for example, the Viceroy demanded its return unopened, fearful that the War Office might interfere in plans for reducing its strength.[57] Even attempts to remodel plans using nomenclature and methods of staff work agreed at the Imperial Defence Conferences, meant that Haig and his staff were accused of endeavouring to 'drag the Indian Army at the heels of Whitehall'.[58] Efforts at developing closer links with the armed forces of the self-governing Dominions were more successful, with the Indian General Staff participating in officer exchanges, attachments and interchanges of officers.[59]

While the Military Operations Directorate did not have such extensive geographical responsibilities as its much larger counterpart at the War

Office, it still had to deal with a wide range of potential 'threats'. As Major-General A. Hamilton Gordon, the Director of Military Operations (DMO) in India, explained on 1 November 1913:

> In the first place 'War' at home is practically limited to war with one or more first-class Powers, whereas in India we have to be prepared for expeditions of all sorts, major and minor, the latter often being passed unnoticed except by those who are immediately interested. Our whole land frontier of nearly 7,000 miles is liable to raids, to deal with which the local police and troops have to be constantly ready. At home the sea and the prestige of our Navy take the place of the Indian frontier troops. Within our frontiers it is undeniable that we maintain a fixed proportion of British troops, and the reason is based on the oft disputed saying that our rule rests on British bayonets. In any case we have to be constantly ready for outbursts which, in their more serious form, can never be contemplated in England ... These differences and the special conditions under which General Staff work in India has to be carried out are not fully appreciated by those not actually engaged in the work, and are scarcely understood by those who only look at India from a distance, or study its conditions on paper.[60]

The maintenance of internal security in India was a complex problem for the General Staff, prompting detailed planning for dealing with a wide spectrum of social, political and religious unrest that might threaten the colonial regime. Despite the need for close consultation with the local political authorities, rapid progress was made in preparing guidelines and plans for maintaining internal security.[61] In 1911 a detailed analysis of conditions in India and Burma was prepared, for example, discussing key points to be held in the event of a major uprising in India. This noted:

> It is the object of this study to determine both the areas and the communications leading thereto from our bases on the sea coast, on which our attention must from the first be directed, so that their safety will be secured to the last, in the event of a rising developing into a general rebellion and taxing our resources to the utmost.[62]

An essential part of the General Staff's duties also involved close scrutiny of the organisation, equipment and morale of the Indian Army itself, as it always represented the single greatest threat to the security of British rule.

The General Staff Branch also looked further afield in terms of planning and preparing schemes for operations on or beyond the Indian frontier. It played a key role in preparing plans, for example, for various minor operations carried out by the army in India before 1914. These included the Abor Expedition in 1911–12 and the larger arms traffic expedition on the Mekran Coast, involving joint operations between the army and the East Indies Squadron. As Hamilton Gordon observed: 'The officers of the Abor Expedition have said that it was the best organized affair that they have been on. Colonel Delamain who commanded the Arms Traffic troops said he was perfectly satisfied with the organization and arrangements.'[63] The prospect of war with Imperial Russia had always loomed large in the minds of Indian defence planners. Following the Anglo-Russian convention, the likelihood of conflict had declined so much that in 1911 the General Staff were instructed by the government of India not to prepare any detailed plans for a war with that country.[64] Although study of strategical conditions on the North-West Frontier continued, it now did so on the basis of war with Afghanistan and the increasingly heavily armed frontier tribes. During 1912, for example, the existing strategical study of conditions on the North-West Frontier of India prepared by the Chief of Staff's Division was revised.[65] Although Haig had arrived in India aiming to modernise the army in India so that it would be available for imperial purposes, little headway was made.[66] In fact, the study and preparation of plans dealing with the deployment of the Indian Army in the Middle East or in Europe was specifically banned by the Government of India and at the India Office by Lord Morley. As Haig's most recent biographer, Gerard de Groot, has written: 'When he tried to devise plans for mobilising the Indian Army in the event of a European war, the Viceroy, Lord Hardinge, intervened and ordered the destruction of the plans.'[67] This did not completely prevent such schemes being studied, however, which was carried out at AHQ under a different name and dressed up as an academic staff exercise in strategy and organisation.[68]

The work of the Intelligence Branch reflected the diverse military commitments of the army in India, in terms of the information it collected, collated and supplied to the other departments of the General Staff. A large part of its work dealt with the 'internal threat'. Detailed intelligence was required, for example, about the armies of the Princely States and political, social and religious movements, in addition to information about routes and local resources.[69] In accordance with earlier agreements with its counterpart in London, it had responsibility for intelligence gathering in certain regions adjacent to India.[70] Much of its work, however, dealt with only partly explored regions outside India about whose topography and inhabitants information was scanty. A large part of its attention accordingly focused on the production of route guides and gazetteers pieced together from reports, travellers and occasional military expeditions.[71]

The new Directorate of Staff Duties and Military Training built upon earlier reforms instituted by Lord Kitchener since 1902. It oversaw military education of the staff, training, manoeuvres, as well as supervising the organisation, development and training of signal companies, musketry, cavalry and flying schools.[72] Perhaps the most important element of its work of wider application were efforts to standardise fighting and training methods between the British Army and the army in India, on the lines laid down by the Imperial Defence Conference in 1911. The provisions of *King's Regulations* were adopted in India, for example, for the first time for promotion examinations. Perhaps more importantly, in India Army Order no. 282 of 1911, *Field Service Regulations*, the Training Manuals of the various arms, *Training and Manoeuvre Regulations*, Musketry Regulations and the *Field Service Pocket Book*, issued to the regular British Army, were adopted as standard texts in India.[73] This important step brought organisation, administration and training for the first time into line with that in the UK. Whenever necessary a modification or supplement was made to official manuals, however, making them applicable and relevant to the Indian Army's needs. Indeed, following the formations of the General Staff all drafts of new manuals were sent to India for comment and amendment before publication.[74] In 1912 a revised edition, for example, of *Field Service Regulations Volume I* appeared incorporating sections dealing with mountain warfare, the employment of pioneer battalions, and pack transport.[75]

The now flourishing Staff College at Quetta made a notable contribution to the development of the Indian General Staff, providing a steady flow of badly needed 'pscs' to fill local appointments. Indeed, considerable competition from British and Indian service officers, attracted by coveted staff appointments and accelerated promotion, occurred for the limited number of vacancies on each course. Under the command of Lieutenant-Colonel Walter Braithwaite, relations between staff and students mellowed considerably.[76] Following a visit in October 1911 the Chief of the General Staff in India (CGSI) noted:

> I was much struck with the friendly feeling existing between Braith and his Staff, and the Officer students. This was not the case last year. In fact there was a gulf between T. Capper & 'the lads' ... He was too full of nerves and too much of a crank to get the best out of officers.[77]

Amongst its Directing Staff were several officers destined to reach high rank, including Lieutenant-Colonel Archibald Montgomery, a future CIGS, and Lieutenant-Colonel Andrew Skeen, another high flyer destined to be CGSI between 1924 and 1928. Earlier fears that it would create a 'separate school of thought' proved ill-founded, with its curriculum and syllabus closely co-ordinated with that of its 'parent' in the UK. As Brigadier-General Walter Braithwaite, Commandant of Quetta during 1911–14, noted in October 1912:

Naturally, in accordance with the eternal fitness of things, the Staff College, Quetta, models itself on the mother college at Camberley. Different climatic conditions impose certain modifications, but, apart from these, the underlying principles of Staff College work, and of Staff College spirit, at Camberley and at Quetta, differ in no particular.[78]

By 1914, 218 new pscs had graduated from Quetta, including officers from the self-governing Dominions, including among their number the future Field-Marshal Sir Thomas Blamey.[79]

The ongoing professional development of General Staff officers serving at AHQ, the Staff College, armies, divisions and independent brigades, was carried out at a series of conferences and staff rides directed by the CGSI. Based on similar meetings in the UK, the first of these periodic meetings had been held at Agra in January 1909, directed by Beauchamp Duff, devoted to discussing staff duties in India, as well as considering the system used by the British Army at home.[80] Following the appointment of Sir Douglas Haig, this system was continued in January 1910, when the opportunity was taken to disseminate news about the new staff organisation and to sound out the views of senior officers, brought together from commands scattered over the subcontinent. Such gatherings enabled officers to study current military problems, specific General Staff questions and to an extent ensure unity of thought on strategical and tactical principles throughout the army in India in accordance with wider imperial needs.[81] A series of practical staff tours were held during the winter of 1909 and 1910. The first covered the concentration and handling of an army mobilised under normal Indian conditions in Asia and the second discussed the employment of an imperial army drawn from several portions of the empire in co-operation with the army in India in the subcontinent. A third, held in May–November 1911, dealt with an increasingly sensitive subject for the army in India, involving a study of a contingent being sent overseas to co-operate with other imperial troops. Such exercises provided a valuable chance for staff officers to undertake duties required of them in wartime, as well as an opportunity to standardise doctrine between the UK and India on the lines of *Field Service Regulations*.[82] As Haig explained: 'I have tried to preach "the doctrine" as laid down in F.S.R. Vol I. and have quoted chap & verse so that the General Staff here may interpret the Regns in the way in which I believe is intended.'[83]

The new General Staff organisation proved generally successful, although growing political pressure for reductions in the strength of the army in India hindered its full development. It did not, however, function completely smoothly or escape criticism before the outbreak of the First World War. Perhaps the most detailed criticism was levelled by the majority report submitted by the Army in India Committee, appointed to investigate reducing military expenditure. Field Marshal Sir William Nicholson, a former CIGS, and Sir William Meyer, Member of Council of the Finance Department, accused it of being over-staffed and of interfering with administrative duties of other departments at AHQ. This was strongly refuted by the C-in-C in India. As General Sir O'Moore Creagh declared:

> I am further satisfied that the marked improvement in the efficiency of the Army in India of late years has largely been due to the institution of a General Staff. I can speak from my own experience of the difficulties of the situation, and of the inadequate grasp of staff work in 1887–98 and generally before 1910 ... there is great leeway to be made up, both in information and intelligence, in organisation of the army and in its training for war. These are the arrears of twenty years and more, to be made up by a General Staff which has not yet been four years in existence. I fancy that both the Foreign Department and the Home Department would back me up when I say that I think that they also have felt the advantage of an efficient General Staff. I most strongly deprecate, therefore, any reduction in the General Staff Branch at Headquarters until a permanent organisation has been adopted for the army and until the Chief of the General Staff can say he has caught up all arrears and has the work reasonably in hand.[84]

The outbreak of hostilities in August 1914, however, meant that no reductions in its strength occurred. Indeed, it was now fully occupied in preparing the army in India for despatch overseas.

The creation of the General Staff in India in April 1910 was a major innovation and an important reform of the military in British India. For the first time an effective 'brain' for this large garrison had been created, devoted to planning systematically and preparing it for war during peacetime and conducting operations during hostilities. While organised generally on the same lines as the UK, it differed in detail from the Imperial General Staff to which it owed only loose allegiance. Unsurprisingly its work was more restricted in scope than at the War Office, focusing primarily on Indian problems: the defence of the North-West Frontier and internal security. It was not a completely new idea grafted onto the Indian military at the direction of the War Office in London. The establishment of the General Staff in India built upon the foundations laid by Lord Kitchener, in terms of establishing the Staff College at Quetta, separating administrative duties from preparing for war and the formation of the Division of the Chief of Staff. Although Kitchener had a circumscribed view of its duties, he was not opposed to the idea of a General Staff and gave considerable thought to the concept before submitting his own proposals in 1907 differing from the model followed in the UK.[85]

The appointment of Sir O'Moore Creagh as C-in-C, with Haig as his Chief of Staff, however, ensured that the final General Staff scheme followed the general lines agreed for the Imperial General Staff, introducing a remarkable degree of uniformity between India and the UK in terms of higher military organisation. Although the General Staff in India remained fully under the control of the government of India, this was a major step forward. As one officer remarked in the *Army Review* in 1912:

> It would indeed have been little less than a calamity if the formation of the General Staff in India had introduced any divergence from the principle of unity of organization which has been accepted by the rest of the Empire.[86]

During the short period before 1914 the Indian General Staff did much to prepare its troops for its tasks of waging war on the North-West Frontier, internal security and mounting an occasional small-scale overseas expeditions. Like its counterpart at the War Office, it oversaw the adoption of definite training principles, contributed to practical staff work and acted as a 'thinking department' for the Indian military.[87] Much work still remained outstanding, however, largely due to growing political pressure for financial retrenchment that from 1910 onwards hampered efforts to increase the preparedness for war of the army in India.

In terms of planning and preparing the army in India for wider imperial purposes it was less successful. Until July 1914 it was not allowed to develop plans for sending troops to Europe or the Middle East, thus hampering its early efforts when the First World War broke out.[88] Some guidance, however, was available. The despatch of Expeditionary Force 'A' to Egypt and Europe, for example, was partly based on the hurriedly 'dusted off' unauthorised plans prepared at Haig's direction.[89] The fact that it was not better organised and equipped for war against a conventional European opponent can be firmly blamed on British politicians and administrators who, in seeking cut-backs in military expenditure, had stymied the efforts of the military to prepare itself adequately for modern war. It was the acceptance of imperial regulations in terms of the system of command, staff duties, *Field Service Regulations* and other training manuals that paid most dividends for the army in India during 1914–18, allowing its units to operate comparatively easily alongside troops from other parts of the British Empire during the First World War.

5

The British Army, its General Staff and the Continental Commitment 1904–14

Hew Strachan

I

After the First World War, Lord Haldane, anxious to refurbish his reputation as Secretary of State for War between 1905 and 1912, published a self-justificatory memoir, *Before the War* (1920). His army reforms were, he claimed, an integrated whole, unified by a single strategic conception. That conception was 'how to mobilize at a place of assembly to be opposite the Belgian frontier, a force calculated as adequate ... to make up for the inadequacy of the French armies'.[1] This was the continental commitment, and its origins were dated to January 1906, the moment in the first Moroccan crisis when the Foreign Secretary, Sir Edward Grey, impressed upon the War Office the need to bolster French resolve by demonstrating Britain's readiness to provide military support. Joint staff talks began in December 1905 and continued until May 1906.[2]

Haldane's claim was both a vindication and an accusation. If it was substantiated, he was the man who had presciently prepared the British Army for the greatest war in which it had ever been engaged. But at the same time he exposed his country to A. J. P. Taylor's charge that in 1914 the foreign policies of the European powers had been hijacked by General Staff planning, with the result that Europe had gone 'to war by railway timetable'. In any literal sense that statement – untrue even for Germany and Austria-Hungary – was inapplicable to Britain. But what was true was that both Cabinet and Parliament had assumed on 2 and 3 August 1914 that Britain's principal effort in the war on which they were about to embark would be maritime. The argument that Britain's policy in the event of war was determined by the army's notion of strategy was not without foundation.

Haldane's interpretation and chronology were accepted by the first generation of scholars to have access to the papers, Nicholas d'Ombrain and J. McDermott.[3] The former believed that the Royal Navy had ceased to exercise its preponderance over the CID in 1905–06, and that thereafter the army's General Staff had usurped the policy-making function of both. Relieved of the threat of a Russian attack on India, first because such an invasion was logistically impossible and secondly – after 1907 – because of the diplomatic settlement between the two powers, the army had latched onto Germany as the justification for its existence. For d'Ombrain the Anglo-French staff talks in 1905–06 did at least provide a policy-making pivot for an argument that was largely driven by bureaucratic politics. McDermott took this point even further than d'Ombrain. He contended that the shift from expecting to fight Russia in India to planning a war with Germany in Europe had begun in 1904, even before the first Moroccan crisis.

McDermott published his article in 1974. In the same year John Gooch's *The Plans of War: The General Staff and British Military Strategy, c. 1900–1916* not only examined the creation of the General Staff as an institution but also drew attention to those of its plans which were never implemented as well as those which were. Gooch abandoned McDermott's vocabulary of revolution for that of gradualism, dubbing the period 1902–07 as one of 'strategic reorientation'. For him 1910, not 1906, let alone 1904, was when this process of change hardened. In August of that year Sir Henry Wilson was appointed DMO.

> Wilson's drive, enthusiasm and complete conviction about the necessity to render effective land support to France were to provide the stimulus to move military strategy on from the period of consideration and of deciding between alternatives to that of detailed planning for action.[4]

In the foreword to his collection of essays, *The Prospect of War* (1981), Gooch was even more forthright in condemning the work of d'Ombrain and McDermott.[5]

Edward Spiers's study of Haldane as an army reformer, published in 1980, endorsed Gooch's view. Spiers dismissed Haldane's claim that he had set about the creation of a British Expeditionary Force (BEF) in 1906 with a view to fulfilling the army's continental commitment in 1914. The BEF, Spiers insisted, was a force designed for intervention anywhere in the world, not just in Europe. It was the solution to a long-standing dilemma: the pressure to scatter British regular forces around the empire in penny packets as opposed to the need to create a central strategic reserve. At least until 1907 and the Anglo-Russian entente, and even implicitly thereafter, the continent for which the BEF seemed to be destined was Asia, not Europe, and its putative opponent Russia rather than Germany.

Spiers, like Gooch, pinpointed Henry Wilson's arrival as DMO in August 1910 as the moment of change.[6]

Gooch and Spiers were making explicit a claim bruited from the moment Charles Callwell published his revealing and in some ways indiscreet biography of Wilson in 1927. Callwell had quoted freely from Wilson's diaries. A passionate man, a Unionist and a Francophile, Wilson was indeed a forceful advocate of the continental commitment as it came to be implemented, that is to say, direct support for the French army with its implicit subordination of the BEF to French suzerainty, rather than an independent British operation in Belgium based on Antwerp. One of the first academic scholars in the field, J. E. Tyler, in *The British Army and the Continent, 1904–1914* (1938), had accepted elements of the Haldane argument by beginning his study with the plans of 1906, but had pointed out that two continental options rather than one were in play between 1906 and 1910, and that what Wilson had achieved was a definite commitment to France rather than to Belgium as the basis for General Staff planning. Tyler declared that Wilson's enthusiasm for France 'verged on the fanatical'.[7]

For Tyler, as for Gooch and Spiers, the meeting of the sub-committee of the CID on 23 August 1911 was when the French version of the continental commitment was accepted as British strategy. Asked to present the army's mobilisation plans in the midst of the second Moroccan crisis, Henry Wilson displayed his familiarity with French thinking while dismissing the Belgian option. Moreover, he left his naval opposite number reeling. The exposition of the First Sea Lord, Sir Arthur Wilson, was – according to Henry Wilson himself – 'pitiful'.[8] Gooch described the meeting as a 'victory' for Henry Wilson. The Prime Minister, Asquith, committed Britain to a military rather than a naval strategy, with the result that the latter was no longer an option when war broke out in 1914.[9]

That was not the conclusion of Maurice Hankey, the secretary of the CID, who wrote to the former First Sea Lord, Jackie Fisher, on the day following the meeting of 23 August 1911: 'The great point is that no decision was arrived at'.[10] D'Ombrain pointed out that Asquith had assured Reginald McKenna, the First Lord of the Admiralty, that he personally opposed a continental strategy, and that it was only a suggestion, not a settled policy.[11] The CID's attention between 1911 and 1914 was focused not on the BEF and its possible deployment, but on the Royal Navy, blockade and home defence.[12] The only clear outcomes from its meeting on 23 August were the replacement of McKenna as First Lord by Winston Churchill, and the latter's brief to create a naval General Staff. Henry Wilson's performance had scotched the navy's lingering advocacy of amphibious warfare but it had done so at the price of reinvigorating the search for a more effective naval strategy. It was the 1912 Anglo-French naval agreement, not the army staff talks, which provided France with leverage over Britain in the July crisis of 1914. On 1 August 1914 the Cabinet was proposing not to send the BEF to France, and when Grey addressed the House of Commons two days later he assumed that Britain's role in the coming war would be maritime. Even on 5 and 6 August, when a rump CID met to discuss British strategy, the key decisions regarding the employment of the BEF – whether it was to go to Belgium or to France, and whether it was to take its full complement – were all reopened.[13]

The basis for seeing 23 August 1911 as pivotal is Henry Wilson's own version of events. But, as Wilson himself realised, his very advocacy of the commitment to France jeopardised not only his own position but also the strategy which he represented. The 'peace party of the cabinet', he wrote in his diary on 16 November 1911, 'are calling for my head. Dirty ignorant curs. They think I forced the pace during the crisis, & they quote all my Teaching at the S[taff] C.[ollege] as evidence of my villainy'.[14] Significant here is Wilson's branding of those who opposed him as the 'peace party'. He named Morley, Crewe, Harcourt and McKenna, but of these only Morley would resign at the beginning of August 1914. The others, notably McKenna, represented not so much a policy of peace *per se*, as an alternative strategy. McKenna had worked hand in glove with Jackie Fisher to overhaul the capabilities of the Royal Navy: in the climate of Edwardian Britain few would describe him as a pacifist. Wilson's opponents were less the 'peace party' and more those who adumbrated other ways of fighting a European war should one occur. The paradox of Wilson's performance on 23 August was that he persuaded some cabinet ministers to adopt a continental strategy which involved the deployment in Europe of an army still structured for colonial operations. His glibness convinced them that six divisions could swing the balance, and so it was not only the Belgian option but also the issues of conscription, operational doctrine and higher command that were conveniently ignored.

The General Staff was a new creation; it was not the capital body identified by Dallas D. Irvine;[15] its chief had to compete with pre-existing peers, like the Adjutant-General and Quartermaster-General. Nor was Henry Wilson its sole spokesman. As his diaries make clear, his vituperation was not reserved solely for the little Englanders within the Liberal government. It embraced many of his professional colleagues and superiors – including Kitchener and Sir John French. Institutionally, the army was not a monolith, a point the Curragh 'mutiny' was both to prove and to deepen. In 1914 the armies of France and Germany were focused (at least in so far as external enemies were concerned) on a possible war against each other to be fought on their joint frontier or in Belgium, and had prepared themselves accordingly. Within Britain elements of the General Staff had given such an eventuality very serious consideration for over a decade, but the schemes that had resulted had not permeated the army institutionally, and had failed to change either its ethos or its structure.

The debate about when the British General Staff adopted continentalism is important, and will be considered in the second section of this chapter. But, whatever the difference in dating – 1904 or 1906 or 1910 or 1911 – its decision to do so had not become the basis of national policy by 1914. A far more significant issue is the fact that Britain should have condoned the General Staffs' continentalism without willing the means to the ends. The General Staff accepted a plan for war in Europe without managing to create a European army.

II

Henry Wilson had plenty of enemies within the army. His politicking and scheming alienated those who took a more conventional view of civil–military relations. But self-evidently he also had friends. His final elevation, to become CIGS in 1918 and a Field-Marshal, can of course be attributed to the patronage of politicians. But the fact that he was appointed DMO in 1910 and that he held that post throughout the ensuing four years shows that he also enjoyed the support of some soldiers. Wilson was at the centre of controversy in 1910–14 – not only because of the CID meeting of 23 August 1911 but also because of the Curragh 'mutiny' of March 1914 – and yet he did not change his spots in that time. His Francophilia and his relish for political intervention were both proven by 1910: he became DMO because of these attributes, not in spite of them. Wilson was not *sui generis*, and nor was his brand of continentalism.[16]

At the broadest level every thinking and literate soldier in the late Victorian army was European in outlook. Military history and military theory venerated the examples of Napoleon and Moltke, not of the Afghans and Zulus. J. F. Maurice has been dubbed 'the second pen' of Sir Garnet Wolseley: he was a member of the latter's 'ring' that established itself as a prototype field staff for the successful execution of colonial operations. In 1891 he published as a separate volume his essay on 'War', originally written as an entry for *Encyclopedia Britannica*. To it he added 'an essay on military literature and a list of books'. Maurice's departure point for the examination of modern war was the campaigns of 1866 and 1870, and the works he recommended were predominantly French and German. A short section of his bibliography was devoted to 'minor British wars since 1815', and included his own account of the 1882 Egyptian campaign, but – like other British military writers – his actual discussion of colonial warfare was severely restricted. A page on the 'method peculiar to campaigns in uncivilised countries' was largely confined to their logistical difficulties.[17]

Theoretically Wolseley's army was posted on the Rhine, but its practice and its strategic assumptions remained firmly imperial. The Stanhope Memorandum of 1888 considered the despatch of forces to the continent the remotest of all possible contingencies.[18] Wolseley, as C-in-C of the army between 1895 and 1900, devoted much attention to its capacity for rapid mobilisation, but the expeditions which he had in mind were to Africa rather than to Europe.

In 1899 that ability was tested on exactly those terms which Wolseley had anticipated. The Boer War exposed many deficiencies in the army. The reforming efforts which followed were therefore intended to render the army better able to fight a similar war should one occur, not a war on the European continent. And yet by late 1904 a change had taken place. In January 1905 J. M. Grierson, the DMO, ordered a strategic war game to be conducted in April and May, whose assumption was that Germany had violated Belgian neutrality in the course of a war with France. The foundations of the Stanhope Memorandum had been significantly modified, if not overthrown. The explanations for the change are both bureaucratic and personal.

The bureaucratic argument has been rehearsed by McDermott, and its key point is that it links the intellectual foundations of British military thought to the final establishment of a General Staff in 1904–06. Henry Campbell-Bannerman had used the platform of the Hartington Commission in 1890 to oppose the creation of a General Staff for fear that such a body would prepare for a continental war, and so enlarge British military policy.[19] Those within the army who opposed the establishment of a General Staff did so for reasons that were the corollary of Campbell-Bannerman's: in peacetime a staff needed to plan, and it would tend to concentrate on the single but remote scenario of a big war rather than on the day-to-day immediacies of unpredictable but relatively minor imperial crises. Both lines of criticism were not without foundation. When the decision to create a General Staff was promulgated Britain did indeed take on the trappings of a continental army. In 1905 the War Office published a translation of Bronsart von Schellendorff's *The Duties of the General Staff*, and that remained the principal official publication on the subject until the outbreak of the First World War. The role model, therefore, was German. And yet the planning assumptions which framed the professional mission of the German General Staff were very different from those of Britain. Germany's most likely threat was war on its own frontiers. In Bronsart von Schellendorff's volume of 567 pages, only seven were devoted to co-operation between the army and navy, and a further seven to colonial warfare.

The British assumption of the German model was in some ways unremarkable. The idea of a General Staff had been promoted by the military commentator and academic, Spenser Wilkinson, in *The Brain of an Army*, 'a popular account of the German General Staff', published in 1890. In his preface Wilkinson quoted the words of another member of the Wolseley ring, Henry Brackenbury. In his evidence to the Select

Committee on the Army and Navy Estimates in 1887, Brackenbury had described the German General Staff as 'the keystone of the whole system of German military organization ... the cause of the great efficiency of the German army ... acting as the powerful brain of the military body, to the designs of which brain the whole body is made to work'.[20] Wilkinson's book went on to describe the history and characteristics of the Prussian General Staff against the background of the wars of 1866 and 1870.

The Wolseley 'ring' was therefore happy to live with a contradiction. Their own battlefield experience was colonial, but their model for a General Staff – whose formation they supported – was continental. Maurice's strategies in the event of war with a European power embraced amphibious operations and a continental alliance. This was what Liddell Hart would later call 'the British way in warfare'. It was not continentalism as it would be defined in the run-up to, let alone the aftermath of, the First World War, but it was the nearest that late Victorian military thinkers came to it. And many did not. Maurice criticised *Imperial Defence* (1892), written by Wilkinson in conjunction with Sir Charles Dilke, for its rejection of a European alliance. Wilkinson believed that the Royal Navy would be Britain's primary arm in a European war. He favoured a 'forward' policy in India against Russia, and this therefore was the scenario in which a General Staff modelled on European lines was likely to find service. But the key point, common across the spectrum of military thought, was that before 1900 advocacy of a General Staff did not of itself presuppose the deployment of a British army on the continent. To understand this development, the weight of explanation needs to shift from structures to personalities.

Wilkinson's own military career was confined to the Volunteers: his experience, such as it was, related to home defence, not colonial conquest. Moreover, his writings as a military historian focused on France and Germany, on Napoleon and Moltke. In 1899 he castigated Wolseley for the setbacks in South Africa. By then his interest in the defence of India had already resulted in a close relationship with Wolseley's great rival, Lord Roberts. Like that of Wolseley, Roberts's focus in the early 1890s was on the empire, albeit in India rather than Africa. But, unlike Wolseley, Roberts saw the ultimate enemy as likely to be a major European army. The threat to India was Russia.

The personal conversion that was at the heart of the British General Staff's espousal of continentalism between 1900 and 1905 was that of Roberts. A man whose reputation was founded on India, and made at the head of a predominantly sepoy army, became the advocate of preparedness against Germany and of conscription within Britain. His friendship with Wilkinson was perhaps one factor in effecting this change. Eyre Crowe, the most trenchant harbinger of the German threat among Foreign Office clerks, was Wilkinson's brother-in-law, and the arguments in Crowe's memorandum of 1 January 1907 on British relations with Germany were a summary of those already published by Wilkinson.[21] In 1904–05 Roberts moved from being the army's last C-in-C, via the CID, to becoming the president of the National Service League. His influence in the senior echelons of the army was still pivotal in 1914, in the Curragh crisis. With one rising officer above all he had a particularly close relationship: for Henry Wilson, Roberts was always simply 'the chief'.

Wilson was only the most voluble, not the most important, army advocate of continentalism. His diary entry for 28 October 1904 still saw France and Russia as Britain's putative enemies, and the volume for the following year, 1905, was devoid of references to the diplomatic and wider strategic context in which his enthusiasm for the General Staff might be set. Others both anticipated him and were more adroit in their political handling.

Pre-eminent was J. M. Grierson, the General Staff's first ever DMO. Like other serious students of his profession, Grierson was a long-standing admirer of the German army, so much so that in 1890 one German officer said of him that he was 'almost as well known at Berlin as at Woolwich'.[22] As a gunner he had received his military education at the Royal Military Academy, where the bracket above his bed held a statuette of Moltke. In 1897 he published anonymously, first in German and then – two years later – in English, a study of the British Army, presciently bound in khaki. *The British Army* is virtually devoid of any other anticipatory quality: it is a description of the army as it was on the eve of the South African War, not as it might become in its aftermath. Its assumptions are Wolseleyan. And yet the colour illustrations betray the continental influences operating on Grierson, for they are the work not of Richard Simkin or Harry Payne, the fashionable military artists of the day, but of the German illustrator of uniform, Richard Knotel.

In 1896 Grierson went to Berlin as Britain's military attaché. His experiences over the ensuing four years ended his love-affair with the German army. The anglophobic tirades of its officers, and particularly of the Kaiser, convinced him that war between the two countries was likely.[23] In 1900 he was relieved to be appointed to Lord Roberts's staff in South Africa. The move showed how permeable both the 'rings' of the late Victorian army were. Grierson never ceased to regard Wolseley as 'the best soldier of my time':[24] his first campaign had been Egypt in 1882, and he had served Henry Brackenbury in the Intelligence Division thereafter. But, like Henry Wilson (to whom he handed over the Quartermaster-General's Department in South Africa), he called Roberts 'the chief'.[25] Grierson's hopes that Britain would create its own General Staff had been stoked by the Hartington Commission in 1890. The lessons which he drew from the South African War began with the staff question: 'We must have big annual manoeuvres', he wrote from Pretoria on 7 July 1900, and have our staffs properly trained. We don't seem to grasp anything higher than a division. And we must have 'staff journeys' to teach the control of armies in the field. If we take the field with a force the size of this one against a European enemy and continue in our present happy-go-lucky style of staffing and staff work we shall come to most awful grief. There is no system about it and without a system a large army cannot be properly handled.[26]

Therefore, by 1900, well before the Anglo-French entente and its ensuing staff conversations, Grierson was both anticipating war between Britain and Germany and talking about the creation of a British Army organised and staffed on European lines. The two elements of continentalism had converged.

Grierson's patronage swept up Lieutenant-Colonel William Robertson. Robertson was another product of Brackenbury's Intelligence Division who had served on Roberts's staff in South Africa. In 1900 he was appointed head of the foreign section of the Intelligence Division – part of the Directorate General of Mobilisation and Intelligence. In his memoirs, Robertson wrote of this period of his life that 'it is not possible, and should not be necessary to try, to prepare at one and the same time for half-a-dozen different wars'. His conclusion, therefore, was that 'soldiers charged with the duty of preparation aim at making ready for the greatest and the most probable war in which their army may become engaged'.[27] Herein were the intellectual origins of the shift from continentalism as method to continentalism as strategy.

In 1898 Robertson had written an essay at the Staff College for his mentor, G. F. R. Henderson, in which he declared that 'conflict with Russia must come sooner or later'.[28] For a man who had passed most of his commissioned service in India, such views were no more than orthodoxy. But by 1902 he was penning a paper destined for Roberts's desk in which he challenged the assumption that a continental war meant a war in Asia against Russia. 'It is not an exaggeration to say', he wrote, 'that in no other European country is hatred of England so general or so deeply-rooted as in Germany.' The greater security need was to preserve the balance of power in Europe, 'and in playing it at the present time we should recollect that a new preponderance is now growing of which the centre of gravity is Berlin'.[29]

Robertson had never been nearer Germany than a tour of the 1870 battlefields in the Meuse valley. His conversion to anti-Germanism was in part the result of his rejection of the feasibility of a Russian invasion of India. He needed to find another enemy who could become the focus for the army's peacetime preparations. But it is not fanciful to see the influence of Grierson on Robertson. Grierson employed Robertson as the commander of the German force in his 1905 staff ride. In the same year the two of them visited the Franco-German frontier. In January 1906 Grierson drew up a memorandum – which, significantly, is to be found in the Robertson papers – on possible contingencies in which military forces might be deployed overseas. It envisaged six scenarios, one of which, a war with France against Germany, was deemed 'possible'. In such circumstances, after an initial commitment of at least four cavalry brigades and three army corps, 'it might be desirable to send troops to an unlimited extent'.[30] In a lecture apparently given in about 1906 on 'the true standard of our military needs', Robertson declared that 'that standard must be looked for nearer home, if the *entente cordiale* is to be regarded as having any meaning, and if we are to hope for its continuance'.[31]

Robertson had little truck with Henry Wilson, who is not even mentioned in his autobiography, *From Private to Field Marshal*. But even allowing for personal animus, it is clear that the grooves along which Wilson travelled as DMO after 1910 were not his own but were set earlier and by others. Grierson it was (and here Robertson was explicit) who believed 'that the only policy consistent with the interests of the Empire was an active alliance with France and Belgium', and who 'did more than any other officer of his time to establish good relations between the French and British armies'.[32]

To argue that the momentum of continentalism was lost because the Anglo-French staff talks were suspended between 1906 and 1910 ignores two points. The first concerns continuity. Grierson's successor as DMO, Sir J. Spencer Ewart, also saw war with Germany as a matter of time, and sustained contacts with the French. He kept warm both continentalism as a strategy and the chair of the DMO as its focus.[33] The second concerns the conclusions of the sub-committee of the CID set up to examine 'the military needs of the empire' in 1908. It included within its brief situations 'in which the British Army might be called upon to operate either alone or with other powers'. In 1909 that sub-committee approved the General Staff's plan to send an army to France. Admittedly, it simultaneously asked for plans for expeditionary forces to Belgium and Holland, and it stressed that no decision had been taken with regard to a single continental strategy, or indeed to any continental commitment. But Sir William Nicholson, the CIGS between 1908 and 1912, argued that the 23 August 1911 debate was a storm in a teacup because the continental strategy had been settled two years previously.[34]

The limitations of Wilson's achievement in 1910–11 can be further appreciated by shifting the focus from London to Delhi. In 1902 Robertson's most pressing need was to undermine the legacy of Roberts's determination that Britain's principal military threat lay on the North-West Frontier of India. In due course Roberts himself was converted, but Roberts's legacy had in the interim found a doughty advocate in Lord Kitchener, as C-in-C in India from 1902 to 1909. Realists involved in military planning reckoned that a Russian invasion through Afghanistan was a logistical impossibility – a conclusion reached by the Russians as long before as the late 1880s.[35] But in the end neither logistics nor diplomacy could shift the assumptions of the Indian Army. The 1902 Anglo-Japanese agreement provided scant relief to planners in either India or Britain. For the former, there was the impossibility of Japan deploying troops on the North-West Frontier; for the latter, as Grierson observed in 1905, the agreement was irrelevant as the threat from Germany was greater than that from Russia.[36] The 1907 Anglo-Russian agreement might have made more difference, but it did not. Douglas Haig was appointed Chief of the Indian General Staff in 1909. Fresh from working as DSD under Haldane, Haig was determined to integrate the Indian Army with the BEF concept. He instituted a close study of German army organisation and looked at the possibility of sending an Indian expeditionary force to Europe in the event of war. The Viceroy, Hardinge, blocked Haig, and ordered his plans destroyed. It was the discovery of the Indian schemes that alerted the Cabinet to the machinations of Henry Wilson in October 1911.[37] The 1912 Army in India Committee concluded that India should not be called upon to maintain troops specifically for war outside the sub-continent. Instead, its army should be geared for the needs of internal security and frontier warfare. In 1914, if the Indian Army had any European army in its sights, that enemy was still Russia – by now Britain's ally. Its equipment was – according to the Mesopotamia Commission in 1917 – less appropriate for war against a European opponent in 1914 than it had been before the South African War. In the event India did of course send four expeditionary forces overseas when war broke out; every one of them was improvised and all of them suffered accordingly.[38]

The sorry tale of Indian planning makes two key points relevant to the argument that centres on Henry Wilson and the CID meeting of 23 August 1911. The first relates to personalities. Douglas Haig set about 'trying to do a Wilson' before Wilson had become DMO: in other words he, like Grierson and Robertson, anticipated Wilson because continentalism was established in British General Staff thought before 1910. The second is institutional. The writ of the British General Staff did not extend very far. It never established control over its partners in India before the First World War. From the perspective of Delhi, none of 1904, 1906, 1910 or 1911 denotes any development of significance in relation to strategy. A total of 53 infantry battalions served in India at some point in 1913;[39] this was where active service was most likely to be found, and it was where ambitious but impoverished subalterns wished to be posted. And yet continentalism had not entered the intellectual horizons of the army in which they served. This was not because the War Office General Staff was not continentalised, but because the General Staff was not the dominant force within the British Army.

III

The status of the General Staff within Wihelmine Germany has been much exaggerated. In peacetime its chief had often to play second fiddle to the Prussian war minister; the latter, not the former, had a greater say in the establishment and size of the army. The training of the army, by which its ideas on war achieved a degree of universality, was in the hands not of the General Staff but of the individual commanders of corps districts. Nevertheless, it is to the German General Staff that military thought, before the First World War, as still today, is indebted for the idea of a capital General Staff – an institution which provides the leading ideas which animate the army as a whole and whose intellectual coherence creates an institutional and politically independent identity. To all intents and purposes Britain has never possessed such a staff. Before 1914 some reformers aspired for it to do so, but three major obstacles stood in their path.

First, the status of the German General Staff had been hallowed by victory: the wars of unification had vested the General Staff with a degree of independence that it had not enjoyed before 1866. In 1914 the British staff had no such legacy on which to draw; after 1918 it would be branded with responsibility for the nature of the First World War and so advocates of the General Staff idea (pre-eminently William Robertson) could be pilloried by such influential critics as Basil Liddell Hart.[40]

Secondly, the British supporters of a General Staff often misunderstood the model on which they were basing their designs. They believed that the German General Staff was the author of doctrine, and that it was doctrine which gave the staff its dominant and unifying role in the army. They therefore argued that the job of the General Staff was first to develop doctrine and then to teach it.[41] But doctrine was not the German General Staff's method of instruction: it taught by way of concrete examples. Throughout the twentieth century the British Army tended to impute to the German General Staff a more cerebral and more principled approach to the study of war than it did in fact implement. German staff training concentrated on practicalities more than theories.

The confusion arose because the German army's strategic problem – the defence of its western and eastern frontiers – was clear-cut. This was the third obstacle to Britain's comprehension of the German General Staff idea. The German General Staff seemed to have a single doctrine because its grand strategy was simple. It developed a number of operational possibilities but it did so within a much narrower policy framework than that which could ever be embraced by the British General Staff. The latter's call for continentalism was in many ways a summons for simplification. Wiser heads knew that the world – and Britain's role in it – demanded political flexibility, and hence greater complexity.

Grierson's memorandum of January 1906, which deemed war in alliance with France against Germany as 'possible', listed five further scenarios for war. Two – war with France and war with the United States – were reckoned to be 'improbable'; one, war with Russia, became less likely after 1907 but never went off the agenda in India; and two, a Boer rising in South Africa and a general category of 'small wars', were the baggage of empire which the European alliances were designed to alleviate but which they could never remove. The drift of Grierson's memorandum was of course to minimise all but the German threat. He could not however discount the danger outside Europe, and indeed one could prompt the other: in 1914 the Boers did rebel after war broke out against Germany. He thought that most small wars could be conducted with the army still on a peace footing, but some more serious dangers, such as conflict with China, or mutiny in the Egyptian army, or a rising in the Sudan, would need a greater effort. The trouble was that Britain was never sufficiently at peace between 1870 and 1914 for its army to concentrate exclusively on the threat in Europe.[42]

Planning for these colonial contingencies was not primarily a function of operational thought. The tasks were administrative and logistical; the issues were medical, cartographical and calorific. Thus, as an imperial power, Britain needed a staff which put as much weight on administration as on command. This was the nub of the deeply divisive debates between 1904, when the scheme for a General Staff was promulgated, and 1906, by which time it was put in place. Henry Wilson, for example, was terrified that the Adjutant-General would 'put a very senior officer in as head of Administrative Staff & a junior as General Staff'.[43] This did not happen, but the result was still a compromise. The first CGS, Sir Neville Lyttelton, lacked the authority to establish the supremacy of the new office. It did not become the dominant appointment in the army, the putative C-in-C in the field or the country's principal adviser, but more a *primus inter pares*. It was squeezed from above and below, as well as from the sides.

On top was the CID. The broader policy context, which so trammelled the General Staff's demand for simplification, was precisely why the CID had been created. Its principal instigator, Lord Esher, favoured a maritime strategy, and had envisaged that the CID would embrace naval and political as well as military dimensions and so would develop into a department which would itself 'fulfil the main functions of a General Staff'. Esher had seen the General Staff of the army as an intelligence division locking into this wider framework. Instead, by 1906, he was damning it as a 'Frankenstein', usurping functions for which it had not been designed and perverting Britain's strategy in the process.[44] If Britain had created a capital staff before 1914, it would have grown from the CID, not from within the War Office. The fact that the CID never developed as Esher hoped it might should not obscure the fact that formally the army's General Staff, however powerful it became, was ultimately a subordinate organisation in planning terms.

To the sides were the administrative aspects of staff work, kept separate and answerable to departments of much greater antiquity and well-established status. Manpower and discipline were subordinated to the Adjutant-General, and logistical and material matters to the Quartermaster-General.[45] This divided structure was repeated in field formations. The commander of an expeditionary force had not one principal adviser, as was the case in the German army, but three – the Chief of Staff, tasked with operations and intelligence; the Adjutant-General (or 'A' branch), responsible for men and their needs; and the Quartermaster-General (or 'Q' branch), charged with supplies, movements and accommodation. The field commander therefore had a dual function: the conduct of operations and the co-ordination of the administrative and fighting branches of his headquarters.

At the conference of General Staff officers held in Camberley in January 1909, the consequences of the split were made explicit by Colonel J. P. Du Cane. He reckoned that, with its attention now 'concentrated on Northern Europe', 'the centre of gravity in which the British may be called upon to conduct warlike operations has changed in recent years'. He pointed out, however, that the regulations for supply did not seem to contemplate war on the continent of Europe. Du Cane attributed this division to the organisational separation of the General Staff from the Quartermaster-General's department.[46] Du Cane's point was well made. The split was enshrined in the *Field Service Regulations* promulgated in 1909. It meant that Henry Wilson's presentation to the CID on 23 August 1911 was largely a paper exercise. Wilson's task was mobilisation and deployment, the stuff of administration, not of the conduct of operations in the field. Its implementation was therefore not in his hands as DMO but those of the Adjutant-General's and Quartermaster-General's departments. The former was responsible for the call-up of personnel, the latter for remounts, railways and supplies – not only of food but also of fuel.[47]

In Germany all these functions were subordinated to the CGS; in Britain they depended on co-operation between departments. Between 1912 and 1914 Sir John Cowans, as Quartermaster-General, gave Wilson that co-operation.[48] Similarly in 1914 itself when mobile warfare revealed the total impracticality of the administrative–operational divide, the situation was saved when Robertson, then the Quartermaster-General in the BEF, subordinated himself to the CGS.[49] But Sir Ian Hamilton, as Adjutant-General in 1910, effectively withheld that co-operation. In *Compulsory Service*, published as a refutation of the arguments for national service, Hamilton openly rejected a continental strategy: for him command of the sea was the pivot of national defence, the army was the navy's projectile, and its organisation should be framed to meet the needs of imperial defence and of joint warfare in the event of European war.

The fact that the theoretical separation of responsibilities was not practicable had already become evident before the war. Henry Wilson, then Commandant of the Staff College, had responded to Du Cane's challenge by pointing out that the staff rides of both 1907 and 1908 had focused on supply. He was right. The objective of the 1908 exercise, centred on operations in a 'neutral country between Scotland and Holland' (and therefore further evidence of 'continentalism' before 1910–11), was to test the lines of communication and maintenance services, not to explore the operational or strategic framework. Staff work was therefore increasingly interpreted as confined to administrative aspects.[50]

Henry Rawlinson reflected this concern at the General Staff conference of January 1908, when he urged the Staff College not to forget that its tasks should include training for command in war, not just for the exercise of administrative duties.[51] But that was by no means received wisdom. Just as General Staff duties were meant to be distanced from administration, so they were also deemed to be distanced from the frictions of command. The Chief of Staff might head the most significant of the three administrative branches of a field headquarters but he was in no sense a surrogate commander. 'There is an essential distinction', wrote Colonel Hubert Foster in 1911 in a work designed to supplement and popularise the *Field Service Regulations* of 1909,

> between the action of *Commanders* and that of *Staff Officers* however capable. It is true that Staff Officers are not mere clerks or messengers ... But it is outside the scope of the Staff to interfere with the exercise of Command ... Only one man can command.[52]

Foster's own treatment of *Staff Work*, published in the following year, was principally concerned with administration and devoted nearly half its length to the movement of troops.

Thus neither the Staff College nor service in staff appointments was necessarily an avenue to high command. This too was a consequence of the 1904–06 debate. Those who had intended the General Staff to be an elite had been defeated by those who favoured a more open body, whose corporate identity derived not from the existence of a series of posts designated as those of the General Staff, but solely from its members having passed through the Staff College and thus having acquired eligibility for (but not exclusive rights over) staff appointments.[53] Many jobs which might be deemed staff posts were not held by Staff College graduates.

The exercise of higher command in a pre-1914 European army was focused at the level of the corps. But in the British Army, Aldershot was the only area where two or more divisions could be assembled for manoeuvres, and therefore the only command in which the training of a corps was possible.[54] The Army Council discussed whether or not to create the corps as a command with a permanent staff in 1906, but rejected the idea in favour of large divisions, of three brigades rather than two. The decision was driven by rejection of continentalism. Sir William Nicholson, then the Quartermaster-General, feared that the adoption of corps command would be tantamount to preparing the army for one contingency only. The fact that the BEF was structured around the division not the corps, so that its organisation was compatible with that of the Indian Army, was clear evidence of the strict limits placed round the penetration of General Staff-inspired continentalism.[55]

The effect was to vitiate yet further the training of British commanders for European warfare. Having separated staff duties and staff training from preparation for the exercise of command, the prewar army now ensured that higher command itself would not be a subject for serious study. At the General Staff conference in January 1908, Haig spoke of the impossibility of one man commanding six divisions (the anticipated size of the BEF) in the field.[56] Nevertheless, the *Field Service Regulations* of 1909, for which he is given principal credit, established the division as the highest subordinate field command. Moreover, a survey in 1908 suggested that even at this level there was little by way of common practice. The keynote in divisional training within the home commands was decentralisation. Units were judged by results rather than the application of common methods. Training was one of the key prerogatives of command, and therefore was in the hands of individual divisional generals and their enthusiasms, rather than of staff officers schooled in shared modes of thought.[57]

Command expertise was acquired by practice. The principle of instruction through allowing officers to exercise command in the rank higher than their current one was not widely accepted. Moreover, in the pre-1914 army, the command in which most officers honed their leadership skills was not as high as the all-arms division but was the single-arm, single-battalion regiment.

The ethos of the Victorian army, determined by its dispersal overseas in colonial garrisoning, was mediated through the regiment. The creation of the General Staff presented a challenge to the regiment's dominance, which the Army Council attempted to defuse by declaring in December 1906 that nothing in the creation of the General Staff was 'intended to relieve [regimental] Commanding Officers of their prime responsibility for the efficiency and proficiency of their officers in educational and professional respects'.[58] The note of protest was significant: the General Staff was fighting for acceptance.

For most regimental commanding officers the existence of the General

Staff remained in many ways a dead letter. The creation of the BEF and the acceptance of the continental commitment (regardless of whether the latter preceded or followed the former) ought to have resulted in a redistribution of infantry battalions away from the imperial periphery towards Britain itself. This would have had two effects. First, it would have brought more battalions within the purview of the General Staff, with its physical concentration in Camberley, London and Aldershot. Secondly, it would of course have created immediately available reinforcements should an expeditionary force be sent to Europe. But what is striking about the distribution of the infantry battalions between 1870 and 1914 is the evenness of the pattern. For all the dire warnings of imminent collapse, the so-called Cardwell system of linked battalions proved remarkably resilient. Grierson was right: most small wars could be accommodated within the peacetime pattern, because they were of a scale where one or two regular battalions supplemented by locally raised units would suffice. Only twice did the system bend and even buckle – during the 1882 Egyptian campaign and during the South African War. The abandonment of the Stanhope memorandum and the diplomatic realignments of 1904–07 produced no change in the pattern of regimental postings. Nor did Wilson's alleged triumph in the CID. In July 1914 the infantry battalions of the regular army were as firmly wedded to the distribution of imperial garrisoning as they had been twenty or thirty years previously. The continentalism of the General Staff not only failed to move laterally, to the Adjutant-General's and Quartermaster-General's departments, it also failed to percolate downwards to the parts of the army that were responsible for the actual business of fighting.[59]

The continentalism of the General Staff therefore had to balance its own expectations of future war with the reality of the army's current practices and commitments. Herein was the reason for the British General Staff's rejection of the German pattern of training and instruction through specific examples, through case studies and staff rides. In January 1911 junior officers asked that the General Staff consider sanctioning a book on applied tactics. If Henry Wilson's focus on France really had provided the leading idea around which the army as a whole could have been shaped, there would have been no harm and much merit in the scheme. Significantly the precedent cited by Captain C. A. L. Yates in making the case was German. However, the General Staff response was unequivocal:

> We must remember that our officers must be prepared to fight in every country on the globe. Arrangements that are desirable in England, or even on the continent of Europe, will be very different from those which will be necessary in South Africa, or on the North-Western Frontier of India'.[60]

Therefore, the British Army studied war through the medium of principles. William Robertson may have wanted to concentrate Britain's planning effort on a single contingency, but even he would not depart from the idea that training should be by way of general principles.[61] For him, as for Douglas Haig, this was what a General Staff was for – to enunciate general principles, on the basis of which officers should work out responses adapted to individual circumstances.[62]

The promulgation of general principles in war was hardly a new approach to military theory. Their origins lay in the Enlightenment's search for universal rules for most human activity, and they had found their embodiment in Jomini. But it was the British Army which used principles as a substitute for doctrine, and which ensured their high priority in twentieth-century military thought.[63] The *Field Service Regulations*, drawn up under the supervision of Douglas Haig while he was DSD, and published in 1909, asserted the primacy of the principles of war, although confusingly they did not spell out what those principles were. They reflected ideas which Haig had formulated in 1896–97 while at the Staff College and against the background of colonial warfare, and they included a chapter on warfare against an uncivilised enemy.[64] The criticism voiced by the military correspondent of *The Times*, Charles à Court Repington, that they should have been more directly geared to the specific application of British troops in a European war, was not without foundation: indeed, it went to the nub of the dilemma which the General Staff's continentalism exposed.[65] But Haig defended the line he had taken both on general and on specific grounds. The former embraced the refrain of every military commentator since G. F. R. Henderson: to go further than general principles and espouse specific doctrines ran the risk that the army would find itself fighting the wrong sort of war. The latter rebutted the notion that, because the principles were therefore as applicable outside Europe as within it, they were somehow invalid. Haig was clear that the *Field Service Regulations* were geared for the eventuality of major war, and when the First World War broke out he continued to see them as his benchmark. They remained applicable right through to 1918.[66]

By then continentalism had transformed the character of the British Army. It had ceased to be a small, regular, professional force, and had become a conscripted citizen army. National service, even more than the system of higher command, or the patterns of military doctrine, was the key denominator in European warfare.

The General Staff advocates of continentalism were fully aware of this. In January 1906, Grierson, in sketching out the pattern of possible support for France in a war against Germany, spoke of sending 'troops to an unlimited extent'.[67] Robertson, writing at around the same time, was more specific. Britain needed to put in the field 'a contingent of at least the same proportionate strength as those we supplied when fighting in alliance with other Powers in a similar cause a hundred years ago'. He wanted to be able to move 100,000 men to the continent within fourteen days, and to have at least 500,000 ready for instant employment. The corollary of a continentalist scheme was a continental army: 'any scheme for the creation of a National Army', he warned, 'must be based on European and not on Asiatic conditions, otherwise it may prove to be both worthless and disastrous'.[68]

Henry Wilson was of course as firm an advocate of compulsory service as his mentor, Lord Roberts. But he was slower than Robertson to put it in a specifically European context. Not only publicly but also privately both Wilson and Roberts tended to justify the need for conscription in terms of home defence or of the empire rather than of the manpower needs of a British Army on the continent.[69] But by 12 September 1911 Wilson too had squared this particular circle, cornering Lloyd George and linking in a single package the need for a friendly Belgium, for mobilisation that was simultaneous with that of France, and for conscription in peacetime.[70]

In this conversation Lloyd George was, according to Wilson, 'quite in favour of war now'. Wilson himself, however, seems to have been entirely reactive in terms of the international situation. To construct a conspiracy theory from Wilson's diary – that he either sought to use the Moroccan crisis to argue for preventive war, or that he was anxious for European war in itself – would be an uphill struggle. Not even the July 1914 crisis itself seems to have caused Wilson to leap from the advocacy of a firm commitment to France if war broke out to an expectation that a continental strategy predetermined Britain's policy. As an Ulsterman, Wilson's own sights in July were focused on Ireland. On 27 July he thought there would not be war, and when on 30 July he concluded that war was inevitable his diary entry smacks of resignation rather than jubilation. However tendentious the conclusions of the CID meeting of 23 August 1911, they can hardly be made to carry the weight of interpretation and expectation now loaded on the so-called 'war council' of 8 December 1912 in Germany.

The burden of this chapter has been to de-emphasise the place of the meeting of 23 August 1911 in Britain's preparations for the First World War, and by extension to reduce the role which Henry Wilson ascribed to himself and to which others have also subscribed. Wilson's intervention did not inaugurate continentalism in British General Staff thinking; instead it gave a push towards that continentalism taking a French rather than a Belgian form, but that in itself was as much the product of Belgium's own decision to distance itself from Britain and to reaffirm its neutrality. Moreover, that preference for rapid military support to France was not the basis for consistent British policy between 1911 and 1914. As J. E. Tyler recognised long ago, Wilson's intervention generated as much confusion as it did certainty. He strapped British strategy to French planning, but he did so before he knew in detail what France's plans were. He managed it by arguing that six divisions could have a decisive effect. However, as the debate in August 1914 revealed, the old assumptions – that only four divisions would go to the continent and that two would be held back for home defence – were not thereby superseded.[71]

In 1914 the BEF suffered a shattering defeat. The army survived, but it did so by effectively reverting to the idea of a limited liability on the continent of Europe – at least until 1916.[72] It had no option, for the General Staff had embraced a continental strategy without creating a continental army. That was true organisationally and doctrinally, but above all true in terms of recruitment. Britain had no other option from the autumn of 1914 than to mark time, for it now had to create the mass army which its strategy demanded of it.

The legacy of the decade 1904–14 extended far beyond the opening years of the First World War. The General Staff would continue to see continental warfare as the gold standard both in the interwar period and in the later stages of the Cold War, but it persisted in doing so despite the fact that it did not have the manpower resources of a truly European army. Moreover, the institutional weakness of the General Staff within the British Army was also not eradicated. Robertson, and his successors, worked to establish a capital General Staff within Britain in the 1920s but they were undermined both by those who equated such thinking with continentalism (like Liddell Hart) and by those who continued to see the regiment as the army's true centre of gravity. And, finally, this delegation of authority to the periphery consistently undermined efforts to create doctrine that was truly continentalist in its thrust. Tied to colonial campaigning and to counter-insurgency, the British Army sought an approach to war that could be universal: the upshot was a preference for general principles, and a rejection of specifics. In espousing a theoretical approach that was one stage removed from the particular, the British Army allowed its subordinate formations to produce solutions peculiar to themselves and which lacked the imprint of a General Staff mentality.

6

The General Staff and the Paradoxes of Continental War

William Philpott

Britain's General Staff, soon to be renamed Imperial General Staff, was created at a time when Britain's military orientation was changing. Paradoxically, one of the first tasks of this imperial staff was to prepare the British Army for continental war. This task, prominent in the first decade of the General Staff's existence, reappeared in the 1930s with a clear sense of *déjà-vu*, and with the same inherent problems. Within the planning process for a 'continental commitment' there existed a number of lesser paradoxes. Firstly, how could practical military preparation be reconciled with political detachment? Secondly, how could Britain's small volunteer army be effectively deployed amongst the mass conscript armies of the continental powers; and could Britain retain, as later political dogma defined it, a 'limited liability', or did continental war mean unlimited commitment? Thirdly, how should a British army be employed on the continent? Could British military support for her principal ally, France, be reconciled with defending traditional British strategic interests in the Low Countries, or indeed with Britain's 'blue water' amphibious strategic traditions? These paradoxes were not easy to resolve, and, arguably, in the General Staff's preparation for continental war they never were. Nevertheless, in their approach to the political, strategic and practical dilemmas of continental war the General Staff demonstrated a high level of independent judgement and professional common sense in dealing with an uncertain and politically sensitive set of variables.

It has been said that modern Britain has lost an empire, but has not found a role. It might also be said of the British Army in the first half of the twentieth century, that having won an empire they had lost a role. After consolidating British rule in Asia and Africa, was their role to be 'imperial defence',[1] or had Britain's first line of defence, as Sir John French put it in his war memoirs, become the fields of Flanders,[2] or even, as Prime Minster Stanley Baldwin later declared, the banks of the Rhine?[3] In the last decade of the nineteenth century a continental role for the British Army had been at the bottom of the list of priorities identified by the well-known 1888 Stanhope Memorandum, after home defence, relief of imperial garrisons, and operations in the colonies.[4] By 1904, the year that the General Staff was created, the political and military climate was changing. The reform of army administration and reorganisation of the army that followed the Boer War coincided with a political and diplomatic revolution as Britain aligned herself with the Dual Alliance against the threatening Central Powers. Central to this realignment was the 1904 Entente Cordiale with France, a colonial agreement which rapidly developed European and military dimensions.[5] Even before the full implications of this entente became clear during the 1905 Moroccan crisis, the new General Staff, searching for a role for the British Army, had seized on the opportunity presented to explore the military ramifications of this *rapprochement* with France, initiating what one analyst has termed a 'revolution in British military planning'.[6]

Before any formal military contacts with France were initiated, a General Staff wargame held in January 1905 within the Directorate of Military Operations, the section of the staff responsible for military planning, investigated the possibility of despatching a British military force to the continent to support the French army in a war against Germany.[7] The wargame presupposed, as had long been the case, that any British army sent to the continent would go there in response to a German violation of Belgian neutrality. Nevertheless, in attempting to examine strategic assumptions critically for the first time, the wargame began the process of replacing nebulous ideas with practicable military options. From this study emerged the paradoxes which were to preoccupy the staff in their future planning. Firstly, the idea that British military intervention might be more effective if a British army was sent directly to support the French army, rather than deployed in Belgium or used in independent amphibious operations against the German coast, was mooted, if not endorsed, because 'politically such an indirect method of protecting Belgian territory might embarrass the British government'.[8] Secondly, the small size and slow mobilisation of any British army was identified;[9] could a British army arrive in time and in sufficient strength to make an impact on the outcome of the campaign?

With Britain still officially committed to an amphibious strategy, and with no formal political endorsement of military support for France, much of the analysis of January 1905 was mere hypothesis. Soon the Moroccan crisis of 1905–06 was to force a realistic appraisal of British strategic policy. Against a background of heightened tensions between France and Germany, and strong British diplomatic support for the former, General Staff planning for a continental campaign received its first unofficial political endorsement. A Committee of Imperial Defence subcommittee on combined operations foundered in the face of inter-service rivalries. Instead, the secretary of the CID, Sir George Clarke, recommended to the Prime Minister, Arthur Balfour, that the General Staff should study the possibility of sending an expeditionary force to Antwerp, adding, revealingly: 'A study of this kind is just what the G[eneral] S[taff] would like, and they might (perhaps), be able to achieve more success than in dealing with the Indian frontier.'[10] Clarke, who had been a member of the Esher Committee that had created the General Staff, was hoping to strengthen and focus the new military organisation, and free it from subordination to the navy. In practice Clarke's initiative allowed the staff to dust off their unofficial January 1905 study and present its conclusions, with refinements, to the CID; as an alternative to the possibility of amphibious operations against the German coast, the General Staff were now considering 'a Strategic Stroke in the Theatre of Operations in co-operation with the French army'.[11] Against a background of political uncertainty as Liberals replaced Unionists in power, the General Staff were given a relatively free hand, with the outcome that their plan for direct intervention on the continent was endorsed by the *ad hoc* sub-committee of the CID that met, between December 1905 and January 1906, to review Britain's strategic options. Although this hastily improvised continental strategy was never adopted, then or later, as official policy, in the absence of other guidelines the General Staff chose to interpret it as such.[12] Nevertheless, there was equivocation on whether the British Army should go to France or Belgium.[13] The sub-committee's real objective was to ensure that as large a British force as possible would reach the continent as soon as possible, and to facilitate this the first politically sanctioned staff talks were initiated with the French and Belgian General Staffs.[14] By the spring of 1906 the issues with which the General Staff were to wrestle until 1914, and again after 1936, had been delineated.

Whenever continental military involvement was mooted, the General Staff had to manoeuvre within sensitive political parameters. Official military planning was circumscribed for reasons of both diplomacy and domestic politics. After the Moroccan crisis, officially sanctioned staff talks were cancelled. Such informal contacts as were continued through the Directorate of Military Operations were confined closely within the Foreign Secretary, Sir Edward Grey's, initial parameters, that they be conducted 'unofficially and in a non-committal way'.[15] Such official information as was subsequently provided to the French by the General Staff, it was made clear in 1907, was only 'an expression of the views of the British General Staff as to what might, under certain circumstances, be done, and ... not binding on the Government'.[16] Official General Staff information remained limited, and had to be supplemented from unofficial, but in French eyes reliable, sources.[17]

Diplomatically, not only did the British government not want to surrender its traditional free hand by getting involved in a formal alliance with France, but there also remained the desire to keep open the option of rapprochement with Germany.[18] Domestically, both pacifistic Liberal public opinion and Little Englander voices in the Cabinet had to be appeased. Only at a time of renewed crisis, again over Morocco in 1911, could more formal links with the French general staff be re-established, but this in itself provoked trouble in the Cabinet.[19] When the prospect of a second war loomed, the same restrictions applied. Crises led to staff talks, after the 1936 Rhineland occupation and the 1938 Munich crisis, but these were half-hearted and limited to low-level exchanges on 'technical' details. Diplomatically the appeasement of Germany, and indeed the restraint of France, would not be served by a formal British military commitment to France. Political and public opinion was strongly behind a policy which promoted European peace; 'limited liability' and 'no more Sommes' were the mantras of the National Government when it came to military rearmament. Only in March 1939, as Germany and Italy demonstrated their unwillingness to be appeased, were formal high-level staff talks finally sanctioned.[20]

Consequently, when military co-operation was being considered, contacts between the British and French armies normally existed in the grey area between official policy and unofficial activity. In the absence of clear political guidance, the General Staff was obliged to develop the 'military entente' through other than formal diplomatic channels. Before the First World War three men did more than any others to prepare the British Army for war on the continent. Major-General Sir James Grierson, DMO and a member of the 1905–06 CID military planning sub-committee, oversaw the 'revolution in British military strategy' and did much to establish close informal contacts between the two armies. 'Très enthousiaste de l'armée français',[21] he maintained a close relationship with the French army in his later commands, visiting French army manoeuvres regularly after 1906 and frequently reciprocating French hospitality at his own Aldershot manoeuvres.[22] By 1914, Grierson had both a deep understanding of French operational methods and considerable experience of handling large bodies of troops, something which the French identified as a weakness in the British senior officer corps.[23] His untimely death on the way to take up the command of the II Corps of the BEF was a great loss to the French army as well as the British.[24]

It was thanks to the efforts of Winston Churchill, the First Lord of the Admiralty, that the navy was ready in August 1914. Owing to the efforts of Sir John French, the army was also ready. General (later Field-Marshal) French, commander of the Aldershot Army Corps and a permanent member of the CID, and subsequently Inspector-General of the Forces and CIGS, did more than any other British officer to prepare the army for continental war before 1914. As C-in-C designate of the BEF, French took pains to ensure that a British army still licking its wounds from a colonial setback would be equipped, trained and organised for a war which its leaders expected would come sooner or later. He and his senior sub-ordinates, including Grierson, were, 'très anxieux de mettre l'armée anglais au niveau des armées continentales', one French guest at the British Army's 1910 manoeuvres reported.[25] Over the years from 1906 he cultivated a close relationship, perhaps even amounting to a 'special relationship', with the French high command. He attended French manoeuvres whenever he could after 1906, and reciprocated French hospitality at his own manoeuvres.[26] This arrangement allowed the British and French armies to get an insight into each other's operational methods, and to become accustomed to working together, should they ever find themselves side by side on the battlefield. This indirect approach certainly worked.[27] Over time the French came to appreciate both the dedication of the General to France, and the value of his army in a future conflict. Appointed to the most senior post in the British Army in March 1912, French brought a new dynamism to preparing the army for war, in contrast to his more circumspect predecessor Sir William Nicholson.[28] The French army, in particular, welcomed his appointment as CIGS,

> car on sait la grande sympathie que le Général éprouve pour notre pays. Placé à la tête de l'Etat Major Général, avec le Général Wilson, ... pour le seconder dans son rôle de préparation à la guerre, il aura certainement, en ce qui nous concerne, une influence des plus heureuses.[29]

French's resignation over the Curragh incident was understandably a disappointment to them.[30]

Brigadier-General Sir Henry Wilson, the third architect of the military entente, is best known to posterity for the preparation of detailed time-tables for the mobilisation of the BEF and its transportation to France, when DMO after 1911. The importance of Wilson's timetables has been overemphasised. The Prime Minister, Herbert Asquith, had always been suspicious of the detail of Wilson's planning, for both strategic and political reasons,[31] and the two waged an undeclared war over Britain's military commitment to the continent in the years leading up to war. Wilson's objective was to force Asquith – 'Sqiff', as Wilson contemptuously dubbed the Prime Minister in his candid diary – into accepting a formal British military commitment to France. For example, in March 1913 he was appalled to learn that Asquith and his 'Cabinet of cowards, blackguards and fools' had announced to the Commons that 'we were not going to help the French on land',[32] and retaliated with a detailed minute on the steps already taken to prepare to assist the French, dubbed his 'bombe d'Asquith'.[33] Despite his repeated and strenuous efforts to browbeat the

Liberal Cabinet, Wilson's planning did not commit the British government, morally or otherwise, to military intervention in support of France.
On the eve of war Asquith could state with a clear conscience that,
although Germany had begun preparations to invade France, and naval
precautions to assist the French were under way, 'the despatch of the
Expeditionary Force to help France at this moment is out of the question
and w[oul]d serve no purpose'.[34] Wilson's timetables for moving the BEF
to France proved valuable when it was decided that the army should go
to the continent; but they did not constitute a binding British military
commitment to concentrate the BEF rapidly on the French left wing, as
Wilson had always preached.[35]

Conversely, Wilson's role in educating the British Army and political
establishment for continental war has been underestimated.[36] The process
began before he became DMO, when he was Commandant of the Staff
College, and set about building a school of thought based on the principle
'readiness against Germany in alliance with France'. Wilson spent his
spare time cycling round the French and Belgian frontiers with French
officers and members of his directing staff and he used this experience to
refocus the Staff College curriculum away from small-scale colonial campaigns towards large-scale European warfare. He introduced syndicate
studies of war on the Franco-Belgian frontier and embarkation exercises
into the Staff College curriculum, practising the despatch of a British force
to the continent before any formal timetables had been drawn up.[37]
His message was disseminated throughout the army – large maps of the
Franco-Belgian frontier appeared on classroom walls throughout regimental establishments.[38] Wilson's approach would seem to have worked.
On the eve of war, the French Military Attaché reported, 'Au War Office
on est parfaitement convaincu de la nécessité pour l'Angleterre de dire
franchement qu'elle marchera avec la France si les circonstances l'exigent'.[39]
Wilson assiduously developed further links between the British and
French General Staffs, to supplement those between the field officers
encouraged by Grierson and French. Most famously he cultivated the
friendship of his opposite number at the French *Ecole Supérieure de
Guerre*, General Ferdinand Foch, and introduced some of his methods
into the training at Camberley.[40] But he also did much to encourage closer
liaison between the armies, often on his own initiative. As well as his
personal visits to the French General Staff in Paris during the 1911 crisis
and afterwards,[41] he created opportunities to proselytise his message of
Anglo-French co-operation. During a visit to Berlin in March 1911 he
made a point of meeting the French military attaché to discuss Anglo-
French co-operation, in the knowledge that this would get back to
France.[42] Equally he entertained French officers at Camberley, and later
in London, where the same message of Anglo-French military co-operation
was preached. At times, as in December 1910 when he took Foch to visit

the new Permanent Under Secretary at the Foreign Office, Sir Arthur Nicolson,[43] these French contacts would be used to press his point of view in political circles.

The French naturally expected much of Wilson when he moved to the War Office,[44] and they were not disappointed. Wilson was determined from the moment he took up his appointment as DMO to formalise military plans and proselytise his message as far as was possible within the existing parameters of civil–military relations and British foreign policy.[45] He strove in particular to spread his message amongst British politicians as well as French generals. At the time of the Agadir crisis he engaged in a lengthy correspondence with Churchill, then Home Secretary, on the merits of his plan to send the BEF to the French left.[46] Similarly, after the idea of a continental role for the British Army had been approved in principle by the CID in the summer of 1911, he strove unsuccessfully to persuade Grey, through the intermediaries Arthur Nicolson and the Secretary of State for War, Lord Haldane, to place Britain's relations with France on a more formal footing.[47]

Although Anglo-French military contacts remained for the most part informal and unofficial, it is clear that the General Staff's activity before 1914 had political sanction at the highest level. Grey and Haldane had initially sanctioned the talks.[48] Grey, and later Churchill, took an active interest in military preparations and strengthening the links between the British and French armies. The special treatment accorded to visiting French military dignitaries was extended to include 'political' contacts. For example, the 1907 French military mission to the British manoeuvres were, reported its head General Michel, 'l'objet d'attentions exceptionelles'. Met on arrival at the station by the whole Army Council, they were received by the King, the Prince of Wales, the Prime Minister, the Foreign Secretary and the Secretary of State for War, and decorated with the Royal Victorian Order. Nevertheless military contacts remained a sensitive issue; politicians, Huguet reported, showed more reserve in dealing with the French military than the British officers.[49]

In the 1930s this tacit political support for contacts between the armies was lacking. In the Cabinet, dominated by Prime Minster Neville Chamberlain, the idea of a continental role for the British Army was stoutly opposed; with the Middle East in turmoil, Britain's Field Force, such as it was, was to be equipped for imperial operations.[50] 'Limited liability' would best be achieved by curtailing formal high level contacts between the British and French armies – not simply a political decision, but a practical one given the low priority given to preparing the army for war in Britain's rearmament programme.

In the British General Staff there were no thrusters pushing for a clear military commitment to France – the senior officers had all experienced at first hand the consequences of the last, and were furthermore well aware that the army was inadequate for the task. Prewar staff talks, it was felt, were one of the factors which had contributed in general to the outbreak of the previous war, and in particular to what amounted to an open-ended commitment of British manpower, and lives, to the Western Front. Any talks that were to be authorised should therefore be limited to technical matters, in order not to restrict Britain's freedom in time of war.[51] While formal and informal contacts, on the lines of those developed by Grierson, French and Wilson before the first conflict, were renewed, before 1939 at least they were pursued with none of the vigour or sense of purpose that had existed before 1914. In sharp contrast to Wilson, Major-General Sir Henry Pownall, later to become DMO in 1938, regarded the resumption of staff talks in March 1936 as 'more of a political gesture to please France than as of any real practical value'.[52] He had no affection for the French, and was pleased that the renewed conversations were to be limited to 'interchange of information of strengths and facilities, but *no* joint planning'.[53] Nevertheless, there was dissatisfaction at the directions received from Whitehall, and the restrictive parameters within which the army had to work. As did Wilson before him, Pownall had a sound appreciation of the realities of the political and military situation. As the international situation deteriorated he came to appreciate clearly the need unreservedly to back the French militarily, and to be adequately prepared if British military action was to be effective; and like Wilson he railed against the politicians' failure to reconcile strategic reality with military policy.[54] Exasperated, he resorted to the political impropriety of hinting to the French that they should raise the subject of military co-operation in Anglo-French political conversations.[55]

General Lord Gort, CIGS from December 1937, had the same role as Sir John French, to prepare the army for war. Gort resisted as far as was possible the downgrading of the British Army to a home and imperial defence role, although there was nothing he could do to reverse the policy of 'limited liability'.[56] Personally, Gort believed strongly in the need for a continental commitment, but shied away from the sort of commitment implied by formal staff talks.[57] The change of the political climate over the winter of 1938–39 belatedly allowed Gort to address the deficiencies in the Field Force's equipment and organisation for continental war. A new round of high-level staff talks in March and April 1939, conducted in a spirit 'of cordiality and frankness on both sides', allowed each army to get a clear perception of the other's preparedness and plans. Gort set about rebuilding the close relationship between the armies which had been allowed to atrophy, notably by regular meetings with his opposite number, General Gamelin, and by taking the salute as British guardsmen marched down the Champs Elyssés in the 1939 Bastille Day parade.[58] But there was too little time to rebuild the amity which the British and French armies had enjoyed before 1914.

In 1939, the French military leadership lacked the confidence that they had had in their own and the British armies before 1914. To some extent this must be attributed to the British failure to create and sustain a harmonious military entente in the late 1930s. After their earlier experience of coalition war, the British General Staff had greater reservations about working closely with the French, and they were also circumscribed by tighter political restrictions. Balancing military preparedness with political non-commitment again proved impractical.

Within these restrictive political parameters, the General Staff had to prepare the army as best they could for effective intervention on the continent, wrestling with two further paradoxes: firstly the question of resources – how to maximise the force Britain could put in the field and its military effectiveness; secondly the question of strategy – how these forces should be employed, given the dual, and often conflicting, requirements of Allied support and defence of British interests.

Between 1906 and 1914 Britain's regular army was reorganised and re-equipped for continental warfare. Yet the rationale behind the organisation of a well-trained and equipped regular army expeditionary force was essentially financial and political, not military.[59] For the General Staff before 1914 the strategy of support for France and the size and organisation of Britain's military forces were out of alignment. In default of political commitment to compulsory service, Wilson could rationalise the policy of despatching the BEF by numerical sleight of hand – the presence of six divisions on the French left, he argued, would be enough to tip the balance of forces at the decisive point in the Allies' favour.[60] Nevertheless, the General Staff recognised that Britain's predominant navy would count for little in a continental war. Wilson's predecessor as DMO, Major-General Spencer Ewart, minuted in 1909 that the development of overland communications had seriously compromised the threat posed by traditional amphibious operations, and 'robbed of this enhancement of her military power the United Kingdom can no longer hope to maintain the relative importance of her assistance in a land campaign without substantial increase in the forces available for action overseas'.[61] For the General Staff this meant '[working] to get the size of the army fixed according to that required for the task in front of it'.[62] Wilson, in particular, strove to get the Liberal Cabinet to recognise that Britain's army was wholly inadequate for the task contemplated, putting forward many elaborate arguments, such as the dubious assertion, in a time of arms races and tit-for-tat army service laws, that '[were] Britain … to put forth her military strength … it would be final and decisive: there would then be full security for the peace of Europe'.[63] Compulsory service, the not-so-hidden agenda behind Wilson and the General Staff's lobbying, was, as the French military attaché recognised, unlikely in the existing political climate.[64] The General Staff were therefore obliged to contemplate continental war with what they considered inadequate force.

The rational alternative was to make the best of what was available. It seemed that a symbolic token of British military commitment and potential counted more to the French than the actual force offered – 'one single private soldier, and we would take good care that he was killed', Foch memorably quipped when asked by Wilson what military support Britain should send to France.[65] In the absence of a political commitment the French could not really count on the arrival of a British reinforcement of any size, although they expected some token force on the outbreak of war.[66] Nevertheless, they carefully watched the British Army's preparations, and one of the important consequences of the close relationship developed between the two armies before 1914 was that the French had a clear awareness of the size, readiness, speed of despatch and potential for expansion of the BEF should the British government decide on war. Plans to accelerate the despatch of the BEF, so that all six divisions could be concentrated for action by 17 days after mobilisation, when the General Staff had calculated that the decisive battle would take place, were put in place.[67] A seventh regular division, cobbled together from colonial garrisons, was a small but carefully monitored immediate addition to the force. Haldane's plan to create an imperial army of 46 divisions was also welcomed, even though it was expected to have little immediate impact on the military situation.[68] Whether the BEF could be sent abroad on the outbreak of war, and whether it could be reinforced in the medium term, depended particularly on the new metropolitan reserve, Haldane's Territorial Force, and so its numbers, training and readiness were closely monitored.[69] Generally, as war approached, the French grew increasingly optimistic about the numbers and quality of the BEF and its reinforcing contingents. It was clear that the British General Staff were doing their utmost to maximise the military support they could offer to their ally.[70]

Roles were reversed in the 1930s: rather than forcing their army into the French line of battle, the General Staff had to fend off increasingly strident French demands for an effective British military commitment. In the 1930s the British military cupboard was much barer, and so the General Staff were less willing to open its doors.[71] It is symptomatic of the more distant relations between the two armies in the 1930s that French knowledge of the British Army was more speculative before the second conflict, and that their conclusions on its quality and readiness became more pessimistic rather than optimistic as war approached.[72] The French began seriously analysing the military potential of the British Army in 1935, as their relative military ascendancy declined through a combination of German rearmament and a shortage of French manpower. What they discovered was not encouraging.[73] Since any British reinforcement would inevitably be small, the French, who had been favourably impressed by the British Army's experiments in mechanisation in the early 1930s, began to hope that the British could rapidly provide a modern and highly mobile force of two divisions able to act effectively in a striking or counter-attack role, thereby filling a perceived gap in the French battle line.[74] The British General Staff were far from sanguine. The force the French hoped for was unobtainable, and they were well aware of the inadvisability of sending the small and ill-equipped British force which could be fielded before 1939 to take on the modern and powerful German army. They were not averse to lobbying their political masters to create a force which could hold its own alongside the French army – it was a good stick to beat them with and Pownall pressed the point on the Secretary of State for War, Leslie Hore-Belisha, in his interview for the job of DMO.[75] But they lacked both the naivety, and enthusiasm for continental war, of their predecessors, having fought through the consequences of the earlier continental commitment.

As with rebuilding the military entente, there was a belated attempt in 1939 to rebuild the British Army.[76] The announcements of peacetime conscription, the doubling of the Territorial Army and the re-equipment of the first echelon of the Field Force were naturally welcomed by both Allied staffs. Yet in practical terms there was little that could be done in the short to medium term to improve the support Britain could give to the French. A doubling of the first contingent from two infantry divisions to four, and an acceleration of mobilisation, so that the first British contingent could reach the front in time for the first engagements if there was an immediate German offensive against France, resulted from the renewed Anglo-French staff talks. Yet the 'mobile division', the most significant British formation in French eyes, only existed on paper.[77] Moreover, imperial strategy, in particular defensive needs in the Mediterranean, exercised a hold over the General Staff's planners which had not been seen in 1914.[78] When war came in September 1939 the small and as yet incompletely equipped BEF proceeded smoothly to France as it had done once before. Yet it was a shadow of its former self, being composed, as one French official document put it, of hardly trained divisions of questionable value.[79] An army which had defied the contempt of its enemy in 1914 justly deserved the contempt of its ally in 1939.

Much of the General Staff's attention was devoted to getting the army ready for continental warfare, and getting political backing for such a strategy. The third problem that exercised them was what to do with the BEF once it had reached the continent. In addressing the paradox of operational strategy the General Staff wrestled with, but perhaps never adequately resolved, the tensions between direct support for France, and independent action in the Low Countries. The latter exercised a strong psychological pull over military planners before 1914 and again before 1939, yet practical preparation for action in Belgium was impossible, mainly as a consequence of Belgian reluctance to compromise her neutrality by intimate military contacts, but also because military and maritime realities had changed. Conversely, the relative ease with which logistical arrangements could be concerted with the French General Staff swayed General Staff opinion behind a strategy of direct support to France, although reservations remained even after war broke out.

The defence of Belgium, to which Britain was pledged by treaty, furnished the *causus belli* in the initial 1905 General Staff study of continental intervention. Militarily such a strategy had much to recommend it, as the British Army would be defending the traditional invasion coast directly, as well as posing a threat to the flank of German armies advancing through Belgium against France.[80] However, when reviewed alongside the option of direct support to France in the winter of 1905–06 the strategic imponderables resulting from uncertainty about Belgian intentions were obvious.[81] On the other hand, the Belgian option had much to recommend it politically – it represented military independence, rather than a contingent role for the British Army in a French battle plan, something on which Sir John French and the Whitehall Gardens planners were determined.[82] The first round of staff talks which ensued were held with both the French and Belgian General Staffs. The latter allowed some of the strategic imponderables to be addressed, which merely confirmed Grierson's initial conclusion that, politically and strategically, in the event of a German violation of Belgium it was preferable to support the Belgian army directly rather than deploy the BEF either on the left of the French line of battle or in a reserve role behind the French army. What did, however, emerge from the talks was confirmation that the maritime strategic position meant that to get to the continent the BEF would have to disembark in French rather than Belgian ports, wherever their final destination.[83]

In practice the first round of staff talks settled nothing beyond the route the BEF would take to the continent. Subsequently, owing to a growing realisation that Belgium's attitude to invasion was uncertain, and that the Belgian army was militarily inefficient, the idea that the defence of British interests in the Low Countries would be better served by helping the French army to defeat the Germans in the main theatre gained ground at the War Office. It was given tentative endorsement by the CID Military Requirements of the Empire sub-committee which reviewed British strategic policy over the winter of 1908–09, although the sub-committee's final report, strongly influenced by Sir John French, recognised that there were still two operational options.[84]

Wilson interpreted the sub-committee's conclusions as an authorisation to formalise arrangements for the despatch of the BEF to French ports on the immediate outbreak of war between France and Germany, the violation of Belgian neutrality not withstanding. He effectively disregarded the CID's directive that 'the possibility of [the BEF] being called upon to cover Antwerp has not been lost sight of, and plans will also be worked out for landings in Belgium with a view to this operation'.[85] Wilson's six-month investigation of the strategic situation,[86] more thorough than any that had gone before, did not get beyond the arrival of the BEF on the French left wing – indeed this was one of the principal caveats expressed at the famous CID meeting of 23 August 1911 when, *faute de mieux*, Wilson's planning was favoured over the Royal Navy's.[87]

Yet it would be wrong to assume from this that Britain's future operational strategy was determined. The debate over a Belgian versus a French deployment rumbled on until war was actually declared in August 1914.[88] The former had both political and military advocates, and Wilson himself was anxious to clarify the position of Belgium to remove this imponderable from the strategic equation. When after the August 1911 CID meeting Churchill subjected Wilson to a series of searching examinations on the strategic value of Anglo-Belgian military co-operation, the latter showed clear sympathy with the idea, to such an extent that he earned a rebuke from the CIGS, Nicholson, for endangering the General Staff's close relationship with France.[89] Such a rebuke was undeserved. Wilson's objective was always to give the most effective support to France, although careful examination of his correspondence and strategic appreciations, which appear confused and contradictory on the subject of Belgium, indicates that he himself was undecided on the role the BEF should play if Belgium declared for the Allies. It was axiomatic for Wilson that 'we must have a friendly Belgium';[90] he did not believe that the BEF should go to the direct support of the Belgian forces unless it was certain beforehand that the Belgians would come in on the Allied side, and they could cover British deployment north of the river Meuse. Disingenuously, Wilson was prepared to argue that the need to offer Belgium effective support necessitated increasing the size of the British Army, and that if it was clear that Britain would send its army to France on the outbreak of war Belgium was more likely to declare for the Entente.[91] Paradoxically, he also believed that an immediate Belgian call for British support would furnish the *causus belli* for immediate British intervention, allowing the British to arrive on the Sambre in time to save the French.[92] Wilson remained determined to send the BEF to 'the decisive point at the decisive time',[93] wherever that might be; but without a formal arrangement with the Belgians, and the close logistic arrangements which would be possible to maximise British support, that point remained the French left wing.[94]

Others were more decided that action in Belgium was the best strategy, despite the logistical uncertainties. Asquith, who did not like the scheme Wilson presented on 23 August 1911, clearly inclined to the Belgian option, which, on Sir John French's prompting, he instructed be properly worked out.[95] Although Wilson's General Staff colleagues realised the utility of the logistical arrangements for despatch of the BEF, they also questioned where they should go and what they should do once they were in France.[96] Sir John French in particular was partisan to what historians have dubbed 'the Belgian option', something which naturally alarmed the French.[97] No doubt acting on Asquith's instructions, soon after taking post as CIGS in 1912 French attempted to clarify the uncertain Belgian situation. He instructed the British military attaché in Belgium, Colonel Tom Bridges, to approach the chief of the Belgian General Staff with a view to reopening staff talks on despatching the BEF to Belgium.[98] It is indicative of the split within the General Staff that while French instructed Bridges to inform the Belgian Staff that the British were prepared to land troops at Ostend, Zeebrugge and Antwerp to come to the direct support of the Belgian army, Wilson was far more circumspect. He briefed Bridges that the Belgians were to be told nothing of ports of embarkation, or planning with the French; just that Britain could 'put 150,000 men at the decisive point and time'.[99] The Belgians, now committed to strict neutrality, rebuffed this advance, forestalling a potential counter-revolution in British strategy.[100]

It is clear that before 1914 there was no consensus within the General Staff on the best plan for intervention in a continental war. Wilson, despite his own uncertainties, convinced himself that without Belgian co-operation his plan was ultimately more practicable, if not preferable. Others continued to hunt for something better, or at least different, although the CID failed to make a final decision between a 'Belgian' or 'French' strategy.[101] When war broke out a decision had finally to be taken,[102] and Asquith called a war council to consider 'a situation ... [which] was not unlike one which had constantly been considered, but with regard to which no decision had ever been taken'. The discussion explored the full range of issues that had exercised the staff for the previous decade, only to conclude that 'the decision as to what our line of operations should be is postponed', pending consultation with the French.[103] Disgusted at 'an historic meeting of men, mostly entirely ignorant of their subject ... discussing strategy like idiots', Wilson put his other talent, for political lobbying, to work to save the 'with France' plan. It took six days of hectoring to persuade Sir John French and the new Secretary of State for War, Lord Kitchener, both partisans of a reserve deployment at Amiens, to follow the arrangements for concentration on the French left wing he had so carefully prepared.[104] This was a momentous decision, which was to have repercussions when the prospect of war reappeared.

It was axiomatic to the officers who came to reconsider Britain's strategic options in the 1930s that Wilson's logistical plans had bound the British too closely to the French in 1914, and it was a mistake that they were determined not to repeat. The CIGS, General Sir Archibald Montgomery-

Massingberd, minuted when the possibility of a continental commitment was reassessed:

> [The Army] should not be committed to a rigid, preconceived role as was the case prior to 1914; they should not be committed beforehand to the defence of any particular line. On the contrary their mobility and training should be exploited by regarding them as a strategic reserve for employment as circumstances may require.[105]

Britain's strategic interest in the Low Countries remained; indeed with the development of air power the need to control that region, a potential base for German bombers, appeared even more vital.[106] Not surprisingly, Antwerp was once again suggested as the best destination for any British army despatched to the continent; and it appeared that the French, with their own memories of co-operation in 1914, and more confidence in their fortified frontier defences, agreed with the idea of using the BEF in an independent counter-attack role in Belgium.[107] The first round of informal staff talks, involving the Belgians as well as the French, were intended to develop this idea.[108]

Two factors stood in the way of realising these plans. The first, the failure of rearmament to turn the BEF into a mobile striking force, has been indicated above. The second, as before 1914, was the uncertain attitude of the Belgians, who as the international situation deteriorated retreated once again into strict neutrality. In these circumstances the General Staff's planners fell back on the only other contingency, despatching the Field Force to French ports, and concentrating it on French soil, where it could be used to support the French army or to go to the assistance of Belgium should the latter's neutrality be violated. However, for a long time the plans lacked the practical detail that had distinguished Wilson's preparations. The initial 1936 studies were merely paper exercises,[109] and Pownall, officially responsible for military planning, had no desire to take them further. Following an interview with the French military attaché, General Lelong, in February 1938, in which Lelong had expounded at length on French plans, Pownall confided to his diary; 'What they want really is staff conversations – they want to get us nicely committed and tied by the leg – not merely militarily but politically as well.'[110] This pressure he resisted, although by 1939 he had been forced to prepare the detailed logistical arrangements necessary for the speedy despatch of the BEF to France. The role it was to play once it got there remained, however, undecided. At the early meetings between the British staff and Gamelin after the declaration of war it became clear that Pownall's caution had changed nothing. The French were in charge, and history was repeating itself. Pownall ruefully recorded:

> Gamelin clearly hinted that if French troops were sent to help the Belgians and hold up the German advance in front of an organised line, he would like British troops to take part ... I fancy the French expect us to fall in on the left, i.e. north-west of Lille ... None of us are too keen on that idea. For one thing we had a pretty fair bellyful last time of fighting in the Flanders plain with its mud and slime, not to mention its bad memories.[111]

In 1914, the General Staff had at least made a positive decision to support France; in 1939 there was no real decision or desire to do so again, and only by default did the BEF find itself back on the well-trodden road to Flanders.

The British General Staff's attitude to continental war before 1914 proved more positive and well ordered than in the late 1930s. In the first instance support to France represented a new and potentially defining challenge for the new military institution, whereas the second time around changed political and international circumstances undermined the General Staff's confidence in their ability to meet the familiar challenge. Personality too played a part. There were no architects of a 'military Entente' with the enthusiasm and ability of Grierson, Wilson and French in the 1930s. For Pownall and Gort their memories of 1914–18 were too strong for an unqualified and dynamic push to rebuild the Anglo-French military relationship, although both in time came to accept the inevitability of a return to France and the need to be properly prepared.

Before 1914 the military were clearly more bellicose than their political masters, and set about preparing the army for their continental role despite lacking clear political endorsement for their strategy. Aware that there was strong sympathy for the Entente in the Liberal Cabinet, the General Staff, and Wilson in particular, constantly solicited such an endorsement, resorting at times to unconstitutional behind-the-scenes machinations, although without success. If successful, Wilson would have reconciled the gulf that existed between policy and strategy, and General Staff planning could have been predicated on an alliance with either Belgium or France. Without that Britain's continental strategy remained 'hypothetical and non-committal',[112] and essentially undecided. While the relationship between policy and strategy was better defined in the 1930s, it was increasingly divorced from the realities of the European strategic situation. Planning, such as it was, was until March 1939 not only hypothetical and non-committal, but also unrealistic.

There was certainly more political support for a continental strategy, if not a military alliance, before 1914 than before 1939. In the first instance this allowed the General Staff to make better progress in organising and equipping the BEF for its potential continental role. Conversely in the

1930s the General Staff accepted, even if they did not welcome, this lack of political commitment. They were themselves less enthusiastic about developing the military Entente, and rearmament priorities prevented them turning an imperial army into a modern mobile force which could realistically expect to hold its own in a Franco-German war.

Against this political background the General Staff wrestled with the problems of operational strategy, should the decision be taken to send the BEF to the continent. The attitudes of their potential allies – Belgian neutrality on the one hand, French pressure for support on the other – naturally influenced their assessments of the practicability of a Belgian or French deployment. Somewhat by default, the General Staff were sucked into an operational strategy of direct support to France; enthusiastically before 1914 because they believed in the need to support France, reluctantly before 1939 because they were aware of the consequences of supporting France. It is to the General Staff's credit that they were ready to act immediately on both occasions when the balloon went up. However, they never knew beforehand if or how they would be asked to act, since the decision to send the army was a political rather than a military decision, which could only be taken once the actual circumstances of war were known, in consultation with Britain's principal ally. This did not stop the General Staff, or more precisely Wilson, trying to pre-empt this decision. But ultimately the General Staff remained the government's military advisers. They advised that the government should reconcile policy and strategy; they advised that the British Army should be large enough and equipped to play a decisive military role on the continent; they advised on where and how to use the BEF once it reached the continent. If politicians had been willing to act on this advice, then Britain's and Europe's military history might have been very different.

7

The Australians at Pozières: Command and Control on the Somme, 1916[1]

G. D. Sheffield

The first action of the Australian Imperial Force (AIF) on the Somme has an evil reputation. At Gallipoli the Australians lost about 23,000 officers and men in eight months in 1915. At Pozières and Mouquet Farm in July–August 1916 Australian divisions lost approximately similar numbers in only six weeks.[2] Private J. T. Hutton of 17th Battalion (2nd Australian Division) recorded his impressions of the battle in a series of terse diary entries: 'Its just like hell pure & simple'; 'Murder bloody murder'; 'Wipe the scenes away they are awful'.[3] Charles Bean, the war correspondent and Australian official historian was convinced that the shelling at Pozières was worse than at the third Battle of Ypres in 1917.[4] The commander of 6th Australian Brigade wondered whether the losses of the summer fighting would have the same impact in Australia as the initial news of the casualties at Gallipoli, and bring in more volunteers for the AIF.[5] In short, Pozières was, in Bean's words, 'one vast Australian Cemetery'.[6]

Some Australian soldiers looked upon these operations as worthwhile. 'Australia is keeping her name up & doing exceptionally good work', noted one other rank.[7] 'Pozières', a piece of doggerel written by 'Fray Bentos' that appeared in a trench journal, concluded by emphasising that the battles had taught 'these haughty Prussians' a lesson.[8] Yet the verdicts of historians on these operations have been harsh. One states that the operations around Pozières and Mouquet Farm were 'ill-conceived in the extreme'. The commanders of Reserve and Fourth Armies 'hardly ever co-ordinated their attacks'. Moreover, 'the fronts of attack were too narrow; and the inability of the artillery to perform tasks essential to any advance was never taken into account by the command. The ground captured proved to be of little importance to the overall campaign, although the Germans were impressed by the tenacity of the Australian attacks.'[9] These are powerful indictments of commanders and staff work, both

British and Australian. This chapter examines Australian command and staff work during the operations on the Somme in July–August 1916, seeking to place the Australian experience into the wider context of that of the British Expeditionary Force (BEF) on the Western Front.

The divisions of the AIF arrived in France from Egypt in March 1916. The first major Australian battle on the Western Front was 5th Division's bloodily abortive attack at Fromelles on 19 July. The battle of the Somme began on 1 July, and on 23 July 1st Australian Division attacked the village of Pozières. This was vital ground. Pozières was perched on one of the highest points on the ridge on which the German Second Line was located, and sat astride the Roman road that ran from Albert to Bapaume. From Pozières windmill the defenders could look north-east to the fortress of Thiepval, a British objective of 1 July that was still firmly in German hands, and east to High Wood, the last major wood in the southern sector of the Somme. Possession of Pozières would be an important step towards allowing the British to attack Thiepval from the rear, while a relatively small advance in the south would make a considerable part of the German Second Line untenable, at a time when the German Third Line was still under construction. Both sides realised the importance of Pozières.

1st Australian Division's attack on 23 July was successful.[10] By 25 July the village had fallen and the line had been advanced 1,000 yards. However, the ferocious German bombardment cost the division 5,285 casualties. The next major series of attacks around Pozières were carried out by 2nd Australian Division. The initial assault, on 29 July, failed. A second attempt was rather more successful, but in all 2nd Australian Division's operations cost 6,848 casualties. Beginning on 9 August, 4th Australian Division entered the battle, attacking towards Mouquet Farm, in the direction of Thiepval. A series of attacks in this area were carried out by 4th, 1st and 2nd Australian Divisions, the last on 3 September. Three were outright failures; four resulted in gains. Then the Australians were sent to another sector, away from the Somme – for the moment. Mouquet Farm finally fell to the British 11th Division on 26 September.

After the war Lieutenant-General Sir John Monash, commander of the Australian Corps in 1918, claimed that the key to success in battle was to develop a carefully choreographed plan like a musical score.[11] Recent scholarship lends some weight to this view, at least as far as the Western Front was concerned. Such an approach rests very largely on competent command and, especially, efficient staff work. With this in mind, it is important to examine the upper echelons of the AIF in July 1916.

Before the war Australia had a small number of permanent soldiers and a sizeable militia, backed by compulsory military training for youths (or 'Boy Conscription').[12] Eventually, Australia was to put five infantry divisions into the field, together with mounted forces in the Middle East and a number of other troops. Like the BEF as a whole, the AIF faced the problem of finding higher commanders and staff officers for a force on a scale far beyond anything planned for prior to 1914. The senior officers of the AIF were a mixture of British and a few Australian Regulars, and Australian militia officers. Places at the British Army Staff Colleges at Camberley and Quetta had been made available to Australian officers in 1905. In all there were eight officers with the psc (passed staff college) qualification available to Australian forces in 1914; two of the total were seconded from the British Army.[13] The eight included Regulars such as Tom Blamey, Brudenell White and John Gellibrand (the latter was an Australian who had served with the British Army, retiring to Tasmania in 1912).[14] There were a few other Australians who could claim to be staff trained or who had staff experience: John Laverack, an Australian officer whose Camberley course was interrupted by the outbreak of war; J. G. Legge, who had served as Australian representative on the Imperial General Staff in London from 1912 to 1914; and W. T. Bridges, the first Australian to reach general officer rank. Bridges was the first Commandant of the Royal Military College Duntroon, which opened in 1911 with the aim of providing Australia with staff officers, but in 1914 Duntroon graduates were used for regimental duties.[15] Moreover, during the war, talented Australians were sometimes given posts in the wider BEF, the most prominent being White, who followed Birdwood to Fifth Army in 1918 to become its chief of staff,[16] but also E. C. P. Plant, who served on Fourth Army Staff in 1918, and S. G. Savige, who ended up in Persia as part of Dunsterforce.[17]

A number of very high quality ex-militia officers came to hold command and staff positions in the AIF, including William Glasgow, James Cannan, H. E. 'Pompey' Elliot, J. J. T. Hobbs, and of course John Monash, who commanded the Australian Corps as a Lieutenant-General in 1918. Monash was one of a number of militia officers who benefited from the 'War Courses' began by Bridges in 1908, which gave at least a smattering of staff training.[18] Hobbs took a military science course at the University of Sydney in 1909. By no means all militia officers took their hobby so seriously but such men, like some of their Territorial Force counterparts in Britain, clearly did. Indeed, one historian has suggested that Monash was not 'handicapped educationally' by his non-attendance at Staff College; that diligent personal study, his engineering background and his everyday work as a militia officer compensated for lack of a psc.[19] Clearly, Monash was an exceptional soldier, and the wider question of the effectiveness of staff training at Camberley and Quetta lies outside the scope of this chapter.[20] However, it is fair to say that the best militia officers had some training and experience that proved valuable on active service.

Tim Travers has demonstrated that the Edwardian British Army was 'strangely personalized', the upper echelons being marked by factionalism.[21] The fledgling Australian forces also had their fair share of cliques and feuds. In part this was related to nationalistic tensions. In July 1916 a number of key posts, including command of I (Birdwood) and II (Godley) ANZAC Corps, and 1st (Walker) and 4th (Cox) Australian Divisions remained in the hands of British (or Indian Army) officers. In early 1916 Birdwood and White, his chief of staff, were sometimes suspected of preferring British officers to Australians, although Bean and White claimed that, if anything, Birdwood was 'always prepared to try an inferior Australian officer rather than a British officer who he knows to be more capable'.[22] There is certainly evidence that Birdwood was keen to promote Australian talent,[23] but this had to be balanced against the need for trained staff officers, as senior Australian commanders recognised.[24] Australian officers were, however, by no means a band of brothers. There were clashes of personalities, frustrated ambitions and tensions between militia and regular officers: all of these factors were involved when Elliot was passed over by White for command of 3rd Australian Division in favour of Gellibrand.[25] Perhaps the most controversial Australian commander was Legge (2nd Australian Division) who had a number of enemies within the AIF.[26] There were tensions between White and Gellibrand, whom the former may have perceived as a potential rival in 1914–15.[27] In 1918 Bean and another journalist, Keith Murdoch, opposed Monash's appointment to command of the Australian Corps and carried out a 'sordid intrigue' to replace him with White.[28]

Pozières had been attacked several times by British formations before 23 July. Why did 1st Australian Division's attack succeed, while previous attacks had failed? One study of the battle concludes that the key factor was 'the quality of the troops used in the assault'. 1st Australian Division was fresh, well trained, and experienced (it had served on Gallipoli).[29] There is undoubtedly much in this explanation, but it does not go far enough. Several other factors must also be taken into account.

The first relates to staff work.[30] 1st Australian Division drew upon the hard-won lessons learned by British formations in the first three weeks of the Somme battle. In his official history Bean discusses this in general terms,[31] but it is worth devoting more attention to this subject. On 14 July, that is, nine days before the first Australian assault on Pozières, Lieutenant-Colonel T. A. Blamey, the chief of staff of 1st Australian Division, issued General Staff Memorandum no. 54. This consisted of a series of lessons from recent fighting passed on by British 7th and 19th Divisions. Blamey had taken the trouble to consult with his opposite numbers in nearby British divisions, and discuss their tactical experiences.[32] Blamey's choice of divisions consulted is interesting. It may have been chance, or it may have been because both formations had been conspicuously successful. A New Army formation, 19th Division, was in reserve on 1 July, and had taken La Boisselle on 2 July, using a 'Chinese' barrage against Ovillers to divert attention from their real target, followed by a rush across No Man's

Land that took the Germans by surprise.[33] On 1 July, 7th Division, a Regular formation, had attacked and captured the fortified village of Mametz. It then participated in the successful dawn assault of 14 July on Bazentin Ridge. C. T. Atkinson, the perceptive author of the division's history, summarised the reasons for success on 1 July as effective use of artillery in wire cutting and accurate barrages; all arms co-operation, the product of 'careful and systematic training'; and the 'lessons' taught by the GOC and the staff.[34]

These lessons were enshrined in Blamey's memorandum of 14 July, and no. 56, issued four days later; the latter may have drawn on the experience of other British divisions. Blamey instructed that attacks should not be launched from more than 200 yards from the enemy line. If No Man's Land was wider, a 'jumping off place' needed to be established, or troops should 'form up under cover of darkness within this distance'. Rather than simply advancing as far as they could, 'definite objectives' were to be set for the infantry. Each phase of the battle was to be 'covered in turn by an artillery barrage'. Particular attention needed to be paid to mopping up enemy positions, 'P' smoke bombs being recommended for dealing with dugouts. Blamey also offered practical advice on what to do once a position was captured, on matters such as the delivery of rations and ammunition, the need to equip some troops with picks and shovels for consolidation of captured positions, and the need to push forward parties of sappers and pioneers as soon as possible. Lewis guns were to be pushed forward, in part to give the infantry cover while they were consolidating. Finally, he stressed the importance of communications; of contact patrols by the RFC and of providing an officer to liaise between brigade HQ and divisional HQ, as well as forward units, who was actually to go forward and see for himself the situation on the ground.[35] All of this was excellent advice, much of which 1st Australian Division was to put to good use on 23–26 July.

The attack on 23 July, although successful, revealed several tactical limitations. Two British battalion commanders of 48th Division commented that 1st Australian Division crowded their trenches, leading to unnecessary casualties.[36] Despite the insistence of their British tutors on the importance of consolidation, and Blamey's memos on the subject, in their excitement, some attacking infantry threw away their picks and shovels – evidence, apart from anything else, of poor battle discipline. More positively, 1st Australian Division's papers reveal them struggling to come to terms with one of the major problems of trench warfare – command at low levels. In July and August 1916 the Australians were fighting 'bite and hold' or 'step by step' operations: that is, limited battles, dominated by artillery, which aimed not to break through the enemy positions and reopen mobile warfare at one fell swoop, but to inflict heavy casualties on the enemy in taking a piece of key ground from which to launch another similar attack. This was the most appropriate method for the BEF to use in 1916, given its level of training and experience, the strength of the German defenders, and the absence of a usable instrument of exploitation. However, on at least two occasions in the first two weeks of the Battle of the Somme rigid application of the bite and hold approach, or diffidence about exploiting enemy weaknesses, led to the missing of important opportunities to make significant advances. The first came on 1 July, when the success of Rawlinson's right flank gave the British a golden opportunity to, at the very least, seize and occupy the woods behind Montauban ridge. These woods – High Wood, Delville Wood and the rest – were to cost the BEF dearly in casualties over the next few months. Similarly, after the success of the dawn assault of 14 July, High Wood was there for the taking, but delays in following up the initial assault allowed the Germans to reinforce their positions in the wood. It is against this background that we should examine Blamey's General Staff Memorandum no. 59, of 1 August 1916, which examined the lessons of the recent actions at Pozières.

This document stressed the need for thorough preparation before each successive advance, and that troops must have specific objectives, and not advance beyond them but consolidate captured positions (this included reorganising the assaulting troops). Pressing on must be left to follow-up waves. This was of some importance, because it seems that 'many' of the attacking infantry did not understand that the attack was essentially limited, and dictated by the pace of the artillery barrage: some men said that the 'artillery did not lift quickly enough for them to get on'. 'Numerous' casualties resulted.

However, sticking to pre-arranged objectives had to be balanced against the seizing of opportunities – such as the taking of terrain features abandoned by the enemy. Patrols were to be pushed forward, but, in Blamey's words, the 'principle' to be observed was for the captured position to

> be made strong against counter-attacks while no opportunity must be lost for want of initiative. It is to be noted that the initiative if uncontrolled and if based on hope as to what the enemy may be doing may easily become dangerous. A subordinate commander who pushes forward without having thoroughly examined the situation by means of patrols incurs a grave risk.

Of great importance was the need to report on actions taken, and to tell neighbouring units so that they might co-operate with the additional forward move.[37]

This document shows 1st Australian Division groping towards the principles of devolved command, known today as 'mission command'. If 'top down' command was applied rigidly, it could stifle initiative and sacrifice tactical opportunities. Conversely, lack of 'grip' by commanders could lead to leaving newly captured positions too weak to resist the inevitable counter-attack that formed an integral part of German tactical doctrine, and to Australian troops advancing into their own barrage.

Blamey's efforts at collating and disseminating tactical advice should be placed in the context of the BEF's culture of innovation and improvisation. The creation of doctrine was a dynamic process. Units at all levels examined operations to try to learn lessons, and such information went up to higher levels of command,[38] and came down in the form of doctrinal pamphlets and semi-informal notes, often issued when operations were still in progress. Before Pozières, 2nd Australian Division issued a 'lessons learned' document on raids, and Australian units received 'primers' on subjects such as the use of artillery and infantry tactics.[39] After its operations in the Pozières area, 4th Australian Division issued a 'lessons learned' report,[40] and I ANZAC Corps issued its own summary of lessons at the end of the Somme campaign.[41] These documents reflect similar debates in formations across the BEF, and played their part in the reshaping of tactical doctrine at the beginning of 1917 that made the BEF a more effective force during the battles of that year than it had been on the Somme.[42]

Robin Prior and Trevor Wilson's seminal *Command on the Western Front* has established something of a new orthodoxy that correct use of guns was a vital factor in achieving success on the Western Front.[43] For its attack on 23 July, 1st Australian Division (and 48th Division attacking on its immediate left) was supported by a substantial concentration of artillery. In addition to organic divisional artillery, the assault was supported by the artillery of 25th Division, whose infantry had been pulled out of the line, and 'the bulk of the X Corps medium and heavy guns'. XLV Heavy Artillery Group, consisting of the British 36th and 108th Siege Batteries, and the Australian 55th Siege Battery armed with 9.2-inch howitzers, was 'at the direct call of 1st Australian Division from 21st July'.[44] The 1st Australian Division's Operation Order no. 31 of 21 July also talks of the heavy artillery of Reserve Army assisting the attack.[45] This was a powerful concentration of artillery on a limited front.

The mere possession of large numbers of guns did not guarantee success, but clearly the artillery support for the attack of 23 July was very effective. 'The systematic bombardment' of the village commenced on 19 July at 2.00 a.m., reducing it to rubble.[46] Counter-battery fire was good. In his after-action report of 3 August, 'Hooky' Walker, the commander of 1st Australian Division, noted that the heavy artillery 'responded quickly' to requests for aid: 'on each occasion the enemy's fire diminished steadily and the infantry obtained a respite'. As for the attack itself, Walker recorded that 'The barrages were most effective', and praised the 'accurate shooting' of his divisional guns, stating that the infantry had pushed up to within 50 yards of the barrage in the assault.[47] A Chinese (i.e. feint) barrage to the west of Pozières attempted to deceive the defenders as to the direction of the assault.[48]

On 23 July the use of artillery compared favourably to that provided for previous attempts to seize Pozières. An unsuccessful attack was carried out on 14 July by 'strong patrols' of 34th Division, in the mistaken belief that the defenders were pulling out. But as 'three different artillery staffs [III Corps, X Corps, 34th Division] were issuing orders for it [the preliminary bombardment] much difficulty was found in ensuring that the barrage should fall clear of attacking troops'.[49] On the following day 34th Division attacked Pozières in greater strength on two occasions. Although Rawlinson assumed that the seizure of Pozières would be accomplished with relative ease,[50] according to the British official historian, the assaulting troops believed that 'the artillery preparation and support were quite inadequate'. The second bombardment, while visually impressive, was a case of too little, too late. Although the divisional artillery fired from 5.00 p.m. to 6.00 p.m., with 100 heavy guns (40 from X Corps, Reserve Army) adding their voices at 5.30 p.m., the bombardment failed to suppress the German machine gunners, who were observed by a British airman emerging from shelters and sprinting for their machine guns. The British attackers were not following the barrage closely enough, and thus lost the race to the wire. Yet another attack by 34th Division, this time on 17 July, also failed, in part because machine gun fire was not suppressed.[51] A report of a reconnaissance carried out by a X Corps staff officer on the following day stated that the trenches contained unburied dead.[52]

These earlier attacks had obvious benefits for Walker's men on 23 July. They enjoyed the cumulative effects of the bombardment on the German positions at Pozières in terms of destruction, and perhaps more importantly, the gunners supporting the Australians had the benefit of knowing where their targets actually were. This was particularly significant when one examines a primary reason for the failure of Fourth Army's attacks on 22/23 July: that they were assaulting a position located largely on a reverse slope. This meant that extensive aerial reconnaissance was needed to allow the artillery to register its guns. However, the weather in the days leading up to the attack was poor, making aerial observation difficult. In sharp contrast to the artillerymen supporting 1st Australian Division's attack, Fourth Army's gunners had precious little time to register their pieces. The accuracy of the bombardment – and subsequently the attacking divisions – suffered as a result. Another spin-off of the poor weather was the delay of the general assault, which gave the Germans time to prepare to be attacked.[53]

Another of Prior and Wilson's major themes is that narrow front attacks usually failed, not least because they allowed the defenders to concentrate their artillery fire against a single target. There was a third advantage enjoyed by Walker's division that was denied to previous attackers of Pozières. The Australians attacked not on a narrow, one or two divisional front, but, in theory, as part of a simultaneous, broad front attack which stretched, from the left of Pozières, across the inter-Army boundary right across to the extreme right flank of Fourth Army. In reality the six participating divisions attacked at four different times, lessening the impact of a concerted push. However, on the left flank, there was a simultaneous assault in the Pozières area, although it must be admitted that this was more through luck than judgement. The two Reserve Army divisions – 48th and 1st Australian – attacked at 12.30 a.m. The left-hand formation of Fourth Army, British 1st Division, also attacked at this time to conform to the assault on Pozières. However, 19th Division had been ordered to attack an hour later, at 1.30 a.m.; but when a new German position (Intermediate Trench) was belatedly discovered in No Man's Land, through RFC reconnaissance, Fourth Army ordered this position to be attacked at 12.30 a.m. before launching the main assault at 1.30 a.m. Had the order to do so been received, 51st (Highland) Division would also have attacked Intermediate Trench at 12.30 a.m. As it was, four divisions attacked, simultaneously, side by side.[54]

Intermediate Trench was a major factor in the failure of 19th Division's attack. Allocating a mere 60 minutes to its capture was a hopelessly optimistic decision by Fourth Army. It was later claimed that Corps and Army headquarters at first refused to believe reports of Intermediate Trench's very existence, and it was therefore omitted from the artillery fire plan. More generally, lack of preparation – 19th Division were still trying to locate the exact front line on the 21st – the absence of surprise, sacrificed by the preliminary bombardment which then failed to do its job, and unsuppressed machine guns put paid to 1st and 19th Division's attacks.[55] The comparison with 1st Australian Division's well-prepared attack, supported by an effective bombardment, is all too stark.

The attack of 2nd Australian Division on 29 July likewise offers a sad contrast with that of Walker's division. Brigadier-General Philip Howell, a senior staff officer of II Corps (another Reserve Army formation) wrote in his diary:

> Last night's attack by Australians on trenches E of Pozières reported a ghastly failure: too rushed: inadequate preparation & reconnaissance: attempting too much at once.[56]

This verdict is fair. The attack was not mounted as part of a concerted, broad front attack. Instead, it was a classic example of 'penny-packeting'. On their left flank, one battalion of 12th Division tried, and failed, to take a position on the flank of 23rd Australian Battalion, which as a result was left out on a limb. On their right, a single battalion of 23rd Division made a successful attack; elsewhere, there were minor operations by 5th and 51st Divisions. The artillery support for the attack was substantial – once again, 25th Divisional Artillery added its weight, as did the heavies of II Corps (which had just relieved X Corps), I ANZAC Corps and Reserve Army. But the heavy guns dispersed their fire, shelling not only targets around the OG Lines at Pozières, but also Mouquet Farm and Courcelette, thus dissipating the effect of the bombardment.

It may also be relevant that there is no evidence of Blamey's tactical memoranda, or their equivalent, in the war diary of Legge's 2nd Australian Division. The suspicion that 2nd Division did not have the benefit of tactical advice offered by experienced formations is strengthened by a terse note of a conference held later on the 29th, presided over by Birdwood, and attended by White, Legge, and his chief of staff:

> Decided to repeat the attempt to capture enemy's position in OG1 and OG2 after more thorough preparation had been made and all details worked out ... Trench to be dug within 200 yards of enemy's line as a jumping off place. OG1 and OG2 to be subjected to heavy bombardment under Special programme.[57]

If it is indeed the case that Legge's staff had failed to seek out tactical advice, this reflects poorly on 2nd Australian Division, but the failure to share information also raises questions about staff work in 1st Australian Division and I ANZAC Corps. It is perhaps significant that the commander of 4th Australian Division, Major-General H. V. Cox, made a point of consulting with other formations before his division was committed to battle. On 18 July he spoke to Horne, the commander of XV Corps, which had enjoyed some success in the battle thus far, and then, like Blamey, visited the headquarters of 7th Division 'and got much information'. After 1st Australian Division's successful attack on Pozières he lunched with Walker 'and talked to him about the battle' and on 31 July he talked with Legge and the commanders of 23rd and 12th Divisions. In operations on 9 and 12/13 August, 4th Australian Division successfully captured trenches around Mouquet Farm. After the first operation, Cox met with Walker and Blamey. Clearly, Cox, like Blamey, believed in consultation and learning from the success and failures of other formations, and this seems to have been a factor in his division's achievements.[58]

One of the most controversial aspects of the entire battle were the respective roles of the commanders of Reserve Army and I ANZAC Corps, Hubert Gough and William Birdwood. The story of Gough's behaviour before 1st Australian Division's attack on 23 July is reasonably well known. According to Bean, on arriving at Reserve Army's front on 18 July, Walker was told by Gough 'I want you to go into the line and attack Pozières tomorrow night!'[59] Walker was appalled at what he described in his diary as 'Scrappy & unsatisfactory orders from Reserve Army', going on to write 'Hope shall not be rushed into an ill-prepared ... operation but fear I shall'.[60] I ANZAC Corps headquarters had not yet arrived, and clearly, little more than a day was hopelessly insufficient time for preparation. Walker and White successfully argued against Gough and dissuaded him from ordering what would almost certainly have been a premature attack that would have been a bloody failure. Apparently, this was not the only battle Walker had to fight against Gough before the 23 July attack. In 1928, Walker recorded how he had to seek more artillery, as the initial allocation was insufficient, and only succeeded in being allowed to attack from the south-east, rather than the south-west, the route of the unsuccessful pushes launched in the past, by taking 'Moses' Beddington, a Reserve Army staff officer whom Gough trusted, up to the front, to show him the ground. Walker's verdict on Gough was scathing: 'the very worst exhibition of Army commandship [sic] that occurred during the whole campaign, though God knows the 5th army was a tragedy throughout'.[61] Gough angrily rejected this version of events when he was shown a draft of Bean's Australian official history, in which Bean claimed that Gough was 'temperamentally' inclined towards rushed attacks: 'I can hardly believe a word of this story about my meeting with General Walker' Gough wrote in 1927. 'I was not "temperamentally" addicted to attacks without careful reconnaissance and preparation.'[62]

This is not the place for a full-scale assessment of Hubert Gough's role as commander of Reserve Army on the Somme.[63] There is, however, a considerable body of evidence that suggests that Gough was a prescriptive, 'hands-on' commander. Andrew Simpson's study of Corps Command on the Western Front has demonstrated that Gough treated Corps as little more than 'post boxes'; that is, as methods of passing down to divisions detailed orders drawn up by his Army headquarters.[64] During the Battle of the Ancre Heights (1 October–11 November 1916), Gough issued a seven-page memorandum on attacks, for the edification of divisional and brigade commanders.[65] Tim Travers has highlighted the case of 32nd Division, whose commander Major-General Rycroft was 'terrified' of Gough, with bad effects on the division's operations. During the Ancre battle of November 1916, Gough seems to have been commanding the division by remote control.[66] This was a rather different approach from that favoured by Rawlinson, the commander of Fourth Army, who was inclined to set broad objectives and then leave corps and divisional commanders to get on with it. Indeed, if Gough can be criticised for breathing down the necks of his subordinates, Rawlinson stands condemned for lack of 'grip'. Gough's approach caused a good deal of friction between Reserve Army headquarters and subordinate commanders.[67] At the end of the Somme campaign, Reserve Army's chief of staff Neill

Malcolm issued a memorandum in which he condemned the 'marked tendency to disregard, or to dispute the advisability of order[s] issued from Army Headquarters' and went on to defend the issuing of such orders.[68]

What impact did Gough's command style have on Australian operations on the Somme? It has been suggested that as an army commander Gough disliked having a level of command between him and the battlefield.[69] Therefore it is possible that on 18 July 1916 Gough was keen to get Walker to attack before Birdwood and I Anzac Corps headquarters arrived to (from Gough's point of view) complicate matters. In fact I Anzac Corps did not take over responsibility for 1st Australian Division's sector until noon on 23 July – that is, after the attack had been launched.[70] The fact that Gough dispensed with I ANZAC Corps headquarters on 23 July was, in one sense, not necessarily a bad thing, since the artillery support that a Corps headquarters would normally have co-ordinated was present in abundant measure. Even after the Corps headquarters was in place, Gough continued to exercise direct control of operations.[71]

Our knowledge of the role played by Birdwood in the operations at Pozières is tantalisingly incomplete. There is no record of his reactions to the planning for the attack of 23 July.[72] While Birdwood wrote descriptions of the battle in letters to Lord Derby and the Australian Governor-General in which his choice of the words 'we' and 'my boys' implies responsibility for the victory, his input into 1st Australian Division's attack appears to have been minimal.[73] The occasion on which he (and White) did seem to have an influence was in obtaining a delay in the attack, when they were, in Bean's words 'most courteously consulted' by Reserve Army.[74] However Bean stresses that Walker and White were primarily responsible for dissuading Gough from his original plan.

This was not the only occasion on which Gough pressurised Australian commanders. When Brigadier-General Howell of II Corps met Legge after 2nd Australian Division's unsuccessful attack on 29 July, he found him 'furious with the [Reserve] army: at least 1000 men lost for nothing'.[75] After the war Legge himself stated that 'Any apparent haste' he had shown in attacking 'should be properly ascribed to the daily pressure of the Reserve Army Commander.'[76] There is little doubt that Gough pressurised Legge into attacking on 29 July before preparations were fully complete.[77] In the official history Bean blamed Legge for buckling under, and said that White blamed himself for not standing up to Gough. Bean's verdict was followed by Peter Charlton in his 1986 study of Pozières.[78] However, one should take this with a pinch of salt. White and Legge had fallen out by early 1916, and Bean was not an impartial witness. As one Australian historian has noted, a 'schoolboy sense of hero-worship was never far from Bean', and Bean described White as 'the greatest man it has been my fortune intimately to know'.[79] To place the blame on Legge is, C. D. Coulthard-Clark has argued, 'grossly unfair'. I ANZAC Corps in the shape of White and Birdwood did not specifically oppose 2nd Division's operation against Pozières on 29 July and therefore gave it 'tacit endorsement'.[80] Whatever Legge's abilities as a commander,[81] to put a mere divisional commander up against an army commander – particularly one with Gough's abrasive and bullying style – was not a fair competition. I ANZAC Corps should have acted as a buffer zone between Reserve Army and subordinate formations.[82]

Bean believed that in 1916 2nd Australian Division's 'general staff was weak'. Gellibrand considered that Legges's chief of staff, Lieutenant-Colonel A. H. Bridges, gave poor service.[83] However, this was not the only occasion on which Australian staff work in this period came in for criticism. To pick just one, minor, example, a Grenadier Guards subaltern was scathing about the way an Australian battalion carried out a relief,[84] but the most serious criticism can be levelled at the staff work of I ANZAC Corps. Birdwood leaned heavily on White, whom he praised in September 1916 as 'one of the best officers it has ever been my good fortune to have with me'.[85] This compliment appeared in the context of an explanation of why Birdwood considered it more important to keep White at I ANZAC Corps HQ than to put him in command of a division. White was privately critical of Birdwood, resenting the heavy burden of staff work placed upon him.[86] However, Eric Andrews has highlighted White's weaknesses as a staff officer during the Bullecourt fighting in 1917, and Bean's role in glossing over his hero's frailties.[87] Similar criticisms can be made of I ANZAC Corps staff work in 1916. Philip Howell was critical, implicitly or explicitly, of Birdwood and White on several occasions, while Gellibrand believed that I ANZAC Corps should have provided Legge with an effective staff.[88] Rawlinson was similarly unimpressed by I ANZAC Corps staff work.[89] Similar criticism could be levelled at many British formations at this period; in general, the BEF's staff work was to undergo a distinct improvement in 1917–18.

If there was indeed a question mark over Australian staff work in 1916, this puts one of Haig's comments in a new light. Following the failure of 2nd Australian Division's attack on 29 July, the British C-in-C criticised the preparations and bluntly told Birdwood and White 'You're not fighting Bashi-Bazouks now – this is serious, scientific war, and you are up against the most scientific and most military nation in Europe'. Haig clearly feared, with some reason, that the experience of Gallipoli had not been good preparation for the rigours of the Western Front. Earlier, on 22 July, he had worried whether Gough had given 1st Australian Division a straightforward job. Unlike Walker and Blamey, Legge's staff had made serious errors in the preparation for their attack. According to Bean, White, stung by Haig's 'Bashi-Bazouk' comment, stood up to the C-in-C. He had earlier failed to take such a strong line against Gough.[90]

During the Hundred Days offensive of 1918 the five-division Australian

Corps emerged as an elite force. Bean's explanation for the impressive performance of Australian troops in 1918 amounted to the fact they were superior soldiers, emerging from a democratic, egalitarian frontier society very different from that of Britain, that encouraged the soldierly virtues of 'determination, endurance, and improvisation'.[91] In recent years this 'Anzac myth' has been challenged.[92] Current scholarship, while not denying the excellence of the 'battle culture' of the Australians, has placed it within the context of a BEF-wide improvement in command and staff work, the emergence of the all arms battle, and the application of scientific methods of warfare, particularly as regards gunnery, to tactics.[93]

Edmonds criticised Bean for being 'inclined to write as if the Australian divisions were in 1916, when they arrived in France, the perfect instrument they were in August 1918, and to attribute their earlier failures in 1916 to British generals'.[94] This comment contains a measure of truth. While Gough's performance as a general must be taken into account when assessing I ANZAC Corps's operations on the Somme, it is clear that Australian formations went through the same steep 'learning curve' as their British, and for that matter other Dominion, counterparts. 1st Australian Division, which was experienced and well led, and had the benefit of good advice from other divisions, performed more effectively than 2nd Australian Division, which lacked these advantages but learned from its mistakes. Many comparisons could be made with British divisions. On 8 August, 55th Division, a Territorial formation from West Lancashire, made a number of elementary mistakes in their first, unsuccessful, attack on the Somme; they too learned from their mistakes and, indeed, became an elite 'storm' formation later in the war.[95] Australian divisions in 1916 were no better, and no worse, than comparable British formations. Operational effectiveness was the product of factors such as training, leadership and artillery support, not national origin.

We have seen that in 1914 the AIF had a very small pool of trained staff officers on which they could draw. Arguably, the situation was not very much better for the British Army, which in August 1914 had 908 active officers with the psc qualification. By the beginning of 1916, as many as 90 of these men had been killed. Given that the BEF had increased from 6 infantry divisions in 1914 to about 60 in 1916 – not forgetting other units and formations on other fronts – it can be seen that trained staff officers had to be spread very thinly indeed.[96] In July 1916, Australian and most British divisions suffered from a common lack of trained staff officers and commanders accustomed to operating at the appropriate level. Over the next two years Australian and British commanders and staff alike were to acquire more experience, in the process of which a rough meritocracy emerged from the personalised prewar armies. Many commanders were 'degummed' – deprived of command – en route: Legge, for example, returned to Australia in 1917. During these years Australians progressively replaced British officers in Australian formations. Monash implied that this enhanced the efficiency of staff work within the Australian Corps.[97] Edmonds came to believe that by 1918 the staff work of Australian formations was better than that of the rest of the BEF. Interestingly, he excluded 2nd Australian Division from this compliment, even though the seizure of the Mont St Quentin position on 31 August 1918 by this formation surely rates as one of the finest feats of arms in the entire war.[98] The historical spadework necessary to substantiate, qualify or refute these assertions has yet to be undertaken.[99] However, one might with confidence assert that the most important factors in the success of Australian staff work were experience and competence, regardless of the national origin of individual staff officers, and the crucial fact that the Australian Corps always had the same divisions under command, enhancing teamwork between higher and lower formations. Moreover, in contrast to the situation with Birdwood in 1916, in 1918 the Australian Corps was more obviously a national army. Monash was prepared to fight his corner against higher command, and was perhaps held in higher regard by his superiors. British corps did not enjoy these advantages. As Edmonds wrote to Bean in 1928, it might have been more efficient if 'Haig had kept British divisions permanently in corps … But don't try to persuade the Australian public that in 1916 the Australian Corps was the fine instrument it was in 1918'.[100]

8

The British General Staff
and Japan, 1918–41

Philip Towle

Historians often argue that the Western nations underestimated Japanese military power before Pearl Harbor. According to Alvin Coox, 'the West was dismally ignorant, in civilian as well as military circles, of Japan's military proficiency on the eve of the Pacific War ... The Japanese armed forces were shallowly evaluated; they were underrated at best, despised at worst'. Coox believed that this was due to Japan's secrecy, to the paucity of Western attachés and language officers, to the slovenly appearance of Japanese troops and to racism.[1] Christopher Thorne quoted Air Chief Marshal Sir Robert Brooke-Popham, the British Commander in the Far East, dismissing the idea that the Japanese could field an 'intelligent fighting force' after seeing their troops across the frontier from Hong Kong.[2] Similarly, Arthur Marder argued that the Royal Navy underestimated the Imperial Japanese Navy and rated it only as efficient as the Italian fleet. The Japanese were wrongly thought to be poor shipbuilders and aviators, slow thinking, badly trained and unable to cope with crises. Ignorance and racial prejudice seem to have been the main causes of such inaccurate assessments.[3]

These failings applied to the Royal Navy and the RAF rather than to the General Staff which made more effort to learn about the Japanese army than about the American, Soviet, German or French. The military experts on Japan, such as Malcolm Kennedy, Major-General F. S. G. Piggott and Colonel G. T. Wards, had a very high appreciation of its army and warned constantly of the need to conciliate Tokyo to protect British interests in Asia.[4] They were neither racists nor bigots, they often liked their Japanese counterparts, socialised extensively with them and served for long periods with Japanese units. They influenced the Intelligence Department of the General Staff with their assessments of Japanese strength and from 1936 the General Staff struggled spasmodically to persuade the Foreign Office to make what terms it could with Tokyo, to sacrifice China and to concentrate Britain's limited forces against Germany. In the event, the

General Staff failed to alter British foreign policy, but this was because of the inherent political problems not because of the underestimation of Japanese power by the General Staff. In this, British military and diplomatic representatives in Tokyo were generally in agreement. As early as 1920 the Ambassador there, Sir Charles Eliot, forecast, 'in a few years, if her naval and military programme is executed, she will be very strong ... I do not think we can afford to risk the enmity of Japan'. The last British Ambassador in Tokyo before the Second World War, Sir Robert Craigie, accepted this assessment and did his best to reduce Anglo-Japanese antagonism.[5]

The popular British impression of the Japanese army in the 1920s and early 1930s was created by fading historical memories of the Russo-Japanese War and by occasional newspaper articles. Japanese co-operation with international agreements and its peaceful foreign policy in the 1920s meant that the British media and politicians turned their attention to other issues. The occasional parliamentary questions about Japan in the mid-1920s usually raised economic concerns. Even the specialist journals, such as the *Journal of the Royal Institute of International Affairs*, devoted very little attention to Japanese politics. However, it did periodically review books about Japan and the Institute's annual *Survey of International Affairs* had a number of prescient articles about Japanese politics.[6]

The *Journal of the Royal United Services Institute* focused on the Chinese conflicts which seemed in the 1920s to present the main threat to Asian stability and British trade. When the Institute did have a lecture on Japan in 1927, it was told by Malcolm Kennedy, by then retired from the army, that 'even a brief survey of the main outstanding facts should help to disprove that Japan need be regarded as a military menace, or that she is not sincere in her avowal that she would welcome the opportunity to cut down her armaments still further and thereby reduce expenditure'. Similarly, the Japanese chargé assured the Institute in December 1928 that, while the East was gaining more self-confidence, his country was committed to peace and disarmament and that it still regarded Britain as its 'oldest and surest friend and former ally'.[7] Coverage of Japan was no greater in the other leading British military journal, the *Army Quarterly*.[8]

If there was only limited interest in Japan in the 1920s, it cannot be said that the articles published underestimated Japanese martial qualities. Typically, Major Alford of the Royal Artillery asserted

> with absolute certainty that the Japanese have had the lessons [of the First World War] drummed into them and that the training and organisation are as perfect as skilled instructors can make them. Indeed it may safely be stated that in numbers, in fighting efficiency, in equipment and training for war, the Japanese Army is the most powerful fighting force in the world today.[9]

Neither of the two leading British military journals, nor the Chatham House publications, could be accused of underestimating Japanese military power.[10] The underestimation, if underestimation there was, came from elsewhere.

Another mistake for which the British Army has been blamed in this period was its failure to predict the brutality which the Japanese armed forces were to demonstrate only too frequently between 1931 and 1945. Here there is a good deal of validity in the criticism. British officers could not normally observe the harshness of Japanese behaviour in Korea, Manchuria and later in China at first hand. They often also sympathised with Japanese colonial endeavours and felt the means were justified by the end. Typically, Kennedy noted in his diary, 'as the nations of the world seem set on raising both immigration and tariff barriers against Japan, it seems essential to let her have a favourable outlet somewhere, and where better than in Manchuria ?'[11] It was the journalists and missionaries who generally had the most accurate notion of what was going on.[12]

Army officers distrusted journalists' accounts which they suspected of exaggeration if not invention, and thus there were plenty of contemptuous asides in their books and articles about press commentary on the Japanese empire. Kennedy himself became for a while Reuters' correspondent in Japan and the experience only convinced him 'that the majority of papers in all countries do far more harm than good when international politics and understanding are concerned'. He bitterly criticised those journalists who warned of Japanese expansionism, dismissing their reports as 'utter bilge'.[13] Similarly, Piggott wanted *The Times* to tone down its reports on the Sino-Japanese War in the 1930s because of the damage they were doing to Anglo-Japanese relations.[14]

Army officers deeply admired Bushido. Major B. R. Mullaly, a former language officer serving with the 10th Gurkha Rifles, wrote in the *Army Quarterly* in 1928 of

> that wonderful code of ethics upon which the greatness of Japan has been built and which is still her inspiration – Bushido, the way of the Bushi, or warrior-knights. Loyalty, frugality, death rather than dishonour and death in battle is the greatest honour of all – these are the essential tenets of Bushido.[15]

It was easy for British army officers to forget that in Europe these military virtues were balanced by centuries of Christian and humanist teaching which stressed the supreme value of gentleness and kindness.[16] In Japan the West came up against a civilisation where patriotism and military necessity were everything, and where Western restraints did not operate.

Finally, Kennedy, Piggott and other British officers were very close socially to Japanese officers.[17] It was difficult for them to imagine that their well-mannered friends were capable of brutality. The Assistant Military Attaché, Major Wards, was unusually observant about contemporary Japanese when he told the GSO2 in London in March 1936,

> when they want to be so, they can be as charming, as considerate and helpful as any people in the world. They can, at the same time, if they want to, be just the opposite and it is a peculiarity of the race that the same person can conduct himself either way.[18]

The language officers attached to the Japanese units sent regular reports to the General Staff about their experiences. Moreover, despite the junior rank of the officers concerned, their papers often went to the Director of Military Intelligence (DMI), sometimes to the CIGS and occasionally even to the Foreign Secretary. It was possible for readers to focus on the criticisms made of the Japanese forces and to ignore the praise, but there is no evidence that the more critical assessments were better received. Certain conclusions were common to the various reports, others were unique. For example, Lieutenant Stockton of the Royal Artillery was attached to the artillery regiment of the Guards from September 1926 to March 1927. Typically, he stressed the trouble taken by the regiment to see to his comfort and to show him hospitality, reflections of Japanese manners and of their desire for good relations with Britain. Stockton was impressed by the endurance of the soldiers but not by the equipment which was only just being modernised. Where Stockton was unusual was in his observation of a number of examples of disobedience to orders, but he concluded more typically, 'during marches and practice camp the men proved that they would be excellent fighting material if well led'.[19]

In 1929 Lieutenant S. R. Hunt of the Staffordshire Regiment was attached to the 7th Infantry Regiment of the 9th Division in the north of Japan. It was generally a very unpleasant experience given the prevalent cold, but Hunt was all the more impressed 'by the apparent cheerfulness of all ranks and their complete disregard of the elements and by the unconcerned way in which they carried on even in the midst of a blizzard'.[20] On the other hand, he noted that they did not practise musketry and their march discipline was sometimes poor. Generally their officers had, in turn, a very low opinion of the efficiency of the British Army. They criticised Britain for opposing Japanese exploitation of China and they 'absolutely ridiculed any suggestion that China might object to being exploited or might make any resistance, and they gave me the impression that they are confident of their ability to control the country'.[21] Hunt's observations were particularly significant over both the Japanese attitude to China and towards the British Army, but they were to be frequently echoed by the language officers in the next decade.

In April 1931 Captain Ainger of the 3rd King's Own Hussars reported on his attachment to the Cavalry School of the Imperial Japanese Army.

He made the common observation that Japanese officers were 'far more mentally studious and far less physically active than officers of corresponding rank in the British army'.[22] Nevertheless, they put up with intense cold and other discomforts without complaint. There was also close comradeship amongst the officers despite the fierce competition between them. As a result of their patriotism and hardihood, they expected to be able to march greater distances in wartime than other armies. They would move their cavalry and other forces very rapidly at night prior to a morning offensive and such attacks would be pressed to the utmost because the Japanese army was deeply imbued with aggressive tactics, whatever the cost in casualties. Major-General A. C. Temperley thanked Ainger for the excellence of his report on behalf of the CIGS, but, unfortunately, Ainger's emphasis on the use by the Japanese of night movements and rapid marches was, nevertheless, not passed on to the generality of British army officers.[23]

In 1935 Lieutenant J. D. P. Chapman was attached to the 13th Infantry Regiment in Kumamoto which had recently returned from operations in Manchuria, a campaign which it regarded as an easy victory. In contrast to Stockton, he believed that discipline was very good and there was no crime. Like many of his predecessors, he noted that bayonet training was stressed more than musketry and mobile rather than trench warfare. The Japanese army emphasised co-operation between the artillery and infantry and, while march discipline appeared slack, the results were good. The General Staff was particularly impressed with this report. Colonel Hastings Ismay was delighted and the DMI particularly asked for Chapman to be thanked.[24]

Early in 1936 Lieutenant P. M. Johnson of the Royal Artillery was attached to the 4th Field Artillery regiment near Osaka. The experience left him one of the most sceptical language officers about Japanese strength. The officers he found very polite and pleasant but slow thinking. The NCOs were excellent, their control of their men admirable and their relationship with their officers equally impressive; 'the men struck me as being so much more like their British counterparts than I could have imagined'. Johnson said he found it difficult to compare the army with others.

> I regard their discipline, keenness and morale generally to be excellent, and probably as good or better than anybody else's; their actual physical resistance to be merely average; their indifference to danger and prowess at 'sticking to their post to the last man' to be to a certain extent mythical.[25]

The training of the Japanese artillery without maps would be very helpful in trackless countryside such as forest or jungle. Night operations and marches were frequently practised and speed was emphasised. Johnson concluded by giving the Japanese 75 or 80 marks compared with 100 for a modern Western army. Johnson was thus atypical in downgrading

Japanese physical endurance and he was mistaken to dismiss their indifference to danger. His observations about their training to fire without the use of maps was particularly noteworthy, given the terrain in Burma where the British and Japanese were to fight, while his general underestimation of the Japanese compared to the European armies was unfortunate.

Later in 1936 Johnson was attached to the 8th Medium Artillery Regiment. Johnson was more impressed by the non-commissioned officers (NCOs) than the officers, as it was the NCOs who carried out the bulk of the training. He was surprised by Japanese concerns about safety as he and other officers were made to hide in a dugout during artillery practice. They had tried spotting for the guns using aircraft but found it ineffective and the radio had broken down. Nevertheless, 'the actual observation of fire is of a distinctly high order and would excel that of the average British officer', Johnson reported.[26] Ranges in the area were thickly wooded and this made firing much more realistic than in British artillery practice on Salisbury plain. Johnson believed that the officers were inclined to be too slow and noted that they felt despised by the infantry.

In 1937 Piggott's son, Francis, was attached to the 2nd Regiment of the Imperial Guards Division. Like Johnson, he found the NCOs were effective and their bullying did not seem to worry the troops. The men were also often well educated and good at passing verbal messages. They were capable of marching for 11 hours and then drilling afterwards. The regiment expected war with Russia in Manchuria and hoped for an encounter battle which they would win by dash and determination.[27]

Similarly Lieutenant Pender-Cudlip of the Royal Artillery concluded, after serving with the Japanese mountain artillery, that officers' professional knowledge and ability left little to be desired. The ordinary soldiers were healthy, strong and intelligent, the NCOs were very 'keen' and their relations with the officers were excellent. The main Japanese deficiencies were lack of imagination and over-centralisation which would disadvantage them in a war against a first-class European army. Two years later, after attachment to a cavalry regiment, Pender-Cudlip reported, 'conversation with the Adjutant and with more senior officers confirmed the impression of contempt for the British army'. He also noted ominously that the Japanese had benefited greatly from their experiences in China.[28]

Later in 1938 Lieutenant T. H. Winterborn of the Royal Corps of Signals spent a month with the 43rd Infantry Regiment which had recently returned to Tokushima from China. Winterborn stressed the stamina of the soldiers, the indifference of their marksmanship, their competence with camouflage and the lack of initiative which he felt the officers showed. The commanding officer, General Hanaya, was a good linguist; 'although he was in no way actively anti-English, he was frankly contemptuous of the British army and navy, but was slightly impressed by air force expansion'.[29] The General Staff may have felt that Japanese assessment of the

British Army was simply the product of their pro-German leanings. It upset neither the Staff nor the language officers but, perhaps as a result, there was no general post-mortem on Japanese estimates. These may have derived from memories of Britain's poor performance in the joint operations against German troops in China in 1914 or from the reports by Japanese officers in Britain on the British obsession with sport, but there was a missed opportunity to subject their criticisms to close analysis and to rectify deficiencies.[30]

In November 1938 the Imperial Defence College in London prepared an exercise on the situation in the Far East. The briefings produced with the assistance of the General Staff stressed that

> the Japanese higher commander is usually a man of strong character, capable of great concentration and detachment. He is dignified, calm and rather obstinate ... To judge by history he would be bold in action and at times inclined to rashness.[31]

The Japanese General Staff was described as highly trained, 'intelligent and hard working' though sometimes lacking in imagination. Regimental officers cut themselves off from the nation by their single-minded concentration on their duties. NCOs and warrant officers treated their men well 'without harshness and are friendly without being familiar'. Such conclusions were clearly based on the reports from Japan, though they ignored the references quoted above to slow-thinking Japanese officers. They were in no way patronising, racist or ignorant of Japanese qualities. British officers who attended such courses had no excuse for dismissing Japanese power or for ignorance of their tactics.

Inevitably British assessments were influenced by the changes which officers were struggling to understand in the military profession as a whole. During the interwar period, warfare was becoming far more diverse. In China Mao Tse Dong was evolving his ideas on people's warfare which were to become so devastatingly effective against the Japanese and the Nationalists in his homeland and, when used by Giap and Ho Chi Minh, against the French and Americans in Indochina after 1945.[32] At the same time, European warfare was coming to be dominated by armoured vehicles and aircraft, while warfare in the Pacific was of an amphibious nature and turned on ability to land forces rapidly and to support them with ships and aircraft in jungle and broken terrain. The Japanese excelled in this last type of warfare.

The Japanese were also the first regular soldiers to encounter people's warfare and, because the Europeans totally underestimated its power and deprecated Chinese military efficiency in general, this led many to underestimate the Japanese since it took them so long to control the Chinese mainland. Moreover, the Japanese never became proficient in armoured warfare, though it was only when they challenged the Russians at the battle of Nomonhan on the Mongolian plains in 1939 that their deficiencies were exposed.[33] The fact that the General Staff had a high estimate of the value of the Japanese army, despite its failings in guerrilla and armoured warfare, is a tribute to the competence of the young officers who were attached to the Japanese and reported so lucidly on their strengths and weaknesses.

Reports to the General Staff on Japanese efficiency during the Sino-Japanese War varied dramatically. On one side was the assessment by Major Wards who went on a tour to Shanghai with a group of attachés in November 1937 to observe the effects of the recent fighting. Wards's experience there confirmed his belief in the efficiency of the Japanese and their hostility to Britain. At the opposite extreme was the assessment by the Captain of HMS *Tamar* in Hong Kong who regarded the Japanese with contempt.

Wards's analysis was not based on the sympathy with the Japanese felt by his superior, Piggott. He believed that Japan had decided on the elimination of all foreign nations from Asia and that it respected only military strength. He was impressed by Japan's speed and efficiency in amphibious operations:

> I do not think that any other nation could have carried out such moves of such large bodies of men [across the sea from Japan] so quickly and so efficiently, combined with such secrecy and apparently an almost total lack of fuss and inconvenience to passenger traffic.

Ominously, he reported that he saw only about 1,000 Chinese prisoners. 'I imagine that Japanese policy is to avoid taking prisoners whenever possible, otherwise they would have tens of thousands to feed and look after.'[34]

Wards heard foreign officers say that the Japanese army was not as efficient as its European equivalents:

> I cannot subscribe to these views, and consider that, not only are they incorrect as regards the Japanese army as a whole, but also very dangerous. In some respects the Japanese is clearly not up to the standards of a first class power in Europe, but if the various factors which are considered necessary for the success of any army in war are tabulated, it will I submit be found that the Japanese army as it is today is a formidable force, well able to cope with any opposition likely to be met with at the present time in the Far East.[35]

The weak side of the army was its firepower, equipment and lack of experience of defeat. Against this was its morale, the unity of the nation, mobilisation arrangements, efficiency of the high command, endurance, ability to maintain secrecy, experience in hand-to-hand fighting and large reserves. Recent operations in China would have improved its tactics and in the Far East it would have obvious advantages over any opponent. Wards's report was sent by Sir Robert Craigie not only to the General Staff but to the Foreign Secretary, Anthony Eden. However, while he might have paid attention to Wards's assessment of Japanese strength, he could hardly have been expected to understand the thrust of Wards's analysis which was that the Japanese had fashioned a force quite peculiarly suitable to the terrain in which they might challenge Britain and the other colonial powers.[36]

There were many British soldiers who disagreed with Wards's assessment of Japanese prowess. One former language officer was sent to North China to try to observe the fighting. He speculated that the Japanese might panic after setbacks; 'after all the Japanese are Orientals!' However, he agreed with Wards's political judgement that they were determined to expel the British from China. Their only concern was with the threat from Russia. Their strategy would be rash in any country but China because they advanced very rapidly leaving exposed and vulnerable supply lines. Nevertheless, Japanese discipline was good and although their soldiers had originally alienated the Chinese by their behaviour, looting had now been stopped.[37]

Colonel Burkhardt reported from Hong Kong in August 1938 on what he had discovered of guerrilla resistance to the occupation forces. Guerrilla attacks forced the Japanese to move in groups of about 100 and even then parties were sometimes ambushed. In many areas the Japanese controlled only the roads, and their reprisals with bombers were ineffective. The Japanese were particularly bad at vehicle maintenance and new trucks turned into unrecognisable wrecks within a few weeks. Other reports suggested that this was due to guerrilla attacks on the roads. Unfortunately Burkhardt's assessment of the efficacy of people's war was treated with some scepticism by the General Staff in London which believed he exaggerated the results of the guerrillas' resistance.[38]

The General Staff also received information from the Captain of HMS *Tamar*. His assessment of the Japanese armed forces reflected the Royal Navy's general underestimation of Japanese prowess. 'The general impression that an observer gains after watching the Japanese in action over a period of two months is that they are a people too little educated to handle or co-ordinate properly the highly technical machinery of modern warfare.' The officers seemed like 'wooden-headed automatons' and a numerically inferior British force should have no problem dealing with the Japanese; 'to many who have watched and conversed with the Japanese in Shanghai, the bogie of their superiority in battle has vanished and it appears improbable that they can rank as a first class fighting power until they have learnt how to properly educate their people'.[39] Given the very high levels of literacy in Japan, compared with Britain, this seems a particularly inappropriate comment and shows the danger of badly informed officers making snap judgements. It directly contradicted the high appreciation in the language officers' reports of Japanese NCOs and their ability to communicate easily with their men.

Such bias and condescension had to be set against the numerous reports from other observers, like the one from the Yangtse Valley in 1937 or from Harbin for the six months from March to September 1938. The first report warned that the Japanese would soon have far more experience of amphibious operations than almost any other armed force and that their practice was to land on a hostile beach and move inland as rapidly as possible. The second concluded, 'all the Japanese units seen here are composed of first line men of action, that their equipment and discipline are admirable and that movements are carried out with remarkable speed and secrecy'.[40] With such contrasts between assessments it was difficult for the General Staff to reach a balanced appreciation of the Japanese armed forces. The critics may have reduced the impact of the favourable reports from the British officers in Tokyo, but the tendency throughout the period was for the General Staff to push for a rapprochement with Japan because of the threat it represented.

The British were well aware that Japan was a militarised society in the 1930s and that this greatly complicated their relations with other countries. The Ambassador in Tokyo pointed out in January 1931 that the army dominated the country historically, that the people were passionately committed to Japan's 'mission in China' and were 'not likely to be deterred by fears of international complications'.[41] Military Intelligence produced an appreciation of 'the Influence of the Army on the Government and People of Japan' in June 1934. It stressed the effectiveness of the million-strong Reservists Association which diffused militaristic ideas amongst all classes. When the chairman of the Dairen Chamber of Commerce referred to the Japanese army as the 'watchdog' of Manchuria he and his colleagues were compelled to resign. 'In fact, if not in name' Japan was a military dictatorship.[42] The burden of the paper was that outside pressure would further unite Japan, while the best hope was that political scandals or failure in Manchuria would discredit the army. In the meantime, it was wise to reaffirm Britain's friendship with Japan to 'convince our former allies that every man's hand is not against them, and so blunt the edge of the most powerful weapon in the armoury of the military party – an appeal to the fanatical patriotism and latent xenophobia of the Japanese people'. Ismay wanted the paper sent to the CIGS and the Secretary of State, and the CIGS did see the assessment.[43]

The appreciation was highly topical because there was a great deal of diplomatic activity between the two countries in 1934. The Chancellor of the Exchequer, Neville Chamberlain, and the Permanent Secretary to the Treasury, Warren Fisher, were behind the despatch of a mission to Japan from the Federation of British Industries (FBI) in September 1934 to try to develop economic links. The Japanese Foreign Minister had also discussed the possibility of negotiating a non-aggression pact with Sir Robert Clive, the British Ambassador. Clive was told to probe Japanese attitudes cautiously because of the difficulties a bilateral pact would present for relations with China and the United States. Thus the Japanese would have to give some assurances over China, 'failing that we would appear to be giving carte blanche to Japan and that would be an impossible position for us. Even the future of the Netherlands East Indies is a matter of vital concern for us'.[44] In the end, neither the FBI mission nor the proposal for a non-aggression pact had any impact.

Meanwhile, the Intelligence Division of the Naval Staff in London under Admiral Dickens were trying to persuade the DMI, Sir John Dill, of the necessity of a rapprochement with Tokyo and thus of convincing the Foreign Office to change British policy.[45] The Japanese navy was preparing for war by increasing its manpower from 89,000 to 112,000 and such a war could be against Britain, given London's hostility to Japanese policy in China and the encouragement given by Britain to the USSR to join the League of Nations. The Naval Staff paper argued in favour of recognising the newly established Japanese colony of Manchukuo and accepting that British policy had to be tailored to take into account 'our military strength'.[46] Dill replied in October 1934 that 'for military – if for no other reasons – we should retain – or should I say regain – the friendship of Japan. Her power to injure us is almost unbounded'. He also agreed that Japan was preparing for war on a vast scale, although he did show a complacency about Japanese competence which did not reflect the attachés' views. 'In our judgement', he wrote with Ismay's encouragement, 'the Japanese army is at present below European standards.' In the event of a Russo-Japanese War, which seemed likely, he predicted a Soviet victory but, in any case, such a war would 'clip the wings of both antagonists'. Dickens agreed that Japan might not attack Britain for a long time but he did not believe that it would be spending so much on naval preparations if the Russians were the intended enemy. One day the Japanese might attack the Dutch East Indies and Britain would be dragged into the conflict. The General Staff put this down in part to special pleading because of the delays in the completion of the Singapore base, but it agreed that Britain ought to remain on friendly terms with Japan at least until Singapore was ready. This was one of the rare occasions during the 1930s when the Naval Staff was more anxious than the General Staff about Japanese power and intentions. It may be that the Naval Staff was responding not only to general concerns about the state of the Royal Navy but to the warnings by Sir Frederick Dreyer, C-in-C on the China Station from 1933 to 1936 and one of the naval officers who had an accurate appreciation of Japanese naval power. Dreyer made four visits to Japan in the period, mixed frequently with Japanese officers and was very impressed by their gunnery practice.[47]

Despite General Staff caution over the Admiralty's paper in 1934, the CIGS prepared a memorandum on the importance of Anglo-Japanese friendship which was circulated to the Cabinet in January 1936. It emphasised both Japanese hints that they would like better relations and the dangers of not coming to terms, particularly if both Germany and Japan were hostile; 'the chances of our being able permanently to station large numbers of forces in the far east appear so remote at present that the General Staff are of opinion that other methods should at least be given a trial'.[48] But the Foreign Office regarded such a rapprochement as impossible given Japanese policy in China, and the Cabinet simply urged the two departments to compose their differences.[49] This was all part of the complex struggle between British ministries over policy towards Asia. In September 1935 Chamberlain and Fisher had backed another attempt at economic diplomacy when the mission under Sir Frederick Leith-Ross was despatched to stabilise the Chinese economy and encourage Anglo-Japanese co-operation there. Like the 1934 FBI mission it reflected Treasury naivety. The Japanese wanted to drive British economic interests from Asia, not co-operate with them, and they had no interest in rehabilitating China until their domination was complete. Not surprisingly, the Leith-Ross mission made little progress in Tokyo and simply encouraged the Foreign Office in its scepticism about Japanese intentions.[50]

By chance the General Staff also came across a paper written on 5 December 1935 by the British Ambassador in China, Alexander Cadogan, who was to come to the Foreign Office as Deputy Under Secretary in 1936. Cadogan urged the continuation of the policy of protesting to Tokyo about its actions in China because otherwise the Japanese would feel that Britain had lost interest in the area. Colonel Ismay and other General Staff officers thought that it was disastrous to go on encouraging the Chinese to provoke Japan. The DMI, Sir John Dill, agreed that there was a gulf between Foreign Office and General Staff assessments, but said that it was an inappropriate moment to try to change government policy so soon after their paper had been rejected.[51]

After its rebuff in January 1936 and the failure of the two economic missions to Japan, the General Staff decided to see what 'military diplomacy' could achieve. Major-General F. S. G. Piggott would return to Japan in 1936 as military attaché and use his close connections with senior Japanese officers to improve relations. This was hardly an absurd notion given the role which the army was playing at that time in Japanese politics and certainly not as naive as the Treasury's initiatives.[52] Piggott did socialise closely with the higher ranks of the Japanese army but this did not necessarily make them understand British objections to their actions in

China. He was impressed by the social graces of his Japanese colleagues and by the courtesy which they showed even to junior language officers.[53] Piggott was much less aware than Wards and Craigie of the ability of the Japanese at that time to behave in very contradictory ways in different circumstances.[54]

In his first report to the British Ambassador after becoming attaché in June 1936, Piggott admitted that the Japanese army had changed since he had served as Attaché from 1922 to 1926. It was now much more faction-ridden than it had been. Senior officers, like the former military attaché in London, General Tanaka, surprised Piggott by saying that their younger colleagues had to be humoured and that they were hostile to all foreign nations. What neither Piggott nor any other outsider could judge, or influence, was the tense and complicated struggle within the Japanese military to fashion a coherent security policy. The new military attaché simply wanted to believe that relations between Britain and Japan could be improved. Sir Robert Clive was more sceptical and by November the extent of his disagreement with Piggott was clear. Piggott argued that there was an opportunity to achieve a degree of rapprochement because 'friendly feeling towards Great Britain is widespread amongst all classes of Japanese'. Clive admitted that the Japanese disliked their isolation but pointed out that they wanted a free hand in China, the right to export freely to all parts of the British Empire, and British neutrality in the event of a war with the Soviet Union. Sir George Sansom of the Embassy staff agreed that Japanese and British policies in China were fundamentally opposed. The only policy open was to wait on events and the diplomats in the Embassy believed that time was on Britain's side.[55] It is an ironic comment on this assessment and, indeed, on Piggott's hopes, that it was in 1936 that the Japanese armed forces added Britain to the list of their potential enemies.[56]

Clive's successor, Sir Robert Craigie, was more sympathetic to Piggott's efforts, and historians have tended to link Piggott and Craigie in their desire to appease Tokyo. There was, however, a difference between Piggott and Craigie and indeed between the War Office and Foreign Office about the best way to handle the Japanese. Piggott believed that Britain should avoid provoking Tokyo over China. Craigie commented, 'one day it is true Japanese friendship may be of vital interest to us in the Far East but experience goes to show that this country has a greater respect for those who stand up to her than for those who do not'.[57] We now know that Piggott was right to point out the dangers of alienating Japanese nationalists. Imperial Naval Staff minutes accused London of exacerbating Japanese problems with China and influential naval officers asserted that Britain was waging diplomatic warfare against the Japanese.[58]

The dispute between Piggott and Craigie was a curious reversal of normal military and diplomatic propensities: the military usually believe that power and toughness earn respect, diplomats advocate compromise and caution. Over Japan in the 1930s the positions were inverted, perhaps because Piggott and the language officers had a better idea of the temper of the Japanese armed forces. Of course, once the European war began in September 1939, Japan was more influenced by its ebb and flow than by any actions which Britain took in Asia and by the tone of British protests. It was the march of European events and increasing US determination to use economic tools to prevent Japanese expansion which determined the course of events in Asia, rather than the nuances in British policy.[59]

In the meantime, Piggott's more ambitious schemes were curbed. He was warned by the DMI, General Haining, in the autumn of 1936 that he must conform with British policy:

> I can assure you that we are watching your efforts to promote better relations with the Japanese army with great interest and sympathy … I realise that such efforts must often lead you into conversations on subjects of policy and politics where you have to tread delicately. As you say, I am sure you will always be a 'model of discretion'. I do hope that this aspect of your work is not going to prove such a tax on you that you will not be able to give the time it deserves to the purely military side of your work, especially the collection of information for the handbook which is much behind.[60]

Piggott promised to heed the warning. Indeed he had already told the CIGS, Sir Cyril Deverell, in July that 'the very fact that I am persona grata with the Japanese, though in one way of great help in carrying out the policy of the General Staff as explained to me last Spring, at the same time necessitates the exercise of a lot of tact'.[61] Typically, when he suggested that the British could ingratiate themselves with the Japanese by offering to help demarcate the frontier between Manchukuo and the Soviet Union, he was quickly disillusioned by the Japanese who wanted prior recognition of Manchukuo.[62]

Piggott remained in the Embassy until the outbreak of the European war. In his memoirs Craigie deplored his recall both because of his friendship and his knowledge of Japan. Piggott himself seemed to feel that he had been withdrawn because of the jealousy of officials in the Foreign Office.[63] For the next two years he joined Kennedy in lecturing on Japan and advocating Anglo-Japanese friendship. Towards the end he tried to persuade Lord Hankey, the Paymaster General, that a letter (drafted by himself) from the King to the Japanese Emperor or a visit to Japan by Hankey might change the course of events. It was the last gasp of the pro-Japanese lobby in Britain.[64]

Enough has been written to make clear that the British General Staff had a mass of information on which to base its assessment of the Japanese army between the world wars, certainly as much as it had on any other, simply because the language officers served so closely with their Japanese counterparts and considerably more than the RAF and Royal Navy had about their Japanese equivalents. The Royal Navy had had very close relations with the Japanese before the First World War and had a better appreciation of Japanese strength at that stage than the British Army.[65] The navy had the chance to renew these contacts in the 1920s but rejected them because it believed that it would have to give more information than it received.[66] Japanese secretiveness would have handicapped efforts to learn about their dramatic advances in military aircraft, torpedoes, amphibious warfare and battleship construction, but British army officers did gain a good deal of information from their attachments. The navy's hesitations were a major error and turned the Imperial Japanese Navy towards Germany.[67]

What the General Staff failed to do was to pass the language officers' reports on Japanese tactics to British forces in Hong Kong, Singapore and India. After the Russo-Japanese War, reports from British officers accompanying the Japanese forces had been printed and circulated widely. No similar circulation was made between the wars. Had it been and had such reports been read, British forces in Malaya and Singapore would have been aware that the Japanese would make great use of night attacks; that they would advance far more rapidly than any other infantry to throw their adversaries off balance; that they would take great risks with their supply train and that their artillery was used to practising in trackless and unmapped forest. Above all they would have been aware of the Japanese experience with amphibious operations, the professionalism of their officer corps and the absolute determination of the whole army to win or perish in the attempt. Of course, the Japanese army was by no means perfect, its marksmanship was generally regarded as inferior to British, and the risks which it was prepared to take would not always be justified. It failed to develop an effective armoured force, though this was more than counterbalanced in Asian conditions by the efficacy of its aerial support. The RAF's utter failure to appreciate the sophistication of Japanese aircraft and the quality of its pilots was to have dire implications for British forces across the whole of Asia.

With rare exceptions, such as Wards's observations on Japanese treatment of Chinese prisoners, reports from the military attachés and language officers in Tokyo failed to emphasise Japanese brutality. They also contrast with later historical accounts of the Japanese army in that, although they refer to bullying by NCOs and officers, they did not give the impression that the men felt crushed or alienated by this behaviour. If, in many ways, their blindness to brutality was their greatest omission, the greatest failings of the General Staff in London were to propagate the tactical observations of the language officers, to investigate the reasons for the low esteem in which the British Army was held by the Japanese and to impress on its political masters that the Japanese were benefiting from their experience in China. The problem was not ignorance or racism but inability to communicate.

The British army officers who knew Japan best struggled to reconcile the two countries both because they had a healthy respect for Japanese power and because they believed that such reconciliation was possible. By the mid-1930s its price was clearly the abandonment of China to Japanese control. The General Staff argued that this was simply to accept the correlation of forces. It was no good pretending to protect China when this was beyond British power. Conversely, the Foreign Office argued that, although the British Empire was vulnerable, Japan and the Soviet Union might come to blows, or the United States would eventually stand up to Japan and the Japanese would either be deterred or defeated. This was indeed how events turned out, but the price paid was the allied disasters in South East Asia in 1942, the repression of the South East Asian peoples from 1942 to 1945, and the rapid collapse of the European empires after 1945.

9

J. F. C. Fuller:
Staff Officer Extraordinary

A. J. *Trythall*

THE BRITISH GENERAL STAFF

The invitation to write this chapter has provided me with the incentive to revisit the whole subject of 'Boney Fuller', which I first visited, with the help and encouragement of Brian Bond, over thirty years ago. The result of that visitation was my biography, *'Boney' Fuller: The Intellectual General*,[1] and a whole lot else besides: a new dimension in my life, a changed way of looking at the world. A great deal of all this I owe to Brian Bond. The result of this revisitation is not so much revision of my original views and conclusions, but the opportunity to relate them, not to Fuller's general military and historical significance, as I did in the biography, but to the creation and nature of the British General Staff during his military career.

It has often been said that the British Army does not exist, that it is in fact only a loose federation of military tribes. This is usually in order to explain its peculiarities to American military colleagues and is said only half in jest. I well remember once, as Director of Army Education, asking a small boy in a Services Children's School in Cyprus if his father was in the army. 'No', he replied, 'he's in the Greenjackets'. 'Why', Americans often ask, 'do you not all wear the same uniform?' It might also similarly be asked whether the British General Staff also exists, although Fuller, one of its chief ornaments, undoubtedly did. It is certainly not a fixed body of officers whose function throughout their careers is to form a staff, and perform staff work and nor has it ever been, even when all staff officers, of whatever rank, wore red gorgets, or tabs, as they did until after the First World War. There always has been, and is today, movement between staff and regimental appointments. Indeed this was the intention in the pre-1914 German army where staff officers were supposed to return to regimental duty from time to time although neither of the Moltkes commanded even a company.[2] The British General Staff is in fact a corpus of appointments filled for periods of time, normally three years, by officers from the regiments and corps of the army who continue to regard themselves as members of a regiment or corps and continue to wear its badges. This arrangement only ceases if or when the officer is promoted to the rank of colonel. There are, however, two other major ambiguities. The first is that until relatively recent times there were also 'A' (Adjutant-General) and 'Q' (Quartermaster-General) Staffs as well as the General Staff and these were responsible for administrative and quartermaster matters, whereas the General, or 'G', Staff covered the more prestigious matters of intelligence, operations and training. There were, and are, also specialist staffs dealing, for example, with medical, legal and educational matters. There is also the fact that from the 1920s onwards, as was indicated above, all officers of the rank of colonel upwards left their regiments and corps and became officers of the Staff Corps, discarding, except for the odd button, their regimental uniforms and insignia. Moreover, when these officers filled command appointments they remained, and still remain, members of the Staff Corps. Thus C-in-C Land is both a commander and staff officer and wears Staff Corps uniform. When an officer of the Staff Corps becomes colonel of his regiment or colonel commandant of a corps he may, while functioning as such, wear colonel's badges of rank on a regimental or corps uniform even though he is, for instance, a lieutenant-general in the Staff Corps. There is in this custom a very British touch of inverted snobbery together with an echo of older systems of organisation and hierarchy.

Until the beginning of the last century the British Army had no formally constituted General Staff. As H. O. Arnold-Foster, Secretary of State for War, wrote in a memorandum in 1902

> A good officer is not necessarily an expert in Defence questions. He may be a good flag officer, a good gunner, a good disciplinarian, a good frontier leader or merely a brave and active-minded man; but he may be all or any of these things without necessarily being an expert in the great science of war, or acquainted with the methods by which, under the complicated conditions of our Empire, preparation for war can most effectively be made.[3]

Hindsight inclines one to wonder if Arnold-Foster had a premonition about Fuller. Following the recommendations of the Esher Committee in 1904 the General Staff was established in 1906. The previous year, the Secretary of State had laid down that General Staff officers should receive accelerated promotion and be appointed for three years initially but that there should be no separate Staff Corps.[4] The objects of the establishment should be 'To gather the ablest men in the Army together, and by some system of advancement and promotion, to make sure that the fortunes of the Army are always in their hands' and 'By means of these men, to form a school of military thought, which shall be abreast, or ahead, of that of any other Army.'[5] In Special Army Order 233 of 12 September 1906 the purpose of the General Staff was defined as:

> To advise on the strategical distribution of the Army, to supervise the education of officers, and the training and preparation of the Army for war, to study military schemes, offensive and defensive, to collect and collate military intelligence, to direct the General policy in Army matters, and to secure continuity of action in the execution of that policy.[6]

Eventually, as with the German model, this staff was used to think, plan and advise at the War Office and to form the staff of commanders in the field. The General Staff also produced *Field Service Regulations*, first published in 1909, which aimed to impose a tactical doctrine on the Army. They also defined the role of the staff in the field and were careful to lay down that staff officers, as such, 'were invested with no military command' but had responsibility for assisting the 'commander in the supervision and control of the operations and requirements of the troops, and transmit his orders and instructions' and for giving 'the troops every assistance in his power in carrying out the instructions issued to them'. They laid down, moreover, that staff officers were to wear a distinctive uniform and were to be organised into three branches: General, AG and QMG. The *Regulations* also provided a detailed delineation of the duties of the General Staff which actually fought shy of specifying that they should actually devise new methods of fighting battles or study or develop the science of war. Such matters, it can be assumed, were considered more appropriate for commanders – if they were necessary at all.[7] These developments caused great outcries from the regiments, particularly of course the introduction of accelerated promotion, but they nevertheless had many beneficial effects in the First World War, although the image of the pampered and distinctively uniformed staff officer, living a life of sybaritic luxury in a chateau well behind the lines, while ordinary officers and men in regiments suffered and died a short distance away in the muddy trenches and amidst the wire and shell-holes of No Man's Land, has coloured attitudes to the staff ever since, as did class-based attitudes towards those whose work involved inky fingers. The then Major-General Ironside wrote in 1928:

> If we study the history of the Army we see that there has been very strong opposition to special training for the staff, due to one or two important factors. The first factor seems to have been the regimental system which existed and still exists in the Army; the second that war had come to be looked upon rather as sport than business. As a result, foreign officers were used on the Staff.

Ironside recalled that in the nineteenth century a certain C-in-C looked 'on time spent at the Senior Department of the Royal Military College as so much leave of absence under most favourable circumstances'. After 1902, he wrote, 'certain first class regiments ... took pride in not sending officers to the Staff College, their view being: " We are regimental officers; we have a wonderful regiment and we do not send officers to the Staff College."' In 1907 a commanding officer said to Ironside when he was in hospital and had two military books on his table, 'What the devil are you reading those for? You are a horse artilleryman; what more do you want?' Ironside believed that the staff officer 'is the best of the regimental officers that we can get'. He 'must not remain on the Staff for the whole of his service; he must go back to troops' and he 'must have commanded in his career, while the other' (the regimental officer) 'should know something of the difficulties of the Staff'. In the 1920s Fuller and Ironside knew each other well and so it is not surprising that in some of this there are clear echoes of Fuller's colourful thinking on the subject.[8]

An officer writing under the *nom de plume* of 'Siege-Gunner' wrote in the *United Services Magazine* in 1920:

> It seems to be a settled policy to make any wearer of coloured tabs a superior being to the fighting officer, whereas it clearly ought to be the other way about, the wearers of tabs being necessary evils or intermediaries between the general and his fighting men.

Staff officers he categorized as 'a quill driver behind the line'.[9] A more balanced view appeared in an editorial in the *Army Quarterly* in the same year:

> The staff officer in the Army in war has none of the responsibility and deserves none of the laurels of the commander; he faces far less instant danger and deserves none of the laurels of, say, the infantry soldier. But, despite uninstructed opinion to the contrary, his work is exceedingly arduous and absolutely increasing ... Yet on the efficiency of the staff depends the smooth running and efficient action of the whole military machine ... It is a pity that the staff, in the Army at least, is prejudiced by two things; first by being decorated beyond what it either desires or deserves – or beyond what it should desire and does deserve; and secondly, by being too much overworked to be able to spend sufficient time in close and personal contact with troops.

In an article on 'The Staff' in the same issue it was claimed that in the First World War there were never enough staff officers to go round and many were kept against their inclination. 'Some clashing of allegiances must come' the writer thought, 'to every staff officer at times in the course of his work, and the more original and strong-minded he is the more often it comes.'[10]

It is against this background that Fuller's military career must be evaluated. Although covered in my biography and in his own and others' memoirs and writings, a brief account of that career is necessary here in order to provide within this chapter itself a basis for the evaluation.

Fritz Fuller, so called until his letters from France were censored in 1915, went as a fee-paying gentleman cadet to Sandhurst in September 1897 and was commissioned in August 1898 into the Oxfordshire Light Infantry, the 43rd Foot. He joined the 1st Battalion in Ireland and left with them for South Africa via Plymouth, Aldershot and Southampton on 22 December 1899. Once there the battalion moved up country and Fuller heard his first gun fired in anger. He fell ill with appendicitis, was operated on back in Cape Town and invalided home to the UK. In October 1900 he again sailed for South Africa where he was eventually given command of 70 native soldiers serving under white agents. When the war ended he returned to Chatham with his battalion and then went with it to India in the autumn of 1903, where he became fascinated with Indian culture and made contact with Aleister Crowley, the mystic, and began to write articles for the *Agnostic Journal*. In late 1905, in Lucknow, he went down with enteric fever and was in due course invalided again and took a year's sick leave back in England where he met Crowley. He also met Magaretha Auguste Karnatz, subsequently known as Sonia and of Polish-German extraction, whom he married in December 1906. This marriage would have made a return to his regiment in India very difficult. Edwardian army officers in good regiments did not normally have Polish-German wives of somewhat ambiguous backgrounds and particularly ones who behaved as rudely as Sonia Fuller sometimes did. For the next few years Fuller became a Volunteer and subsequently Territorial adjutant which allowed him time to write and edit an occult journal! He failed the Staff College exam in a trial run in 1912, rejoined his regiment (Sonia notwithstanding, but the battalion was no longer in India) and was made a company commander, in those days a captain's appointment. He also acted as Railway Transport Officer for Aldershot Command and Machine Gun Officer for 5 Infantry Brigade. He had begun to write seriously on military topics before finally passing into the Staff College at the beginning of 1914.

At the Staff College Fuller was criticized for a paper he wrote on penetration which ran counter to the prevailing belief in the tactics of envelopment. The Commandant, Brigadier-General L. E. Kiggell, who was to become Haig's Chief of Staff in the BEF, considered that the paper lacked military judgement. The tool of Fuller's early penetration thesis

147

was artillery but this proved mistaken. At Camberley he also began to develop his life-long interest in the principles of war. However, war broke out on 4 August and his staff course dispersed. Fuller became an Assistant Embarkation Staff Officer and Deputy Assistant Director of Rail Transport at Southampton, probably because he had published an article in the *Army Review* in July 1914 entitled 'Notes on the Entrainment of Troops to and from Manoeuvres'. His very long career as a staff officer had begun. In December 1914 he became General Staff Officer Grade Three (GSO3) to HQ Second Army, at that time in the war very much a non-job. He planned the evacuation of sheep in the event of invasion! After some months he engineered a posting to France and in July became GSO3 to VII Corps located ten miles behind the line at Doullens. There he also did not have much to do but while visiting the trenches he began to think about the tactics and strategy of the war on the Western Front. In September he wrote an article about the application of the principles of war to the campaigns of 1914–15 and this was published in the *Journal of the Royal United Services Institute* of February 1916. He was promoted to major at the somewhat advanced age of 37 while at VII Corps and invited to work out a syllabus for a Third Army refresher course for officers and NCOs; he wisely declined, on grounds of inexperience, the offer of command of the school set up to run these courses. In February 1916 he was posted as GSO2 to 37 Division based at Marieux in a Versailles-type chateau. A French withdrawal saw HQ 37 Division move to Bavincourt. Again his work was somewhat humdrum but he became involved in running one-week courses for commanding officers withdrawn from the line. In July the Division was broken up and he then became a GSO2 in Third Army HQ at St Pol. It was while he was there that Captain F. H. E. Townsend showed him a paper he had written on penetration, 'The MS in Red Ink'. Townsend did not indicate what the tool of this penetration was to be. However, on 20 August 1916 he and Fuller saw their first tank. On 26 December Fuller took up the appointment of GSO2 Heavy Branch of the Machine Gun Corps and a few days later was awarded the DSO and thus became a member of the decorated staff.

The Heavy Branch, based at Bermicourt, was, of course, the name given to the embryo Tank Corps; it was responsible to the War Office through GHQ. Thus began Fuller's life-long total immersion in armoured warfare, coupled in his later years with political thought and the study of history. His good fortune in being given such a post at such a time was immense; he was handed probably the greatest opportunity for stardom ever presented to any officer of the British General Staff, an opportunity which he subsequently, in 1927, failed to pursue in a direction which might have led to almost galactic fame and even, in some degree, changed the course of history. Although in no way the tank's inventor, or the first officer to think about their use in war, his new job was simply to plan just that. He was in on the ground floor with a vengeance and his fertile brain, his great originality as a thinker, his previous study of and writing about tactics enabled him to make, for the time being, the greatest possible use of that opportunity.

At Bermicourt Fuller met Colonel Hugh Elles, the head of the Heavy Branch, who soon became a brigadier-general, together with Captains Uzielli, Martel and Hotblack, also on the Heavy Branch staff. On 1 April Fuller, aged 38, was appointed GSO1 and promoted lieutenant-colonel although he remained a substantive major. At the end of July the Heavy Branch became the Tank Corps and Fuller served as its GSO1 until 1 August 1918. During those 16 months he wrote 'Training Note No. 16' and 'Projected Bases for the Tactical Employment of Tanks in 1918', a pamphlet on tank tactics. He was involved as the principal tank staff officer in the planning and even conduct of the Battles of Arras, Messines, Passchendaele, Cambrai, Hamel and Amiens. At the same time he was involved in continuous discussion and argument with his brother officers, with GHQ, with the War Office which he visited on several occasions, with Churchill, Henry Wilson, the new CIGS, and Lord Milner, the new Secretary of State. On 24 May 1918 he wrote 'Plan 1919' which proposed that the war should be won in 1919 by mounting a massive surprise attack on a front of about ninety miles using a total of some 2,000 of the as yet unproduced Medium D tanks with a range of 150–200 miles, a maximum speed of 20 miles per hour (mph) and the capability of crossing a 13–14 foot gap. There would also be over 2,500 heavy tanks participating in the offensive. To preserve surprise there would be no preliminary artillery bombardment. The primary objective would be the area between the German divisional and army headquarters, while the secondary would be the area between their front line and their guns. The German Western GHQ would be bombed and the attack would be 'morcellated', that is sections of the front would be penetrated and the unattacked sections subsequently enveloped. This was 'brain warfare', the rendering inoperative of the enemy's military organisation by putting his power of command out of action. Here, although not entirely original, were the seeds of *Blitzkrieg*, not to be given a trial in 1919 because the war ended before it could. Paul Harris believes that Plan 1919 was in many ways 'preposterous'.[11] In terms of success in 1919 I believe that the jury will always be out because it is impossible to know what factors would have emerged to further inhibit its success; however, viewed as a piece of inspired staff work it was quite remarkable and contained the seeds of much military history for the next half century or more.

After leaving France Fuller became a member of the General Staff in the War Office for the next four years, filling the posts of Head of Section 7 or Deputy Director of Staff Duties (DDSD) (Tanks), at first as a temporary colonel, then as a brevet colonel and, finally, from 31 August 1920, as a substantive colonel. Later he became Head of SD4, responsible for all training throughout the army. In these posts he was initially concerned with trying to make something of Plan 1919 and was then instrumental in the permanent establishment of the Tank Corps although this did not finally take place, together with the award of 'Royal' in its title, until 13 months after he had left the War Office. While at the War Office he wrote and lectured about armoured warfare and war generally; the zenith was reached when he lectured at the Royal United Services Institute on 11 February 1920 on 'The Development of Sea Warfare on Land and its Influence on Future Naval Operations.'[12] This was brilliant, maverick and visionary in essence. He published *Tanks in the Great War* and won the Royal United Services Institute's Gold Medal Prize Essay for 1919 with an essay on 'The Application of Recent Developments in Mechanics and Other Scientific Knowledge to Preparation and Training for War on Land.'[13] This essay was published in the *Journal of the Royal United Services Institute* in May 1920 but was regarded as 'violent military Bolshevism'[14] and resulted in a turning of the tide against Fuller's ideas in a large section of the military establishment particularly because it contained the suggestion that the cavalry would be displaced by tanks. Fuller followed this up by three articles in the *Cavalry Journal*[15] which concluded with the opinion that cavalry, as men on horseback, were doomed. For good measure he also won the 1920 Naval Prize Essay but was refused the medal and publication in the *Journal of the Royal United Services Institute* when it was discovered who the author was. It was also at this time that he first met Liddell Hart. In July 1922 he left the War Office and went on half pay while awaiting appointment as a chief instructor at the Staff College in January 1923. During this time he finished writing *The Reformation of War* which was published soon after his arrival at Camberley.

Service at Camberley was regarded as a General Staff appointment and Fuller's time there between 1923 and 1926 can therefore be considered as a continuance of his staff employment. He devised and gave there a very academic course of lectures which he wrote up into *The Foundations of the Science of War*, one of his less happy ventures, the undoubtedly significant meaning distorted and obscured by occult, theoretical and philosophical clouds. The CIGS, Lord Cavan, refused him permission to publish while he remained an officer of the General Staff and thus under Cavan's control, on the grounds that an officer on the active list should not be allowed to publish books on military subjects because young officers reading them might find they did not agree with the Manuals; Fuller asked for his Staff College tour to be reduced to three years.[16]

At the beginning of 1926 Fuller continued his staff odyssey and became, thanks to the intervention of Liddell Hart, Military Assistant to the CIGS, by now Sir George Milne, who appears not to have shared Cavan's views on publication. In fact Fuller was more than simply an assistant. Fuller was a colonel; the post was for a lieutenant-colonel. Although the post was essentially that of private secretary, Fuller used it as a means for pursuing his quest for mechanisation; in some ways he acted as a chief of staff to the CIGS. Naturally enough it did not work because the tensions between the two men appear to have been too much for Milne who, after only nine months, arranged for Fuller to visit India without giving any specific instructions as to what he was to do when he got there. Perhaps the CIGS wanted a rest? Also soon after he moved to London *Foundations* was published. It received some balanced and partially favourable criticism, but the *Army Quarterly* ridiculed it venomously and this did not do him much good, especially, one imagines, in the eyes of the CIGS.

On his return from India Fuller handed in a report but little action resulted. Eventually in 1931 he published *India in Revolt*. On 18 December Milne told Fuller that he had selected him to command the Experimental Mechanised Force. Then there began the most tragically unfortunate and difficult to explain episode in Fuller's career. The creation and command of such a force represented the culmination and justification of his life's work, the opportunity to make a lasting and supremely important mark on the theory and practice of war, a step, perhaps, in a process which might even have diminished or prevented the easy victories of Hitler before and during the Second World War. But it was not to be; Fuller turned down the appointment and the Experimental Mechanised Force went off with a whimper; the mechanization of the British Army had to wait a decade. Perhaps even Fuller could not, in the event, have pulled it off against the forces of conservatism, cavalry prejudice, revulsion from 'militarism', economy and inertia, but he would have had a chance.

Why did Fuller do it? The truth is that we will never be quite sure. The appointment was to the post of Commander 7 Infantry Brigade, not Commander of the Experimental Mechanised Force. Fuller thought this was a mistake, particularly as he had been involved in devising a different plot before he left for India, and he accepted the post. He soon found out that it was not a mistake since the War Office took the view that a temporary organisation had to be linked to something more permanent. I told the story at length in my biography.[17] Suffice it here to say that Fuller tried to get the CIGS to change his mind and this process involved giving Milne a list of complaints and suggested changes. The complaints were that the new appointment involved the command of both mechanised and unmechanised forces, that the Force itself had no stable organisation, and that the commander had insufficient staff and had also to act as a garrison commander whose duties 'largely increases entertaining, and so not only adds expense to the Brigadier but reduces his time'. The suggestions included that he should be relieved of command of the three unmechanised infantry battalions in the brigade, or given a second-in-command to train them, that the garrison be handed over to the cavalry brigade commander or an administrative commandant, that a staff captain be provided to release the Brigadier for his experimental work, that one clerk be replaced by a shorthand typist and that the Brigadier be given an entertainment allowance.[18] The CIGS would not budge, told him not to be silly and refused to read the paper, so Fuller eventually resigned, a resignation only in the end withdrawn on the understanding that he be not asked to command 7 Infantry Brigade.

Whom the Gods wish to destroy, they first make mad. There is not space to go into all the stupidities of this affair. The kindest thing that can be said is that Fuller was so imbued with the importance of the appointment and the task that he fought to make sure everything was right and used the threat of resignation to make the CIGS put them right – and this inevitably misfired; the unkindest is that the reason he did not want the job, or that Sonia persuaded him not to take it, was the expense involved or very understandable fears that she would not do well as a garrison commander's wife. My own judgement, over 25 years after writing the biography, is still that, driven by almost fanatical belief in mechanisation, he was being, as he sometimes was, too clever by half and thought that his threats and suggestions would bring about the changes he desired and thought essential for his cause. There is not inconsiderable evidence that highly intelligent men and women sometimes make similar mistakes which those a little less cerebrally well-endowed seem to avoid. Perhaps the real error is to believe that those who oppose you think and behave with the same sort of rationality with which you credit yourself. Indeed, perhaps even the clear light of Fuller's rationality may have suffered some obfuscation over this affair, since a career soldier and staff officer of his experience should have been pretty confident that once in command of 7 Brigade he could have achieved the small changes he deemed essential without undue difficulty on the ground.

The result of what became known as the Tidworth Affair, since that was where 7 Brigade was located, was a rather humdrum posting to another general staff appointment as GSO1 to 2 Division, which Ironside commanded. The Divisional HQ was located at Aldershot and here Fuller carried out his duties satisfactorily and wrote numerous articles on military subjects. In July 1929 he was promoted brigadier and posted to Weisbaden in Germany to command 2 Rhine Brigade. This was the end of Fuller's enormously lengthy spell of staff appointments since he became a commander although still, of course, an officer of the Staff Corps. This appointment, however, lasted only three months since Rhine Army was evacuated, an event which may or may not have been expected by those who sent him there.

In October he arrived in Catterick and took command of 13 Infantry Brigade, another four-year appointment like 2 Rhine Brigade, but one year later he was promoted major-general and went on half pay again on

1 November 1930. This proved to be effectively the end of his army career. He went on holiday to Switzerland where he received a letter from the Military Secretary offering him the command of a second-class district in India. He discovered that the district was Bombay where his command would comprise an AA battery, a heavy battery, an infantry battalion, a Royal Army Medical Corps (RAMC) company and a deputy assistant director of pathology.[19] Understandably this was too much for the father of tank warfare and he therefore refused the appointment. He gave as his principal reason his lack of confidence in the government of India and this was a tactical error since political reasons for refusing appointments were obviously not acceptable.[20] He was never employed again and was retired on 14 December 1933 at the age of 55. In the period between leaving the War Office and retirement he published no fewer than seven books including *On Future Warfare, The Generalship of Ulysses S Grant, Lectures on FSRII, Lectures on FSRIII, Dragon's Teeth* and *War and Western Civilization*.

EVALUATION

That Fuller was the essence of staff officership, both with troops and in the higher echelons, the very Gilbertian model of a staff officer, must be readily apparent, as is the fact that he was certainly an extraordinary staff officer in the sense of being enormously above the average. He fitted perfectly Arnold-Foster's definition; he was 'an expert on the science of war' and was well-acquainted 'with the methods by which, under the complicated conditions of our Empire, preparation for war can most effectively be made'. On the ground he was also an excellent planner and thinker and an invaluable aid and adviser to those he served. He carried the profession of the General Staff to the extremes of its purpose and usefulness – far beyond what one imagines many officers hoped and intended would occur. While doing this he was highly regarded by those he served and received numerous splendid confidential reports. He could not have progressed as he did between 1917 and 1923 without such approval and was given very favourable reports by Sir A. Lynden Bell, his Director of Staff Duties in the War Office, and by Ironside and Sir T. A. Cubitt, his commanders in 2 Division. The later two were written after Tidworth.[21] What then was the problem, for problem there was since Fuller failed to achieve the high rank and significant appointments which his ability merited.

There was not, of course one problem but many. However, before analysing these it is necessary to dismiss one alleged problem as not a problem at all. It has often been said that Fuller never commanded anything at all and so was unfitted for high rank. In fact, Fuller did command, a company of his regiment and two brigades. What he did not do was to command a battalion, or similar unit, and traditionally this is regarded as a supreme disqualification from active command at any higher level. In Fuller's case, however, it would have been very difficult for him to do so because he left the Staff College at the beginning of the First World War and then quite properly performed his allotted stint on the staff. By the time he had done so for three years he was filling what was probably the most important grade one staff job in the British Army, and to have given him command of an infantry or tank battalion would have removed him from a far more important role. Long before his next staff tour was completed the war ended. Fuller was a brevet colonel; he could have taken a step down to his substantive rank but there were many temporary brigadiers looking for commands and he was filling an important staff post. However on 31 August 1920 he became a substantive colonel and so was ruled out for a battalion command. For not dissimilar reasons Wavell served throughout the First World War on the staff, although from November 1914 until June 1915 as a brigade major he was close to troops, but no closer than Fuller, perhaps, at Bermicourt. Brooke similarly remained on the staff during the war except for a few weeks in late 1914. Wavell commanded a company for six months in 1921 but was then made a substantive colonel and held staff appointments until he was given command of a brigade in 1930. He was made a major-general in 1933 and went on half pay. Brooke did not command a field unit or formation until he was given command of a brigade in 1934 although he did command the School of Artillery from 1929 to 1932. Fuller's failure to achieve command of a battalion was therefore by no means unique. It is just possible that in his case his personality and marriage would not have helped had a command been otherwise on the cards, particularly in his own regiment, a future constituent of the Greenjackets. However his lack of command experience at battalion level did not prevent him from being given two brigades after serving a penitential three years in 2 Division after the Tidworth fiasco.

The real problems, I believe, lay deep in the nature of the British Army and in Fuller's own nature and developing personality, and in the dissonance between them. It was the obverse of these same problems which enabled him to do well as a junior and middle-piece staff officer, especially in view of the desperate nature of the military environment in which he found himself.

In the first three and a half decades of the last century, the period covered by Fuller's active service, the British Army's regimental system was its most notable characteristic, as to a lesser degree it still is. The most important fact about any officer was to which regiment he belonged, and regiments were not only distinguished as being infantry, cavalry or artillery, or even corps like the Engineers or Signals, but also because they drew their officers from different areas of society; the men might come from particular parts of the country, as did some of the officers, especially in 'Celtic' regiments, but what the officers had most in common was social class. Moreover regiments differed widely as regards the social elevation within the officer class from which their officers came. Thus Grenadiers might be as good as Lancers, but most line infantry regiments were not. Gunners were acceptable, particularly Horse Gunners, but Engineers were a bit intellectual and Signallers did not count socially. As regards reaching very high rank this was largely the preserve of officers from 'good', that is socially acceptable, regiments; there were, of course exceptions, of which William Robertson, the wartime CIGS, was an early example, but they were rare. The establishment of the General Staff cut across this regimental hierarchy and this led to its unpopularity in many quarters. Moreover staff officers had to possess and practise skills which were not regarded as socially desirable by many of the less able officers in good regiments, that is, thinking professionally, writing papers and working hard. Such activities tended to interfere with the proper activities of officers such as hunting, riding, shooting, fishing and attending prestigious social functions. Finally any attack on the horse and its place on the battlefield was resented deeply by the horse-owning and horse-riding classes. The Great War had necessitated conscription and the commissioning of many temporary gentlemen, but peace in 1918, it was fervently hoped, would return things to normal and expose trench warfare as a deviation from the norm and relegate the tank to a position of only passing importance. In this army, therefore, as in life generally, extreme cleverness, leading as it did to proposals for radical change, was not a desirable characteristic.

Fuller's high intellectual ability was therefore a problem. Fuller's intellect had similarities to that of Enoch Powell, who shared others of Fuller's characteristics including a propensity to chase rationality to its irrational extremes. There is abundant evidence of Fuller's intelligence throughout his life – his quickness of mind, his ability to think laterally, his ready grasp of the essentials of new problems, his speed and breadth of reading, his incisive conversation, and his annoying propensity generally to be right. This very high IQ was of great value to him when thrust into the burgeoning world of the tank and enabled him to seek out the possibilities of armour; it also helped him to establish the Tank Corps amidst the jungles of conservatism in the army and the War Office; it enabled him to deal with the eminent and to make sense of disaster, notably the Allied retreat in the spring of 1918 which led to his perception that brain warfare, the destruction of the enemy's command structure, could bring victory, and led also to such nice points as the recommendations that the enemy's communications should not be disrupted in an attack in order to encourage the dissemination of alarm, and that artillery preparation should be dispensed with in order to preserve surprise and prevent the terrain of the advance being rendered impassable to tanks. It would be possible to put forward many other examples; Fuller, as Azar Gat says, had an ingeniously creative mind.[22] His intelligence, married to his singular experience as chief staff officer of the Tank Corps, helped him to develop his revolutionary theories about mechanized warfare and to become the mentor of another highly intelligent officer, Basil Liddell Hart. Later in life, when he began to write books on military theory and history, it led to the production of notable insights and theories, particularly the Law of Military Development, the Constant Tactical Factor and the ultimate abolition of war through weapon development.

The obverse of this quality, however, was that he found it difficult, except in Sonia's case, to suffer those less intellectually well-endowed than himself; he offended the average and the slow by being right; he made them hate him in reaction to his wit and perception; he just did not know how to be a diplomat. Sir Archibald Montgomery-Massingberd, who succeeded Milne in 1933, hated him so much that he refused to read his books. It is very easy to hate those who make you feel intellectually uncomfortable. Moreover, perhaps it is a limitation of the very clever if you are just not quite clever enough to perceive the offensive – and hence self-defeating – effect your cleverness may have on others. Also cleverness was not so socially acceptable in the 1920s and 1930s as some like to convince themselves it is today. In fact, although Fuller joined a 'good' regiment, he was a very untypical member of it.

One other reason why Fuller's intelligence let him down was that he was 'driven'. He had a powerful singleness of mind and purpose and he had visions, although near the end of his life he denied being a visionary. Plan 1919 was a vision; his Royal United Services Institute Prize Essay was visionary in the extreme. 'I see', he said, 'a fleet operating against a fleet, not at sea but on the land – My astral form follows one side and I notice it is in difficulty; it cannot see; there appears an aeroplane and gives it sight'. He concluded, 'Let us think forward to 1930, or we shall become pillars of salt – There is nothing too wonderful for science – we of the fighting services must grasp the wand of this magician and compel the future to obey us'.[23] There were to be many more similar visions in his life. To an extent these visions helped the cause of mechanisation but they also stiffened the opposition and opened him up to ridicule. Extraordinary staff officers may be visionaries, but if the object of the staff is to get the best possible things done, that attribute may not always be effective. Also visionaries are not comfortable companions in the mess or the club. It was all this which helped to turn him into what Azar Gat[24] calls a proto-fascist and eventually led him to join the British Union of Fascists. Fuller had no time for democracy, or at least not for democracy as we understand it. He saw the empire threatened, believed that it could only be protected by a machine-age, mechanised army, and was a Positivist

with no time for sentiment or unprovable beliefs. This increasingly strident streak in his beliefs began to upset sections of the military and
political establishment and cannot have helped his career. It certainly
prevented his re-employment in 1939 and but, I believe, for Churchill's
protection, would have led to his imprisonment under Defence Regulation 18B. His belief in the occult was related to his fascism and his
activities in this field were also unhelpful. Another characteristic, of
nurture not nature, was that he was, as Gat points out, an 'autodidact'.[25]
He was never subjected to the rigours of a traditional tertiary education,
although from an early age he read widely and voraciously particularly
in the fields of philosophy and psychology. This meant, again to quote
Gat, that he had an 'untrained, self-taught' mind.[26] As a staff officer and
armoured protagonist this probably did not matter much but it began to
have an effect when he started to write books. It is an unanswerable
question whether he would have been a more successful army officer had
he been to Oxbridge. Perhaps, but it did not happen much in his day and
it might have blunted his originality and creativity.

Another characteristic which both helped and hindered his career was
his undoubted ability as a writer with a prolific literary and polemic
output. He was an industrious producer of papers, a dedicated pamph-
leteer and a writer of innumerable books. His writings contained many
flashes of brilliance and not a few stupidities, notably the Threefold Order
in *Foundations*. His writing helped him to make his points, achieve success
on the staff and, often, to offend and irritate his superiors. A man of such
literary brilliance is not a comfortable subordinate.

And then, finally, there was Sonia who was simply unable to fit into
the military society of the time. Fuller was immensely loyal to her but she
made life very difficult for him outside the home. Estelle Fuller, her sister-
in-law, told me that 'John was loved by us all, a kind, generous and most
gentle character.'[27] Obviously this was not his public persona but it lends
depth to our understanding of him. Without the burden of his wife, whom
Estelle Fuller described as 'the most insulting person I knew',[28] he might
have been more generous and gentle in public, and this might have
made him a more acceptable officer and a more effective protagonist for
a mechanised army, or it might have blunted the edge of his very sharp
intellectual sword. We cannot know.

So in the end it is not surprising that Fuller did not reach the pinnacles
of the military profession. Indeed it is legitimate to wonder whether the
General Staff and the army, at least in peacetime, could have survived
Fuller's appointment to very high office. Only imagine a triumvirate of
Fuller, Liddell Hart and Leslie Hore-Belisha in 1939. Would he have been
acceptable today? Perhaps thinkers of his power and incisiveness are not
acceptable within any organisation; they have to have unchallengeable
authority or to exist outside the organisation in order to be effective. As

a serving officer in the 1920s and 1930s Fuller was too clever, too driven and dedicated, too prone to infelicitous publication, too undiplomatic, too politically extreme, too odd, too uncomfortable, too unclubbable. And yet he was a most accomplished staff officer and fitted all the requirements laid down in the first decade of the century for the British General Staff, who demonstrated in his career almost all the attributes of high rank. One feels that if he had been German he might have got much further. However, the British Army was too hard a nut for him to crack and so Fate gave him the opportunity, before he became old and tired, to become a military theorist of the highest order and probably the greatest and most original military thinker of the twentieth century. Too extraordinary in the end for the General Staff, too extraordinary for high command, he was none the less extraordinarily effective as a theorist and philosopher of war.

Let me conclude with Fuller's own words which show a perhaps unconscious awareness of his own problems as a staff officer. He wrote in 1933, as he finally left the army: 'No soldier can doubt the immense value of a general staff if it is the general's servant – the general alone should and must decide.' Milne decided, but Fuller was too extraordinary a staff officer to take that in good part and continue on the team. Perhaps staff officers, unlike great leaders and thinkers of genius, have to be good team players.[29]

10

'An Extensive Use of Weedkiller':[1] Patterns of Promotion in the Senior Ranks of the British Army, 1919–39

David French

In a note written in October 1936, the journalist and military commentator Basil Liddell Hart cast a disappointed eye over the senior officers of the British regular army. Eight of the 21 Generals and Lieutenant-Generals were 'dud', ten 'show signs of deteriorating', only five were ever 'first rate' and only three 'are now really capable of commanding in the field'. Of the 70 Major-Generals, he awarded the accolade of being 'first-rate' to only 10 (and he had reservations about five of those) and 19 were 'good second rate'.[2] The root of the problem was that too many of them were too old. In September 1937 he publicised his conclusions in an article in *The Times*. It showed that on average divisional commanders were nearly four years older, generals holding the major home commands were nearly six years older, and Military Members of the Army Council were five years older than they had been in 1914.[3]

Liddell Hart's was not the only voice raised in favour of younger generals. His article evoked a letter to the paper's editor from Colonel C. E. Vickery complaining that the cause of the problem was that too many senior officers had remained on the active list after 1918 and had blocked the promotion prospects of promising younger officers. 'The game of musical chairs has gone on long enough and in the interests of the Army it should be stopped.'[4] As Vickery had himself been prematurely retired in 1935 it might be easy to dismiss his letter as the bitter cry of a disappointed officer who had seen his own career unfairly terminated. But his charge was taken up by another officer against whom that accusation certainly cannot be made. Writing in 1958, Field Marshal Montgomery accused many senior officers of the interwar army of clinging to office for too long, 'playing musical chairs with the top jobs but never taking a chair away when the music stopped'. In his opinion, 'an extensive use of weedkiller is needed in the *senior* ranks after a war; this will enable the first class younger officers who have emerged during the war to be moved up. This did not happen after the 1914–18 war.'[5]

Critics argued that the appointment of aged senior officers had three adverse effects on the army. Liddell Hart believed that elderly commanders would be found wanting because 'under the conditions of modern mechanized warfare, the strain on commanders in the field was likely to be much greater than in the last war when operations moved at foot-marching pace – if they moved at all – and headquarters were comparatively immune from hostile interference'.[6] Alfred Duff Cooper, Secretary of State for War between November 1935 and May 1937, complained that 'the existing military members of the Army Council were incapable, through age or growing inertia, of an effective effort to rearm adequately on modern lines to meet the growing dangers abroad'.[7] And in Montgomery's opinion the result of the army's failure to appoint younger generals in the interwar period was that 'the Army entered the Second World War in 1939 admirably organised and equipped to fight the 1914 war, and with the wrong officers at the top'.[8]

This chapter will investigate these allegations by examining the career patterns of the senior officer cadre of the British Army between 1919 and 1939. It will explain the formal rules governing the appointment and promotion of senior officers, it will examine how those rules were applied in practice by successive interwar Secretaries of State and CIGSs to discover whether favouritism outweighed merit and whether senior officers did indeed rotate around a small number of appointments. And finally it will offer some largely speculative remarks about the impact on the army of the pattern of promotions and appointments.

Liddell Hart based his charges upon an analysis of a very small sample of officers, the commanders of the five regular Field Force divisions, the General Officers Commanding-in-Chief (GOC-in-C) of the Aldershot, Southern, Northern and Eastern commands in the United Kingdom, and the four Military Members of the Army Council, the CIGS, the Adjutant-General, the Quartermaster-General and the Master-General of the Ordnance. This chapter will base its conclusions upon a rather larger group of regular officers who formed the senior officer cadre of the interwar regular army. It will look at all officers appointed to the following positions between March 1919 and the middle of August 1939: a seat on the Army Council; command of a regular or territorial army Field Force division; GOC-in-Cs of the six home commands (Aldershot, Southern, Eastern, Western, Northern and Scottish Commands); GOC of Northern Ireland District or London District; one of the three General Staff Directorships under the Chief of the Imperial General Staff (CIGS), the Director of Military Operations and Intelligence (DMO&I), the DSD and the DMT; and Commandant of the Staff College at Camberley.[9] The sample does not include officers appointed to command Indian Army and

Dominion divisions and Anti-Aircraft divisions in the United Kingdom. But it does encompass all those senior officers who were responsible for organising and training the Field Force in the United Kingdom for overseas operations, and who therefore played a part in preparing the BEF for service in 1940.

Liddell Hart thought that favouritism was the real reason why the army's promotion and appointment system had failed. His particular *bête noir* was Sir George Milne, who held the post of CIGS for an unprecedented seven years between 1926 and 1933. He accused Milne of advancing the careers of his friends and blocking those of men who had crossed him.[10]

Liddell Hart was not alone in thinking this. Even an officer like Sir Charles Bonham-Carter, who had worked closely with Milne, who admired his good qualities and had benefited from his patronage, agreed that 'he would sometimes give way to the pressure of old friends and comrades' and that 'He was "very vindictive" – never forgave'.[11] The accusation that CIGSs were prone to nepotism clearly stung, for no less than three of them, Milne, his predecessor, Lord Cavan (CIGS 1922–26), and his successor, Sir Archibald Montgomery-Massingberd (CIGS 1933–36) felt compelled to deny it.[12]

The formal process by which officers were promoted and appointed to the senior ranks of the army was intended to make favouritism impossible. The selection of officers for promotion to the ranks lieutenant-colonel to lieutenant-general was the task of the Selection Board. Throughout the interwar period it retained a core membership of the CIGS, who sat as its president, the Adjutant-General and the GOC-in-Cs of the Aldershot, Eastern and Southern Commands. The Military Secretary and his Deputy acted as its secretaries. Sir Henry Wilson (CIGS 1918–22) added to this core group the GOC-in-Cs of all of the remaining home commands plus the GOC-in-C of the Rhine Army, but Milne removed the GOC-in-Cs of the Northern, Scottish, Western Commands and the Rhine Army. Further changes took place in December 1937 when the Secretary of State for War, Leslie Hore-Belisha, carried out a major overhaul of the system, making the Board responsible for both promotions *and* appointments. Hitherto the Selection Board had dealt with appointments to commands, but a separate Staff Selection Board, consisting of the Military Members of the Army Council, had dealt with all staff appointments up to the level of General Staff directors. The result of this division between promotions and appointments had been the ludicrous situation in which some officers had been promoted but immediately placed on half pay until an appointment fell vacant for them.[13]

The Selection Board's regulations were designed to ensure that it acted with the utmost impartiality. In deciding who was to be promoted from colonel to major-general, it acted upon the principle of seniority tempered by rejection of the unfit. It did not try to identify particularly meritorious candidates and promote them over the heads of competent, but less meritorious colleagues.[14] The board considered the claims of each individual officer in order of seniority, taking into account his record and the recommendations in his recent confidential reports.[15] Members were forbidden to discuss the merits of any officer whose case came before them with anyone outside the board. The board would normally be guided in its deliberations by the written confidential reports that every officer was required to write on his subordinates.[16] If the written information before the board was incomplete, only the Military Secretary had the authority to make further enquiries and other board members were forbidden to enter into private correspondence about an officer's eligibility.[17] *King's Regulations* strictly forbade officers from lobbying on their own behalf, although they could not always prevent tactless friends or relations from trying to do so.[18] At every step on the promotion ladder the case of each officer was considered only once. Those who failed this test faced automatic retirement.[19]

In practice, however, it is clear that a candidate's suitability to fill an appointment at the next highest rank was not always the only criterion that members of the board considered. Friends in high places were not one of the prescribed attributes which successful officers were supposed to require. But the Selection Board system left considerable scope for the operation of nepotism. Much depended upon the accuracy and impartiality with which senior officers completed confidential reports. But, as every officer was shown his annual report, some senior officers may have been less than frank in what they wrote in an attempt to avoid embarrassment. This encouraged members of the Selection Board to favour the claims of officers they knew personally, rather than rely upon incomplete and misleading written information about officers that they did not know.[20] The fact that the CIGS was the president of the board was of great significance, because a CIGS with strong personal preferences could usually get his own way. As one member of the board remarked in 1937 when Sir Cyril Deverell was CIGS and vacancies were about to occur at Aldershot and in Northern Command, 'The position was entirely in Deverell's hands.'[21] Other members of the board could also sometimes significantly influence decisions. In October 1938, Major-General D. G. Johnson took command of 4th Division largely because of the strong support he received from Sir Edmund Ironside.[22] Shortly after he became Military Secretary in 1937, Lord Gort minuted that, 'It would seem possible that occasional promotion in the past has been given as recognition for good work in a lower rank, and that later it is difficult to find suitable employment in a higher rank for these officers.'[23] This may explain the reason why in 1936 the members of the Selection Board 'had gone right down the Major-General's List and had been shocked to find how weak a list it was'.[24]

The attributes that the army sought in its senior officers were defined in 1925 by a committee led by Lord Plumer, the former commander of Second Army on the Western Front. They fell into three categories. The first, which it was assumed would remain constant throughout an officer's career, were honesty, trustworthiness, loyalty, sobriety, zeal, energy and cheerfulness. The second, which it was hoped would increase with age, were industry, initiative, the capacity to command, tact and a sense of humour; and the third, which the committee thought could be allowed to diminish with age, were physical activity and powers of endurance.[25] This opened the way for the continuation of the careers of officers who were clearly past their physical prime.

Most Secretaries of State were content to accept without question the recommendations of the Selection Board for promotions and appointments up to and including major-general. The two exceptions were Churchill and Hore-Belisha. Churchill played an active role in deciding which major-generals should be given divisional commands in 1919. However, his intervention caused little disquiet, perhaps because he was attempting to give such commands to officers who had clearly proved their abilities as divisional commanders in the field.[26] The very opposite was the case with Hore-Belisha.[27] In 1937–38 he thoroughly overhauled the promotion and appointments system. He dismissed the CIGS, Adjutant-General and Master-General of the Ordnance in part because they opposed his desired appointees. His actions caused great disquiet because, as he later privately admitted, 'he had exceeded his province as S. of S.' and acted contrary to accepted practice by taking advice about the abilities of individual officers from Liddell Hart, an outside adviser who bore no official responsibilities for his actions.[28] However, Liddell Hart's power to advance the careers of particular officers in 1937–38 should not be exaggerated. Whilst some men, identified by him as 'outstanding', such as Wavell, Gort and Sir Ronald Adam, did climb the promotion ladder at this time, he complained bitterly to Hore-Belisha that he had done little or nothing for others, such as Hobart or Tollemache, whilst giving good jobs to men like Laurence Carr, who was 'static'.[29]

Above the rank of major-general the Secretary of State had clearly defined constitutional powers. Officers were not considered for promotion to the ranks of lieutenant-general or general, unless, in the opinion of the Selection Board, they were 'considered fully qualified for the highest commands or appointments in the Army'. The board presented three names in order of seniority to the Secretary of State and the final choice was his. To ensure that he could not wreck the career of an officer on a political whim, if he did not choose the most senior candidate those passed over remained eligible for further promotion.[30] Similarly the final choice of who was to become the CIGS lay with the Secretary of State for War. However, he was usually constrained by constitutional practice to make his choice from amongst those generals who had reached or been selected for promotion to lieutenant-general, and it was the Military Selection Board who determined who should reach that level and thus come into the Secretary of State's purview.[31]

It is not difficult to discover examples of nepotism governing senior appointments and promotions. The first batch of postwar appointments to command regular and territorial divisions was heavily weighted towards officers who had served on the Western Front. This was hardly surprising, as Haig was the chairman of the *ad hoc* board that had selected them. Officers who had served at Salonika received their opportunity when Milne served as CIGS from 1926 to 1933. Lieutenant-General Sir W. Gillman, who had served as Milne's Major-General, General Staff (MGGS) at Salonika, became Master-General of the Ordnance in 1927 and GOC-in-C, Eastern Command, in 1931. Other officers who had served at Salonika and who received preferment at Milne's hands included Major-General C. G. Fuller (GOC 48 Division, 1931–35), Major-General J. Duncan (GOC 1 Division from March 1928 until his resignation in December 1928), Major-General C. E. Corkran (GOC London District, 1928–32) and Major-General G. A. Weir (GOC 55 Division, 1932–34). Other officers who had served with Milne on the staff of 4 Division at the start of the war and whose careers now prospered were Major-General G. F. Boyd (Military Secretary, 1927–30) and Lieutenant-General B. F. Burnett-Hitchcok. Having commanded 55 Division between 1926 and 1928 the latter then went to India as GOC Deccan District between 1928 and 1930. He was not a conspicuous success. Milne could not save his career and he was retired in 1933, but he did console him with promotion to lieutenant-general.

Milne also had a reputation for being vindictive towards officers who had crossed him. One such was Lieutenant-General Sir George Cory. Cory had also served with Milne at Salonika before going to India and serving as Deputy CGS there under Sir Henry Rawlinson. Rawlinson had a good opinion of his ability, but in 1931 Cory was retired because, according to an officer who had served with him at Salonika, 'Cory had been carrying on with Lady Milne' and Milne had never forgiven him.[32] Liddell Hart thought that 'the victim's record was so notable that the action in singling him out, alone of his rank, for shelving, was too palpable to be missed'.[33]

But Milne's willingness to help his friends and harm his enemies was not unique. Other interwar CIGSs advanced the careers of promising officers who had served under them and blocked the careers of those they disliked. Gort effectively ended the careers of at least two officers, Sir Charles Broad and Colonel E. Tollemache. Gort's relations with Broad had broken down in the mid-1920s when Gort was an instructor at the Senior Officer's School and Broad had criticised one of his schemes.[34] He had no time for Tollemache, even though he was a fellow Guardsman, because he had 'funked during the war'.[35] Tollemache's fate underlined the need for aspiring senior officers to have patrons on the Selection Board, for although he had received excellent confidential reports he had served under only one of the members of the board that passed him over in 1937, and they gave more weight to Gort's opinion than to the written reports before them.[36]

In June 1922 Cavan appointed a fellow Grenadier Guardsman who had served as his Brigadier-General, General Staff (BGGS), J. F. Gathorne-Hardy, to be DMT. Two years later Colonel W. Kirke was promoted to major-general at the very early age of 48, partly because he had an excellent record as a staff officer during the First World War, but also probably because he had served as a colonel at Aldershot under Cavan. Sir Harry Knox probably owed his appointment as Adjutant-General in March 1935 partly to the fact that he had served as one of Montgomery-Massingberd's brigade commanders when the latter had commanded 1 Division at Aldershot between 1923 and 1926.

However, despite the example of Cavan's patronage of Gathorne-Hardy, and despite the strength of the regimental system in the British Army, CIGSs do not appear to have gone out of their way to patronise officers from their own regiments. Neither Henry Wilson (Rifle Brigade) nor Deverell (West Yorkshire Regiment) appointed a single officer from their own regiment. Cavan and Gort (both Grenadier Guards) each appointed only a single Grenadier. Milne and Montgomery-Massingberd, who were both gunners, might at first glance appear to be exceptions to this rule. Milne filled 16 of his appointments (18.8 per cent) with gunners and Montgomery-Massingberd 8 of his appointments (21.1 per cent) with them. However, as Table 1 shows, when these figures are compared with the total number of appointments each man made, and to the proportion of gunner officers in the regular army, it is apparent that their appointments did no more than reflect the proportion of gunners in the army as a whole.

Line infantrymen dominated the senior ranks of the army. They received nearly one out of every two appointments. Over the entire interwar period appointments to the senior officer cadre of the army appear to have fairly closely reflected the balance between the arms of the service in the cavalry and the artillery. This was also almost the case for the line infantry. However, Guardsmen were considerably over-represented at the top of the army, filling nearly one in eight of all senior appointments. Their good fortune came about at the expense of the technical arms, and in particular the Royal Engineers (RE), whose officers were under-represented. This may have been because, except for a brief period during 1927–30, their entry into the Staff College was deliberately restricted.[37] Royal Tank Corps (RTC) officers were also under-represented, probably because the RTC was only established as a separate arm of the service in

1923. And RASC officers were entirely excluded from the senior officer cadre, perhaps because, having passed through the Staff College, they tended to be posted to fill administrative, rather than command appointments.

Table 1: Officers Holding Senior Appointments by Arm of Service as a Proportion of all Appointments between the Wars

Arm of service	Appointments by arm of service as a percentage of all appointments made	Establishment of regular officers by arm of service as a percentage of the regular officer corps on 1 April 1933
Cavalry	6.6 (16)	6.1
Guards	12.3 (30)	3.6
Line Infantry	54.1 (132)	47.6
Royal Artillery	21 (51)	19.7
Royal Engineers*	5.7 (14)	14.8**
Royal Tank Corps	0.4 (1)	3.6
Royal Army Service Corps	0	4.5

Notes:
* Included one officer who transferred from the Royal Engineers to the Royal Corps of Signals in 1919.
** Royal Engineers = 10.4%; Royal Corps of Signals = 4.4%

Sources: *Army List*; 'Statistical review of officers and other ranks of the regular army, regular army reserve, supplementary reserve, Territorial Army for the financial year 1932–33', PRO WO 33/1323.

Many patron–protégé relationships were established at the Staff College. In 1919 Wilson appointed Sir George Harper as GOC-in-C Southern Command. Harper had instructed at the college when Wilson was Commandant before the war, and then followed him to the War Office as Deputy-Director of Military Operations during 1911–14. Milne appointed his Staff College contemporary, Major-General Sir C. F. Romer, to be GOC 1 Division in 1926 and then advanced him, as a Lieutenant-General, to be GOC-in-C Western Command in 1928, GOC-in-C Southern Command in 1931 and finally to a seat on the Army Council as the Adjutant-General on the day he himself retired in February 1933. Romer succeeded another of Milne's Staff College contemporaries in that post, Sir Walter Braithwaite. Montgomery-Massingberd pursued a similar course with Sir John Dill, who had been a pupil at the College when Montgomery-Massingberd had been an instructor on the eve of the war. They served together again in 1922–23 when Montgomery-Massingberd took command first of 53 Division and then of 1 Division. Dill served as one of his brigade commanders in both divisions.[38] In 1934 Montgomery-Massingberd secured Dill's appointment as the DMO&I and his subsequent promotion to lieutenant-general. Deverell also used his power to advance the careers of those he knew and trusted. In 1937 he made Kirke the Director-General of the Territorial Army because he 'is a most loyal helper and friend who can get a move on and who has experience based on my ideas in the Western Command'.[39] To the resentment of many officers he appointed another friend, Sir William Bartholomew, to Northern Command in October 1937.[40] As Military Secretary, and then as CIGS, Gort was determined to advance the careers of a group of young major-generals and colonels, such as Brooke, Marshall-Cornwall, Mackesy, Neame, Thorne, Eastwood, Evans, Martel and Loyd whom he had met when he was a student and later an instructor at Camberley.[41]

As might be expected, such overt use of patronage caused resentment amongst those outside the charmed circle and even some qualms from those who were within it.[42] Shortly after becoming the Commandant at Camberley, Dill wrote that 'I do not altogether relish going over people's heads'.[43] Charles Broad, who had been relegated to the post of Major-General, Administration, at Aldershot, lamented in July 1939 that, 'The Army had never been so full of cliques as today, and the unfortunate result was that people were suspecting each other of intriguing for promotion.'[44]

However, it would be quite wrong to suggest that all appointments were guided by nepotism or that the CIGS and Selection Board exercised their powers to the exclusion of the meritorious. This can be illustrated by an incident in the career of Sir Archibald Wavell that took place in 1936. Although Deverell recognised that Wavell was a protégé of Sir John Burnett-Stuart, and that Wavell would have preferred the latter to be CIGS, he recognised Wavell's undoubted talent and offered him the job of DMT. It was only when Wavell himself refused it that he was posted to Palestine.[45]

A more general examination of the senior officer cadre makes clear the limits of nepotism, for it shows that the senior officers of the interwar army were selected from men who had prepared themselves as thoroughly as they could for their profession and who had already distinguished themselves in the field. As rewards for distinguished service in the Boer War, the First World War and a score of lesser colonial campaigns, the 168 officers in the senior leadership cadre had amassed between them a large number of rewards for gallantry and leadership before reaching the rank of major-general. Their distinctions included 187 brevet promotions, 13 Military Crosses, 126 Distinguished Service Orders, 5 Victoria Crosses, 96 Companions of the Bath, 87 Companions of the Order of St Michael and St George, and 34 Knight Commanders of the Bath. Added to these they had also gained numerous foreign decorations, ranging from the fairly common Legion d'Honneur to the much more unusual Order of the Rising Sun (fifth class), awarded to Major-General C. D. H. Moore, (GOC 42 Division, 1927–28) for his part in the capture of the German naval base at Tsingato on the coast of China in 1914.[46]

Table 2: Senior Officers who were Staff College Graduates
as a Proportion of all Senior Appointments Made by Each of the Interwar CIGS

CIGS	Percentage of officers appointed to senior posts who were Staff College graduates
Wilson	47.4
Cavan	69.2
Milne	74.1
Montgomery-Massingberd	84.2
Deverell	100.0
Gort	95.2

Source: *Army List*

Table 2 shows the proportion of officers appointed by each of the interwar CIGS who had graduated from the Staff Colleges at Camberley or Quetta. In 1913, as many as 60 per cent of the senior officer cadre were Staff College graduates, although the proportion of infantry division commanders who had passed staff college (psc) was slightly lower, at 50 per cent. Two out of four Military Members of the Army Council, three out of three General Staff Directors, six out of eight Command or District commanders and ten out of 20 divisional commanders were pscs in 1913. Despite the rapid expansion of the army during the First World War the latter figure remained constant, and of the 212 officers who commanded infantry divisions during the war, 104 (49.1 per cent) had passed staff college.[47] Staff College graduates had obviously proven their worth in action for, as Table 2 shows, the interwar Selection Board made great efforts not merely to return to the prewar proportion, but they very soon exceeded it. As early as 1924 Sir Henry Rawlinson, home on leave from India, was struck by the fact that, 'As regards the Army at home, there is generally a more professional spirit than there was before the War.'[48] There was a growing trend in the interwar period towards reserving senior posts for Staff College graduates until, by the late 1930s, it had become almost impossible for an officer to reach a senior position without having the psc qualification. This development might have taken place even more rapidly but for the fact that over 200 of the 628 Staff College graduates on the Army List in 1914 were killed during the First World War and the limited size of the postwar entry to the colleges meant that by 1928 the number had only risen to 671.[49]

It is reasonable to conclude that although nepotism did guide some appointments and promotions, in general patronage was used by the Selection Board to advance men of proven merit rather than to reward the worthless. It is, however, more difficult to refute the charge that the senior ranks of the army were becoming a gerontocracy in the interwar period. As Table 3 shows, Liddell Hart was correct to suggest that the average age of members of the senior officer corps crept upwards after 1918. Until the second half of the 1930s, Boer War veterans dominated senior posts in the army, as 162 of the 200 appointments made by the first four interwar CIGSs (Wilson, Cavan, Milne and Montgomery-Massingberd) were given to them. The minority of senior appointees who had escaped service in South Africa had done so because they were serving elsewhere, not because they were too young. It was only after 1936, with the appointment of Deverell and Gort as CIGSs, that the post-Boer War generation of officers began to reach senior levels in the army. Of the 39 appointments made by Deverell and Gort only seven had served in South Africa, most of the remainder having been too young to do so.

Table 3: Average Age on Appointment of Senior Officers, 1919–1939

CIGS	As Divisional Commander	As GOC-in-C Home Home Command or GOC London or Northern Ireland District	Army Councillor	General Staff Director or Commandant of Staff College
Wilson	52	54	52	50
Cavan	54	56	57	48
Milne	54	58	58	52
Montgomery-Massingberd	55	58	59	54
Deverell	55	58	–	52
Gort	52	55	55	52

Sources: *Army List*; *Who Was Who*; *Dictionary of National Biography*.

The reasons why senior officers tried to remain on the active list for as long as possible are not difficult to discern, for the retirement regulations gave them a positive incentive to do so. This was partly because their pension grew with their years of service.[50] But it was also because of the way in which the retirement regulations operated. In 1881 compulsory retirement ages for major-generals was fixed at 62 and for lieutenant-generals and generals at 67. Officers who had been on half pay for more than three years were compulsorily retired on a pension, but any senior officer who voluntarily retired before he was compelled to do so forfeited his retirement pay.[51] Any reforms intended to encourage senior officers to retire before they were compulsorily retired would entail an increase in the money which would have to be set aside for pensions, 'not a vast sum', Deverell admitted in August 1937, 'but it is certain to be opposed by the Treasury'.[52]

There is also some justification for the charge that a handful of officers played 'musical chairs' by rotating from one senior appointment to another. However, the number concerned was small. Of the 52 officers who were appointed to posts as a GOC-in-Cs or as Military Members of the Army Council between March 1919 and August 1939 and held the ranks of lieutenant-general, general or field-marshal, only 12 were pluralists in that they held more than one of these appointments. They included each of the four CIGSs appointed between 1919 and 1937. The problem only appears to have reached serious proportions under Milne, when no fewer than six officers moved directly from one such senior appointment to another.[53] The most likely explanation for this problem was that advanced by Sir Edmund Ironside, one of the younger generation of officers who became frustrated in the early 1930s as they saw their promotion prospects increasingly blocked by their elders. In July 1933 he complained that

> They tell me that [Major-General E. W. E.] Harman [GOC 1 Division 1930–34] cannot be 'saved'. They are always thinking of saving people from the age limit and then keeping them for years on half pay. There will be no drastic clearing out under Montgomery-Massingberd any more than under Milne. Only if the politicians interfere will there be change.[54]

Ironside was correct in thinking that little would change without intervention by the politicians. Various attempts had already been made to ease the passage of younger officers to senior posts, but with little success. In 1919, Churchill wanted to hasten the promotion of younger officers by reducing the normal period of command from four to three years, but was dissuaded by the Army Council.[55] In 1925 the Plumer Committee was critical of the Selection Board's excessive reliance on the principle of seniority and persuaded the Army Council to reserve the right to ask the Selection Board to consider promoting especially meritorious colonels before their turn. Three years later the Army Council again tried to facilitate the promotion of meritorious colonels by offering immediate promotion to six of their older contemporaries provided they immediately retired.[56] But, the impact of these and other measures was largely nullified by the fact that the number of appointments open to general officers was strictly limited by the army's establishment, which was laid down by the Treasury, and by the Treasury's refusal to fund a large-scale retirement programme. For most of the interwar period the establishment stood at 10 generals, 20 lieutenant-generals and 75 major-generals. These figures included a margin of officers deliberately kept on half pay to allow for some flexibility in the selection of suitable men to fill appointments as they fell vacant. Thus in 1926 there were only 7 appointments for generals, 14 for lieutenant-generals and 58 for major-generals.[57] By the late 1920s only between one in five and one in six colonels could hope to become a major-general.[58]

The politicians' first attempt to break the log-jam failed. In 1934 the Stanhope Committee recommended the abolition of the 'ghost system' under which, when a general retired, his appointment was not filled for several years. It also attempted to end the system of 'musical chairs' by classifying all new major-generals into one of two categories. The first group were to be given one appointment and then retired and the second group were to be earmarked for further promotion. But again the impact of this reform was nullified because the Treasury insisted that to meet the extra pension costs involved, the Army Council had to reduce the establishment of general officers by one general and two lieutenant-generals.[59] It was not until the Hore-Belisha reforms of 1937–38 that major changes occurred. Hore-Belisha brought the political weight and sense of urgency to the problem that had hitherto been absent. 'All promotions and appointments', he insisted in August 1937, 'must be guided by the urgent sense that we are preparing for a war not only having the material but the men ready.'[60] Encouraged by Liddell Hart, he was determined to eliminate the idea that appointments and promotions should be governed by 'the comradely principle of "Buggin's turn"'.[61] As part of a package of measures to improve the promotion prospects of younger officers, Hore-Belisha, with the support of Gort, first as Military Secretary and then as CIGS, attempted to break the log-jam for promotions and to check the apparently inexorable rise in the age of senior officers. He reduced the compulsory retirement age for major-generals to 57 and for lieutenant-generals to 60. The half-pay system was abolished. A system of time-promotion was introduced for officers up to the rank of major. Above that rank, officers would only be promoted if a definite vacancy existed for them. In order to hasten the appointment of the right men to the right posts, the normal tenure of staff and command appointments was reduced from four to three years, and in early 1938 the Treasury reluctantly agreed to a temporary increase in the establishment of lieutenant-generals and major-generals to ease the path of younger officers upwards. However, they did so on the understanding that by the end of the year the establishment would have been reduced to its normal figure as older officers retired.[62]

Gort wanted to secure the appointment of divisional commanders who were in their early fifties and Liddell Hart claimed that Hore-Belisha succeeded in reducing the average age of the top level of the army by a whole decade.[63] But the measure of his success depends upon the definition of the 'top level' and he carefully refrained from defining it. The figures in Table 3 suggest that his assertion must be taken with a pinch of salt. Gort (aged 51) was indeed eleven years younger when he was appointed as CIGS than Deverell (aged 62). The appointment of divisional commanders like H. R. Alexander or W. G. Holmes, who were only

47 and 46 respectively when they took command of 1 and 46 Divisions in February 1938, did grab the newspaper headlines. But Gort's appointees to divisional commands were only three years younger than those made by Deverell and were older than those made by Henry Wilson between 1919 and 1922. They also hardly compared favourably with the men commanding divisions at the Armistice in 1918, whose average age was only 46.7 years, a figure which was not again approached until the closing stages of the Second World War.[64]

Liddell Hart supposed that the army needed younger senior officers than those it had possessed in 1914 because by the late 1930s warfare had become more mobile. Battles would be more physically exhausting and the advent of air power would expose generals to greater physical hazards than in 1914. His contentions were superficially plausible, but they rested upon the unwarranted assumption that the senior officers of the First World War had lived in comfort and safety far behind the lines. In fact ten major-generals and three lieutenant-generals died at the front and one lieutenant-general and 19 major-generals were wounded.[65] Generals in 1914 probably underwent at least as much physical strain as their successors in 1939, if only because the former rode horses and the latter were driven about in motor cars. Duff Cooper's suggestion that the army failed to rearm in the mid-1930s because its senior officers were inert and elderly does scant justice to the fact that those same officers were urging the government to prepare a modern army for a continental land war, only to have their advice ignored by their political masters.[66] It is difficult to imagine how younger officers would have been any better able to persuade the Baldwin and Chamberlain governments to adopt this course of action. There were political barriers to innovation and preparation that were effectively insurmountable before March 1939 no matter what the age of the officers trying to overcome them. Furthermore, the connection between relative youth and success on the battlefield was not as obvious as Liddell Hart implied. The fact that Gort was younger than all six of the commanders of the German armies that attacked France and the Low Countries in May 1940 availed him nothing. The performance of D. G. Johnson in 1940 also suggests that there was no automatic connection between age and competence. On the eve of the German invasion of France, Brooke, the GOC II Corps, had decided to replace Johnson, the GOC of 4 Division, because at 56 years of age, he considered he was too old to withstand the strains of active operations. However, the German attack came before he could act, Johnson remained, and at the end of the campaign Brooke had no regrets that he had done so.[67]

The system also had at least one other major fault. Senior officers were not properly trained to fulfil their role as commanders in battle. Troops and their commanders spent a large part of their careers in isolated colonial garrisons where the opportunities for formation training were limited. The training of formations in the United Kingdom was hampered by the fact that units were perennially short of troops, equipment and manoeuvre grounds. Only twice in the interwar period, in 1925 and 1935, did the army hold manoeuvres in which two corps headquarters together with all of their subordinate divisions, were pitted against each other. This problem was compounded by the fact that the British Army had no formal training courses for brigade, divisional, corps or army commanders. The Staff College trained officers to be both staff officers and commanders but, as Major-General Sir Charles Gwynn, Commandant at Camberley between 1925 and 1931 recognised, by the time the comparatively junior officers who attended the Staff College had attained sufficient seniority to put what they had learnt into practice as commanders, much of it was probably out of date.[68] Gwynn's predecessor, Ironside, had suggested that what the army needed was a War College. Promising junior officers could go to the Staff College in their early thirties for a course lasting a year (rather than the existing two years) which would fit them to become junior and middle-ranking staff officers. Those who were a success in such appointments and showed real promise of becoming good commanders could return in their late thirties or early forties for a second year-long course which would train them specifically for that role.[69] But Milne rejected his suggestion. He decided that it would suffice if, at the outbreak of the next war, the army avoided the mistake it had committed in 1914 when it shut the Staff College and allowed too many trained staff officers to be killed serving in the front line.[70] It was not until March 1939 that the War Office announced it was about to establish a higher commander's course for lieutenant-colonels, which was too late to have any impact before the outbreak of war.[71]

Responsibility for training senior commanders lay with their immediate superiors. Senior officers were trained by 'experience and by working out practical and theoretical problems at exercises carried out under the direction of the War Office or commands'.[72] But the *Training Regulations* were vague about how this should be done, beyond recommending some combination of exercises with and without troops, conferences and discussions.[73] This lack of system placed a great deal of responsibility on individual senior officers. Some were better suited to discharge it than others, and the quality of what they had to offer often lacked realism. In July 1939, for example, Aldershot Command held a three-day skeleton corps exercise which included an 'armistice' lasting for several hours 'to give the various Headquarters time in which to consider, and if necessary effect improvements in the organization and running of their own office'.[74]

The fact that some senior officers were not doing all they could to train their immediate subordinates as commanders was recognised as early as

173

1926. But little was done to rectify the matter until late 1937, when Deverell tried to inaugurate a two-year training cycle.[75] Recognising that the best way for senior officers to learn the art of command was to practise it in full-scale army manoeuvres, he decided that they would be held every two years and that in the intervening years skeleton army and corps exercises would be conducted. However, the war came before his reforms could have any real impact. The result was that in 1939 too many of the senior officers who were to command formations in the early part of the Second World War lacked practice at leading troops in the field.[76]

As CIGS from 1941 to 1945 Brooke blamed the sometimes mediocre performance of British generals on the fact that too many potentially outstanding commanders had been killed during the First World War. His assertion cannot be proved or disproved. But there is no guarantee that outstanding company officers of the First World War would necessarily have made outstanding generals in the Second. It also overlooks the fact that the interwar army had to make the best of the officers it had, and that for a variety of reasons it failed to do so. The promotion system was partly blocked in the early 1930s by ageing senior officers playing 'musical chairs'. 'Weedkiller' was needed, and it was applied with some gusto by Hore-Belisha. Some competent officers did find their careers blighted if they had offended a senior officer who was in a position to do them harm. Aspiring senior officers certainly did find their paths upwards made easier if they had a powerful patron. But the kinds of men who attracted patronage had probably already proven their competence in action before they reached high office, and they had demonstrated a commitment to their profession by passing successfully through the Staff College. The army's problem was not that it lacked appropriate human resources, but that it systematically failed to cultivate them by training officers for high command. Reflecting on the situation in August 1939, Ironside, who had just been belatedly appointed Inspector-General of Overseas Forces, commented that 'I have been thinking over the words of my Instructions. It is to supervise "the higher training" of the Army ... The War Office have no idea of the importance of this training. They have simply played at it.'[77]

11

The British General Staff
and the Coming of War, 1933–39

J. P. Harris

A General Staff has been described as 'the brain of an army'.[1] In the 1930s, the responsibilities of the General Staff in the British War Office included the formation of military policy, the collection and collation of military intelligence and, indeed, most aspects of the preparation of the army for war.[2] The importance of the thought and action of this institution in the period between Hitler's becoming German Chancellor in January 1933 and the outbreak of the Second World War in September 1939 needs no emphasis.

Though a better balance has been achieved over the last two decades,[3] the British General Staff of the thirties received, for about four decades, an extremely bad press.[4] A number of reasons for this could be suggested. A certain disdain for the army is traditional in Britain. In the thirties this was compounded by the anti-military reaction which had set in following the terrible losses of the First World War.[5] Early defeats during the Second World War seemed to show conclusively that those responsible for the British Army had not prepared it adequately for modern warfare. More purely intellectual influences were at work also. For many years the military critic and prolific author, Sir Basil Liddell Hart, had a major impact on many of those who wrote about the British Army in the inter-war period.[6] Liddell Hart was concerned to emphasise his own qualities of insight and foresight, even prophecy, and was a merciless critic of the General Staff.[7] Since the publication of Brian Bond's study of Liddell Hart's military thought in 1977,[8] historians have been more cautious about echoing the judgements of this great pundit. But even now it is difficult to say there has been an equivalent rehabilitation of the General Staff.[9]

Amongst the criticisms which have been made of the British General Staff of this period, some of the most serious and specific are the following: that though it wanted to send a Field Force to the continent in the event of a war with Germany, it had not adequately weighed the risks of such a policy;[10] that it remained to a great extent insular and imperial in outlook and did not keep up with continental, particularly German, military doctrine;[11] that it failed to understand the importance of armoured forces and their potentially revolutionary impact on war;[12] and, finally, that it underestimated the potential of strategic bombing and opposed the development of the anti-aircraft defences of Great Britain.[13] While the performance of the General Staff of the 1930s was by no means beyond criticism, it will be argued below that these particular attacks upon it are all largely invalid.

In the mid-1930s the General Staff was one of four military branches of the War Office, the government department in charge of the army. The others were: the Adjutant-General's department which dealt with personnel matters; the Quartermaster-General's which handled housing, the peacetime movement of troops and stores, transport, food, fodder and the care of animals; and the Master-General of the Ordnance's department which controlled the development, procurement and manufacture of military hardware. All the heads of these military branches were also members of the Army Council, the body which had overall responsibility to the Cabinet for the control and administration of the army.[14] The General Staff, under the overall control of the CIGS, was divided into three directorates. The Director of Military Operations and Intelligence was charged with the making of strategy, planning and the control of operational and intelligence activities, the Director of Staff Duties was concerned with the organisation of the army, officer education, staff training and the maintenance of standards of staff work, while the Director of Military Training dealt with collective military training, the technical training of officers and all aspects of the training of other ranks.[15]

In some continental armies the General Staff constituted an elite body within the officer corps, rigorously selected for intellectual capacity and administrative skill. Once an officer became a member of this elite he remained so until he left the army, and in a certain sense for the rest of his life, and this group had a very strong identity as a distinct group within the army.[16] The case was rather different in the British Army. Though most of those holding major appointments on the General Staff in the War Office at this period were expected to have passed the Staff College at Camberley, access to that institution had never been so competitive as to the famous German *Kriegsakademie*. The letters 'psc' ('passed staff college') appeared next to appropriate names in the British *Army List*. But in other respects Camberley's products were not obviously distinguished from brother officers who had never attended the institution.[17] In practice the British General Staff consisted simply of those officers holding General Staff appointments at any given time, either in the War Office or in the headquarters of formations.

In the period 1933 to 1939, moreover, there was a fairly high turnover of personnel in the senior General Staff positions in the War Office.

Between November 1933 and September 1939 there were three CIGSs, four DMO&Is, four DSDs and four DMTs.[18] It might be expected that the lack of the status of a distinct elite and the high turnover in senior positions would have led to a breakdown in continuity of purpose in the development of strategic policy and in the preparation of the army for war. In general this was not the case. Though there were inevitably some differences of opinion between its members, the General Staff in the War Office, throughout this period, collectively demonstrated a high degree of consistency in its strategic outlook, in its sense of purpose and in its order of priorities.

Until 1933, though the British Army was minute in relation to the size of the empire it was charged with defending, and was frequently stretched very tight by overseas emergencies,[19] there was no clear long-term enemy against which the British Army had to prepare. Such arrangements as the General Staff had made for the mobilisation of an expeditionary force in time of war were framed in response to a possible Soviet threat to India via Afghanistan and were termed 'The Defence of India Plan'.[20] But the speed with which this contingency disappeared into the background once a more serious threat arose nearer home, suggests that it was never taken particularly seriously. Up until 1933, certainly, imperial defence was the primary role of the army. Yet, as we shall see, the General Staff kept a careful eye on military developments on the continent, particularly in Germany. The fact that the British were world leaders in thought about and experimentation with armoured formations until the early 1930s[21] also suggests that Britain's military leadership never lost sight of the possibility of having to engage in technically sophisticated European-style warfare.

For some senior officers who had fought in the 1914–18 war, fear (and even loathing) of the Germans never died. In 1925, the year of Locarno, and the date between the two world wars at which international relations were apparently at their most harmonious,[22] the CIGS, Lord Cavan, told a meeting of the CID that the General Staff regarded the German nation as 'a primitive people, scientifically equipped ... vigorous, prolific and unscrupulous, combining the height of modern efficiency with the mentality and brutality of the Middle Ages'.[23] Cavan's successor, General Sir George Milne (CIGS 1926–33), was also concerned about Germany and demanded detailed reports on military developments there.[24] Intelligence from MI3, the branch of the General Staff responsible for monitoring western and central Europe, indicated that, even before Hitler became German Chancellor in January 1933, some degree of German rearmament was covertly taking place.[25]

As with everything the General Staff did in the early thirties, it drew its intelligence picture of Germany on a tight budget, MI3's principal sources apparently being military attachés' reports, German publications of various sorts and liaison with the intelligence services of friendly powers.[26] The British government system as a whole was slow to react to the intelligence MI3 was producing, but even a stringent critic of British intelligence at this period is obliged to concede that the General Staff in the early thirties 'had done its homework' and 'entered the Nazi era with a good grounding in German developments'.[27] When, in November 1933, a general enquiry began into defence deficiencies, the CIGS, General Sir Archibald Montgomery-Massingberd, came armed with an appreciation of the threat of another war in Europe a good deal more sophisticated than any available to the other chiefs of staff.[28]

Montgomery-Massingberd, who became CIGS in February 1933, played a vital role in shaping the whole approach of the General Staff during the period of rearmament before the Second World War. He retired slightly early, probably frustrated by the obstacles to rearmament which he was encountering, and stating that he wished to hand over to a younger man.[29] In most respects, however, the War Office's rearmament effort ran on the lines of strategic thought which he had laid until December 1937, when it was temporarily forced onto a different track by Treasury and Prime Ministerial pressure. Even after December 1937 the General Staff wanted to return to the original track,[30] but was only allowed to do so in February 1939.

Montgomery-Massingberd was, at first sight, a dubious choice for CIGS in 1933. Though highly experienced as a staff officer, he had never commanded a large formation in war.[31] Up to the point at which he took over as CIGS, moreover, he had not been identified with the principal advocates of mechanisation. Serving on War Office committees to examine the future of the cavalry and the artillery, he indicated that he still saw a role for the horse, particularly in conveying mobility in difficult terrain where motor vehicles might not be suitable. Not initially an opponent of the great Experimental Mechanised Force trials commencing in 1927, he felt it wrong to allow the Force to continue to flaunt its superiority over the other arms after 1928, by which time it had proved its point. Though by deciding on the permanent establishment of the 1 Tank Brigade in November 1933 he proved that he had been converted to a belief in the need for independent armoured formations, in 1928 he had advocated a greater emphasis on preparing the infantry and cavalry for war and to that end had favoured the termination of the Experimental Mechanised Force.[32] There is no doubt that Montgomery-Massingberd was a natural conservative. He extolled values such as tradition and loyalty[33] of which the modern liberal mind tends to be suspicious and this may partly account for the harsh treatment he has had at the hands of some writers.[34] Yet a careful analysis of his thought and actions as CIGS suggests a reasonably able military mind at work.

The process of adjusting the British armed forces to meet the challenge of a resurgent Germany began with the Defence Requirements inquiry of

November 1933 to February 1934, before which the armed services had been obliged to operate on the assumption that there would be no war for ten years. This inquiry (conducted by the Chiefs of Staff and the Permanent Under Secretaries of the Foreign Office and the Treasury)[35] and the Cabinet's reaction to it were vital for the future of the army and of British defence policy as a whole.

Early in the proceedings a decision had to be made on the relative priority to be given to the German and Japanese menaces. Montgomery-Massingberd advised strongly that Germany should be considered as the main threat and that British rearmament should be based on this conclusion.[36] On this issue he was strongly supported by Sir Warren Fisher of the Treasury and Sir Robert Vansittart of the Foreign Office, both intensely Germanophobic. These civilian members, acting together with the CIGS, steered the Defence Requirements Committee (DRC) to its conclusions that Germany was the 'ultimate enemy' against whom all long-term planning should be directed.[37]

The DRC concluded that the Japanese were unlikely to attack British possessions in the Far East unless there were the 'sudden temptation of a favourable opportunity arising from complications elsewhere, and elsewhere means Europe, and danger to us in Europe can only come from Germany'. The DRC recommended a show of (primarily naval) strength in the Far East coupled with an attempt to reach an accommodation with the Japanese.[38] All this went with the flow of General Staff thinking. Montgomery-Massingberd regarded the abandonment of the Anglo-Japanese alliance, unaccompanied as it was by any guarantee from the Americans, as 'insensate folly', and Milne, his predecessor, had looked back with nostalgia to the friendly relations with Japan which had prevailed in the pre-1914 period.[39]

It was also important for the DRC to give a time-scale for the development of the German threat. Here again the General Staff's influence on the committee's findings appears to have been crucial. Montgomery-Massingberd came to the committee armed with an MI3 paper entitled 'The War Menace in Western and Central Europe'. This pointed to German designs on Czechoslovakian and Polish territory and endorsed an assessment by the French Deuxième Bureau that the Germans might consider themselves in a position to push their claims to the point of war within five or six years. When asked by Vansittart and Fisher for his personal opinion, Montgomery-Massingberd (the only one of the three chiefs of staff prepared to offer such an assessment) opted for five years[40] – not a bad guess as it turned out. The DRC endorsed this figure and recommended that the deficiencies they outlined in the three defence services be made good by 1939.[41]

The DRC agreed a £40 million expenditure programme for the army, the bulk of which was to be spent on the preparation of a Field Force of four infantry divisions, a tank brigade and a cavalry division for service on the continent. Liddell Hart was to attack the General Staff's policy of despatching an army to the continent in time of war as dangerous and ill-considered.[42] In fact the General Staff offered cogent arguments. One important task of a British Field Force would be to try to help keep Belgium and the Netherlands out of German hands. The defence of the Low Countries against occupation by a potentially hostile foreign power was a long-standing British preoccupation. In terms of seapower the Low Countries were as important as ever, 'as proved by the experience of the Great War, when German destroyers and submarines were a continual threat to our sea communications'.[43] Their importance had been enhanced, not diminished by the growth of airpower.

> Today the Low Countries are even more important to us in relation to the air defence of this country. Their integrity is vital to us in order to obtain that depth in our defence of London which is so badly needed and of which our position will otherwise deprive us. If the Low Countries were in the hands of a hostile power, not only would the frequency and intensity of attack on London be increased but the whole of the industrial areas of the Midlands and the North of England would be brought within the range of hostile air attacks.[44]

It is worth pointing out here that the task of maintaining Belgian integrity (or at least preventing most of the country from being overrun by the Germans) inevitably seemed more feasible to the British General Staff at this juncture than it did even a couple of years later. German rearmament was, of course, still in its infancy, and Belgium in 1934 had a defence agreement with France.[45] This would probably have allowed British as well as French troops access to Belgian soil in wartime before an actual German invasion took place, though helping the Netherlands, a strictly neutral state, would have been altogether more difficult.

But the need to make it hard for the Germans to establish air and naval bases in the Low Countries was not, in any case, the General Staff's only argument for preparing a Field Force for the continent. Montgomery-Massingberd, with the support of the other chiefs of staff, also argued that:

> Assistance on sea and in the air will always appear to Continental peoples threatened by land attack to be but indirect assistance. Refusal on our part to provide direct assistance would be interpreted as equivalent to abandoning them to their fate. The arrival in good time of even the small forces proposed would have an incalculable moral effect out of all proportion to their size.[46]

This was an argument for the support of France even if the Netherlands and Belgium could not be saved. Supporting France made sense even from a purely selfish British point of view, the General Staff argued, because the Germans were likely to concentrate on the defeat of France first and, while France was still in the war, it was unlikely that more than 25 per cent of German airpower would be used against Britain.[47]

The General Staff had a good case. But the Cabinet, on the advice of Neville Chamberlain, the Chancellor of the Exchequer and a dominating figure within Ramsay MacDonald's 'National' Government, effectively overruled it. The rearmament proposals of the three armed services, amounting to some 120 million pounds over five years were, Chamberlain told the ministerial committee which reviewed the DRC report, financially 'impossible to carry out'.[48] At Chamberlain's insistence the Cabinet halved the War Office programme from £40 million to £20 million, while allowing a significant increase in the money to be spent on the RAF.[49]

During the mid-1930s, Chamberlain, advised by Sir Hugh Trenchard, the former Chief of the Air Staff, and Lord Weir, the Scottish industrialist who had played a large part in organising the manufacture of aircraft during the First World War, was, rather than pursuing a balanced programme of rearmament, gradually moving towards a deterrence strategy. He wanted to build up a powerful British strategic bomber force and to use this to deter Hitler from going to war.[50] This was, to say the least, a dubious approach. The RAF was not in a position to do significant damage to targets in Germany from bases in Britain with the technology it possessed in the mid-thirties.[51] While wishing to slash the proposed budget for the army, moreover, Chamberlain was not proposing to spend so much on the RAF that it was likely to be able quickly to transform this technology and develop the awesome offensive power such a strategy required. In his emphasis on airpower and deterrence, Chamberlain was probably thinking more perceptively of the reaction of the British public than that of Hitler. Certainly he believed that the British public had such a revulsion against continental warfare after the 1914–18 experience that it would be extremely reluctant to tolerate involvement in such horrors ever again.[52] Concentration on airpower had the advantage, as far as the National Government was concerned, of being a fashionable policy. Airpower was relatively new and exciting ('hi-tech' in contemporary parlance) and a government which emphasised it might seem forward looking. The preparation of a Field Force for continental war, by contrast, however valid the strategic arguments in its favour, inevitably evoked distressing memories which were potentially harmful politically.

Chamberlain's reaction to the first DRC report was sufficient, owing to the great influence he had in the Cabinet, to delay the start of a really serious rearmament effort for the British Army until 1936. Though the General Staff was not at this stage ordered to discount the long-term possibility of having to send a Field Force to the continent, the allocation of £20 million over five years, which was all the War Office gained in 1934,[53] was sufficient only to correct the most extreme deficiencies in the army.[54]

From 1934 to 1936, however, the General Staff was not inactive. It did not allow shortage of funds to produce mental paralysis. Having taken the decision to establish 1 Brigade Royal Tank Corps as a permanent formation in November 1933, Montgomery-Massingberd gave great encouragement to the training of the brigade the following year, gaining glowing praise from its commander, Brigadier P. C. S. Hobart. A fanatical tank enthusiast, Hobart was, to say the least, not known for sycophancy to superior officers. But writing to Basil Liddell Hart, military correspondent of *The Times* and (though Hobart may not fully have realised this) a bitter personal enemy of Montgomery-Massingberd, he remarked:

> Most of the great ones scoff of course, but we are lucky indeed in having so far seeing, resolute and open-minded a CIGS who is giving us a chance to try and is so remarkably understanding.[55]

In October 1934, inspired by the example of the French General Staff in establishing the first of its so-called *Divisions Légères Mécaniques*, and following various mechanised exercises carried out on Salisbury Plain in that year's training season, Montgomery-Massingberd took the decision to establish a mechanised Mobile Division, to replace the cavalry division,[56] and ordered the cavalry to conduct various experiments in mechanisation.[57] At the same time the General Staff pressed ahead with the mechanisation of both infantry and cavalry supply vehicles, and with the reorganisation and re-equipment of the artillery, as rapidly as the available funding would allow.[58]

In the sequence of events which brought about a (relatively) serious rearmament programme for the British Army, the Abyssinian War of 1935–36 was prominent. Italy had not hitherto been regarded as a likely enemy.[59] The Abyssinian War coupled with the growing threat of German rearmament forced a reappraisal of defence problems. In July 1935 the DRC produced an interim report which drew the Cabinet's attention to the increased dangers of the international situation.[60] After considering this, the Cabinet authorised the DRC to draw up proposals for a somewhat intensified programme of rearmament.[61]

It was against this background that the General Staff composed its most comprehensive policy paper of the 1930s. Entitled 'The Future Reorganisation of the British Army' and completed on 9 September 1935, it was a document of some 38 typescript pages, sweeping in its scope, penetrating in many of its insights and remarkably prescient in some of its predictions. It was divided into three parts. Part 1 analysed the lessons of the 1914–18 war, gave an account of developments in weapons, tactics and organisation since the war, offered a lengthy scenario of the possible course of a future war with Germany and then drew conclusions as to how the Field Force should be trained and equipped for a continental role. Part 2 discussed the peace commitments of the army, possible secondary (i.e. non-continental) war commitments, and the organisation of the Territorial Army. In Part 3, general conclusions were drawn.[62] The purpose of 'Future Reorganisation' seems to have been to aid clarity of thought within the War Office. Though it was circulated to the entire Army Council, its ideas were not presented in quite the same form to inter-departmental bodies, such as the DRC, or to the Cabinet. Perhaps a collective effort by officers of the General Staff, it was signed by Montgomery-Massingberd and fellow Army Councillors reacted to it as representing his ideas.[63]

The introduction spelt out that though it was impossible to ignore 'tasks performed in peace, particularly in our garrisons abroad' which had to be continued 'often in an intensified form' in war, the main emphasis of the paper was (in keeping with the DRC's designation of Germany as the 'ultimate enemy') war against a first-class power in Europe.[64] In an analysis of the lessons of the 1914–18 war, which appears to have drawn heavily on the report of the Kirke Committee,[65] the General Staff emphasised the 'relative superiority of defensive weapons and tactical methods over those of the attack' and especially the power of the machine gun.[66] But, having been the chief of staff of the Fourth Army during the 'Hundred Days', the CIGS was in a good position to know that, by 1918, the balance between offence and defence had been at least partially restored. The General Staff recognised the part that tanks and aircraft had played in this and clearly saw them as crucial instruments of future war:[67]

> The tank provided the most efficient means yet discovered of dealing with wire obstacles and with rifle and machine gun fire. The employment of tanks, when available in large numbers, greatly assisted the impetus of the attack …
>
> The use of aircraft enabled the offensive to be carried beyond the battle zone and into the enemy's country. The effect of this development on the armies was, at first, chiefly felt in the increased facilities afforded for observation and reconnaissance, in the restrictions consequently imposed on movement by daylight and in the more efficient direction of artillery fire. There was towards the end of the war, however, an increasing tendency to use aircraft for offensive operations against the enemy's rearward organisation. It can hardly be claimed that the potentialities of an air striking force acting in conjunction with land operations were ever fully developed, although there were significant instances of effective action against lines of communication and retreating troops.[68]

The main problem for the attacking side in the fighting of 1918 had been the difficulty of exploiting a breakthrough. 'Cavalry which had performed this role in other theatres was never able to perform it on the Western Front'. But means to overcome this problem were now available, the British General Staff believed. 'It seems reasonable to assume that suitable mechanised and armoured formations acting in co-operation with … aircraft could have achieved it.'[69]

The General Staff regarded 'the introduction of a self-contained armoured formation into our field army' (a reference to the Tank Brigade) as one of the most important developments since 1918, recognised that by the mid-thirties armoured vehicles were 'capable of operations widely differing from the close support of infantry for which tanks were originally produced'[70] and went on to indicate that the combined use of armour and airpower would give the Germans their best chances of success in the next war.

The General Staff's 'Forecast of the opening stages of a war with Germany' pointed out that, 'The Great War has left a firm conviction amongst European nations that a long drawn-out struggle is disastrous even for the victor'. There were indications that Germany would make 'strenuous efforts' to obtain 'an early decision' and that the German army was training for mobile operations to this end. The attitude of the French army at the outbreak of war was expected to be defensive and in these circumstances it was expected that the Germans would have three possible strategies for securing a quick victory. They could launch a sudden attack with 'a small, highly trained, highly mobile force' on a selected portion of the French defences on the Franco-German border or by-pass these defences with a sweep either through Switzerland or through Holland and Belgium.[71]

In 1935, with the Rhineland still demilitarised (making a surprise attack on the Maginot Line very problematical), a direct German assault on the Franco-German border seemed to the British General Staff to offer particularly poor prospects of success. It was also considered unlikely that the Germans would attempt to advance through Switzerland. The terrain was considered difficult and the Swiss were expected to be determinedly hostile to any violation of their neutrality. The Germans were therefore expected to seek victory through the Low Countries. The British General Staff believed in 1935 that the Germans would be likely to violate Dutch as well as Belgian neutrality in the next war and thought it important to British security that at least the western parts of the Netherlands and Belgium should be kept out of German hands. The initial role of the British Field Force would be 'to provide sufficient moral and material support to our Allies' to prevent western Holland and Belgium (and ultimately northern France) being overrun by the Germans. To this end it was considered essential to ensure the swift despatch of the first contingent of the Field Force which was to include four infantry divisions and one mechanised mobile division. The General Staff envisaged the role of this British force as being strategically defensive though it might be possible to adopt the tactical offensive at times. If Franco-British forces prevented the Germans achieving the early victory they would seek, then after a period of rough equilibrium the allies might, in the long run, be able to take the offensive.[72]

Montgomery-Massingberd's concept of the use of airpower in the next war is particularly interesting. As early as the first DRC report it was evident that the General Staff had devoted considerable thought to this matter and had come with ideas radically different from those of the RAF. The Air Staff's emphasis was on the 'strategic' use of airpower, on the bombing of enemy cities and industry, and to some extent on defending the British homeland from German air attack. The General Staff, on the other hand, believed, as we have noted, that the scale of air attack on the British homeland would tend to be quite limited until the issue on the continent had been decided.[73] In 1935, the CIGS expressed agreement with the French and Belgian General Staffs that the targets the Germans would select for air attack in the early stages of a war would conform to the objectives of the field armies, 'air action being directed against enemy air bases ... railway nodal points and concentration areas'. In all probability the object would be 'to paralyse the enemy's movements, concentration and administration systems and to make possible a breakthrough by highly mobile land forces'.[74] In 1935 German air doctrine was in fact in a state of considerable flux, but this was a good guess as to how it would turn out by the 1939–40 period. The description of the way the Germans would use their air forces to enable dramatic breakthrough by mobile ground forces was extremely perceptive.[75] Because of the view it took of the way the Germans would use their airpower the General Staff believed it essential to establish 'at the outbreak of the war and in conjunction with allied armies' an effective system of air defence on the continent.[76] Montgomery-Massingberd regarded the existing state of army–RAF relations as extremely unsatisfactory and remarked in a sentence that would no doubt have horrified the Air Staff, that, 'It may be necessary to examine the question of whether a system analogous to that of the Fleet Air Arm would not give better results.'[77]

In the conclusion to this very broad-ranging paper on the future of the British Army, the General Staff, while paying lip-service to the Defence of India Plan and emphasising the need to raise and train more infantry battalions to reinforce depleted garrisons overseas, reaffirmed its commitment to a continental strategy. Its aim was 'to reorganise the Regular and Territorial Armies on such a scale as will enable them to take part in a Continental war'.[78]

The issue of the Territorial Army's rearmament was to trigger a violent controversy between the War Office and the Treasury which, under Neville Chamberlain's leadership, was still not reconciled to expenditure on the scale necessary to prepare it for a continental campaign. In February 1936 the War Office was allowed to proceed with the rearmament of the Regular Army for a continental role, but the Cabinet, in response to the objections of Neville Chamberlain to the large-scale rearmament of the army,[79] decided to compromise by postponing a decision on the rearmament of the Territorials for three years.[80] It was in this situation that Montgomery-Massingberd decided to step down as CIGS. He prepared detailed handing over notes for his successor General Sir Cyril Deverell,[81] and Deverell in most respects continued the policies that his predecessor had laid down.

Though the actual rearmament of the Territorials for the continent had been ruled out by the Cabinet, the War Office made repeated efforts at least to lay down reserve industrial capacity for them.[82] This led to heated controversy with the Treasury. Alfred Duff Cooper, Secretary of State for War in 1936, argued the General Staff's case very valiantly in committee and in Cabinet, a stance that placed him in a direct confrontation with the heir-apparent to the leadership of the (Conservative) political party to which he belonged – the Chancellor, Neville Chamberlain. Predictably, Duff Cooper was removed from the War Office when Chamberlain became Prime Minister in May 1937.[83]

The new Secretary of State for War was Leslie Hore-Belisha. He belonged to the National Liberal Party, a minority party in coalition with the Conservatives and unlikely ever to gain power in its own right. He was regarded as an outsider by most Conservatives and was, therefore, very much dependent on the patronage of Neville Chamberlain.[84] In October 1937 Chamberlain recommended that Hore-Belisha read part of Liddell Hart's book *Europe in Arms* which cast doubt on the need for a Field Force for the continent. Hore-Belisha was thus left in little doubt as to the policy change he was expected to implement. By December 1937 a change in the army's role was being insisted upon by a coalition of forces including the Treasury, the Admiralty, and, reluctantly, the Minister for the Co-ordination of Defence, Sir Thomas Inskip.[85] Hore-Belisha had little choice other than to fall in line if he valued his political career.

In December 1937 Hore-Belisha, leaning heavily on the advice of Liddell Hart, sacked Deverell and virtually the entire Army Council.[86] In the open letter he wrote to Deverell, announcing the latter's dismissal, Hore-Belisha gave as his reason the slow progress made with the army's rearmament and the need to find a younger man to hurry it along.[87] This was distinctly hypocritical and Deverell was understandably outraged by it. Hore-Belisha actually sacked Deverell because, under pressure from Chamberlain, Hore-Belisha wished to implement a new policy by which the army would focus on home and imperial defence[88] and under which preparation for fighting a first-class enemy on land would, in the interests of economy, all but cease. Deverell, as Hore-Belisha explained to the Prime Minister, had indicated his willingness to implement such a policy, but obviously did not believe in it. It was therefore better, Hore-Belisha concluded, to remove him.[89]

The 'New Army Policy' was formally introduced in January 1938. Unfortunately for Hore-Belisha, Viscount Gort, the new CIGS he appointed to replace Deverell, had no real belief in the policy either. The same applied to Major-General Henry Pownall, the new DMO&I, though Pownall's first major task in his new role was to help Hore-Belisha write the paper in which the details of the policy were worked out.[90] Gort and Pownall were quickly on very poor terms with Hore-Belisha whom they regarded as a self-seeking politician careless of the real needs of the army in a likely future war. Though the holder of a new office created by Hore-Belisha, the Deputy CIGS, Lieutenant-General Sir Ronald Adam, was able to maintain better personal relations with the Secretary of State, he no more believed in the New Army Policy than did Gort or Pownall.[91] All those holding key General Staff positions in the period 1933–39 seem to have believed that, if the British government wanted to check German expansion on the continent, it would have to be prepared to send a Field Force to fight alongside the French army. They also dismissed as dangerous nonsense the notion (of which Liddell Hart and Neville Chamberlain were both fond) of 'limited liability' in the conduct of a future European war. During the course of 1938 the General Staff campaigned, with growing vigour, for a reversal of the policy. But it was abandoned and the General Staff allowed seriously to prepare a Field Force for the continent only in February 1939, within seven months of the outbreak of the Second World War.[92]

Liddell Hart is generally regarded as one of the leading advocates of armoured warfare and Hore-Belisha has often been portrayed as a great reforming Secretary of State for War. But one of the effects of the New Army Policy, for which the two were jointly responsible, was to make it much more difficult for the British Army to develop its armoured forces. The War Office's tank programme was an area in which the Prime Minister and the Treasury particularly sought cuts and Hore-Belisha was happy to offer them.[93] Indeed, in October 1937, when formulating the policy, he had suggested to Liddell Hart that the Royal Tank Corps be abolished.[94] Liddell Hart was not in favour of going so far, but neither does he appear to have opposed pruning the tank programme.

The General Staff, however, retained from 1934 to the outbreak of war, through all the vicissitudes of Cabinet policy, a commitment to develop a Field Force capable of taking on a first-class opponent and including a substantial proportion of armour. Montgomery-Massingberd had, as we have noted, established the 1 Tank Brigade as a permanent formation in November 1933 and had taken the decision to establish a mechanised Mobile Division, which would include the Tank Brigade, to replace the cavalry division, in October 1934. In the comprehensive 'Future Reorganisation' paper of September 1935 the General Staff had indicated that, in addition to the Mobile Division (later to become the 1 Armoured Division), it wanted a total of four Army Tank Battalions – one per infantry division – in the first contingent of the Field Force. These battalions, equipped with heavily armoured but slow-moving 'Infantry' tanks (in contrast with the faster medium or 'cruiser' tanks in the Mobile Division) were intended for close co-operation with the infantry in the assault.[95] Mechanisation was the key-note of Montgomery-Massingberd's whole Field Force policy. The transport of all of the infantry divisions was to be mechanised and the General Staff intended to have enough motor transport with the first contingent of the Field Force to lift an entire division if required. At the same time the General Staff moved relentlessly towards the complete mechanisation of the cavalry of the line, most of these regiments being put into light tanks.[96]

After the introduction of the New Army Policy the General Staff fought to hang on to as much as possible of its tank programme by playing up the threat to Egypt from Italian Libya.[97] It was a ploy with which the General Staff had a certain degree of success, despite the fact that the Treasury really knew full well that the General Staff really wanted the armour for the continent. Indeed, the Permanent Under Secretary of the Treasury privately dismissed the whole idea of a desert war as 'merely silly'.[98]

It is true that at the outbreak of the Second World War the armoured forces of the British Army were desperately weak. This was not, however, primarily owing to any lack of vision on the part of the General Staff. The very low priority which the Cabinet gave to the army's rearmament, the virtual ban between December 1937 and February 1939 on preparations specifically made for a continental campaign, the financial stringency imposed by the Treasury, and the consequent difficulty in expanding the very restricted specialist armaments industry, were the main problems.

That the General Staff remained fully aware of the importance of armour can easily be proved. It took great interest in the growth of armoured forces in Germany. MI3's appreciations tended to lack detail on the technical side, because of German security measures, but they contained fairly good analyses of German thinking about armour.[99] It seems evident that these were studied at the highest levels within the General Staff. Lord Gort, the CIGS, minuted to Hore-Belisha in November 1938 that:

> there is no doubt that the German General Staff have great expecta-
> tions from armoured forces. There are a number of interesting
> publications by responsible military authors on the strategy and

tactics of armoured formations which give a reasonably clear picture of the present German doctrine on this subject.

The Germans believe that the power of penetration and mobility of the older arms is not sufficient to enable them to carry an attack so rapidly and to such depth into the enemy organisation that he will not have time to take counter-measures. This the Germans claim, can only be achieved by armoured formations.

German principles of employment of such formations are based on three requirements:

(a) suitable ground
(b) surprise
(c) large masses

A tank attack is envisaged in successive waves, biting deep into the enemy defences. Speed is the essence of such an attack. The Germans insist, however, that the role of the armoured formations is to clear the way for the other arms and that only by co-operation with them can decisive results be achieved. The armoured units punch holes through which the other arms can penetrate.[100]

This analysis might be criticised in some details but was generally a fair account of the way the German army was thinking about armour. In other prewar analyses Gort showed that he was well aware of the importance the Germans attached to airpower as a means of facilitating armoured breakthrough.[101] He thus understood well enough the operational methods the Germans were likely to employ in an offensive on their western front. For most of his period as CIGS, however, the General Staff was virtually banned from making specific preparations for a continental campaign and he did not have access to the funds or the industrial capacity necessary to build the sort of British armoured forces which might have been able to counter German methods successfully.

Though since the Second World War the General Staff's detractors have attacked it more for its failure to develop armoured forces than for anything else, during the second half of the 1930s Liddell Hart, and some other critics, were far more worried about its policy on the anti-aircraft defence of the British homeland. In the second half of the 1930s Liddell Hart seems largely to have lost his earlier faith in the capacity of armoured forces to restore mobility to land warfare. He formed the opinion that the defensive would be supreme on land, that the French army, assisted by its powerful frontier defences, would be able to hold its own without direct British help and that there was therefore no need to prepare a British Field Force for the continent.[102] The real danger came in his view from the air. He shared a widely prevalent fear of a massive German air attack on British cities at a very early stage in a future war, and wanted the War Office to devote a very high proportion of the resources available to it to the anti-aircraft defence of the homeland.[103]

As we have seen, the General Staff had a different conception of the use of airpower in the next war. It was never opposed to spending money on home anti-aircraft defence within a balanced rearmament budget but it was not prepared to devote so much money and industrial capacity to air defence that it had none for the equipment of the Field Force.[104] This was, however, the course of action to which it was constantly being pressed by the combined forces of the Cabinet, the Treasury and the Air Ministry.[105] The General Staff, on the other hand, argued that one of the most effective means of air defence was to keep enemy air bases as far as possible from Great Britain. This meant assisting continental allies to stay in the war. So long as there was a continental campaign to be conducted this was expected to absorb most of the effort of the German air force.[106]

We may conclude that the General Staff's strategic view in the period from 1933 to 1939 was continentalist and that it remained remarkably consistent throughout these years, despite a fairly high turnover of personnel. The General Staff argued that the Low Countries were very important to Britain and thought it vital to prevent the Germans defeating and overrunning France. It did not believe that it was a practical policy to ask the French army to do the land fighting in a future war without British help. The argument put forward by Liddell Hart that the defence was so strong on land that it would be virtually impossible for the Germans to achieve decisive results in an attack on France was consistently rejected. As early as 1935 the General Staff was well aware that the German army was training for mobile operations and described, quite prophetically, how air forces might be used to aid a breakthrough by mobile ground forces.

The continentalist policy of the General Staff was logical. If Great Britain wished to check German expansion on the continent it would need an ally with a substantial army. France was the only continental state that fielded an army with which the British found it at all possible to co-operate. But the French were unlikely to be prepared to go to war to prevent Germany's eastward expansion without the assurance of British military assistance on land. If, in whatever fashion, a Franco-German war came about, there was, moreover, every reason to expect that the French would need and would demand British assistance on land. If France fell, the Germans would dominate most of continental Europe and Britain's ability to survive, over the long term, as a truly independent state would be in doubt.[107] Assuming that the British government did, indeed, ultimately wish to limit German expansion, the General Staff was entirely correct to insist on the preparation of a British Field Force to fight alongside the French army.

Even considering the enormous difficulties under which it laboured, the British General Staff might (to adopt the somewhat schoolmasterly tone to which historians are tediously prone) have done better. Staff procedures in formation headquarters might have been more streamlined on the German model. A portable belt-fed machine gun (like the German MG 34) might have been adopted instead of the magazine-fed Bren gun, and more powerful mortars might have been procured – measures which would have significantly enhanced infantry firepower.[108] The tank situation might have been somewhat improved if more attention had been paid to what manufacturers could produce competently and less to what users thought they required.[109] The procurement of more and better radios should certainly have been given a greater priority.[110] But the British General Staff of these years was by no means as stupid as it has often been portrayed. It can hardly be blamed for having failed to prepare the British army to meet the Wehrmacht in the field. It was never allocated the necessary resources, and during a really critical period its own government virtually banned it from so doing.

12

'A Particularly Anglo-Saxon Institution': The British General Staff in the Era of Two World Wars

John Gooch

In 1920, the American military attaché in London, Colonel L. O. Solbert, prefaced a description of the institution he had been sent across the Atlantic to observe and report on with the warning that 'there is probably no more complex and complicated organization in the world than the British Army'.[1] The uniqueness to which he drew attention applied as much to the General Staff as it did to the regimental system, the social composition and outlook of the officer corps, and the equipment and functions of the army of which it was a part. Its place in the army, its character and make-up, its functions and its influence were determined at least as much by its location in the machinery of government as by its purpose, giving it a unique complexion which made it in many respects dissimilar to any of the continental staffs with which it shared the superficial similarity of a title.[2]

The post of Chief of the General Staff was a European invention which Great Britain adopted only after a characteristically lengthy delay. Helmuth von Moltke the elder had been appointed to the post in Prussia in 1857, and from it had subsequently guided the Prussian-German armies to victory in the German wars of reunification. Moltke won his influence, and the German General Staff gained its commanding stature, from his work in planning, preparing and then directing the great campaigns of 1866 and 1870–71. So remarkable was his success, and so incontestable was the worth of the new military institution he had ushered into prominence, that other powers lost little time in acknowledging the military revolution that had occurred before their eyes, and within a decade France, Russia and Italy all had copies of the new office and the institution it led.

The stimulus for Britain's late turn to continental practices was not success but what was perceived as a palpable failure of existing military structures before and during the Boer War (1899–1902). Thus, when Sir Neville Lyttelton was appointed first chief of the British General Staff in

1904 his post was born out of very different circumstances than that of any of his continental counterparts. This, and the fact that for two years he had no general staff to lead, marked the birth of an institution which was characterised as much by the limitations of its influence over policy and over the army of which it was a part as by its achievements.[3] The British General Staff came into being as a bolted-on addition to a machine which was in the final stages of reconstruction.

Ever since the Crimean War – a military venture whose unhappy conduct seemed to bear a more than passing similarity with the Boer War that followed almost half a century later – the British Army had been the subject of almost incessant scrutiny: between 1854 and 1904, no fewer than 567 committees and Royal Commissions explored various aspects of its structure, workings and performance. The culmination of a process of more or less continuous criticism and tinkering came in the two decades between 1885 and 1904, when a neo-Benthamite quest for efficiency in the public service saw the evolution of a variety of consultative committees into the Committee of Imperial Defence. With that development, the essentials of the architectural structure through which the government would work in the realm of defence policy, and into which the general staff had to fit, were in place and reform at last came to a halt. Save for the creation of the Chiefs of Staff Committee in 1923, the drive to co-ordinate the armed services and refine the manner in which they contributed to the making of defence policy was to get no further until after the Second World War.[4] Thus, the addition of a General Staff to the War Office and to the governmental machinery for debating defence policy was, like the addition of a permanent secretariat to the Committee of Imperial Defence in 1904, in one sense 'the end rather than the beginning of the story'.[5]

The new body fitted into a pre-established structure and a political culture defined by the need of Cabinet government for professional military assistance and by the absolute unwillingness of politicians in Cabinet to go beyond the promotion of consultation and the receipt of advice. This determined the ground rules – unwritten in conformity with much of the British constitution – which would govern the General Staff's political existence. In such a world, neither Lyttelton nor any of his successors could ever hope in peacetime to exercise anything approaching the independent power and influence of a von Moltke, if they should ever wish to do so.

The way in which the General Staff worked in Britain was at bottom the product of the determination of politicians to exercise strong civilian control over all military matters. Collective decision-making appealed to them. It did not much appeal to the leading military personalities who served Queen Victoria in her late years and King Edward VII in his early ones: Lord Roberts, who would lose his post as last Commander-in-Chief of the army in 1904 when the office was abolished in favour of an Army

Council on which the new Chief of the General Staff was but one of four military members, professed to be prepared to work with a board, but his commitment to the new ways was dubious, while his predecessor, Lord Wolseley, favoured an unacceptable version of Cromwellian rule in which a single soldier would carry full authority over and responsibility for the army.[6] Lord Salisbury preferred to weaken military control and increase civilian authority, adopting a structural re-division of responsibility in the War Office in 1895 that had this effect, and was more or less exactly that proposed under the preceding Liberal administration to rein in the soldiers.[7] Salisbury's attitude resulted as much from the poor opinion he held of his generals as it did from his parliamentary constitutionalism. In 1890, referring to the attempt six years earlier to relieve General Gordon at Khartoum, he commented caustically that 'the results [of the military expedition] were not of the most brilliant character', and he can only have been moderately comforted (if at all) when, six years later, he raised doubts about an army in which promotion was too heavily determined by seniority, only to receive the reply from Lord Lansdowne that the younger officers were 'good as a rule' and that 'incompetency among the seniors will become rarer'.[8] The only soldier Salisbury trusted was Kitchener, whose cautious methods fitted with his own predisposition.

The principles which Salisbury espoused were turned into the template under which the General Staff was to operate for the next half century by his nephew and successor as Prime Minister, Arthur James Balfour. Balfour, whose 'lordly nonchalance' masked an acute intelligence and a deep interest in defence matters matched by none of his successors until 1940, was a convinced proponent of advisory committees as the vehicle for determining defence and military policy.[9] By accepting the application of the board principle – which had been the controlling mechanism used at the Admiralty since 1832 – for the army, by enforcing a division of responsibility in which the Chief of the General Staff was one among four military members of the Army Council, all of equal status and power, and by including him as one of a number of members of a defence council that was advisory and not executive and whose membership and agenda was controlled by the Prime Minister, Balfour encased the British General Staff in a system in which its functional role was severely circumscribed.[10] So it would remain, the ebb and flow of its influence determined by the degree to which the international situation put defence questions and issues of military capability to the fore in public life.

It is not often remarked how easily the British General Staff settled into the contributory role allotted to it. Occasionally, a member would rail privately at his subordination to the 'frocks' – Sir Henry Wilson (Chief of the Imperial General Staff [CIGS] 1918–22) fumed in his diary in August 1903, 'The report of this Commn. [the Royal Commission on the South African War] must show up our rotten system of having an army run by ignorant politicians' – but dissatisfactions were individual and not collective, and never amounted to very much.[11] The sole exception to this was the Curragh 'Incident' in the spring of 1914. While the issue of whether the army should and could be used to coerce Unionists who opposed the Liberal government's Home Rule Bill ran far wider than the confines of the General Staff, all three of the directors who worked under the Chief of the Imperial General Staff were prepared to resign in support of Hubert Gough and his brother officers, who refused to be ordered to do what they feared was going to be the government's business in the matter. In the aftermath of the imbroglio Sir John French, who was deeply shaken by it, resigned – the only holder of the post of Chief of the Imperial General Staff ever to do so. A more determined – and less disciplined – leader might have charted a different course: in the immediate aftermath of the affair the Adjutant-General believed that 'it would not have been difficult to get up a revolution had one been of that mind'.[12]

The explanation for the apoliticism of the British Army as a whole, a somewhat neglected facet of the history of the General Staff, has generally been found in the strength of the regimental system. In the case of the General Staff in particular, the explanation for a phenomenon which marks it out in varying degrees from most of its continental companions is also to be found in the relationship between its members and their political environment. Throughout modern times, the divisions between the political parties over matters military were neither sharp enough nor deep enough, and issues of defence policy not central enough to national life, for them to attract senior soldiers into their ranks as active or even symbolic members working on behalf of their profession. Thus there was no equivalent in England of General Maurice Sarrail, darling of the French Socialist Party during the First World War, and no General Maxime Weygand, so profoundly of the right as to be forced to confirm his allegiance to the Third Republic in Parliament before being allowed to take up office as Chief of Staff in 1930.[13] If, before the First World War, there was a preponderance of Conservatives over Liberals among members of the General Staff, then it did not make itself felt in any of their corporate functions.

Between the wars, the army confronted the novelty of Labour governments in 1923 and again in 1929. They accepted the soldiers, and the soldiers accepted them. Lieutenant-General Sir Webb Gilman, Master-General of the Ordnance, and therefore not a member of the General Staff, but seemingly broadly representative of the upper reaches of the War Office in his views, told the American Military Attaché in June 1929 that during the first Labour government the army had 'fared very well', because its members 'knew very little of Army affairs and depended entirely on those in charge at the War Office', adding that 'in a Labor or Socialist Government they [the army] had nothing to fear, except for the occasional extreme Reds one encountered in the Party'. What caused far more bother was the politician of either party who had a smattering of military knowledge and who attempted to use it to impose his views on the army.[14]

One of the tasks of every European general staff was to encourage and forward the evolution within the army to which it belonged of a single operational conception of war, and to help foster the adoption of a body of doctrine that would ensure uniformity in the operations of the forces on the field of battle. The leading lights among the first generation of British General Staff officers were well aware of the need to grasp this nettle: on the first day of the General Staff conference in January 1908, Colonel William Robertson (CIGS 1915–18) stressed the importance of developing uniformity in tactics and training on the basis of common principles, and on the fourth day Colonel Douglas Haig emphasised the need for uniform approaches on the questions of strategy, tactics, organisation and training.[15] The suggestion that every General Staff officer keep a 'Precedent Book' in order to 'conduce to uniformity', put to the next annual conference by Colonel Aylmer Haldane, was an early indicator that practice rather than fiat was more likely to become the lodestone of the army.[16] At the Staff College, Colonel Henry Wilson (commandant 1906–10) pointedly drew the problem to the attention of the next generation of staff officers:

> [T]here has been nobody to teach us the lessons of our wars & the result is that our superior Generals think, & act, differently & the training at Aldershot is not that at Salisbury nor does Ireland agree with either, while the training in other commands is very small indeed.[17]

Wilson used his staff tours to din in the same message, concluding a collective excursion to the battlefields of 1870–71 by emphasising that one thing alone explained the outcomes of all the battles, 'want of purpose on one side & purpose on the other due to a school of thought'.[18]

Haig went to India in 1910 to take up the post of Chief of Staff and thereupon suffered a change of heart, defending what he acknowledged as a failure to develop and impose a common doctrine by stressing the importance of flexibility and pragmatism.[19] This was no doubt partly a reflection of the differences in practice and in outlook across the globe which made the search for general uniformity in empire, dominion and colony something of a fruitless task.[20] The short time that elapsed between the creation of the British General Staff and the outbreak of the Great War, and the size of the task Wilson and others sought to accomplish, explain the fact that no clear, uniform and commonly accepted school of strategic thought existed when war came, a fact that was subsequently bewailed by politicians and their biographers; as Herbert Asquith's bio-graphers noted, 'in all the great emergencies military opinion was deeply and sometimes evenly divided'.[21] It also resulted from a deeply rooted and abiding determination among senior commanders not to be constrained by anyone else when called on to command and direct military operations in the field.

In October 1931, Admiral Chatfield, remarking on the failure of the Chiefs of Staff to approach anything like a commonality of view on defence questions during the previous decade, explained that

> the difficulties of the past were caused by the personalities who composed the Chiefs of Staff Sub-Committee after the war, men who had risen chiefly by their forcefulness of character ... and whose general line of argument was 'what I say is right'.[22]

These were not newly acquired characteristics. Sir William Nicholson, first Chief of the Imperial General Staff (1908–12) was addicted to lurid language and possessed a rich vein of caustic humour, as well as what seems in retrospect to have been a visceral loathing of the navy, a feeling which Admiral Sir John Fisher heartily reciprocated;[23] and the future Lord Burnham, principal proprietor of the *Daily Telegraph*, recorded in 1915 of Kitchener and French (CIGS 1912–14) that 'they are both men of violent tongues & when discussing one another use such adjectives as one hears in the Police Courts'.[24] Not all the chiefs of staff were forceful men – the first, General Sir Neville Lyttelton, was gently upbraided by his wife for his lack of self-assertiveness – but in any case they could not impose anything more than broad strategic designs on the army at large, because very few senior officers likely to take the field in command of large forces were prepared to depart from the view forcefully expressed in the after-math of the South African War by Lords Roberts and Wolseley that no one other than the man on the spot should draw up strategic plans to guide the use of his troops in war.[25]

The principle established in the late Victorian army persisted during the First World War. The devolution of operational strategic planning from Whitehall to headquarters staffs in commands – the practice followed by Haig during the First World War, when he himself set only general objectives for operations – helped ensure that the British General Staff did not resemble some of its continental counterparts. It also led to wide variations of practice, so that a general such as Gough might be breathing down the neck of his staff where a Rawlinson stood too far back.[26]

These attitudes persisted during the interwar years. In the cause of resisting the move to combine the Chiefs of Staff in the summer of 1923 – and the even darker shadow of a Ministry of Defence which loomed behind it – Sir William Robertson reiterated the established view that 'an important cornerstone is that he who makes a plan ought to be responsible for its execution'.[27] Now, however, it was reinforced by a new factor: a general aversion to almost any strategic planning at all. 'Under existing world conditions', Lord Cavan (CIGS 1922–26) told the Cabinet in January 1924, 'we require no plans of campaign (except for small wars incidental to our imperial position)'.[28] There was, he claimed, no need for the Chiefs of Staff to waste time and energy in drawing up hypothetical plans in order to justify their existence as long as a European conflict was plainly not in the offing. The training given to future General Staff officers at the Staff College tended to reinforce this attitude of mind. Sir John Dill, then its commandant, told the American Military Attaché in 1932 that 'the British Army had to be prepared to operate in almost any kind of country and its tactical doctrines and instruction had to conform to this idea'. Thus tactical exercises were held in Wales, because the terrain there was quite like that of the North-West Frontier.[29]

The vein of pragmatism which still ran deep in the veins of the British Army reinforced this stance. Writing for a popular audience in the *Graphic* in 1925, Robertson forcefully reiterated it:

> [W]ars have invariably been accompanied with many unexpected developments and the conqueror has owed his success more to rapidity of mobilisation and adaptability to circumstance, i.e. to common sense, than to any prevision on his part, either as to the character of the particular war in which he was engaged, or the effects of the weapons employed in it.[30]

Nine years later, facing what was now a more obvious threat from Germany but not yet an immediate one, Cavan's successor but one, Sir Archibald Montgomery-Massingberd (CIGS 1933–36), clearly shared something of both views, feeling that 'a detailed plan of operations' for a war which might take place four years hence could not be drawn up, largely because it was impossible to foresee future developments.[31] This was not the stance taken by European general staffs of the day.

As well as being marked out by a pragmatic attitude to preparations for war and a disinclination to develop strategic planning to any degree of detail (a characteristic which the General Staff departed markedly from only during the years 1910–14), the British General Staff differed from its continental confrères in another respect: its inclination, like that of the army's senior commanders at large, to regard administration as the dominant ingredient of staff work.[32] Kitchener, himself the embodiment of the view that both functions could be carried out by one man and were in effect more or less the same thing, acknowledged that a competent General Staff was 'one of the adjuncts the British Army most requires to enable it to hold its own against European forces and to give our soldiers a fair chance in any warfare of the future', but went on to add that advice from it in wartime would be fatal, and that what it should know about was the feeding and supply of troops.[33] Henry Wilson, sensitive as he was to the army's need for a guiding school of thought, shared a part of Kitchener's mindset, pointing out in his opening address to the Staff College that 'it is impossible to be a good General Staff Officer or Superior Commander unless one is possessed of Administrative Knowledge'.[34] In the years prior to 1914, staff work was thus evolving in such a way as to incorporate the practical dimension at the cost perhaps of the theoretical. It was also of necessity sharing its platform with 'command', since there was nowhere else but the Staff College at which to teach that subject.[35]

The experience of the Great War, and in particular the huge increase in the size of the British Army and all the attendant problems that expansion brought in its train, seems to have reinforced the army's opinion that effective administration was what mattered most. This was an understandable reaction to the challenges inherent in the exercise of high command as a result of the unparalleled increase in the scale and complexity of the tasks commanders had to manage; it is worth noting that in 1914 only Kitchener had commanded a force of 12,000 men in the field, whereas four years later Haig commanded one a hundred times that size. The consequence seems to have been to shape the training of the General Staff in the interwar years in a way that reflected both pre-war predilections and the priorities generated by a particular interpretation of the significance of wartime experience: on a visit to Camberley in 1935, the American Military Attaché was told by the staff and the commandant, 'we do not re-examine the World War battles in light of modern weapons, arms and tactics, we study chiefly to learn about leadership, command and logistics'.[36] At the start of the Second World War, Wavell, who had passed into the Staff College at the top of the list in 1908 but who had found the education he had received 'too academic and too theoretical', declared that the most important mental quality a general could possess was a *sens du practicable* and that the 'mechanisms of war', by which he meant topography, movement and supply, were 'the real foundations of military knowledge, not strategy and tactics as most people think'.[37]

Being neither a dominant caste within the army nor an independent player on the political chess-board helped ensure that the General Staff never developed anything like a foreign policy of its own. Its closest flirtation with this siren occurred in the aftermath of the celebrated meeting of the Committee of Imperial Defence on 23 August 1911, when Sir Henry Wilson (Director of Military Operations 1910–14) tried to match the new military strategy with a new diplomatic policy and launched a single-handed bid to generate a defensive alliance with Belgium, France, Denmark and Russia against Germany. Wilson enlisted as his ally Sir Arthur Nicolson, Permanent Under Secretary at the Foreign Office, apparently unaware that Nicolson had lost influence with Sir Edward Grey, and was in any case swiftly brought to heel by the Chief of the Imperial General Staff, Sir William Nicholson.[38] This episode seems to have been unique in the annals of the General Staff; although its members had their own orientations, and although the Chiefs of the General Staff joined with their opposite numbers in the other services from the mid-1930s in pressing the government to appease Germany and Japan in order to gain time for rearmament, there was no other case in which a senior member of the General Staff tried to manoeuvre the government down a path which it, or the military leaders as a collectivity, did not wish to follow.

Wilson's individualistic foray into foreign policy was stimulated by his reaction to what was a key issue for the General Staff throughout the years under consideration here: the proper place of the continent in the British Army's scheme of things. In the decades before the First World War, the undertow exerted by Europe grew gradually until by 1911 it had become the dominant force in strategic thinking. The late Victorian army had been a prey to a variety of cross-currents, among which that inspired by 'continentalists' who saw a European war as both the commanding model and the most severe test Great Britain was likely to face competed with that of the 'imperialists', concerned with its pre-eminent responsibilities and the threats to position and possession in the Mediterranean, in the Indian sub-continent and beyond. The practical results of the interlacing of these forces were that while the mobilisation schemes devised by the War Office at the close of the nineteenth century had a 'European' feel to them and the artillery approached most closely to continental standards of education and technical excellence, infantry training was tailored to colonial requirements, cavalry training reflected study of the American Civil War as well as extra-European experience, and supply and transport arrangements emerged from the crucible of the African campaigns in Zululand and Egypt.[39]

The reforms in defence structure which were put in place during and after the Boer War did not represent an outright victory for the 'continental' school, but rather a further evolution of institutions shaped to Britain's wide-ranging needs and obligations, among which the empire was still very much one of the front runners.[40]

Changes in international circumstances, among them the rise of Japanese naval power and the rise of the French entente, inexorably led to the army replacing the navy as the major fighting force due to its prospective involvement on the continent.[41] Mounting alarm at Germany's hostile international posture can only have been reinforced by the despatches forwarded from Berlin between 1906 and 1910 by the British Military Attaché there, Colonel Frederick Trench, which depicted Germany as an increasingly bellicose and aggressive power – though Trench's preoccupation with the threat of a German invasion of England ran counter to the General Staff's gathering focus on fighting on the continent alongside the French.[42] The result of all these forces – no matter how we ajudge their exact working – was to produce by 1912 a 'continental commitment' in the General Staff, which was unlike anything that had preceded or would succeed it in peacetime.

The consequences of that commitment left their mark on the interwar years, when the General Staff was only pulled back towards a continental involvement by major crises.[43] In 1923, the Secretary of State for War, Lord Derby, told the Cabinet that the Great War was not exceptional 'but the greatest lesson we ever had', but three years later Sir George Milne, newly installed as CIGS (1926–33) told the chiefs of staff that war with Germany was 'abnormal'. The continental 'undertow' had once again disappeared and the move away from contemplating a military involvement in Europe resulted, as Brian Bond has noted, in the fact that throughout most of the interwar years there was 'no systematic attempt to grapple with the greatest strategic lesson of the war: that Britain's security was inextricably involved with that of western Europe'.[44] The General Staff was, as Milne pointed out, without a defined role and 'until such time as the Cabinet had decided on the policy it was not possible to frame any proposals in regard to details.'[45] Politics once again determined the General Staff's attitude and actions. With no equivalent of the prewar Liberal Imperialists with whom to side, there was nothing to be done but to go back to imperial concerns and to grapple with the most pressing professional problem of the day – the question of mechanisation and the future role of the tank in war.

Whether it was advantageous to the General Staff in tackling this complex question to have the benefit of the futuristic predictions of prophets of armoured warfare such as J. F. C. Fuller is far from clear.[46] While his value as a populariser of ideas and a 'blue-skies' thinker was undoubtedly high, Fuller's predictions could mislead. Speaking to the British Legion in February 1933, and plainly having imbibed a deep draught of Fullerian rhetoric (with perhaps more than a dash of Liddell Hart as well), General Sir Ian Hamilton forecast that the next war would last not four years but only four weeks.

> The first encounter [of mechanised forces] will almost certainly decide the war. The victorious tanks and aeroplanes will eat up the hostile infantry and artillery as half a dozen heavily armoured knights of the wars of the Jacquerie could and did eat up a thousand armed, but unarmoured, peasants. Then they will begin to lap up the civilian population as a cat laps up cream ...[47]

Tethered to reality by such things as a severe shortage of funds and the possibility that a future disarmament conference might abolish the tank altogether, or at least severely restrict it in ways yet to be determined, the General Staff had perforce to tread more cautiously. As the Director of Staff Duties explained in 1929, its 'problem' was 'to think and to experiment now, and to train our officers so that they will be able to use the machines when they are provided ...'[48]

Milne trod carefully in introducing the concept of mechanisation to the army, reassuring an audience at the Royal United Services Institute in November 1927 that changes in methods and weapons did not mean changes in 'the principles that have won all our wars in the past', which he explained consisted in men, matériel and reserves 'and most of all men'.[49] Nevertheless, a quiet revolution was under way. It was spotted by the American Military Attaché, Colonel John R. Thomas, who reported during Milne's third year in office that, 'The whole atmosphere of British military thought, insofar as it can now be gauged, is charged with "mechanization".'[50]

Deep within the policy and process of mechanisation features can be found which suggest that while the interwar General Staff no longer favoured a 'continental commitment' as such, they did foresee and were preparing so far as they could and if needs be to undertake a possible continental involvement of some kind. Justifying the rationale for the mechanised force in 1927, Milne cited as an example the dash to Antwerp in 1914. 'Had this force been mechanised,' he argued, 'it would have considerably reduced their losses.'[51] His successor as CIGS, Archibald Montgomery-Massingberd, believed in the 'incalculable moral effect' of the arrival on the continent of even a small British contingent – a notion very much akin to that propounded before the war by Henry Wilson in justification of the marginal addition of force represented by six divisions of the British Expeditionary Force.[52] Montgomery-Massingberd, whose reputation has been rescued in recent years from the opprobrium heaped on it by followers of Liddell Hart's hostile judgements, went a little further than his predecessor:

> So long as Great Britain maintain[s] an Army capable of intervening if there was any trouble on the Continent, such as now exist[s] in the Saar, that was the surest assistance that this country could give to peace. It must always be remembered that they might be faced once again, as they were in 1914, with a very dangerous threat to Empire.[53]

Montgomery-Massingberd's successor, Sir Cyril Deverell (CIGS 1936–37), stuck to the General Staff line as it had evolved by the mid-1930s. While the first purpose of the army was still, as it had been since early in the previous decade, to defend and police the overseas empire, it intended to provide a prompt expeditionary force for continental land warfare and serve as a training cadre for a much larger force. For this, mechanisation was an essential.[54]

While the General Staff at Whitehall, and its offshoots in the various commands, laboured over the complexities of mechanisation and the puzzles of national strategy, its representatives overseas sent back a stream of information about the armies with which Great Britain might one day find itself fighting a war, either in alliance or as opponents. With the exceptions of Germany and Japan, their contributions to the making of General Staff policy have yet to be the subject of any sustained examination.[55] As with mechanisation, a careful examination of the record suggests a picture that is more nuanced and less unfavourable to the staff than some of the cruder generalisations have sought to present. The difficulties of correctly interpreting what had been observed, and of avoiding the pitfall of applying inappropriate standards to foreign armies, threatened to cloak appreciations with inaccuracy.[56] Nevertheless, it is evident that skilled and experienced observers were able to report back to Whitehall in remarkably accurate terms on foreign armies, even if their reports then faced the hurdles of competition from alternative sources, collision with ethnocentric prejudice and effective communication to those who needed to know.[57]

Looking back across the era spanning the first four decades of the twentieth century during which the British General Staff was created and established, and which Brian Bond has made very much his own, it is perhaps most appropriate to regard that evolutionary experience as one of 'punctuated equilibrium'. A purge of the War Office was necessary to create the General Staff, and another was attempted in 1937 to rejuvenate the high command and shed what were regarded as antediluvian attitudes. The beneficiary of the latter, Lord Gort (CIGS 1937–39), had no doubts but that such actions were sometimes necessary: writing to a fellow soldier about the situation in the Indian Army, he observed that '[t]he whole place needs a purge as we have had at home even though it may cause some misgivings and heart burnings'.[58] Although cliques persisted and influence was still exerted to advance some and block others, the professionalism of the General Staff gradually spread throughout the army as the number of Staff College graduates among higher commanders and among middle-rank officers slowly but inexorably increased.[59] The test came with the Second World War, during which the General Staff combined discreet but effective bureaucratic activity on innumerable Whitehall committees with an approach to conducting the war that was as much pragmatic as it was the product of strategic principle. The revolution that had begun in 1904 was thus a quiet one, and the pace at which the General Staff advanced during the succeeding 35 years was not dramatic. In this, and in many other respects, it was a particularly Anglo-Saxon institution.

Notes

Introduction

1. Brian Bond, *Liddell Hart: A Study of his Military Thought* (London: Cassell, 1977), pp. 1–2.
2. Brian Bond, *Judgment in Military History: An Inaugural Lecture* (King's College, London, 1987).
3. Brian Holden Reid has noted this tendency in the writing of his biography of T. E. Lawrence, see *Studies in British Military Thought* (Lincoln, NE: University of Nebraska Press, 1998), p. 154.
4. Although Bond has always been more drawn to J. F. C. Fuller's hero, Grant, rather than Liddell Hart's favourite, Sherman. See his 'Appomattox: The Triumph of General Grant', *History Today* (May 1965), pp. 297–305.
5. A second edition of this work appeared as *Britain, France and Belgium, 1939–1940* (London: Brassey's, 1990).

1: Planning for War in the Final Years of Pax Britannica, 1889–1903

1. Cambridge to Cardwell, 21 Nov. 1869, in W. Verner, *The Military Life of HRH George, Duke of Cambridge*, 2 vols (London: John Murray, 1905), vol. I, p. 407.
2. E. M. Spiers, *The Late Victorian Army, 1868–1902* (Manchester: Manchester University Press, 1992), p. 44; T. G. Fergusson, *British Military Intelligence, 1870–1914* (Frederick, MD: University Publications of America, 1984), p. 46; I. F. W. Beckett, 'Edward Stanhope at the War Office, 1887–92', *Journal of Strategic Studies*, vol. 5 (1982), pp. 278–307.
3. Memorandum attached to the 'Report of the Royal Commission to Inquire into the Civil and Professional Administration of the Naval and Military Departments' [Hartington Commission], c. 5979 (1890) 19, Churchill, 15 May 1889.
4. 'Report of the Hartington Commission', para. 69.
5. Ibid., paras 71–2, 94.
6. 'Dissent to the Report of the Hartington Commission', Campbell-Bannerman, 10 Feb. 1890.
7. Campbell-Bannerman to Hartington, 12 Jan. 1890, Devonshire mss, 340.2225, Chatsworth.
8. Wolseley to Ponsonby, 10 April 1890, in G. E. Buckle and A. C. Benson (eds), *The Letters of Queen Victoria*, 3 vols (London: John Murray, 1932), 3rd series, vol. I, pp. 594–5.
9. 'Evidence to the Hartington Commission', Wolseley, Q. 197, Wolseley Private Papers, W/MEM/3, Hove.
10. H. M. Kochanski, *Sir Garnet Wolseley* (London: Hambledon, 1999), pp. 195–6.
11. Ponsonby to Queen, 4 March 1890, in Buckle and Benson, *Letters of Queen Victoria*, p. 577. Stanhope to Cambridge, 28 April 1890, Stanhope mss, 0254/3, Kent Record Office. Ponsonby to Cambridge, 5 April 1890; Stanhope to Cambridge, 6 June 1890; Buller to Cambridge, 20 Sept. 1890, all in Verner, *The Military Life*, vol. I, pp. 356–60.
12. G. Chesney, 'The "Confusion Worse Confounded" at the War Office', *Nineteenth Century*, 30 (August 1891), pp. 237–57. C. Dilke and S. Wilkinson, *Imperial Defence* (London: Macmillan, 1892), p. 209. C. Dilke, *The British Army* (London: Chapman & Hall, 1888), p. 318. Roberts to Cambridge, 3 May 1890, Roberts mss, 7101-23-100/3, National Army Museum.

13. Spiers, *Late Victorian Army*, p. 48.
14. 'Draft Order in Council relative to the War Department', Campbell-Bannerman, June 1895, Public Record Office (PRO), War Office (WO) 33/56.
15. 'Changes consequent upon the retirement of HRH the Duke of Cambridge', Lansdowne, 12 Aug. 1895, PRO, CAB 37/40.
16. Wolseley to Lansdowne, Aug. 1895, in F. Maurice and G. Arthur, *The Life of Lord Wolseley* (London: Doubleday Page, 1924), p. 278; Wolseley to Lansdowne, 2 and 3 Oct. 1895, Lansdowne mss, British Library (BL), L(5) 37.
17. A. V. Tucker, 'Army and Society in England, 1870–1900', *Journal of British Studies*, vol. 2 (May 1963), pp. 110–41.
18. For further details on this see Kochanski, *Sir Garnet Wolseley*, pp. 218–19.
19. J. A. S. Grenville, *Lord Salisbury and Foreign Policy* (London: Athlone, 1964), p. 18.
20. H. O. Arnold-Forster, *The War Office, the Army and the Empire* (London: Cassell, 1900), p. 81.
21. W. S. Hamer, *The British Army: Civil–Military Relations, 1885–1905* (Oxford: Clarendon, 1970), p. 31.
22. 'Memorandum on the Transvaal Boers from a Military Point of View', Ardagh, Oct. 1896, Ardagh mss, PRO 30/40/14.
23. Lansdowne to Salisbury, 9 April 1897, Salisbury mss, Hatfield House; Salisbury to Lansdowne, 21 April 1897, in Lord Newton, *Lord Lansdowne* (London: Macmillan, 1929), p. 145.
24. Wolseley to George Wolseley, 1 Dec. 1899, Wolseley mss, Duke University.
25. 'Memorandum on the defence of South Africa', Goodenough, 30 Sept. 1896; Stopford to Wolseley, 9 Dec. 1898; Stopford to Butler, 21 Dec. 1898; 'Plan for the Defence of South Africa', Butler, 14 June 1899; all in PRO, WO 32/6369. W. Butler, *An Autobiography* (London: Constable, 1911), p. 385.
26. 'Evidence to the Royal Commission on the military preparations and other matters concerned with the war in South Africa' [Elgin Commission], c. 1789–92 (1901) XL, XLI, XLII, Lansdowne, QQ. 21219, 21289; *Report of the Elgin Commission*, para. 45.
27. 'Evidence to the Elgin Commission', Lansdowne, Q. 21170.
28. 'Memorandum on the military strength in South Africa', Wolseley, 8 June 1899; Wolseley to Lansdowne, 7 July 1899, both in PRO, CAB 37/50.
29. This committee was established on 13 July 1899 as the C-in-C's Committee to Consider Questions Relating to Operations in South Africa. The membership was wider than that of the Army Board. On 11 September it was renamed the Proceedings of the Army Board for Mobilisation Purposes, still with a wide membership. On 11 June 1900 the committee was abolished and the Army Board took over its functions.
30. 'Memorandum on the military strength in South Africa', Wolseley, 8 June 1899; Buller to Lansdowne, 6 July 1899, Wolseley to Lansdowne, 7 July 1899; 'Prepared for both', Lansdowne to Wolseley, 27 Aug. 1899; all in CAB 37/50. Wolseley to Lansdowne, 28 Sept. 1899, Lansdowne mss, L(5) 37.
31. Lansdowne to Wolseley, 20 Aug. 1899; Wolseley to Lansdowne, 24 Aug. 1899; both in CAB 37/50.
32. Buller to Salisbury, 5 Sept. 1899; Wolseley to Lansdowne, 5 Sept. 1899; both in PRO, CAB 37/50. Buller to Wolseley, 7 Sept. 1899, Buller mss, Devon Record Office, 2065M/SS4/14.
33. Wolseley to Lansdowne, 8 Sept. 1899, CAB 37/50. Wolseley to Lansdowne, 28 Sept. 1899, Lansdowne mss, L (5) 37. Wolseley to Ardagh, 23 Sept. 1899, Ardagh mss, PRO 30/40/3. 'Memorandum on South Africa', Lansdowne, 25 Sept. 1899, CAB 37/51.
34. L. S. Amery, *The Times History of the War in South Africa*, 7 vols (London: Sampson Low, 1900–09), vol. II, pp. 103, 466.
35. 'Memorandum on the Ordnance Branch', Brackenbury, 15 Dec. 1899, Elgin documents; Wolseley to Lansdowne, 29 Dec. 1899, PRO, CAB 37/51; 'Memorandum on the Ordnance Branch', Brackenbury, 9 Jan. 1900, PRO, WO 32/6360.
36. For details of these battles see T. Pakenham, *The Boer War* (London: Futura, 1979), pp. 201–42; H. Bailes, 'Military Aspects of the War', in P. Warwick (ed.), *The South African War* (London: Longman, 1980), pp. 77–84.
37. Lansdowne to Salisbury, 10 Dec. 1899, Salisbury mss; Wolseley to Bigge, 14 Dec. 1899, in Buckle and Benson, *Letters of Queen Victoria*, 3rd series, vol. III, p. 433; Wolseley to Lansdowne, 17 Dec. 1899, Lansdowne mss, L(5) 37.

38. 'Memorandum on the position of the C-in-C', Wolseley, 17 Nov. 1900, CAB 37/53.
39. Ibid.
40. Debate on the War Office administration, 4 and 5 March 1901, *Hansard*, fourth series, 90; debate on Lord Wolseley's memorandum to Lord Salisbury, 15 March 1901, ibid., 91.
41. Brackenbury to Roberts, 17 Dec. 1900, Roberts mss, 7101-23-11/166; 'Memorandum on the role of the C-in-C', Roberts, 27 Dec. 1900, CAB 37/53; 'Memorandum on the organisation of the War Office', Brodrick, 19 Jan. 1901, CAB 37/56.
42. 'Report of the Committee appointed to enquire into War Office administration', cd. 580 (1901), XL.
43. Hamer, *The British Army*, pp. 187–92; anon, 'The Position of the C-in-C', *Blackwoods*, vol. 169 (April 1901), pp. 573–84.
44. Fergusson, *British Military Intelligence*, p. 116.
45. Spiers, *Late Victorian Army*, p. 312.
46. Esher to King, 30 April 1903, in M. V. Brett, *Journals and Letters of Reginald, Viscount Esher* (London: Nicolson & Watson, 1934), p. 399.
47. 'Evidence to the Elgin Commission', Ardagh, Q. 4966.
48. Ibid., Wood, Q. 4283.
49. B. Bond, 'The Retirement of the Duke of Cambridge', *Journal of the Royal United Services Institute*, vol. 56 (1961), pp. 544–53.
50. 'Report of the War Office (Reconstitution) Committee', cd. 1932, 1968, 2002 (1904), VIII.
51. Hamer, *Civil–Military Relations*, p. 244; J. McDermott, 'The Revolution in British Military Thinking from the Boer War to the Moroccan Crisis', in P. M. Kennedy (ed.), *The War Plans of the Great Powers, 1880–1914* (London: Allen & Unwin, 1979), pp. 99–117.

2: Towards a Ministry of Defence: First Faltering Steps, 1890–1923

1. Salisbury, 'Report of the Sub Committee of the Committee of Imperial Defence on National and Imperial Defence (with a report on the relations between the Navy and Air Force)', P(arliamentary) P(apers), 1924 x, p. 285; Esher, 'Report of the Committee into Reconstitution of the War Office', pt 1, PP, 1904 viii, p. 106.
2. See J. Sweetman, *Raglan: From the Peninsula to the Crimea* (London: Cassell, 1993), ch. 9, p. 215 *et seq.* and ch. 8, p. 166 *et seq.*
3. Summary of naval changes, W. Jackson and Lord Bramall, *The Chiefs* (London: Brassey's, 1992), p. 10. Secretary of State for War and Secretary at War, see J. Sweetman, *War and Administration: The Significance of the Crimean War for the British Army* (Edinburgh: Edinburgh University Press, 1984), ch. 6, p. 97 *et seq.* Ordnance Department, ibid., p. 59 *et seq.*; 'Order in Council regulating Establishments of the Civil Departments', PP, 1854–55 xxxii, p. 677; 'Order Amalgamating Army of India with the Line', published 10 April 1861, PP, 1861 xlii, p. 225.
4. 'Royal Commission on the National Defences', PP, 1860 xiii, p. x.
5. Admiralty minute, 24 Jan. 1857, P(ublic) R(ecord) O(ffice)/C(olonial) O(ffice) 201/590; Mills' Select Committee, PP, 1861 xiii, p. 1 *et seq.* For an analysis of disputes between the imperial government and colonies, see D. C. Gordon, *The Dominion Partnership in Imperial Defense* (Baltimore, MD: Johns Hopkins University Press, 1965), p. xiii.
6. Canadian fears, see G. F. G. Stanley, *Canada's Soldiers, 1604–1954* (Toronto: Macmillan, 1954), p. 246; F. A. Johnson, *Defence by Committee: The British Committee of Imperial Defence, 1885–1959* (Oxford: Oxford University Press, 1960), pp. 16–18; 26 July 1879, Hicks Beach to Carnarvon, inviting him to head the Royal Commission, PRO 30/6/52; Gordon, *Dominion Partnership*, p. 71. Carnarvon produced three reports, PP, 1887 lvi, p. 3 *et seq.*
7. Gordon, *Dominion Partnership*, pp. 99–100.
8. 5 March 1888, *Hansard* 3rd series, vol. 123, c. 229 *et seq.* and 8 March, ibid., c. 593 *et seq.*; Hamley, 5 March, ibid., c. 267; Churchill, 8 March, ibid., c. 593. Hartington's terms of reference were signed on 7 June and published in the *London Gazette*, 12 June 1888.
9. 'Administration of Military and Naval Departments', Royal Commission preliminary and further reports (with appendices), PP, 1890 xix, pp. v–viii; memos by Brackenbury (21 June 1889) and Churchill (15 May 1889), ibid., pp. xiv and xv–xvii resp.
10. C. Dilke and S. Wilkinson, *Imperial Defence* (London: Macmillan, 1892); 21 December 1893, Dilke to Balfour, quoted in S. Gwynn and G. M. Tuckwell, *The Life of the Rt Hon*

Sir Charles W. Dilke, 2 vols (London: John Murray, 1917), vol. II, pp. 451–2: the letter and Balfour's reply were published in the press on 28 Feb. 1894.

11. Gwynn and Tuckwell, *Dilke*, vol. II, p. 454; Chamberlain, quoted ibid., p. 456; Johnson, *Defence by Committee*, pp. 33–4; Hankey quoted ibid., p. 34.

12. Wolseley's statement, 4 March 1901, *Hansard* 4th series, vol. 90, c. 327 *et seq.*; Salisbury, 5 March 1901, ibid., c. 543 *et seq.*

13. C. Dilke, *Problems of Greater Britain* (London: Macmillan, 1890); Dilke and Wilkinson, *Imperial Defence*; Secretary of State for War and the Commander-in-Chief documents as to their respective duties and authorities, PP, 1868–69 xxxvi, p. 591. Colonial conferences, Gordon, *Dominion Partnership*, pp. 134–63; Johnson, *Defence by Committee*, pp. 50, 54; correspondence relating to a conference between the Secretary of State for the Colonies and the Prime Ministers of self-governing colonies, June–Aug. 1902, PP, 1902 lxvi, p. 451; Brodrick and Selborne, 'The Improvement of the Intellectual Equipment of the Services', 10 Nov. 1902, noted in I. F. W. Beckett and J. Gooch (eds), *Politicians and Defence: Studies in the Formulation of British Defence Policy 1845–1970* (Manchester: Manchester University Press, 1981), p. xii.

14. Elgin Commission terms of reference, report and minutes of evidence, vol. I, PP, 1904 xl, p. 1 *et seq.*; evidence, vol. II, ibid., xli; appendices, ibid., xlii; on Colonial Defence Committee, PP, 1904 viii, p. 103; (Esher) 'Report of the Committee into Reconstitution of the War Office', pts 1–3 (11 Jan., 26 Feb. and 9 March 1904), PP 1904, pp. 101, 121, 157 resp. See, too, Johnson, *Defence by Committee*, pp. 40, 51, 56–9, 67.

15. Balfour, 5 March 1903, *Hansard*, 5th series, vol. 118, c. 1579; Treasury minute, 4 May 1904, PP, 1904 lxxix, c. 111; Johnson, *Defence by Committee*, pp. 82, 93–5, 105; Balfour and Hankey quoted ibid., pp. 74 and 73 resp.

16. Johnson, *Defence by Committee*, pp. 63, 71; N. A. M. Rodger, *The Admiralty* (Lavenham: Terence Dalton, 1979), pp. 123–6; Lord Chatfield, *The Navy and Defence* (London: Heinemann, 1942), p. 34.

17. Esher report, PP, 1904 viii, p. 124. 'Correspondence relating to the proposed formation of an Imperial General Staff', PP, 1909 li, p. 627.

18. Rodger, *Admiralty*, pp. 128–9; R. Rhodes James, *Gallipoli* (London: Batsford, 1965), pp. 24–5; Lord Ismay, *The Memoirs of Lord Ismay* (London: Heinemann, 1960), p. 49; Scott, 22 March 1920, 127 *Hansard* c. 82; Asquith and Lloyd George, quoted Rhodes James, *Gallipoli*, p. 25; Crewe and Fisher, quoted ibid., p. 24; Johnson, *Defence by Committee*, p. 156.

19. The Royal Flying Corps was established by Royal Warrant on 13 April 1912 with a military wing stationed at Farnborough and naval wing at Eastchurch, where the Royal Navy developed its own training centre independent of the Central Flying School on Salisbury Plain. On 1 July 1914, the naval wing was renamed the Royal Naval Air Service, PRO Air 1/361, 15/228/51. On 29 July 1915 Admiralty Weekly Order 1204/15 pronounced it 'an integral part of the Royal Navy', quoted in S. W. Roskill, *Hankey: Man of Secrets*, 3 vols (London: Collins, 1970), vol. I, p. 185.

20. The Inter-Departmental Committee on the Air Service, more generally known as the Joint War Air Committee, met March–April 1916, the first Air Board May–December 1916, the second Air Board February 1917–January 1918. Friction between Churchill and Fisher: Rhodes James, *Gallipoli*, p. 68.

21. Rhodes James, *Gallipoli*, pp. 20–1; Asquith, quoted ibid., p. 69; K. Jeffrey (ed.), *The Military Correspondence of Field-Marshal Sir Henry Wilson, 1918–1922* (London: Army Records Society and Bodley Head, 1985), pp. 16–17.

22. H. A. Jones, *The War in the Air*, 6 vols (Oxford: Clarendon, 1922–37), vol. 6 (1937), pp. 26–7; Bonar Law on Henderson, 15 April 1918, 105 *Hansard* c. 564–5; on Rothermere, 24 April 1918, ibid., c. 1128.

23. Haldane's governmental committee report, dated 14 December 1918, PP, 1918 xii; Jackson and Bramall, *Chiefs*, p. 117; Jeffrey, *Wilson Military Correspondence*, pp. 169, 195; Churchill, 12 February 1919, 112 *Hansard* c. 231 *et seq.*

24. 4 July 1919, memo. by Seely, Lloyd George papers, House of Lords Record Office, F/9/1/2; Seely, 12 November 1919, 121 *Hansard* c. 373 *et seq.* and letter to *The Times*, 26 Nov. 1919. Seely resigned as Under Secretary of State for Air on 10 November 1919 on the grounds that Churchill's continued responsibility for War and Air was detrimental to an Air Ministry.

25. Entries in Wilson's diary for 8, 11, 12, 14 and 16 July 1919, Henry Wilson mss, Imperial War Museum, 73/1/4; Hankey diary, 12 July 1919, quoted M. Gilbert, *Winston Spencer Churchill*, 8 vols (London: Heinemann), vol. IV, *Companion*, pt. 1 (1977), p. 742; 13 July 1919, Wilson to Prime Minister, House of Lords Record Office, Lloyd George mss, F/47/8/26; 14 July 1919, Churchill to Prime Minister, ibid., F/9/1/5; 16 and 31 July 1919, Wilson to Prime Minister, ibid., F/47/8/27 and 29; 4 August 1919, Churchill to Lloyd George, quoted in Gilbert, *Winston Spencer Churchill*, vol. 4, p. 213; Riddell quoted in ibid., p. 213.
26. Geddes Committee on National Expenditure produced two interim reports and a final report, 14 Dec. 1921, 28 Jan. and 21 Feb. 1922, PP, 1922 ix, pp. 1, 173 and 287 respectively.
27. 21 March 1922, Churchill and Wedgwood, 152 *Hansard* c. 390 and 330 resp.; Lord Weir's Committee on the Amalgamation of Services common to the Navy, Army and Air Force reported on 2 Jan. 1923, PP, 1926 viii.
28. Guinness and Hunter-Weston, 15 March 1922, 151 *Hansard* c. 347 and 357 resp.; Lloyd George and Malone, 27 June 1922, 155 *Hansard* c. 1837; Lloyd George and Sueter, 29 June 1922, ibid., c. 2314.
29. 19 Feb. 1923, Hoare to Weir, Weir mss, Churchill College, Cambridge, 8/1; Viscount Templewood, *Empire of the Air: The Advent of the Air Age, 1922–9* (London: Collins, 1957), pp. 55–7; L. S. Amery, *My Political Life* (London: Hutchinson, 1953), vol. 2, p. 363; Salisbury's terms of reference, 9 May 1923, PP, 1924 x, p. 277. The report of Balfour's sub-committee, dated 21 July 1923, was published as an annex to the main Salisbury report, PP, 1924 x, pp. 304–12.
30. Evidence of Robertson, Geddes, Sykes and Haldane, PP, 1924 x, pp. 292, 286, 287; opinion of senior army officers, ibid., p. 287. The Salisbury Committee held 19 meetings and considered 67 memos, 15 March–31 Oct. 1923. Salisbury's conclusion, PP, 1924, X, p. 292.
31. Parliamentary Papers, 1924, X, p. 301, para. 51(f).
32. Churchill, 21 March 1922, quoted by Salisbury, PP, 1924 xx, p.286.

3: 'Selection by Disparagement': Lord Esher, the General Staff and the Politics of Command, 1904–14

1. Ian F. W. Beckett, 'The South African War and the Late Victorian Army', in Peter Dennis and Jeffrey Grey (eds), *The Boer War: Army, Nation and Empire* (Canberra: Army History Unit, 2000), pp. 31–44. Hew Strachan, 'The Boer War and its Impact on the British Army, 1902–14', in Peter B. Boyden, Alan J. Guy and Marion Harding (eds), *Ashes and Blood: The British Army in South Africa, 1795–1914* (London: National Army Museum, 1999), pp. 85–98.
2. John Gooch, 'Britain and the Boer War', in George J. Andreopoulos and Harold E. Selesky (eds), *The Aftermath of Defeat: Societies, Armed Forces and the Challenge of Recovery* (New Haven, CT: Yale University Press, 1994), pp. 40–58; idem, 'Adversarial Attitudes: Servicemen, Politicians and Strategic Policy, 1899–1914', in Paul Smith (ed.), *Government and the Armed Forces in Britain, 1856–1990* (London: Hambledon, 1996), pp. 53–74. Brian Bond, *The Victorian Army and the Staff College, 1854–1914* (London: Eyre Methuen, 1972), pp. 212–40.
3. Churchill Archives Centre, Cambridge (hereafter CAC), ESHR 10/28, Esher to French, 8 Aug. 1905.
4. CAC, ESHR 10/41, Fisher to Esher, 17 Jan. 1904.
5. Royal Archives (hereafter RA), P4/127, Wolseley to Bigge, 14 Dec. 1899. Ian F. W. Beckett, 'Buller and the Politics of Command', in John Gooch (ed.), *The Boer War: Direction, Experience and Image* (London: Frank Cass, 2000), pp. 42–55.
6. Ian F. W. Beckett, 'Command in the Late Victorian Army', in G. D. Sheffield (ed.), *Leadership and Command: The Anglo-American Military Experience since 1861* (London: Brasseys, 1997), pp. 37–56; idem, 'Kitchener and the Politics of Command', in Edward M. Spiers (ed.), *Sudan: The Reconquest Reappraised* (London: Frank Cass, 1998), pp. 35–53; idem, 'Military High Command in South Africa, 1854–1914', in Boyden, Guy and Harding, *Ashes and Blood*, pp. 60–71; idem, 'Women and Patronage in the Late Victorian Army', *History*, vol. 85 (2000), pp. 463–80.

7. Sir Guy Fleetwood Wilson, *Letters to Somebody: A Retrospect* (London: Cassell, 1922), p. 122. National Army Museum (hereafter NAM), 9011-42-13, Nicholson to Wilkinson, 7 June 1894.

8. Beckett, 'Buller and Politics of Command', pp. 42–55. Earl of Midleton, *Records and Recollections, 1856–1939* (London: John Murray, 1939), p. 120.

9. Edward M. Spiers, *The Army and Society, 1815–1914* (London: Longman, 1980), pp. 6–8.

10. For the general background to the administrative changes prior to 1904, see W. S. Hamer, *The British Army: Civil–Military Relations, 1885–1905* (Oxford: Clarendon, 1970), pp. 93–222.

11. Hamer, *British Army*, p. 258. Bond, *Victorian Army and Staff College*, pp. 216–21. CAC, ESHR 10/41, Fisher to Esher, 7 Dec. 1903; 10/47, Esher to Knollys, 19 Oct. 1903.

12. John Gooch, *The Plans of War: The General Staff and British Military Strategy, 1900–16* (London: Routledge & Kegan Paul, 1974), pp. 36–55. Lord Sydenham, *My Working Life* (London: John Murray, 1929), pp. 173–5. Hamer, *British Army*, pp. 239–45.

13. Liddell Hart Centre for Military Archives, King's College, London (hereafter LHCMA), Hamilton, 20/1/1, Jean Hamilton diary, 1 Feb. 1904. NAM, 7101-23-122-7, Roberts to Hamilton, 11 Feb. 1904 and Roberts to Arnold-Forster, 13 Feb. 1904. CAC, ESHR 10/24, Roberts to Esher, 14 Feb. 1904; 10/33, Clarke to Esher, 14 and 15 Feb. 1904. D. S. Macdiarmid, *The Life of Lieutenant-General Sir James Moncrieff Grierson* (London: Constable, 1923), p. 206. NAM, 9011-42-13, Nicholson to Wilkinson, 8 Feb. 1904. Imperial War Museum (hereafter IWM), HHW 13, Wilson diary, 8, 9 and 11 Feb. 1904. Major-General Sir C. E. Callwell, *Field Marshal Sir Henry Wilson: His Life and Diaries*, 2 vols (London: Cassell, 1927), vol. 1, pp. 55–6. Sir Alfred Turner, *Sixty Years of a Soldier's Life* (London: Methuen, 1912), pp. 310–11.

14. CAC, ESHR 10/24, Haig to Esher, 8 Feb. 1904; 10/41, Fisher to Esher, 17 Jan. 1904.

15. Field-Marshal Sir William Robertson, *From Private to Field-Marshal* (London: Constable, 1921), p. 137. NAM, 7101-23-122-7, Roberts to Hamilton, 11 Feb. 1904. LHCMA, Hamilton, 20/1/1, Roberts to Jean Hamilton, 29 Feb. 1904.

16. CAC, ESHR 10/43, Arnold-Forster to Esher, 13 Feb. 1904; 10/33, Clarke to Esher, 14 Feb. 1904. Ian F. W. Beckett, 'H. O. Arnold-Forster and the Volunteers' in Ian F. W. Beckett and John Gooch (eds), *Politicians and Defence: Studies in the Formulation of British Defence Policy, 1845–1970* (Manchester: Manchester University Press, 1981), pp. 47–68. Rhodri Williams, *Defending the Empire: The Conservative Party and British Defence Policy, 1899–1915* (New Haven, CT: Yale University Press 1991), pp. 41–55. British Library (hereafter BL), Add mss 50341, Arnold-Forster diary, 7 Nov. 1903; Add mss 50341, diary, 4 March 1904; Add mss 50340, diary, 17 Oct. 1904. RA, W40/103, Esher to Knollys, 19 March 1907. Midleton, *Records and Recollections*, pp. 144–58. BL, Add mss 50072, Brodrick to Balfour, 29 Feb. 1904.

17. Fleetwood-Wilson, *Letters to Somebody*, p. 77.

18. RA, W39/8, Esher to King, 3 Jan. 1904; W39/27, Esher to Knollys, 26 Jan. 1904. CAC, ESHR 10/28, Esher to Roberts, 31 Jan. 1904; 10/33 Clarke to Esher, 30 Jan. 1904; 10/47, Knollys to Esher, 27 Jan. 1904.

19. CAC, ESHR 10/41, Fisher to Esher, 3 Feb. 1904. NAM, 7101-23-122-7, 'Memorandum by Roberts', 2 Feb. 1904; Roberts to Arnold-Forster, 2 Feb. 1904; Roberts to Hamilton, 11 Feb. 1904; Roberts to Balfour, 12 Feb. 1904; Roberts to Hamilton, 28 Feb. 1904. IWM, HHW 13, Wilson diary for 5, 6 and 7 Feb. 1904.

20. NAM, 7101-23-122-7, Roberts to Hamilton, 28 Feb. 1904. RA, W39/49, Esher to Knollys, 19 Oct. 1904; W39/113, Esher to Knollys, 1 Sept. 1905; W40/43, Esher to Knollys, 6 Aug. 1906. CAC, ESHR 10/28, Esher to Knollys, 30 Oct. 1904. IWM, HHW 13, Wilson diary for 23 and 24 Feb. and 2 March 1904. On the Mediterranean command, see Noble Frankland, *Witness of a Century: The Life and Times of Prince Arthur, Duke of Connaught* (London: Shepheard-Walwyn, 1993), pp. 240–8. Philip Magnus, *Kitchener: Portrait of an Imperialist* (Harmondsworth: Penguin, 1968), pp. 287–90.

21. CAC, ESHR 10/47, Knollys to Esher, 13 Jan. 1904. IWM, HHW 12, 13 Wilson diary, 22 Dec. 1903 and 6 Feb. 1904. NAM, 7101-23-122-7, Roberts to Kitchener, 4 Feb. 1904. Gooch, *Plans of War*, p. 46.

22. NAM, 9011-42-13, Nicholson to Wilkinson, 7 June 1894, 12 Dec. 1894, 23 Dec. 1894 and 24 June 1895. BL, Add mss 49710, Fisher to Sandars, 30 Jan. 1904. RA, W39/22, 105, 132, Esher to Knollys, 16 Jan. 1904, 20 Aug. 1905 and 31 Dec. 1905; W40/111, Esher to

Knollys, 5 May 1907. NAM, 8704-35-159, Esher to Haldane, 1 May 1907. CAC, ESHR 10/41, Fisher to Esher, 17 Jan. and 2 Feb. 1904. NAM, 7101-23-122-7, Roberts to Kitchener, 4 Feb. 1904.

23. John Gooch, 'The Bolt from the Blue', in John Gooch (ed.), *The Prospect of War: Studies in British Defence Policy, 1847–1942* (London: Frank Cass, 1981), pp. 1–34. Gooch, *Plans of War*, pp. 165–94, 278–9. Ian F. W. Beckett, *Riflemen Form: A Study of the Rifle Volunteer Movement, 1859–1908* (Aldershot: Ogilby Trusts, 1982), pp. 231–2.

24. CAC, ESHR 10/41, Fisher to Esher, 17 Jan., 2 Feb., 3 Feb., and 15 Feb. 1904. BL, Add mss 49710, Fisher to Sandars, 23 Jan. 1904; Add mss 49762, Sandars to Balfour, 18 Jan. 1904. Nicholas D'Ombrain, *War Machinery and High Policy: Defence Administration in Peacetime Britain, 1902–14* (Oxford: Oxford University Press, 1973), pp. 42–3.

25. Maurice Brett (ed.), *Journals and Letters of Reginald, Viscount Esher*, 4 vols (London: Ivor Nicolson & Watson, 1934), vol. 2, p. 39. CAC, ESHR 10/41, Fisher to Esher, 17 Jan. and 2 Feb. 1904; 10/47, Knollys to Esher, 1 Feb. 1904. RA, W39/22, Esher to Knollys, 16 Jan. 1904. NAM, 7101-23-122-7, Roberts to Arnold-Forster, 3 Feb. 1904. LHCMA, Hamilton, 20/1/3, Jean Hamilton diary, 13 June 1916.

26. CAC, ESHR 10/24, Repington to Esher, 4 Feb. 1904; 10/47, Knollys to Esher, 13 Jan. and 1 Feb. 1904. RA, W39/22, Esher to Knollys, 16 Jan. 1904. NAM, 7101-23-122-7, Roberts to Arnold-Forster, 3 Feb. 1904; Roberts to Hamilton, 11 Feb. 1904; 7101-23-32, Kitchener to Roberts, 29 Feb. 1904. BL, Add mss 49722, Arnold-Forster to Balfour, 13 Jan. 1904. LHCMA, Hamilton, 20/1/1, Jean Hamilton diary, 3, 4, 18 and 26 Feb., 5 and 27 March, 19 June 1904, and 27 Jan. 1906; 3/2/3, Hamilton to Jean Hamilton, 7, 8, 15, 17 Feb., 7 March, and 15 April 1904; Brodrick to Hamilton, 8 June 1904; 3/2/5, Hamilton to Brodrick, 1 May and 3 Aug. 1904.

27. CAC, ESHR 10/24, Ward to Esher, 13 Nov. 1903 and Kelly-Kenny to Esher, 13 Nov. 1903; 10/28, Esher to Fisher, 19 Nov. 1903; 10/47, Kelly-Kenny to Knollys, 14 Nov. 1903.

28. CAC, ESHR 10/41, Fisher to Esher, 17 Jan. 1904; 10/47, Knollys to Esher, 21 Jan. and 1 Feb. 1904. BL, Add mss 50336, Arnold-Forster diary, 6 Feb. 1904. RA, W23/48, King to Brodrick, 15 Oct. 1902. IWM, HHW 13, Wilson diary, 12 Feb. 1904. BL, Add mss 49710, Fisher to Sandars, 20 Jan. 1904. NAM, 7101-23-122-7, Roberts to Arnold-Forster, 3 Feb. 1904 and Roberts to Hamilton, 11 Feb. 1904. LHCMA, Hamilton, 20/1/1, Jean Hamilton diary, 29 Nov. 1904; 3/2/6, Hamilton to Jean Hamilton, 9 Jan. 1905. Simon Heffer, *Power and Place: The Political Consequences of King Edward VII* (London: Weidenfeld & Nicolson, 1998), pp. 189–90.

29. CAC, ESHR 10/41, Fisher to Esher, 17 Jan. 1904. Ian F. W. Beckett, 'Haig and French', in Brian Bond and Nigel Cave (eds), *Haig: A Reappraisal 70 Years On* (Barnsley: Leo Cooper, 1999), pp. 51–63. William Philpott, 'The Strategic Ideas of Sir John French', *Journal of Strategic Studies*, vol. 12 (1989), pp. 458–78. Richard Holmes, *The Little Field-Marshal: Sir John French* (London: Cape, 1981), pp. 126, 139–42, 196–8.

30. RA, W39/21, Esher to Knollys, 16 Jan. 1904. CAC, ESHR 10/41, Fisher to Esher, 17 Jan. 1904; 10/45, Esher to French, 12 July 1905. RA, W40/128, Esher to King, 26 Sept. 1907.

31. CAC, ESHR 10/19, Surtees to Brett, 16 May 1904; 10/45, French to Esher, 25 Aug. 1904. RA, W40/109, Esher to Knollys, 19 March 1907. IWM, 75/46/3, Esher to French, 20 Nov. 1904 and 25 Dec. 1905. French to Esher, 24 Feb. 1904 quoted in Holmes, *Little Field Marshal*, pp. 126–7. D'Ombrain, *War Machinery and High Policy*, pp. 36, 127.

32. RA, W39/21, Esher to Knollys, 16 Jan. 1904; W39/26, Esher to Knollys, 23 Jan. 1904. CAC, ESHR 10/41, Fisher to Esher, 17 Jan. 1904. BL, L(5)48, Lansdowne to Roberts, 27 July, 21 and 28 Sept. 1900; Roberts to Lansdowne, 9 Nov. 1900.

33. General Sir Neville Lyttelton, *Eighty Years: Soldiering, Politics, Games* (London: Hodder & Stoughton, 1927), p. 268. CAC, ESHR 10/24, Repington to Esher, 9 Feb. 1904 and 18 Sept. 1904. NAM, 7101-23-122-7, Roberts to Kitchener, 4 Feb. 1904. LHCMA, Hamilton, 3/2/3, Hamilton to Jean Hamilton, 10 Feb. 1904.

34. CAC, ESHR 10/33, Clarke to Esher, 23 March 1904. IWM, HHW 13, Wilson diary, 5 April, 27 July, 7 and 9 Oct. 1904. Queen Mary and Westfield College, University of London (hereafter QMWC), mss KL/NGL/705, Katherine Lyttelton to Lyttelton, 6 Nov. 1905. Bond, *Victorian Army*, pp. 241–2, n.16. RA, W39/48, Esher to Knollys, 6 Sept. 1904. BL, Add mss 49718, Esher to Sandars, 12 Dec. 1904; Add mss 49762, Sandars to Balfour, 14 Dec. 1904. CAC, ESHR 10/44 Esher to Clarke, 14 Sept. 1904. Beckett, 'Arnold-Forster and the Volunteers', p. 57. BL, Add mss 50342, Lyttelton to Arnold-Forster, 16 Dec. 1904;

Add mss 49700, Clarke to Balfour, 12 Dec. 1904; Add mss 49718, Esher to Sandars, 12 Dec. 1904.

35. BL, Add mss 49762, Sandars to Balfour, 15 Dec. 1904; Add mss 49765, Sandars to Balfour, 2 April 1907; Add mss 49718, Esher to Sandars, 15 May 1905; Add mss 50339, Arnold-Forster diary, 8 and 12 Jul. 1904; Add mss 50347, diary, 3 May 1905; Add mss 5050352, diary, 16 Nov. and 27 Nov. 1905. CAC, ESHR 10/36, Clarke to Esher, 6 May 1905. RA, W39/106, Esher to Knollys, 22 Aug. 1905. Gooch, *Plans of War*, pp. 77–9. QMWC, NGL/FAM/429, 431, Lyttelton to Talbot, 28 Dec. 1904 and 30 Jan. 1907.

36. IWM, 75/46/3, Esher to French, 20 Nov. 1904, 21 Aug. and 26 Aug. 1906. BL, Add mss 52277B, Repington to Marker, 25 Aug. 1904. A. J. A. Morris (ed.), *The Letters of Lieutenant-Colonel Charles à Court Repington, CMG: Military Correspondent of The Times, 1903–18* (Stroud: Sutton Publishing for Army Records Society, 1999), pp. 20–2. CAC, ESHR 10/25, Kitchener to Esher, 12 Aug. 1905. Brett, *Journals and Letters*, vol. 2, pp. 94–8. Gooch, *Plans of War*, pp. 66, 85–6. BL, Add mss 50341, Arnold-Forster diary, 5 Nov. 1904. Edward McCourt, *Remember Butler: The Story of Sir William Butler* (London: Routledge & Kegan Paul, 1967), pp. 242–3. Archie Hunter, *Kitchener's Sword-Arm: The Life and Campaigns of General Sir Archibald Hunter* (Staplehurst: Spellmount, 1996), pp. 181–2, 187–8. BL, Add mss 49718, Esher to Sandars, 12 Dec. 1904.

37. BL, Add mss 50347, Arnold-Forster diary, 3 and 29 May 1905; Add mss 50349, diary, 7, 9, 11 and 15 July 1905; Add mss 50351, diary, 9 Oct. 1905. CAC, ESHR 10/34, Clarke to Esher, 6 May 1905; 10/42, Fisher to Esher, 26 June 1905. RA, W39/84, Esher to King, 15 July 1905; W39/105, 106 Esher to Knollys, 20 and 22 Aug. 1905.

38. RA, R26/68, King to Balfour, 4 Aug. 1905 (draft); W26/81, French to Knollys, 6 Aug. 1905; W39/103, Esher to Knollys, 9 Aug. 1905. CAC, ESHR 10/28, Esher to French, 8 Aug. 1905; 10/45, French to Esher, 16 July 1905 and French memorandum, 6 Aug. 1905. Holmes, *Little Field Marshal*, p. 135. National Library of Scotland (hereafter NLS), Acc. 3155/334 (e), French to Haig, 6 Aug. 1905. Gooch, *Plans of War*, pp. 100–1, 112–13. Edward Spiers, *Haldane: An Army Reformer* (Edinburgh: Edinburgh University Press, 1980), pp. 120–1.

39. Spiers, *Haldane*, pp. 195–6. Dudley Sommer, *Haldane of Cloan: His Life and Times, 1856–1928* (London: Allen & Unwin, 1950), p. 167. General Sir Aylmer Haldane, *A Soldier's Saga* (Edinburgh: William Blackwood, 1948), p. 248. NLS, MS. 5906, Haldane to Rosebery, 19 Dec. 1905. BL, Add mss 52277B, Repington to Marker, 15 Dec. 1905, 2 Jan. and 29 June 1906; Add mss 43919, Fleetwood-Wilson to Dilke, 22 Jan. 1906. NAM, 8704-35-159, Esher to Haldane, 1 May 1907. CAC, ESHR 10/34, Clarke to Esher, 17 March 1906; 10/41, Fisher to Esher, 17 Jan. 1904. LHCMA, Hamilton, 3/2/3, Hamilton to Jean Hamilton, 25 Dec. 1904. NAM, 7101-23-52, Nicholson to Roberts, 10 Oct. 1904, 4 Jan. and 14 Dec. 1905. RA, W26/101, Haldane to Knollys, 16 Dec. 1905. W39/132, Esher to Knollys, 31 Dec. 1905.

40. CAC, ESHR 10/25, Repington to Esher, 21 Nov. 1904. BL, Add mss 50339, Arnold-Forster diary, 3 Aug. 1904; Add mss 50342, diary, 19 Dec. 1904; Add mss 50343, diary, 29 Jan. 1905; Add mss 50353, diary, 16 Dec. 1905; Add mss 52777, Repington to Marker, 15 Dec. 1905. General Sir Charles Harington, *Plumer of Messines* (London: John Murray, 1935), pp. 55–6, 58–60. LHCMA, Hamilton, 20/1/1 Jean Hamilton diary, 26 Feb. and 17 Jul. 1904 3/2/3, Hamilton to Jean Hamilton, 10 Feb. and 18 April 1904; Edmonds, II/1/163A, Harington to Edmonds, 21 Nov. 1934. Haldane, *Soldier's Saga*, pp. 271–2. Edmonds quoted in Tim Travers, *The Killing Ground: The British Army, the Western Front and the Emergence of Modern Warfare, 1900–18* (London: Allen & Unwin, 1987), pp. 3, 29 n. 11.

41. RA, W40/46, Esher to King, 16 Aug. 1906; W40/111, Esher to Knollys, 5 May 1907. Spiers, *Haldane*, pp. 195–6. NLS, MS. 5907, Lyttelton to Haldane, 12 Aug. 1906; Haldane to Esher, 6 Sept. 1907. LHCMA, Hamilton, 20/1/1, Jean Hamilton diary, 12 May 1905. IWM, 75/46/3, Esher to French, 23 Aug. 1906, and Repington to French, 26 Sept. 1906. NAM, 7101-23-52, Nicholson to Roberts, 14 Dec. 1905.

42. RA, W41/65, 103, Esher to Knollys, 18 Sept. 1908 and 31 Dec. 1909. French to Esher, 2 June 1906, quoted in Holmes, *Little Field Marshal*, p. 135. IWM, HHW 2/70/5, Maxwell to Wilson, 23 April 1911. NLS, MS. 5910, Repington to Haldane, 27 Nov. 1911.

43. Gooch, *Plans of War*, pp. 125–6. Ian F. W. Beckett, *The Army and the Curragh Incident, 1914* (London: Bodley Head for the Army Records Society, 1986), pp. 26, 268, 398 n. 87.

44. Heffer, *Power and Place*, pp. 99–101, 215–18.

4: Lord Kitchener, the General Staff and the Army in India, 1902–14

1. David Omissi, *The Sepoy and the Raj: The Indian Army 1860–1940* (London: Macmillan, 1994), p. 133.
2. See Brian Bond, *The Victorian Army and the Staff College* (London: Eyre Methuen, 1972) and John Gooch, *The Plans of War: The General Staff and British Military Strategy c.1900–1916* (London: Routledge & Kegan Paul, 1974).
3. Kitchener to Roberts, 17 Dec. 1902, Kitchener mss, PRO 30/57/29.
4. See Military Department Despatch no. 138 of 1904, 29 Sept. 1904 L/MIL/7/5451, BL Oriental and India Office Collection (hereafter OIOC).
5. *War Office Systems of Foreign Countries and India 1900* (London: War Office, 1901), pp. 98–115.
6. G. de S. Barrow, *The Fire of Life* (London: Hutchinson, 1941), p. 82.
7. F. G. Fergusson, *British Military Intelligence* (London: Arms & Armour, 1984), pp. 56–9.
8. Military Department Despatch no. 37 of 1903, 5 March 1903, L/MIL/7/7810, OIOC.
9. Lt-Gen. Sir G. F. MacMunn, *Behind the Scenes in Many Wars* (London: John Murray, 1930), p. 58.
10. T. R. Moreman, *The Army in India and the Development of Frontier Warfare, 1849–1947* (London: Macmillan – now Palgrave, 1998), pp. 70–1.
11. Major-General G. de C. Morton to Government of India, Military Department, 15 March 1908, L/MIL/7/7448, OIOC.
12. MacMunn, *Behind the Scenes in Many Wars*, p. 61.
13. Kitchener to Roberts, 4 May 1903, Birdwood mss, mss.Eur.D.686/18, OIOC.
14. See Military Despatch no. 203 to the Governor-General, 27 July 1876, L/MIL/3/2111, OIOC.
15. Bond, *Victorian Army*, pp. 199–200.
16. See Military Department Despatch no. 156 of 1890, 4 Aug. 1890, L/MIL/7/3144, OIOC.
17. Military Department Despatch no. 197 of 1903, 29 Oct. 1903, L/MIL/3/170, OIOC.
18. See 'Report of the Committee on the Proposed Establishment of a Staff College in India', 13 May 1904, L/MIL/7/3153, OIOC.
19. War Office to India Office, 18 July 1904, L/MIL/7/3153, OIOC.
20. Bond, *The Victorian Army*, p. 202 and *Record of Lord Kitchener's Administration of the Army in India, 1902–1909* (Simla: Government Central Branch Press, 1909), pp. 208–9.
21. *Records of the Staff College, Quetta (Established 1905)* (Simla: Government Central Printing Office, 1908) and Brigadier-General Walter Braithwaite, 'The Staff College, Quetta', *Army Review*, 3 (1912), p. 414.
22. Major-General Beauchamp Duff to the Government of India, Military Department, 29 July 1903, L/MIL/7/7467, OIOC.
23. India Army Order no. 246, 'The Higher Training and Military Education of Officers, the Distribution of Staff Duties, and the Responsibility of General and Staff Officers', 11 April 1904, L/MIL/7/7471, OIOC.
24. Ibid.
25. *Record of Lord Kitchener's Administration*, p. 205.
26. Barrow, *The Fire*, p. 98.
27. MacMunn, *Behind the Scenes*, p. 49.
28. Ibid., p. 57.
29. See Finance Department to Secretary of State for India, 23 Aug. 1906 and Army Department Despatch no. 79 of 1906, 6 Sept. 1906, L/MIL/7/7485 and Army Department Despatch no. 79 of 1906, 6 Sept. 1906, L/MIL/7/7485, OIOC.
30. See *A Study of the Existing Strategical Conditions on the North-West Frontier of India. Prepared by the Chief of the Staff's Division. Army Headquarters, India* (Simla: Government Monotype Press, 1909).
31. MacMunn, *Behind the Scenes*, p. 66.
32. Gooch, *Plans of War*, p. 100; Kitchener to Marker, 28 Feb. 1907, Marker mss, BL Add.mss.52276A.
33. Kitchener to Marker, 21 March 1907, Marker mss, BL Add.mss. 52276A.
34. *Record of Lord Kitchener's Administration*, p. 210.
35. Ibid.
36. Kitchener to Marker, 8 Aug. 1907, Marker mss, BL Add.mss.52276A.

37. Military Despatch no. 98 of 1907, 3 Oct. 1907, L/MIL/7/7493, OIOC.
38. Draft Indian Army Order by His Excellency the C-in-C in India, L/MIL/7/7493, OIOC.
39. Military Despatch no. 49 to Governor General, 20 March 1908, L/MIL/7/7493, OIOC.
40. Army Department Despatch no. 55 of 1908, 4 June 1908, L/MIL/7/7493, OIOC.
41. Military Despatch no. 44 to Governor-General, 2 April 1909, L/MIL/7/7493, OIOC.
42. General W. G. Nicholson, 'The Imperial General Staff', 7 Dec. 1908, L/MIL/3/2144, OIOC.
43. Ibid.
44. Army Department Despatch no. 63 of 1909, 10 June 1909, L/MIL/3/7493, OIOC.
45. India Office to War Office, 13 Aug. 1909, L/MIL/3/2144, OIOC.
46. War Office to India Office, 8 Sept. 1909, L/MIL/3/2144, OIOC.
47. Military Despatch no. 117 to Governor-General, 1 Oct. 1909, L/MIL/3/7493, OIOC.
48. Kitchener to Marker, 25 Feb. 1909, Marker mss, BL Add.mss.52276B.
49. MacMunn, *Behind the Scenes*, p. 79.
50. Haig to Kiggell, 24 April 1909, LHCMA Kiggell mss, 1/1.
51. Army Department Despatch no. 52 of 1910, 26 May 1910, L/MIL/7/7493, OIOC, and 'The General Staff in India', *Army Review*, vol. 2 (1912), pp. 15–17.
52. See Lieutenant-General D. Haig, 'Formation of a General Staff in India', Explanatory Note by the Chief of the Staff, Feb. 1910, L/MIL/7/7493, OIOC.
53. India Army Order nos 202 and 203, L/MIL/17/5/252, issued as Special India Army Order by His Excellency the C-in-C in India, 19 March 1910, L/MIL/7/7493, OIOC; and *Army Department Summary of Principal Events and Measures during the Viceroyalty of Lord Minto from November 1905 to November 1910* (Simla: Government Central Branch Press, 1910), pp. 6–7.
54. Circular Memorandum from Major-General R.I. Scallon, 29 July 1910, P/8494, OIOC.
55. Army Department Despatch no. 4 of 1914, 8 Jan. 1914, L/MIL/3/214, OIOC.
56. Army Department Despatch no. 106 of 1913, 14 Aug. 1913, L/MIL/3/1115, OIOC; and *Summary of the Administration of Lord Hardinge of Penshurst November 1910–March 1916* (Delhi: Superintendent of Government Printing, 1916), p. 88.
57. Haig to Kiggell, 10 Aug. 1911, LHCMA Kiggell mss, 1/19; and Haig to Howell, 5 Oct. 1911, LHCMA Howell mss, 2/35.
58. MacMunn, *Behind the Scenes*, p. 84.
59. 'The General Staff in India', *Army Review*, vol. 2 (1912), pp. 21–2.
60. Major-General A. Hamilton Gordon, 'Share of General Staff Work in Preparation for War at Army Headquarters in India', *Army Review*, vol. 6 (1914), pp. 325, 326.
61. Haig to Kiggell, 31 Aug. 1911, LHCMA Kiggell mss, 1/21.
62. See *A Strategical Study of the Conditions in India and Burma with Special Reference to Internal Defence, Part 1. The More Permanent Conditions* (Simla: General Staff, 1911).
63. See *Proceedings of the Army in India Committee, 1912, vol. IV. Minutes of Evidence including Written Evidence and Index* (Simla: Government Central Branch Press, 1913), p. 1081.
64. Ibid., p. 1045.
65. See *A Study of the Existing Strategical Conditions on the North-West Frontier of India. Prepared by the Chief of the Staff's Division, Army Headquarters, India (Revised 1912)* (Simla: General Staff, 1912).
66. Haig to Kiggell, 27 April 1909, LHCMA Kiggell mss, 1/2.
67. G. de Groot, *Douglas Haig, 1861–1928* (London: Unwin Hyman, 1988), p. 137.
68. MacMunn, *Behind the Scenes*, p. 87.
69. See, for example, *Military Report on the 9th (Secunderabad) Divisional Area* (Simla: General Staff, 1911); and *Military Report on the Indus River System* (Simla: General Staff, 1912).
70. See Major-General H. C. Slater, QMG in India (Intelligence Branch) to Military Department, 17 Jan. 1905, L/MIL/7/7812, OIOC.
71. See *Strategical Epitome of Routes on and Beyond the North West Frontier of India* (Simla: General Staff, 1912).
72. Hamilton Gordon, 'Share of General Staff Work', p. 325.
73. India Army Order no. 282 of 1911, L/MIL/17/5/243, OIOC.
74. General Sir O'Moore Creagh, 'The Army in India and the New Field Service Regulations', *Army Review*, vol. 4 (1913), p. 33.
75. See *Field Service Regulations, Part I. Operations, 1909 (Reprinted with Amendments, 1912)* (London: General Staff, War Office, 1912).
76. Barrow, *Fire of Life*, p. 124.

77. Haig to Kiggell, 22 Oct. 1911, LHCMA Kiggell mss, 1/26.
78. Braithwaite, 'The Staff College', p. 413.
79. Bond, *The Victorian Army*, p. 208; and David Horner, *Blamey: The C-in-C* (St Leonards: Allen & Unwin, 1998), pp. 15–23.
80. *Report of a Conference of Staff Officers held at Agra under the direction of Lieutenant-General Sir Beauchamp Duff, January 1909* (Simla: Government Monotype Press, 1909).
81. See *Report of a Conference held under the direction of the Chief of Staff* (Simla: Government Monotype Press, 1910).
82. *Report of a Staff Tour, 1911, held by the Chief of the General Staff, India* (Simla: Government Monotype Press, 1912).
83. Haig to Kiggell, 13 July 1911, LHCMA Kiggell mss, 1/17.
84. *Recommendations by His Excellency the C-in-C, Army in India Committee 1912–13. Introductions and Annexures (General Staff Branch)* (Simla: Government Central Branch Press, 1914), p. 5.
85. Bond, *The Victorian Army*, pp. 202–3.
86. 'The General Staff in India', *Army Review*, vol. 2 (1912), p. 22.
87. See Bond, *The Victorian Army*, p. 239.
88. Army Department Despatch no. 108 of 1914, 30 July 1914, L/MIL/3/1116, OIOC.
89. MacMunn, *Behind the Scenes*, p. 84.

5: The British Army, its General Staff and the Continental Commitment, 1904–14

1. Edward M. Spiers, *Haldane: An Army Reformer* (Edinburgh: Edinburgh University Press, 1980), p. 22.
2. Samuel R. Williamson, *The Politics of Grand Strategy: Britain and France Prepare for War, 1904–1914* (Cambridge, MA: Harvard University Press, 1969), pp. 60–88.
3. Nicholas d'Ombrain, *War Machinery and High Policy: Defence Administration in Peacetime Britain, 1902–1914* (London: Oxford University Press, 1973); J. McDermott, 'The Revolution in British Military Thinking from the Boer War to the Moroccan Crisis', *Canadian Journal of History*, vol. 9 (1974), reprinted in Paul Kennedy (ed.), *The War Plans of the Great Powers 1880–1914* (Boston: Allen & Unwin, 1979).
4. John Gooch, *The Plans of War: The General Staff and British Military Strategy, c. 1900–1916* (London: Routledge & Kegan Paul, 1974), p. 289.
5. John Gooch (ed.), *The Prospect of War: Studies in British Defence Policy, 1847–1942* (London: Frank Cass, 1981), pp. vii–viii, see also pp 105–12.
6. Spiers, *Haldane*, pp. 81–3, 154.
7. J. E. Tyler, *The British Army and the Continent, 1904–1914* (London: Arnold, 1938), p. 97.
8. Sir Henry Wilson diary, 23 Aug. 1911, Wilson mss, Imperial War Museum, DS MISC/80, reel 4.
9. Gooch, *Plans of War*, pp. 292–5.
10. Keith Wilson, 'Hankey's Appendix: Some Admiralty Maneuvres During and After the Agadir Crisis', *War in History*, vol. 1 (1994), pp 81–97.
11. D'Ombrain, *War Machinery*, p. 259.
12. Avner Offer, *The First World War: An Agrarian Interpretation* (Oxford: Oxford University Press, 1989), pp. 242–3, 291–309: d'Ombrain takes the line that the CID was increasingly preoccupied with technical questions only.
13. Williamson, *Politics of Grand Strategy*, pp. 353–70.
14. Sir Henry Wilson diary, 16 Nov. 1911, Wilson mss, IWM.
15. Dallas D. Irvine, 'The Origin of Capital Staffs', *Journal of Modern History*, vol. 10 (1938), pp. 161–79.
16. Brian Bond, *The Victorian Army and the Staff College, 1854–1914* (London: Eyre Methuen 1972), esp. p. 251.
17. F. Maurice, *War* (London: Macmillan, 1891), p.41; see also Jay Luvaas, *The Education of an Army: British Military Thought, 1815–1940* (London: Cassell, 1965).
18. Ian Beckett, 'The Stanhope Memorandum of 1888: A Reinterpretation', *Bulletin of the Institute of Historical Research*, vol. 57 (1984), pp. 240–7.
19. Tyler, *British Army*, pp. 12–13; also W. S. Hamer, *The British Army: Civil–Military*

Relations, 1885–1905 (London: Oxford University Press, 1970).

20. H. Spenser Wilkinson, *The Brain of an Army* (London: Macmillan, 1890), p. v.

21. Luvaas, *Education of an Army*, p. 275.

22. D. S. Macdiarmid, *The Life of Lieutenant-General Sir James Moncrieff Grierson* (London: Constable, 1923), p. 87.

23. Macdiarmid, *Grierson*, pp. 115, 130–4.

24. Ibid., p. 250, see also pp. 19, 47, 62–3.

25. Ibid., p. 165.

26. Ibid., p. 271, see also p. 82.

27. William Robertson, *From Private to Field Marshal* (London: Constable, 1921), p. 132. Obviously, this is not a contemporary reference, but see his observations in a lecture of 1913, Robertson papers, LHCMA 1/3/5.

28. 'Essay for G. F. R Henderson', 1898, p.6, Robertson papers, LHCMA 1/2/1.

29. Report by Robertson, submitted by Sir William Nicholson to the C-in-C, 11 Nov. 1902, pp. 3, 9, Robertson papers, LHCMA 1/2/4.

30. J. M. Grierson, 'Memorandum upon the military forces required for over-sea warfare', 4 January 1906, Robertson papers, LHCMA 1/2/6.

31. 'The true standard of our military needs', *c.* 1906, Robertson papers, LHCMA 1/2/9.

32. Robertson, *From Private to Field Marshal*, pp. 139–40.

33. D'Ombrain, *War Machinery*, pp. 89–94, 149–50.

34. D'Ombrain, *War Machinery*, pp. 97–102.

35. Alexander Graham Marshall, 'Dar al-Harb: the Russian General Staff and the Asiatic Frontier, 1860–1917', Glasgow University PhD thesis, 2001.

36. G. P. Gooch and Harold Temperley (eds), *British Documents on the Origins of the War, 1898–1914*, 11 vols (London: HMSO), vol. 4, p. 127.

37. Tyler, *British Army*, p. 140; see also G. J. De Groot, *Douglas Haig, 1861–1928* (London: Unwin Hyman, 1982), pp. 136–7.

38. This paragraph has benefited from my supervision of the Glasgow University MPhil. thesis of Ben Gillon. See de Groot, *Haig*, pp. 133–9; George MacMunn, *Behind the Scenes in Many Wars* (London: John Murray, 1930), pp. 81–7; F. J. Moberly, *Military Operations: The Campaign in Mesopotamia* (4 vols, London: HMSO, 1923–7), vol. 1, p. 73.

39. This paragraph draws on the painstaking but unpublished work of Corinne Mahaffey plotting the movement of infantry battalions between 1870 and 1914.

40. William Robertson, *Soldiers and Statesmen, 1914–1918*, 2 vols (London: Cassell, 1926); Hew Strachan, '"The Real War": Liddell Hart, Cruttwell and Falls', in Brian Bond (ed.), *The First World War and British Military History* (Oxford: Oxford University Press, 1991), p. 50.

41. Shelford Bidwell and Dominick Graham, *Fire-Power: British Army Weapons and Theories of War, 1904–1945* (London: Allen & Unwin, 1982), esp. pp. 1–4.

42. J. M. Grierson, 'Memorandum upon the military forces required for over-sea warfare', 4 Jan. 1906, Robertson papers, LHCMA 1/2/6, pp. 7, 12.

43. Sir Henry Wilson diary, 14 Oct. 1904, IWM DS, MISC/80, reel 3.

44. D' Ombrain, *War Machinery*, pp. 89–94, 149–50.

45. Gooch, *Plans of War*, pp. 80–2, 99–103.

46. 'Report on a conference of General Staff officers at the Staff College', 21 January 1909, pp. 69–70, Haig papers, National Library of Scotland (NLS), Acc 3155/81.

47. General Staff, War Office, *Field Service Regulations, Part II: Organization and Administration* (London: HMS0, 1909), pp. 38–41.

48. Desmond Chapman-Huston and Owen Rutter, *General Sir John Cowans, G.C.B.: The Quartermaster-General of the Great War*, 2 vols. (London: Hutchinson, 1924), vol. 1, pp. 250–8, 263–74; see also Tyler, *British Army*, p. 149.

49. Ian Malcolm Brown, *British Logistics on the Western Front, 1914–1919* (Westport, CT: Praeger, 1998), pp. 41–75; see also Roberston, *From Private to Field Marshal*, pp. 197–201.

50. 'Report on a staff tour held by the Chief of the General Staff, 26th to 30th Oct. 1908', pp. 5, 9, Haig papers, NLS Acc 3155/77.

51. 'Report on a conference of General Staff officers at the Staff College', 10 Jan. 1908, p. 36, Haig papers, NLS Acc 3155/81.

52. Hubert Foster, *Organization: How Armies are Formed for War* (London: Hugh Rees, 1911), p. 246.

53. Gooch, *Plans of War*, pp. 98–9, 107–8.
54. 'Report on a conference of General Staff officers at the Staff College', 8 Jan. 1908, pp. 17, 25, Haig papers, NLS Acc 3 155/81.
55. Gooch, *Prospect of War*, pp. 108–9; also Andrew Simpson, 'The Operational Role of British Corps Command on the Western Front, 1914–18', London University PhD thesis, 2001, pp. 20–3.
56. 'Report on a conference of General Staff officers at the Staff College', 8 Jan. 1908, p. 25, Haig papers, NLS Acc 3155/81.
57. Ibid., 7 Jan. 1908, pp. 5–13.
58. Ibid., 10 Jan. 1908, p. 31.
59. Based on the research of Corinne Mahaffey.
60. Major-General E. S. May in 'Report of a conference of General Staff officers at the Staff College', 9 Jan. 1911, p. 7, Haig papers, NLS Acc 3155/81.
61. 'Remarks on a visit to battlefields 1912', Robertson papers, LHCMA, 1/2/12; see also 'Notes on strategy by Colonel Henderson Campbell for use of students at the Staff College', Robertson papers, LHCMA, 1/2/10.
62. 'Report of a conference of General Staff officers', 7 Jan. 1908, p. 5, and 10 Jan. 1908, p. 46, Haig papers, NLS, Acc 3 155/81.
63. John I. Alger, *Quest for Victory: The History of the Principles of War* (Westport, CT: Greenwood, 1982).
64. Albert Palazzo, *Seeking Victory on the Western Front: The British Army and Chemical Warfare in World War I* (Lincoln, NE: University of Nebraska Press, 2000), pp. 17–20.
65. De Groot, *Haig*, p. 136.
66. Palazzo, *Seeking Victory*, pp. 8–10, 234; Simpson, 'The Operational Role of British Corps Command', pp. 8–9, 23–7.
67. Grierson, 'Memorandum upon the military forces required for over-sea warfare', 4 Jan. 1906, Robertson papers, LHCMA, 1/2/6, p. 7.
68. 'The true standard of our military needs', *c*. 1906, Robertson papers, LHCMA, 1/2/9.
69. Sir Henry Wilson diary, 30 Dec. 1905 and 21 April 1905, IWM, DS/MISC/80, reel 3.
70. Sir Henry Wilson diary, 12 Sept. 1911, reel 4.
71. Tyler, *British Army*, pp. 115, 119–22, 176–7.
72. Hew Strachan, 'The Battle of the Somme and British Strategy', *Journal of Strategic Studies*, vol. 21 (1998), pp. 79–95.

6: *The General Staff and the Paradoxes of Continental War*

1. For discussion of imperial defence issues see J. Gooch, *The Plans of War, c.1900–16* (London, Routledge, 1974); M. Howard, *The Continental Commitment: The Dilemma of British Defence Policy in the Era of Two World Wars* (Harmondsworth: Penguin, 1974), pp. 9–30.
2. Field-Marshal Viscount French of Ypres, *1914* (London: Constable, 1919), p. 215.
3. Howard, *Continental Commitment*, p. 112.
4. S. R. Williamson, *The Politics of Grand Strategy: Britain and France Prepare for War, 1904–14* (Cambridge, MA: Harvard University Press, 1969), p. 20.
5. K. M. Wilson, *The Policy of the Entente: Essays on the Determinants of British Foreign Policy, 1904–1914* (Cambridge: Cambridge University Press, 1985).
6. J. McDermott, 'The Revolution in British Military Planning from the Boer War to the Moroccan Crisis', in P. M. Kennedy (ed.), *The War Plans of the Great Powers, 1880–1914* (London: Allen & Unwin, 1979), pp. 99–117.
7. 'Records of a Strategic Wargame, 1905', Directorate of Military Operations, General Staff, War Office: Reports and Miscellaneous Papers, Public Record Office, Kew PRO WO (War Office) 33/364.
8. Ibid., p. 47.
9. Ibid., pp. 48, 81.
10. Clarke to Balfour, 17 Aug. 1905, quoted in McDermott, 'The Revolution', pp. 108–9.
11. Drake to Callwell, 30 Sept. 1905, War Office: Directorate of Military Operations and Intelligence, PRO WO 106/46/E2/2.
12. W. J. Philpott, 'British Military Strategy on the Western Front: Independence or Alliance, 1904–1918', D. Phil. thesis, Oxford University, 1991, pp. 31–2.

13. 'Notes of conferences held at Whitehall Gardens', 19 December 1905 and 6, 12 and 19 January 1906, Cabinet Office: CID minutes, PRO CAB (Cabinet) 2/1.
14. W. J. Philpott, 'British Military Strategy', pp. 20–31.
15. Grey to Tweedmouth, 16 Jan. 1906, quoted in J. W. Coogan and P. F. Coogan, 'The British Cabinet and the Anglo-French Staff Talks: Who Knew What and When Did He Know It?', *Journal of British Studies*, vol. 24 (1985), pp. 110–31, p. 112. For the Foreign Office's formal instructions on the staff talks see Lord Sanderson to Grierson, 15 Jan. 1906, in G. P. Gooch and H. Temperley, *British Documents on the Origins of the War, 1898–1914, Vol. 3. The Testing of the Entente, 1904–6* (London: HMSO, 1928), pp. 176–7.
16. Minute by Lyttelton, 26 July 1907, Service Historique de l'Armée de Terre, Vincennes, SHAT, 7N1782.
17. Huguet to Brun, 4 Nov. 1908, ibid.
18. See for example, Wilson diary, 23 March, 9, 13 and 15 May and 10 June 1912, Field-Marshal Sir Henry Wilson papers, Imperial War Museum, London.
19. For the political problems associated with the early staff talks see Coogan and Coogan, 'The British Cabinet', *passim*.
20. For a thorough introduction to the tensions in civil–military relations, and the sensitive nature of staff talks, before the Second World War see Brian Bond, *British Military Policy Between the Two World Wars* (Oxford: Clarendon, 1980), pp. 214–311.
21. 'Rapport du Chef de Battalion Ferrere du 72e au sujet d'un voyage en Angleterre', 22 June 1909, SHAT, 7N1242.
22. 'Notices sur personages: notice sur le Général Grierson', 1913, SHAT, 7N1241; Ministre de la Guerre to Huguet, 19 Sept. 1908, SHAT, 7N1236.
23. See for example 'Effectifs que l'Angleterre serait susceptible de mobiliser et de débarquer sur le continent, dans le cas d'une guerre entre la France et l'Allemagne', Huguet to Ministre de la Guerre, 18 Nov. 1905, SHAT, 7N1222; Huguet to Ministre de la Guerre, 29 July 1909, SHAT, 7N1225.
24. De la Panouse to Ministre de la Guerre, 19 Sept. 1914, SHAT, 7N1228.
25. 'Rapport sur manoeuvres anglaises en 1910', by Capitaine le Merre, 5 Oct. 1910, SHAT, 7N1243.
26. See correspondence on visits to foreign manoeuvres in SHAT, 7N1236; Huguet to Ministre de la Guerre, 6 Sept. 1908 and 12 May 1909, SHAT, 7N1224.
27. 'Notre collaboration avec l'Etat Major Général anglais, est aussi sincère d'un côté que de l'autre': 'Grandes manoeuvres de l'armée anglais en 1912', Panouse to Ministre de la Guerre, 13 Oct. 1912, SHAT, 7N1227.
28. Sir Henry Wilson diary, 14 to 16 March 1912, Wilson papers.
29. 'Prochaines mutations dans le haut commandement de l'armée anglais', Huguet to Ministre de la Guerre, 13 May 1911, SHAT, 7N1226/2.
30. Panouse to Ministre de la Guerre, 1 April 1914, SHAT, 7N1228.
31. Philpott, 'British Military Strategy', pp. 59–62.
32. Sir Henry Wilson diary, 11 March 1913, Wilson papers.
33. Ommaney to Wilson, 3 April 1913, Wilson papers, 3/7.
34. Asquith to Venetia Stanley, 2 Aug. 1914, in M. and E. Brock (eds), *H. H. Asquith: Letters to Venetia Stanley* (Oxford: Oxford University Press, 1982), p. 146.
35. Indeed this option was immediately rejected at the War Council which met to determine Britain's military strategy when war broke out. 'Secretary's Notes of a War Council held at 10 Downing Street, 5 August 1914', Cabinet Office: Cabinet Papers, 1915–16, PRO CAB 42/1/2; W. J. Philpott, *Anglo-French Relations and Strategy on the Western Front, 1914–1918* (London: Macmillan, 1996), pp. 7–9.
36. B. Ash, *The Lost Dictator: Field Marshal Sir Henry Wilson* (London: Cassell, 1968), p. 71. Further, Ash has plausibly suggested (p. 80) that on becoming DMO Wilson tried to create a 'school of thought in national and international affairs'.
37. 'Rapport du Chef de Battalion Ferrere du 72e au sujet d'un voyage en Angleterre', 22 June 1909, SHAT, 7N1242. For examples of the Staff College exercises see 'Senior Division, 1910: Belgian Scheme', in 'Wilson-Foch Scheme: Expeditionary Force for France', PRO WO 106/49c. C. E. Callwell, *Field Marshal Sir Henry Wilson: His Life and Diaries*, 2 vols (London: Cassell, 1927), vol. I, pp. 72–3.
38. 'Note sur la report du Lieutenant Staehling', c. Feb. 1914, SHAT, 7N1243.
39. Panouse to Chef de l'Etat Major de l'Armée, 31 July 1914, SHAT, 7N1228. See also Foch

to Ministre de la Guerre, 28 Oct. 1912, and 2nd Bureau analysis of 'Grandes Manoeuvres Anglaises, 1913', SHAT, 7N1243.

40. Callwell, *Sir Henry Wilson*, vol. I, pp. 77–80.

41. Williamson, *The Politics of Grand Strategy*, pp. 174–8.

42. Pellé to Ministre de la Guerre, 16 Jan. 1911, [?] to Pellé, 26 Jan. 1911, and 'Conversation avec le Général Wilson', Pellé to Ministre de la Guerre, 7 March 1911, SHAT, 7N1110.

43. Sir Henry Wilson diary, 6 Dec. 1910, Wilson papers.

44. '[Wilson] est un homme jeune ... actif, à l'esprit vif et ouvert, et dont l'arrivée au War Office, dans le poste importante qu'il va occuper, ne peut avoir, à notre pointe de vue spécial, que de très heureuses conséquences.' 'Prochaine mutations dans le haut commandement de l'armée anglaise', Huguet to Ministre de la Guerre, 24 June 1910, SHAT, 7N1226.

45. 'Modifications proposées au plan de transport de l'armée W', Huguet to de Ladebat, 4 Nov. 1910, SHAT, 7N1782; Sir Henry Wilson diary, Sept. to Dec. 1910, *passim*, Wilson papers.

46. K. M. Wilson, 'The War Office, Churchill and the Belgian Option: August to December 1911', *Bulletin of the Institute of Historical Research*, vol. 122 (1977), pp. 218–28.

47. Sir Henry Wilson diary, April–June 1912, *passim*, Wilson papers.

48. However, sensitive about the implications of these contacts, Haldane appears to have vetoed a proposed meeting between Grierson and the French Chief of Staff, General Brun, when the former was on personal business in Paris. Huguet to Brun, 23 and 24 Feb. 1906, SHAT, 7N1782.

49. 'Rapport du Général Michel sur le séjour de la mission français en Angleterre, du 24 au 27 Juin 1907', SHAT, 7N672; 'Visite en Angleterre de la mission militaire français', by Huguet, 3 July 1907, SHAT, 7N1223.

50. Howard, *Continental Commitment*, pp. 116–18.

51. 'Staff conversations with France and Belgium', draft of memorandum by the Chiefs of Staff, 21 Jan. 1938, Cabinet Office: Chiefs of Staff Minutes and Memoranda, PRO CAB 53/35; Howard, *Continental Commitment*, pp. 119–20.

52. Pownall diary, 30 March 1936, Brian Bond (ed.), *Chief of Staff: The Diaries of Lieutenant-General Sir Henry Pownall*, 2 vols (London: Leo Cooper, 1972), vol. I, 1933–40, p.107.

53. Pownall diary, 30 March and 3 April 1936, ibid., pp. 107–8.

54. Bond, *British Military Policy*, pp. 290–2. Pownall diary, 27 Jan. 1936 and 1 Jan. to 12 Dec. 1938, *passim*, Bond, *Chief of Staff*, pp. 99, 123–74.

55. Pownall diary, 14 Nov. 1938, Bond, *Chief of Staff*, p. 170.

56. Bond, *British Military Policy*, pp. 266, 271–4.

57. Pownall diary, 14 March and 4 April 1939, Bond, *Chief of Staff*, pp. 139–42.

58. Bond, *British Military Policy*, pp. 319–20.

59. See E. M. Spiers, *Haldane: An Army Reformer* (Edinburgh: Edinburgh University Press, 1980).

60. Williamson, *The Politics of Grand Strategy*, p. 169.

61. 'Value of an alliance with the United Kingdom', memorandum by Ewart, 8 March 1909, PRO WO 106/45/E1/1.

62. 'War with Germany in defence of Belgian neutrality', by Grant Duff, 4 Jan. 1907, PRO WO 106/46/E2/8.

63. 'Memorandum on policy and the army', by Wilson, 1 Jan. 1913, Wilson papers.

64. 'La service obligatoire en Angleterre: Discussion à la Chambre des Lords', Huguet to Ministre de la Guerre, 20 July 1909, SHAT, 7N1225.

65. Callwell, *Field Marshal Sir Henry Wilson*, vol. I, pp. 78–9.

66. Philpott, *Anglo-French Relations and Strategy*, p. 11. In their 1910 manoeuvres the French included two supporting British divisions, perhaps to impress Wilson who was Foch's guest. Sir Henry Wilson diary, 3 Aug. 1910, Wilson papers.

67. Huguet to de Ladebat, 23 Mar. 1911 and 'Memorandum de la conference de 20 Juillet 1911', SHAT, 7N1782.

68. 'Projet de création d'un Etat-Major Général de l'Empire' and 'L'année 1909 en Angleterre au point de vue militaire', Huguet to Ministre de la Guerre, 24 Feb. 1909 and 15 Jan. 1910, SHAT, 7N1225.

69. See for example 'L'Armée territoriale anglaise' and 'Au sujet de l'Armée territoriale anglaise', Panouse to Ministre de la Guerre, 19 Aug. and 26 Oct. 1912, SHAT, 7N1227.

70. 'La cooperation militaire anglaise: hypothèse d'une guerre franco–allemand', Capitaine le

Merre, 2nd Bureau, 15 May 1912, SHAT, 7N1227, and revised copy, June 1914, SHAT, 7N1243.

71. Pownall diary, 15 April 1936, Bond, *Chief of Staff*, p. 109.
72. For an overview of mutual intelligence assessments, see M. S. Alexander and W. J. Philpott, 'The Entente Cordiale and the Next War: Anglo-French Views on Future Military Co-operation, 1928–1939', in M. S. Alexander (ed.), *Knowing Your Friends: Intelligence Inside Alliances and Coalitions from 1914 to the Cold War* (Ilford: Frank Cass, 1998), pp. 53–84.
73. 'Note sur l'appui militaire éventuel de la Grande Bretagne', 2 May 1935, SHAT, 7N2840/1.
74. 'Note sur les accords d'Etat-Major dont la conclusion serait à rechercher par la France', 4 April 1938, SHAT, 2N227/2.
75. Pownall diary, 1 Jan. 1938, Bond, *Chief of Staff*, p. 123.
76. Bond, *British Military Policy*, pp. 312–29, *passim*.
77. 'Situation en materiel d'armament moderne', by Lelong, 26 Jan. 1939, SHAT, 7N2816.
78. Bond, *British Military Policy*, p. 317.
79. 'Information du Général: remarques realtives aux conclusions du Conseil Suprême Interallié du 12 Septembre 1939', 13 Sept. 1939, Daladier Papers, Archives Nationales, Paris, 3DA2/2b.
80. 'Records of a strategic wargame, 1905', PRO WO 33/364.
81. 'Notes of conferences held at Whitehall Gardens', 19 Dec. 1905, PRO, CAB 2/1.
82. Ibid., 19 Dec. 1905 and 19 Jan. 1906; W. J. Philpott, 'The Strategic Ideas of Sir John French', *Journal of Strategic Studies*, vol. 12 (1989), pp. 458–78.
83. 'Memorandum on the military forces required for over-sea warfare', by Grierson, 4 Jan. 1906, PRO, WO 106/44/E1/7; Williamson, *The Politics of Grand Strategy*, pp. 84–5.
84. 'Report of the Sub-Committee on the Military Requirements of the Empire (Europe)', 24 July 1909, Cabinet Office: Committee of Imperial Defence Ad-hoc Sub-Committees of Enquiry, Proceedings and Memoranda, PRO CAB 16/5; Philpott 'British Military Strategy', pp. 34–43.
85. 'Report of the Sub-Committee on the Military Requirements of the Empire', PRO CAB 16/5.
86. Sir Henry Wilson diary, 9 March 1911, Wilson papers.
87. CID 'Minutes of the 114th meeting', 23 Aug. 1911, PRO CAB 2/2.
88. K. M. Wilson, *The Policy of the Entente*, pp. 128–34.
89. K. M. Wilson, 'The War Office, Churchill and the Belgian Option', *passim*.
90. Sir Henry Wilson diary, 15 Sept. 1911, Wilson papers.
91. 'Memorandum on policy and the army', by Wilson, 1 Jan. 1913, Wilson papers, 3/7.
92. Sir Henry Wilson diary, 7 April 1912, Wilson papers.
93. 'Appreciation of the political and military situation in Europe', by Wilson, 20 Sept. 1911, Wilson papers, 3/6.
94. K. M. Wilson, 'The War Office, Churchill and the Belgian Option', *passim*; Philpott, 'British Military Strategy', pp. 50–64, *passim*.
95. Esher journal, 4 Oct. 1911, Esher papers, Churchill College, Cambridge; Philpott, 'British Military Strategy', pp. 59–63.
96. See for example Sir Henry Wilson diary, 17 Nov. 1912, Wilson papers.
97. Huguet to Dubail, 18 Oct. 1911, SHAT, 7N1782; Sir Henry Wilson diary 25 Nov. 1912, Wilson papers.
98. Sir G. T. M. Bridges, *Alarms and Excursions* (London: Longmans, Green, 1938), p. 62.
99. Sir Henry Wilson diary, 7 April 1912, Wilson papers.
100. Philpott, 'British Military Strategy', pp. 63–4.
101. Sir Henry Wilson diary, 6 Dec. 1912, Wilson papers.
102. 'Report on the opening of the war', CID Historical Section, 1 Nov. 1914, Cabinet Office: Miscellaneous Cabinet Papers, PRO CAB 1/10.
103. 'Secretary's notes of a War Council … 5 August 1914', PRO CAB 42/1/2.
104. Sir Henry Wilson diary, 5 to 12 Aug. 1914, Wilson papers; Philpott, *Anglo-French Relations and Strategy*, pp. 7–10.
105. Bond, *British Military Policy*, pp. 209–10.
106. Howard, *Continental Commitment*, p. 108.
107. Chiefs of Staff Committee, minutes of the 125th meeting, 4 May 1934, PRO CAB 53/4; Bond, *British Military Policy*, pp. 202–4, 228.
108. Bond, *British Military Policy*, pp. 228–30.
109. Ibid., pp. 229–32.

110. Pownall diary, 25 Feb. 1938, Bond, *Chief of Staff*, p. 136.
111. Pownall diary, 18 Sept. 1939, Bond, *Chief of Staff*, p. 235.
112. Memorandum by Ommaney, enclosed with 'Minute to CIGS reporting progress of scheme no. E7', April 1913, Wilson papers, 3/8.

7: *The Australians at Pozières: Command and Control on the Somme, 1916*

1. I would like to thank Helen McCartney and Niall Barr for reading and commenting on this piece, and the Australian Army for awarding me a Fellowship that enabled me to undertake archival work in Australia.
2. P. Dennis *et al., The Oxford Companion to Australian Military History* (Melbourne, Oxford University Press, 1995), p. 655.
3. J. T. Hutton diary, 27, 28, 31 July 1916, MML mss 1138, M[itchell] L[ibrary], S[ydney]. See also W. V. Wright diary, 22, 23 July 1916, ML mss 1012, MLS.
4. Bean to Edmonds, 18 April 1934, Bean papers, 3 DRL 7953 item x34, A[ustralian] W[ar] M[emorial].
5. J. Gellibrand to W. Gellibrand, 12 Oct. 1916, 3 DRL 6541 item 2, AWM.
6. Quoted in G. D. Sheffield, '"One Vast Australian Cemetery": The Battle for Pozières, July 1916', *Wartime: Official Magazine of the Australian War Memorial*, vol. 7 (Spring 1999), p. 22.
7. G. B. Hughes, diary, 26 July 1916, ML mss 3923, MLS.
8. *The Oh Pip*, Somme issue, A2771, MLS.
9. Dennis, *Oxford Companion*, p. 655. See also P. Stanley, 'Gallipoli and Pozières: A Legend and a Memorial', *Australian Foreign Affairs Record*, vol. 56, part 4 (April 1985), pp. 285–7.
10. For narratives of the fighting, see C. E. W. Bean, *The Official History of Australia in the War of 1914–1918*, 6 vols (St Lucia: University of Queensland Press, 1982; originally published 1929), vol. 3, *The AIF in France, 1916*, pp. 448–862; W. Miles, *Military Operations France and Belgium, 1916*, 2 vols (London: Macmillan, 1938), vol. I, pp. 115–16, 141–56, 208–28, 282–5; P. Charlton, *Australians on the Somme: Pozières, 1916* (London: Leo Cooper, 1986).
11. J. Monash, *The Australian Victories in France in 1918* (London: Imperial War Museum, 1993, first published 1920), p. 56.
12. J. Grey, *A Military History of Australia* (Cambridge: Cambridge University Press, 1990), pp. 80–1; C. Coulthard-Clark, 'Formation of the Australian Armed Services, 1901–14', in M. McKernnan and M. Browne, *Australia: Two Centuries of War and Peace* (Australian War Memorial in association with Allen & Unwin, Australia, 1988), pp. 128–30.
13. P. Sadler, *The Paladin: A Life of Major-General Sir John Gellibrand* (Melbourne: Oxford University Press, 2000), p. 56.
14. Biographical details are drawn, unless otherwise stated, from Dennis, *Oxford Companion*.
15. C. D. Coulthard-Clark, *A Heritage of Spirit: A Biography of Major-General Sir William Throsby Bridges* (Melbourne: Melbourne University Press, 1979), p. 116.
16. Throughout this chapter the functional title 'chief of staff' is used in preference to more formal titles such as 'Brigadier-General General Staff'.
17. For Gough's views on the desirability of using Australians on the staffs of British formations, see Malcolm to Birdwood, 17 May 1917, AWM 25 515/1, AWM.
18. Coulthard-Clark, *Heritage*, p. 116; P. A. Pedersen, *Monash as Military Commander* (Melbourne: Melbourne University Press, 1992, first published 1985), pp. 27–8.
19. Pedersen, *Monash*, pp. 37–8.
20. For these topics, see Brian Bond, *The Victorian Army and the Staff College, 1854–1914* (London: Eyre Methuen, 1972); Brian Holden Reid, *War Studies at the Staff College, 1890–1930* (Camberley: Strategic and Combat Studies Institute, 1992).
21. Tim Travers, *The Killing Ground: The British Army, the Western Front and the Emergence of Modern Warfare, 1900–1918* (London: Allen & Unwin, 1987), pp. xxi, 3–36.
22. Bean notebook, Feb.–March 1916, pp. 49, 54, 3 DRL 606 item 40(2), AWM.
23. But see E. M. Andrews, *The ANZAC Illusion: Anglo–Australian Relations During World War I* (Cambridge: Cambridge University Press, 1993), p. 113.
24. Birdwood to Sir R. Munro-Ferguson (Governor-General), 3 Oct. 1915, 3 DRL 3376 item

31, AWM; same to same, 23 Jan., 18 May 1916, Birdwood papers, 3 DRL 3376 item 32, AWM.

25. J. M. Bourne, 'The BEF's Generals on 29 September 1918: An Empirical Portrait with Some British and Australian Comparisons', in P. Dennis and J. Grey (eds), *1918: Defining Victory* (Canberra: Army History Unit, 1999), p. 104.

26. Birdwood to Munro-Ferguson, 31 Dec. 1916, Birdwood papers, 3 DRL 3376 item 32, AWM. For Legge, see C. D. Coulthard-Clark, *No Australian Need Apply: The Troubled Career of Lieutenant-General Gordon Legge* (Sydney: Allen & Unwin, 1988).

27. Sadler, *Paladin*, pp. 54–6.

28. P. A. Pedersen, 'General Sir John Monash: Corps Commander on the Western Front', in D. M. Horner (ed.), *The Commanders: Australian Military Leadership in the Twentieth Century* (Sydney: Allen & Unwin, 1984), p. 103.

29. Charlton, *Australians on the Somme*, p. 139.

30. Blamey asserted that the plan was 'chiefly mine'. See D. Horner, *Blamey: The Commander-in-Chief* (St Leonards, NSW: Allen & Unwin, 1998), pp. 43–5 for a discussion of this claim, and some criticism of 1st Australian Division's staff work.

31. Bean, *AIF*, vol. 3, pp. 452–4. See OA 256, 16 July 1916, in war diary of Reserve Army General Staff, WO 95/518, P[ublic] R[ecord] O[ffice]. This memorandum, on the importance of infantry keeping close to the artillery barrage, was sent from GHQ to Reserve Army and subsequently circulated. Bean seems to refer to it in *AIF*, p. 453.

32. Reports on lessons were also sent to Fourth Army, arriving on 19 July: File 47, 'Notes on Somme', Montgomery-Massingberd papers, L[iddell] H[art] C[entre] for M[ilitary] A[rchives].

33. Everard Wyrall, *The History of the 19th Division* (London: Arnold, nd), p. 42.

34. C. T. Atkinson, *The Seventh Division* (London: John Murray, 1927), pp. 276–7.

35. Appx. 7 & 9 to July 1916, war diary, 1st Australian Division, WO 95/3156, PRO.

36. White to Walker, 28 July 1916, AWM 27 354/35, AWM. For the learning of this lesson, see document on lessons learned, nd but *c.* June 1917, Gellibrand papers, 3 DRL 1473 item 101a, AWM.

37. Appx. 2 to August 1916, war diary, GS, 1st Australian Division, WO 95/3156, PRO.

38. See Files 47 and 48, 'Notes on Somme', Montgomery-Massingberd papers, LHCMA. This consists of a number of reports from divisions and corps, based in turn on material from subordinate units, solicited by Fourth Army while the battle was in progress. Similar material was gathered by Fifth Army at the end of the Somme: WO 158/344, PRO.

39. 'Report on minor enterprise …' issued by 2nd Aus. Div., 7 June 1916; 'Notes on artillery' nd but *c.* June 1916; no. S 309, issued by HQ I ANZAC 20 June 1916, all in Monash papers, 3 DRL 2316-22, AWM.

40. Issued by HQ 4th Australian Division on 14 August 1916, Monash papers, 3 DRL 2316-22, AWM.

41. I ANZAC Corps General Staff Circular no. 38, 16 Dec. 1916, Monash papers, 3 DRL 2316-23, AWM.

42. John Lee, 'Some Lessons of the Somme: The British Infantry in 1917', in Brian Bond *et al.*, *'Look to Your Front': Studies in the First World War* (Staplehurst: Spellmount, 1999), pp. 79–87.

43. R. Prior and T. Wilson, *Command on the Western Front* (Oxford: Blackwell, 1992).

44. Miles, *Military Operations France and Belgium, Vol. 2*, p. 142; 21 July 1916, war diary, I ANZAC Corps General Staff, WO95/980, PRO.

45. Appx. 19 [*sic*] to July 1916, war diary of 1 Aus. Div., WO 95/3156, PRO.

46. Bean, *AIF*, vol. 3, p. 491.

47. Appx. 19 to July 1916, war diary of 1st Aus. Div, WO95/3156, PRO.

48. Miles, *Military Operations*, vol. 2, p. 142.

49. Bean, *AIF*, vol. 3, pp. 458–9.

50. Rawlinson diary, 16 July 1916, CAC 1/5, C[hurchill] C[ollege] C[ambridge].

51. Bean, *AIF*, vol. 3, pp. 460–1, 467; Miles, *Military Operations*, vol. 2, pp. 97–8; H. A. Jones, *The War in the Air*, 6 vols (Oxford: Clarendon, 1922–37), vol. II (1928), p. 232.

52. X Corps to Reserve Army, 18 July 1916, AWM 45 [35/7], AWM.

53. Miles, *Military Operations*, vol. II, p. 112; Prior and Wilson, *Command*, p. 212; Jones, *War in Air*, vol. 2, p. 237.

54. Prior and Wilson, *Command*, pp. 211–12.
55. Wyrall, *19th Division*, p. 54; Miles, *Military Operations*, vol. 2, p. 138.
56. Diary, 29 July 1916, Philip Howell papers, 6/2/161, LHCMA.
57. 29 July, war diary of GS, 2 Aus. Div., WO 95/3254, PRO.
58. H. V. Cox, diary, 18, 25, 31 July, 5, 11 Aug. 1916, 1 DRL 0221, AWM.
59. C. E. W. Bean, *Two Men I Knew* (Sydney, NSW: Angus & Robertson, 1957), p. 134.
60. Walker to Bean, 13 Aug. 1928 (quoting diary entry of 18 July 1916); Bean papers, 3 DRL, 7953, item 34, AWM.
61. See note 60 and Bean, *Two Men*, p. 134; P. A. Pedersen, 'The AIF on the Western Front: The Role of Training and Command', in McKernan and Browne, *Two Centuries*, p. 173; T. H. E. Travers, 'From Surafend to Gough: Charles Bean, James Edmonds, and the Making of the Australian Official History', *J[ournal] of the A[ustralian] W[ar] M[emorial]*, vol. 27 (Oct. 1995), p. 19.
62. Edmonds to Bean, 16 Nov. 1927, enclosing 'General Sir Hubert Gough's remarks', Bean papers, 3 DRL 7953, item 34, AWM.
63. See G. D. Sheffield, 'Hubert Gough as an Army Commander on the Somme', in G. D. Sheffield and D. Todman (eds), *Command and Control on the Western Front: The British Army's Experience, 1914–18* (Staplehurst: Spellmount, forthcoming); and I. F. W. Beckett, 'Hubert Gough, Neill Malcolm and Command on the Western Front', in Bond *et al.*, *Look To Your Front*, pp. 1–12.
64. I am grateful to Dr Simpson for sharing the fruits of his research with me. See Andrew Simpson, 'The Operational Role of British Corps Command on the Western Front, 1914–18', PhD thesis, London University, 2001.
65. S. G. 43/0/5, 5 Oct. 1916, WO95/518, PRO.
66. Travers, *Killing Ground*, pp. 168, 189.
67. For details see Sheffield, 'Hubert Gough'.
68. Memo., Malcolm to Corps, 16 Nov. 1916, A&Q Reserve Army, WO95/523, PRO.
69. Anthony Farrar-Hockley, *Goughie* (London: Hart-Davies, McGibbon, 1975), p. 188.
70. Bean, *AIF*, vol. 3, p. 530. For speculation on the form that Gough's directives took, see Bean to Edmonds, 28 April 1928, AWM38 3 DRL 7953 item 34, AWM.
71. Pedersen, 'AIF on the Western Front', p. 174.
72. J. D. Millar, 'A Study in the Limitations of Command: General Sir William Birdwood and the AIF, 1914–1918', PhD thesis, University of New South Wales, 1993, p. 143.
73. Birdwood to 'Eddy' [i.e. Derby], 15 Aug. 1916, Birdwood papers, 3 DRL 3376 item 16; Birdwood to Munro-Ferguson, 15 Aug. 1916, 3 DRL 3376 item 32, both AWM.
74. Bean, *AIF*, vol. 3, p. 483.
75. Diary, 29 July 1916, Philip Howell papers, 6/2/161, LHCMA.
76. Legge to Bean, 25 May 1934, 3 DRL 7953 item x34, AWM. Legge appears to be referring to the August fighting.
77. Gellibrand, however, believed that Legge preferred to attack rather than take casualties while remaining static in the trenches. Gellibrand to Bean, 26 Jan. 1934, 3 DRL 7953 item x34, AWM.
78. Coulthard-Clark, *No Australian*, pp. 147–8; Charlton, *Australians on the Somme*, pp. 174–8, 189.
79. L. Robson, 'C. E. W. Bean: A Review Article', *JAWM*, no. 4 (April 1984), p. 56; Bean, *Two Men*, p. xi.
80. Coulthard-Clark, *No Australian*, pp. 147–8.
81. Coulthard-Clark, *No Australian*, pp. 159–61; Pedersen, 'AIF on the Western Front', p. 174.
82. For further examples of Gough's pressure on the Australians for hasty action, see diary, 1, 5 Aug. 1916, Philip Howell papers, 6/2/161, LHCMA.
83. Bean to Edmonds, 18 April 1934, 3 DRL 7953 item x34, AWM; Sadler, *Paladin*, p. 93.
84. Lieutenant B. Lawrence, letter, Nov. 1916, in I. Fletcher (ed.), *Letters from the Front* (Tunbridge Wells: Parapress, 1993).
85. Birdwood to Hutton, 30 Sept. 1916, Sir E. Hutton papers, BL Add mss 50 089, vol. XII, excerpt in White papers, PR 85/83, AWM.
86. White to wife, 24 April, 22 July, 21 Sept. 1916; White to Gellibrand, 8 June 1917; all quoted in Rosemary Derham, *The Silence Ruse: Escape from Gallipoli* (Armadale, NSW: Cliffe, 1998), pp. 44, 49, 41, 53.
87. E. M. Andrews, 'Bean and Bullecourt: Weaknesses and Strengths of the Official History

of Australia in the First World War', *Revue Internationale d'Histoire Militaire*, no. 72 (Canberra: Australian Commission for Military History, 1990), pp. 25–47.

88. See for example diary, 8 Aug. 1916, Howell papers, 6/2/161, LHCMA; Sadler, *Paladin*, p. 95.
89. Rawlinson diary, 11, 24 Dec. 1916, 13 Feb. 1917, 1/7, CAC. See also E. M. Andrews and B. G. Jordan, 'Second Bullecourt Revisited', *JAWM*, no. 15 (Oct. 1989), p. 43.
90. Bean, *Two Men*, p. 137; Haig diary, 22 July 1916, in R. Blake (ed.), *The Private Papers of Douglas Haig, 1914–1919* (London: Eyre & Spottiswoode, 1952), p. 155.
91. C. E. W. Bean, *The Official History of Australia in the War of 1914–1918, Vol. 6. The AIF in France: May 1918–The Armistice* (St Lucia: University of Queensland Press, 1983; originally published 1942), p. 1079.
92. This has engendered a considerable literature. For a sample of the arguments, see Andrews, *ANZAC Illusion*, pp. 60–3, 144–7, 214–15.
93. S. F. Wise, 'The Black Day of the German Army: Australians and Canadians at Amiens, August 1918', in Dennis and Grey, *1918: Defining Victory*, pp. 25–96.
94. 'Report on work of Historical Section, 1 December 1927 to 30 November 1928', CAB 103/6, p. 4, PRO (I owe this reference to Dr Jenny Macleod).
95. 'Notes from recent operations' [issued by 55th Division] 21 Aug. 1916, WO95/2900, PRO (I owe this reference to Michael Orr); Anon, *The War History of the 1/4th Battalion the Loyal North Lancashire Regiment 1914–18* (privately published, 1921), pp. 80, 107; H. B. McCartney, 'The 1/6th and 1/10th Battalions of the King's (Liverpool) Regiment in the Period of the First World War', PhD thesis, University of Cambridge, 2000, pp. 299–303, 308–11.
96. J. Hussey, 'The Deaths of Qualified Staff Officers in the Great War: "A Generation Missing"?' *Journal of the Society for Army Historical Research*, vol. 75 (1997), pp. 250, 253–5.
97. Monash referred to Blamey, his chief of staff in 1918, as a 'Staff College graduate, but not on that account a pedant'(!), Monash, *Australian Victories*, pp. 295–6.
98. Edmonds to Bean, 14 Nov. 1932, AWM 38, 3 DRL 7953 item 34.
99. As Roger Lee recognises in his pioneering study: 'The Australian Staff: The Forgotten Men of the First AIF', in Dennis and Grey, *1918: Defining Victory*, pp. 115, 129.
100. Edmonds to Bean, 27 June 1928, Bean papers, 3 DRL 7953 item 34, AWM.

8: The British General Staff and Japan 1918–41

1. Alvin D. Coox, 'The Effectiveness of the Japanese Military Establishment in the Second World War', in Allan R. Millett and Williamson Murray (eds), *Military Effectiveness*, 3 vols (Boston: Allen & Unwin, 1988), vol. 3, *The Second World War*, p. 1.
2. Christopher Thorne, *The Issue of War* (London: Hamish Hamilton, 1985), p. 18.
3. Arthur Marder, *Old Friends: New Enemies. The Royal Navy and the Imperial Japanese Navy* (Oxford: Clarendon, 1981), p. 341 ff.
4. For Kennedy's views see *The Military Side of Japanese Life* (London: Constable, 1924), *The Problem of Japan* (London: Nisbet, 1935) and *The Estrangement of Great Britain and Japan, 1917–1935* (Manchester: Manchester University Press, 1969). For Piggott's views see *Broken Thread: An Autobiography* (Aldershot: Gale & Polden, 1950). See also Peter Lowe, 'Great Britain's Assessment of Japan before the Outbreak of the Pacific War', in Ernest R. May (ed.), *Knowing One's Enemies: Intelligence Assessment before the Two World Wars* (Princeton, NJ: Princeton University Press, 1984), p. 473.
5. For British ambassadors' views of Japan see Rohun Butler, J. P. T. Bury and M. E. Lambert (eds), *Documents on British Foreign Policy* (hereafter *DBFP*), 1st series, vol. XIV (London: HMSO, 1966), no. 1818, Sir C. Eliot to Lord Curzon, 12 Dec. 1920; and Sir Robert Craigie, *Behind the Japanese Mask* (London: Hutchinson, 1946). For brief biographies of Piggott, Kennedy, Sansom, Sir Charles Eliot and other key officials see Sir Hugh Cortazzi and Gordon Daniels (eds), *Britain and Japan, 1859–1991* (London: Routledge, 1991).
6. *Journal of the British Institute of International Affairs* (later *International Affairs*) (1922–23), Reviews of Books, p. 204 ff.; *International Affairs* (1932), p. 142 ff. Arnold J. Toynbee (ed.), *Survey of International Affairs, 1920–1923* (London: Humphrey Milford–Oxford University Press, 1925), p. 418 ff.; C. A. Macartney *et al.*, *Survey of International*

Affairs, 1925 (London: Humphrey Milford–Oxford University Press, 1926), vol. 2, p. 210 ff. For the scarcity of parliamentary questions on Japan see, for example, *House of Commons Debates 1926*, vols 191, 192 and 193. Vol. 191 has one reference to Japan in the index on p. 69 on steamship subsidies, Vol. 192 has one reference in the index on cotton on p. 71 and vol. 193 has no reference at all. For a range of opinions on Pacific issues see Fleetwood Chidell, 'The Menace of Japan', *Contemporary Review* (May 1920), p. 655 ff.; T. Okamoto, 'American–Japanese Issues and the Anglo-Japanese Alliance', *Contemporary Review* (March 1921), p. 354 ff.; Robert Young, 'The Anglo-Japanese Alliance', *Contemporary Review* (July 1921), p. 8 ff.; Frederick Anson, 'The Chinese Point of View', *Fortnightly Review* (February 1926), p. 230 ff.; Robert Machray, 'British Policy in China', *Fortnightly Review* (March 1927), p. 289 ff.; K. Kawakami, 'A Japanese View of Anglo-Chinese Relations', *National Review* (April 1927), p. 227 ff.; Sir Henry Pollock, 'British Policy in China', *National Review* (Dec. 1927), p. 525 ff.

7. M. D. Kennedy, 'Japan and Disarmament', *Journal of the Royal United Services Institute* (Feb. 1927), p. 173 ff.; Sadao Saburi, 'Japan's Position in the Far East', *Journal of the Royal United Services Institute* (August 1929), p. 454 ff.

8. A. C. Alford, 'Japan and the United States of America', *Army Quarterly* (1924), p. 286 ff.; Malcolm Kennedy, 'The Korean Frontier', *Army Quarterly* (April 1925), p. 28.

9. Alford, 'Japan and the United States', p. 286 ff.

10. Lieutenant-General Golovin, 'What Forces can Russia Concentrate in the Far East?', *Army Quarterly* (January 1934), p. 274 ff.

11. See the General Staff's reply to the Japanese paper, 'The Base of the Manchurian Dispute', in PRO WO 106/5486. For Kennedy's view see the Kennedy papers, Sheffield University Library, 4/27, pp. 48–9. See also Brigadier-General C. D. Bruce, 'The Situation in Manchuria', *Army Quarterly* (July 1932), p. 298 ff. See also 'China and Japan' by a Special Correspondent, *Journal of the Royal United Services Institute* (November 1931), p. 858 ff.

12. For early missionary and journalists' warnings about the behaviour of the Japanese army see Angus Hamilton, *Korea* (London: William Heinemann, 1904); F. A. McKenzie, *The Tragedy of Korea* (London: Hodder & Stoughton, 1907); Reverend Lord William Gascoyne-Cecil, *Changing China* (London: James Nisbet, 1910); Price Collier, *The West in the East from an American Point of View* (London: Duckworth, 1911), p. 463 ff. For later journalists' accounts see Edgar Mowrer, *Mowrer in China* (Harmondsworth: Penguin, 1938); Hugh Byas, *The Japanese Enemy: His Power and His Vulnerability* (London: Hodder & Stoughton, 1943); Carroll Alcott, *My War with Japan* (New York: Henry Holt, 1943); John Morris, *Traveller From Tokyo* (Harmondsworth: Penguin, 1943).

13. Kennedy papers, 4/27, p. 9. For Kennedy's views on Peter Fleming and *The Times* see 4/30, p. 11.

14. PRO WO 106/5611, Sir Robert Clive to Cadogan, 13 Oct. 1936 and despatch from Sir Robert Craigie, 9 Sept. 1938, describing an interview between Piggott and the Vice Chief of the Japanese General Staff.

15. B. R. Mullaly, 'The Evolution of the Japanese Army', *Army Quarterly* (April 1928), p. 52 ff.

16. Peter Brock, *Pacifism in Europe to 1914* (Princeton, NJ: Princeton University Press, 1972); Frederick H. Russell, *The Just War in the Middle Ages* (Cambridge: Cambridge University Press, 1975).

17. Piggott, *Broken Thread*, p. 265 ff.

18. Wards papers IWM 92/24/1, Wards to GSO2, War Office, 19 March 1936.

19. PRO WO 106/5658, letter from Lieutenant-Colonel Hill enclosing Stockton's report.

20. PRO WO 106/5656, report by S. R. Hunt.

21. Ibid.

22. PRO WO 106/5491, report by Captain Ainger.

23. Ibid. For Temperley see A. C. Temperley, *The Whispering Gallery of Europe* (London: Collins, 1939).

24. PRO WO 106/5656, Chapman's report and covering letter of 7 March 1935.

25. PRO WO 106/5658, Johnson's report and covering letter, 16 March 1936.

26. PRO WO 106/5658, Johnson's report and covering letter, 8 Jan. 1937.

27. PRO WO 106/5656, Francis Piggott's report and covering letter from F. S. G. Piggott, 1 Nov. 1937.

28. Report in the Pender-Cudlip papers, IWM 99/19/1.
29. PRO WO 106/54656, report by Lieutenant T. H. Winterborn.
30. For joint operations in China in 1914 see Richard Storry, *Japan and the Decline of the West in Asia, 1894–1943* (London: Macmillan, 1979), pp. 105–6.
31. PRO WO 106/5684, briefings of Nov. 1938.
32. *Selected Works of Mao Tse-Tung* (Peking: Foreign Languages Press, 1967).
33. Storry, *Japan and the Decline*, p. 155. Tanks did play a role in Japan's conquest of Malaya: see Louis Allen, *Singapore, 1941–1942* (London: Frank Cass, 1977), p. 206 ff.
34. PRO WO 106/5576, Wards's report of 15 Dec. 1937. Wards's report on the fate of Chinese prisoners was supported by the Military Attaché in Shanghai's report on the capture of Nanking, ibid., 2 Jan. 1937.
35. Ibid.
36. Ibid.
37. PRO WO 106/5576, report by Marr-Johnson on visit to North China, 17 Aug. to 3 Dec. 1937 and covering letter of 18 Dec. 1937.
38. PRO WO 106/5576, report by Colonel Burkhardt, GSO1, Hong Kong, 30 Aug. 1938. See also the Pender-Cundlip papers in the IWM. Pender-Cundlip visited North China in Oct. 1937.
39. PRO WO 106/5684, report by the Captain of HMS *Tamar*. For other naval assessments of Japanese naval power see G. Till, 'Perceptions of Naval Power between the Wars: The British Case', in Philip Towle (ed.), *Estimating Foreign Military Power* (London: Croom Helm, 1982), p. 177 ff.
40. PRO WO 106/5854, Harbin intelligence report of 30 Sept. 1938 and report on 'Operations and activities of the Japanese Army in the Yangtse Valley, Aug. 1937 to Jan. 1938', prepared by the General Staff in Hong Kong.
41. PRO WO 106/5478, Sir Francis Lindley to Sir John Simon, 4 Jan. 1931.
42. PRO WO 106/5498, 'The influence of the army on the government and people of Japan', MI2C, 6 June 1934.
43. Ibid.
44. PRO WO 106/5501, despatches to and from Sir Robert Clive, 7 Aug. 1934, 25 Sept. 1934, 5 Oct. 1934. See also Hosoya Chichiro, 'Britain and the United States in Japan's View of the International System', in Ian Nish (ed.), *Anglo-Japanese Alienation* (Cambridge: Cambridge University Press, 1982), p. 18 ff. and Nish, 'Japan in Britain's View, 1919–37', ibid., p. 44 ff.
45. PRO WO 106/5501, minute to the DMI, 29 Sept. 1934.
46. PRO WO 106/5502, Naval Staff paper sent to Dill, 28 Sept. 1934. Dill letter to Dickens, 26 Oct. 1934; Dickens's reply of 30 Oct. 1934.
47. Ibid. For Dreyer's views see Dreyer papers, CAC, 9/2, 'Some strategic notes on the Western Pacific', 10 Feb. 1939.
48. PRO WO 106/5509, printed memorandum by the CIGS, 17 Jan. 1939.
49. Ibid. See also Kennedy papers, 4/30, p. 104.
50. Nish, *Anglo-Japanese Alienation*, pp. 21, 47.
51. PRO WO 106/5509, comments on Cadogan's paper, 29 Jan. 1936. Ismay's autobiography, *The Memoirs of General the Lord Ismay* (Heinemann: London, 1960) is uninformative on this period in his life, so are his papers in King's College, London, though he does show sensitivity in the papers about the loss of Singapore: see 1/14/31, letters between Ismay and General Sir Ian Jacob, 24 Jan. 1959; 11/5/19, letter to Sir John Salmond, 2 Dec. 1963.
52. Peter Lowe, 'Great Britain's Assessment of Japan before the Outbreak of the Pacific War', in May, *Knowing One's Enemies*, p. 464.
53. PRO WO 106/5611, Military Intelligence note of 8 May 1939 and Piggott's letter of 17 March 1939 concerning Captain Winterborn's departure from Japan.
54. PRO WO 106/5611, Esler Dening's letters to Sir Hugh Knatchbull-Hugessen, 2 and 8 Dec. 1936, give some idea of Japanese behaviour to the British in China.
55. PRO WO 106/5513, Piggott to Sir Robert Clive, 2 June 1936; Sir George Sansom's minute of 22 Sept. 1936; and Clive to Eden, 6 Nov. 1936.
56. Fujiwara Akira, 'The Role of the Japanese Army', in Dorothy Borg and Shumpei Okamoto (eds), *Pearl Harbor as History: Japanese American Relations, 1931–1941* (New York: Columbia University Press, 1973), p. 190.
57. PRO WO 106/5614, Sir Robert Craigie to Anthony Eden, 9 Sept. 1937.

58. Asada Sadao, 'The Japanese Navy and the United States', in Borg and Shumpei, *Pearl Harbor*, p. 246.
59. Ibid., p. 248 ff. See also Hosoya Chihiro, 'The Japanese–Soviet Neutrality Pact', in James William Morley (ed.), *The Fateful Choice: Japan's Advance in Southeast Asia, 1939–1941* (New York: Columbia University Press, 1980), p. 40 ff. See also the same editor's *Japan's Road to the Pacific War: The Final Confrontation, 1941* (New York: Columbia University Press, 1994).
60. PRO WO 106/5513, General R. H. Haining, the DMI, to Piggott, 20 Nov. 1936. For Haining see his obituary in *The Times*, 17 Sept. 1959, reproduced in *Obituaries from The Times 1951–1960* (Reading: Newspaper Archive Developments, 1979), p. 322.
61. PRO WO 106/5513, Piggott to Sir Cyril Deverell, 28 July 1936.
62. PRO WO 116/5513, 'Suggested British participation in frontier demarcation commission', 28 July 1936.
63. For Piggott on Craigie see *Broken Thread*, p. 295; for Craigie on Piggott's departure see Craigie, *Japanese Mask*, p. 80. See also the Piggott papers, IWM, Piggott to Hankey, 12 Nov. 1941.
64. Piggott papers, IWM. For Kennedy's lecturing efforts see his papers in Sheffield University.
65. Philip Towle, 'British Estimates of Japanese Military Power', in Philip Towle, *Estimating Foreign Military Power*, p. 129 ff.
66. For proposals for reviving close links between the two navies see PRO FO 371/10958, Admiralty minute of 13 February 1925; for the initial reluctance to help the Japanese develop a naval air arm see *DBFP*, vol. 14, no. 159, Curzon to Eliot, 14 Nov. 1920.
67. For the naval arms race with Japan see James H. Herzog, *Closing The Open Door: American–Japanese Diplomatic Negotiations, 1936–1941* (Annapolis, MD: Naval Institute Press, 1973); Stephen E. Pelz, *Race to Pearl Harbor* (New Haven, CT: Yale University Press, 1974); Christopher Hall, *Britain, America and Arms Control, 1921–1937* (Basingstoke: Macmillan, 1987); Nish, *Anglo-Japanese Alienation*, p. 9.

9: J. F. C. Fuller: Staff Officer Extraordinary

1. A. J. Trythall, *Boney Fuller: The Intellectual General, 1878–1966* (London: Cassell, 1977). The narrative of Fuller's life and career is based on this work and its references.
2. Brigadier-General Sir James Edmonds, 'The German General Staff', *RUSI Journal*, vol. 99 (1954), pp. 54–7.
3. H. O. Arnold-Foster, *The Army in 1906* (London: John Murray, 1906), p. 386.
4. C. Barnett, *Britain and her Army* (London: Allen Lane, 1970), p. 359.
5. See Arnold-Foster, *The Army in 1906*, p. 404.
6. Special Army Order 233 of 12 Sept. 1906.
7. General Staff, War Office, *Field Service Regulations, Part II* (London: HMSO, 1909), pp. 35–6.
8. Major-General Sir W. E. Ironside, 'The Modern Staff Officer', *RUSI Journal*, vol. 72 (1928), pp. 435–43.
9. 'Siege-Gunner', 'Staff and Regimental Officers', *United Services Magazine*, vol. 60 (1920), p. 66.
10. *Army Quarterly*, vol. 1, no. 1 (1920), editorial and p. 31.
11. J. P. Harris, *Men, Ideas and Tanks* (Manchester: Manchester University Press, 1998), p. 170.
12. *RUSI Journal*, vol. 65 (1920), pp. 281–98.
13. Ibid., pp. 17–19.
14. J. F. C. Fuller, *Memoirs of an Unconventional Soldier* (London: Nicholson & Watson, 1936), p. 392.
15. *Cavalry Journal*, vol. 10 (1920), pp. 109–32, 307–22, 510–30.
16. See Fuller, *Memoirs*, p. 420.
17. Trythall, *Boney Fuller*, pp. 120–44.
18. Fuller papers, Rutgers University Library, New Brunswick, New Jersey, Box 2.
19. See Fuller, *Memoirs*, p. 448.
20. Fuller papers, Rutgers University Library, New Brunswick, New Jersey, Box 2.
21. Ibid.
22. Azar Gat, *Fascist and Liberal Visions of War* (Oxford: Clarendon, 1988), p. 40.

23. *RUSI Journal*, vol. 65 (1920), pp. 281–98.
24. Gat, *Visions of War*, pp. 13–20.
25. Ibid., p. 14.
26. Ibid., p. 40.
27. Letter from Estelle Fuller to the author, 18 June 1971.
28. Conversation with Estelle Fuller, 24 Aug. 1971.
29. J. F. C. Fuller, *Generalship, its Diseases and their Cure* (Harrisburg, PA: Military Service Publishing, 1936), p. 65.

10: 'An Extensive Use of Weedkiller': Patterns of Promotion in the Senior Ranks of the British Army, 1919–39

1. Viscount Montgomery, *The Memoirs of Field-Marshal the Viscount Montgomery of Alamein* (London: Collins, 1958), p. 40. Research for this article was made possible by a Small Personal Research Grant from the British Academy.
2. Liddell Hart, 'Analysis of Army List', Oct. 1936, LHCMA Liddell Hart mss 11/1931/45; Liddell Hart, 'Age of promotion', 'Promotions in 1934 and 1935', nd, LHCMA Liddell Hart mss 11/1931/43; Liddell Hart, 'Age of promotion', 'Promotions since Jan. 1st 1936', nd, LHCMA Liddell Hart mss 11/1931/44.
3. 'High Command in the Army', *The Times*, 16 Sept. 1937.
4. Colonel C. E. Vickery, 'Blocked Promotion', *The Times*, 20 Sept. 1937.
5. Montgomery, *Memoirs*, p. 40.
6. B. H. Liddell Hart, *Europe in Arms* (London: Faber & Faber, 1937), pp. 229–30.
7. B. H. Liddell Hart, *The Memoirs of Captain Liddell Hart*, 2 vols (London: Cassell, 1965), vol. 1, p. 379.
8. Montgomery, *Memoirs*, p. 40.
9. This group will be referred to collectively as the senior officer cadre.
10. 'Notes on Milne's regime as C.I.G.S.', nd, LHCMA Liddell Hart mss 11/1933/40.
11. 'Talk with General Sir Charles Bonham-Carter', 12 Dec. 1935, LHCMA Liddell Hart mss 11/1935/114; Bonham-Carter, 'Autobiography, 1921–39', CAC Bonham-Carter mss BHCT 9/3. For Bonham-Carter's generally favourable opinion of Milne see Bonham-Carter to Hutton, 14 Jan. 1954, CAC Bonham-Carter mss 13/1.
12. See Milne's closing remarks to the General Staff Conference on 11 Jan. 1933, 'Report on the Staff Conference held at the Staff College Camberley, 9th to 11th Jan. 1933', PRO WO 279/74; Cavan, 'Preferment and Appointments', nd but *c.* 1932, CAC Cavan mss 1/3/II; Montgomery-Massingberd to the editor, *The Times*, 25 Sept. 1937.
13. War Office memorandum no. 1847, 22 Dec. 1937, PRO WO 32/4469; 'Dinner with Gort at White's Club', 22 Nov. 1937, LHCMA Liddell Hart mss 11/1937/96b.
14. 'Report of the Committee on Promotion of Officers in the Army', 6 Jan. 1925, PRO WO 32/3737; Chetwode to Montgomery-Massingberd, 4 Aug. 1921, LHCMA Montgomery-Massingberd mss 133/1.
15. Précis for the Army Council, no. 1242, Feb. 1926, PRO WO 32/3740.
16. Army Council, *The King's Regulations for the Army and the Army Reserve 1928* (London: HMSO, 1928), pp. 45, 535–7.
17. Military Secretary to Military Members of the Army Council, 10 Nov. 1920, PRO WO 32/12539.
18. Cavan, 'Preferment and Appointments', nd but *c.* 1932, CAC Cavan mss 1/3/II; Army Council, *King's Regulations*, p. 164.
19. Précis for the Army Council, no. 1242, Feb. 1926, PRO WO 32/3740.
20. 'Some comments and opinions on the selection of officers for senior appointments, with some general remarks about generalship', a paper by Major J. K. Nairne, nd but *c.* Feb. 1971, LHCMA O'Connor mss 8.
21. 'Talk with General Ironside', 6 May 1937, LHCMA Liddell Hart mss 11/1937/33.
22. 'Talk with General Liddell', 31 Dec. 1937, LHCMA Liddell Hart mss 11/1937/108.
23. Gort to Military Members of the Army Council, 12 Oct. 1937, PRO WO 32/4469.
24. 'Talk with Major-General J. Kennedy', 11 Nov. 1936, LHCMA Liddell Hart mss 11/1936/98.
25. 'Report of the Committee on the Promotion of Officers in the Army', 6 Jan. 1925, PRO WO 32/3737.

26. Churchill to Military Secretary, 30 April 1919, PRO WO 32/5955.
27. Liddell Hart, 'Talk with Hore-Belisha', 21 Aug. 1937, LHCMA Liddell Hart mss 11/HB/ 1937/14; Liddell Hart, 'Talk with Hore-Belisha', 1 Sept. 1937, LHCMA Liddell Hart mss 11/HB/1937/34.
28. Liddell Hart, 'Talk with Hore-Belisha', 3 Jan. 1938, LHCMA Liddell Hart mss 11/HB/ 1938/1; Liddell Hart, 'Talk with Hore-Belisha', 16 Jan. 1940, LHCMA Liddell Hart mss 11/HB/1940/19.
29. Liddell Hart, 'Points given to Hore-Belisha on telephone', 12 Nov. 1937, LHCMA Liddell Hart mss LH 11/HB 1937/90; Liddell Hart, 'Talk with Hore-Belisha', 3 Nov. 1937, LHCMA Liddell Hart mss 11/HB/1937/77.
30. Précis for the Army Council, no. 1242, Feb. 1926, PRO WO 32/3740.
31. Liddell Hart to Montgomery, 5 Dec. 1958, LHCMA Liddell Hart mss 1/519/109.
32. Liddell Hart diary, 14 Jan. 1931, LHCMA Liddell Hart mss 11/1931/1b; Major-General Sir F. Maurice, *The Life of General Lord Rawlinson of Trent: From his Journals and Letters* (London: Cassell, 1928), p. 340.
33. 'Notes on Milne's regime as C.I.G.S.', nd, LHCMA Liddell Hart mss 11/1933/40.
34. 'Talk with Broad', 12 Feb. 1947, LHCMA Liddell Hart mss 11/1947.
35. 'Dinner with Gort at White's Club', 22 Nov. 1937, LHCMA Liddell Hart mss 11/1937/96b; 'Talk with General Liddell', 31 Dec. 1937, LHCMA Liddell Hart mss 11/1937/108.
36. Liddell Hart, 'Talk with Hore-Belisha', 3 Jan. 1938, LHCMA Liddell Hart mss 11/HB/ 1938/1; Liddell Hart, 'Note for H.-B.', 3 Jan. 1938, LHCMA LH 11/HB 1938/3.
37. CIGS to Military Members of the Army Council', 30 Oct. 1929, PRO WO 32/3102.
38. Montgomery-Massingberd, 'The Autobiography of a Gunner', pp. 48–9, nd, LHCMA Montgomery-Massingberd mss 159/1.
39. Deverell to Bartholomew, 11 Feb. 1936, LCHMA Bartholomew mss 2/4/3.
40. 'Talk with Lieutenant-General B. D. Fisher', 16 Nov. 1937, Liddell Hart mss 11/1937/92.
41. 'Dinner with Gort at White's Club', 22 Nov. 1937, LHCMA Liddell Hart mss 11/1937/96b.
42. 'F. A. P. [ile]', 6 May 1939, LHCMA Liddell Hart mss 11/1939/52.
43. Dill to Liddell Hart, 9 Jan. 1931, LHCMA Liddell Hart mss 1/238/9.
44. 'Talk with Major-General C. N. F. Broad', 11 July 1939, LHCMA Liddell Hart mss 11/1939/63.
45. Deverell to Bartholomew, 22 Dec. 1935 and 11 Feb. 1936, LCHMA Bartholomew mss 2/4/3.
46. These figures include only those awards given to officers before 1919 or before they were promoted to major-general and entered the senior leadership cadre.
47. I am most grateful to Dr John Bourne of the University of Birmingham for supplying me with this information.
48. Maurice, *Rawlinson*, p. 337.
49. 'Report on the Staff Conference held at the Staff College, Camberley, 16–19 Jan. 1928', PRO WO 279/60; B. Bond, *The Victorian Army and the Staff College, 1854–1914* (London: Eyre Methuen, 1972), p. 324.
50. Liddell Hart, 'Measures to improve the officer situation in the army', 31 May 1937, LHCMA Liddell Hart mss 11/HB/1937/8.
51. R. Patterson to ? [illegible], 7 April 1926, PRO WO 32/3785.
52. Deverell to Hore-Belisha, 26 Aug. 1937, CAC Hore-Belisha mss HOBE 5/8.
53. They were: Sir W. Braithwaite, who served as GOC-in-C Scottish Command (1923–26), GOC-in-C Eastern Command (1926–27), and Adjutant-General (1927–31); Sir A. Montgomery-Massingberd, GOC-in-C Southern Command (1928–31), Adjutant-General (1931–33); Sir C. Romer, GOC-in-C Western Command (1928–31) and Adjutant-General (1933–35); Sir W. Gillman, Master-General of the Ordnance (1927–31) and GOC-in-C Eastern Command (1931–33); Sir P. de B. Radcliffe, GOC-in-C Scottish Command (1930–33) and GOC-in-C Southern Command (1933–34); and Sir J. F. Gathorne-Hardy, GOC-in-C Northern Command (1931–33) and GOC-in-C Aldershot Command (1933–37).
54. Ironside to Liddell Hart, 10 July 1933, LHCMA Liddell Hart mss 11/1933/20.
55. Churchill to Military Secretary, 30 April 1919, and Military Secretary to Churchill, 1 May 1919, PRO WO 32/5955.
56. CIGS's periodical letter to Dominions and India, no. 1, 26 Jan. 1928, PRO WO 32/2378.
57. Military Secretary to Adjutant-General, 7 May 1928, PRO WO 32/3734; Précis for Army Council, no. 1261, July 1926, PRO WO 32/3785.
58. 'Report of the Committee on Promotion of Officers in the Army', 6 Jan. 1925, PRO WO

32/3737.

59. Talk with Major-General B. D. Fisher, 22 March 1934, LHCMA Liddell Hart mss
    11/1934/37; Talk with Major-General J. Kennedy, 25/9/35, LHCMA Liddell Hart mss
    11/1935/94; Major-General F. S. Pigott, *Broken Thread: An Autobiography* (London: Gale
    & Polden, 1950), p. 247.
60. Hore-Belisha to Deverell, 27 Aug. 1937, CAC Hore-Belisha mss HOBE 5/8.
61. R. J. Minney, *The Private Papers of Leslie Hore-Belisha* (London: Collins, 1960), p. 66.
62. 'Committee on the Conditions of Service of Officers in the Royal Navy, the Army and the
    Royal Air Force', July 1938, PRO WO 163/608; B. Bond, *British Military Policy between
    the Two World Wars* (Oxford: Clarendon, 1980), p. 54; Hore-Belisha to Gort, 1 Sept. 1937,
    CAC Hore-Belisha mss 5/8; Minute by Military Secretary, 3 Feb. 1938, PRO WO 32/4466.
63. Liddell Hart to Montgomery, 5 Dec. 1958. LHCMA Liddell Hart mss 1/519/109; 'Dinner
    with Gort at White's Club', 22 Nov. 1937, LHCMA Liddell Hart mss 11/1937/96b.
64. I am again grateful to Dr Bourne for supplying me with information concerning the age
    of divisional commanders in November 1918. For the comparison with their successors
    in the Second World War, see D. French, 'Colonel Blimp and the British Army: British
    Divisional Commanders in the War against Germany, 1939–1945', *English Historical
    Review*, vol. 111 (1996), pp. 182–201.
65. F. Davis and G. Maddocks, *Bloody Red Tabs: General Officer Casualties of the Great War,
    1914–1918* (London: Leo Cooper, 1995), *passim*.
66. Bond, *British Military Policy*, *passim*; see also J. P. Harris's chapter in this book.
67. Alanbrooke, 'Notes from My Life', vol. 3; 'BEF. France-Flanders 1939–40', pp. 102, 135,
    LHCMA Alanbrooke mss 3/A/3.
68. Minute by Gwynn, 10 March 1926. PRO WO 32/4840.
69. Ironside, 'Higher education for war', 15 Dec. 1925, PRO WO 32/4840.
70. 'Report on the Staff Conference held at the Staff College, Camberley, 16–19 Jan. 1928',
    PRO WO 279/60.
71. Anon, 'Army Notes', *Journal of the Royal United Services Institute*, vol. 84 (1939), p. 430.
72. Major General Sir C. W. Gwynn, 'The Higher Study of War in the Army', *Journal of the
    Royal United Services Institute*, vol. 76 (1931), p. 483.
73. General Staff, War Office, *Training Regulations 1934* (London: HMSO, 1934), pp. 32–3.
74. 'Aldershot Command Corps skeleton exercise, 11–14 July 1939', LHCMA Liddell Hart
    mss 15/3/43.
75. *Memorandum on Army Training: Collective Training Period for 1926* (London: War Office,
    1926), LHCMA Liddell Hart mss 15/3/23.
76. *Army Training Memorandum no. 19, December 1937* (London: War Office, 1937), LHCMA
    Liddell Hart mss 15/2/23.
77. Colonel R. Macleod and D. Kelly (eds), *The Ironside Diaries 1937–40* (London: Constable,
    1962), p. 87.

11: *The British General Staff and the Coming of War, 1933–39*

1. Spenser Wilkinson, *The Brain of an Army: A Popular Account of the German General Staff*
   (London: Constable, 1913).
2. *War Office List* (London: HMSO, 1935) p. 79.
3. See, for example, Brian Bond, *British Military Policy Between the Two World Wars* (Oxford:
   Clarendon, 1980), *passim*, and David French, *Raising Churchill's Army: The British Army
   and the War Against Germany, 1919–1945* (Oxford: Oxford University Press, 2000),
   passim.
4. R. J. Minney, *The Private Papers of Hore-Belisha* (London: Collins, 1960) *passim*; D. C.
   Watt, *Personalities and Policies: Studies of British Foreign Policy in the 20th Century*
   (London: Longmans, 1965), p. 113; A. J. P. Taylor, *The Origins of the Second World War*
   (Harmondsworth: Penguin, 1964), p. 59. Minney was concerned to portray Hore-Belisha
   as a dynamic and far-sighted minister whose efforts were frustrated by the obscurantism
   of senior soldiers. Watt echoes the Minney version. Taylor writes of 'the most respected
   military authorities' holding 'that tanks were of less use than horses'.
5. See C. L. Mowat, *Britain Between the Wars* (London: Methuen, 1956), pp. 537–8.
6. See John J. Mearsheimer, *Liddell Hart and the Weight of History* (London: Brassey's, 1988),
   pp. 208–17.

7. B. H. Liddell Hart, *The Memoirs of Captain Liddell Hart*, 2 vols (London: Cassell, 1965).
8. Brian Bond, *Liddell Hart: A Study of his Military Thought* (London: Cassell, 1977).
9. Mearsheimer makes frank criticisms of Liddell Hart. But after quoting an intelligent comment by Gort on the possible German use of armoured and air forces, he states, 'One must be careful not to place too much emphasis on selected comments like Gort's because of the danger of painting too favorable a picture of Britain's military leaders': Mearsheimer, *Liddell Hart*, p. 81. But it is gratifying to see that Field-Marshal Sir Archibald Montgomery-Massingberd is now generally receiving a more balanced treatment from historians – notably in Robert H. Larson, *The British Army and the Theory of Armored Warfare, 1918–1940* (Newark: University of Delaware Press, 1984), pp. 162–84, and French, *Raising Churchill's Army*, pp. 111–12.
10. Bond, *Liddell Hart*, p. 92.
11. Liddell Hart, *Memoirs*, vol. II, pp. 279–80.
12. Ibid, pp. 269–72, 279–80.
13. See Liddell Hart's 'Note on the opposition to the development of the anti-aircraft defences of Great Britain', 30 July 1938, LHCMA, Liddell Hart mss H 11/1938/89.
14. H. Gordon, *The War Office* (London: Putnam, 1935), pp. 7–10.
15. *War Office List* (1935), pp. 79–80.
16. Wilkinson, *Brain of an Army*, p. 132.
17. *Army List* (London: HMSO, 1933–39).
18. *War Office List* (1933–39).
19. See the General Staff memorandum, 'The present distribution and strength of the British Army in relation to its duties', 1 Nov. 1927, PRO WO 32/2823.
20. Bond, *British Military Policy*, pp. 82–4.
21. For more on this theme see J. P. Harris, *Men, Ideas and Tanks: British Military Thought and Armoured Forces, 1903–1939* (Manchester: Manchester University Press, 1995), pp. 195–236.
22. R. Albrecht-Carrié, *A Diplomatic History of Europe Since the Congress of Vienna* (London: Methuen, 1958), pp. 418–19.
23. 'Meeting of the Committee of Imperial Defence', 29 Jan. 1925, PRO CAB 4/12.
24. Wesley Wark, *The Ultimate Enemy: British Intelligence and Nazi Germany, 1933–1939* (Oxford: Oxford University Press, 1986), p. 81.
25. See MI3 reports of 19 Feb. 1932, PRO WO 190/140, 24 Feb. 1932, PRO WO 190/143 and 30 May 1932, PRO WO 190/147.
26. For some discussion of the sources of General Staff intelligence on Germany at this period see J. P. Harris, 'British Military Intelligence and the Rise of the German Mechanised Forces', *Intelligence and National Security*, vol. 6 (1991), p. 396.
27. Wark, *Ultimate Enemy*, pp. 29, 81. Though reasonably impressed with MI3's analysis of the German threat up to 1933, Wark argues (*Ultimate Enemy*, pp. 86–92) that in 1935 and 1936 that branch considerably under-rated the speed and magnitude of the German army's expansion. This is certainly correct. But it is to some extent understandable in that many German officers thought the rate of expansion on which Hitler actually insisted was impracticable (W. Deist, *The Wehrmacht and German Rearmament* (London: Macmillan, 1981), p. 40). Wark further indicates that, in 1935–36 a small group of senior officers from the General Staff's intelligence branches argued that there was little choice other than to give the Germans a free hand in eastern Europe. This is also true, though the same officers seem to have been quite determined to defend western Europe against German aggression, such a 'free hand in the east' policy never became an official General Staff or War Office position. Wark further argues that Britain's failure to rearm its army early enough and on an adequate scale can be attributed in large measure to the MI3's underestimation, in the 1935–36 period, of the German army's eventual growth. Though there is not the space to discuss the matter adequately here, this strikes the present writer as dubious. The General Staff's and the Defence Requirements Committee (DRC)'s warnings at the time of the first DRC report had been very strong, yet the proposed programme for the army had been slashed by the Cabinet. Wark accepts that from November 1936 the General Staff (and everyone else in British policy-making circles) realised that the German army was to be expanded to the maximum possible extent. Yet, through the New Army Policy, introduced in late 1937–early 1938, the government sought a massive cut in the army's rearmament programme. This suggests that the British government's willingness to rearm

its own army bore no simple or direct relation to what was believed about German army expansion. Financial, economic and domestic political considerations seem to have been paramount.

28. MI3 memorandum, 11 Nov. 1933, PRO WO 190/230.
29. Field-Marshal Sir A. A. Montgomery-Massingberd, 'The Autobiography of a Gunner', LHCMA, Montgomery-Massingberd mss 10/11.
30. Bond, *Liddell Hart*, pp. 99, 100, 107.
31. Montgomery-Massingberd, 'Autobiography', LHCMA, Montgomery-Massingberd mss. 10/11.
32. 'Experimental Armoured Force Report', GOC Southern Command to Under Secretary of State, the War Office, 24 Nov. 1928, RH 87, RTC: MH.4 (41) Tank Museum, Bovington.
33. On Montgomery-Massingberd's obsession with loyalty see 'Talk with Duff Cooper', 18 Jan. 1936, LHCMA, Liddell Hart mss 11/1936/28.
34. See for example his treatment in Norman Dixon, *On the Psychology of Military Incompetence* (London: Jonathan Cape, 1976), pp. 113–18.
35. Committee of Imperial Defence, 'Defence Requirements Sub-Committee Report' (DRC 14) 28 Feb. 1934, PRO CAB 16/109.
36. 'Statement by the C.I.G.S.', 9 Jan. 1934, DRC 7, PRO CAB 16/109.
37. On the Germanophobia of Fisher and Vansittart see Wark, *Ultimate Enemy*, pp. 29–33.
38. DRC 14, paras. 9–12, PRO CAB 16/109.
39. Montgomery-Massingberd to Sir Maurice Hankey, 11 Sept. 1933, PRO CAB 21/369; 'Present Distribution', para. 2, PRO WO 32/2823.
40. MI3 memo., 11 Nov. 1933, PRO WO 190/230; Minutes of DRC 1 meeting, 14 Nov. 1933, PRO CAB 16/109.
41. DRC 14, Table C, 'Expenditure to meet army deficiencies'.
42. Bond, *Liddell Hart*, pp. 93–5.
43. 'Report of Ministerial Committee on Defence Requirements', CP 205 (34), 31 July 1934, Appendix 3, PRO CAB 16/110.
44. DRC 14, para. 25, PRO CAB 16/109.
45. Albrecht-Carrié, *Diplomatic History*, pp.505–6.
46. Appendix 3 to 'Ministerial Report on Defence Requirements', PRO CAB 16/110.The same argument is reproduced in Montgomery-Massingberd's, 'Notes for my successor', section 1, para. 6 (b), 1936, LHCMA, Montgomery-Massingberd mss 10/6.
47. DRC 7, para. 8, PRO CAB 16/109.
48. 'Ministerial Committee on Disarmament', minutes, DCM(32), 54 Concs., 17 July 1934, PRO CAB 16/110.
49. Cabinet minutes, 31 July 1934, PRO CAB 23/79.
50. On the Chamberlain deterrence strategy see G. C. Peden, *British Rearmament and the Treasury, 1932–39* (Edinburgh: Scottish Academic, 1979), pp. 118–21.
51. Anthony Verrier, *The Bomber Offensive* (London: Pan, 1974), p. 54. The General Staff's scepticism about the effectiveness of strategic bombing is expressed in 'Notes for my successor', section 1, para. 6, LHCMA, Montgomery-Massingberd mss 10/6.
52. 'The role of the army', memorandum by the Chancellor of the Exchequer, CP 334 (36), 11 Dec. 1936, PRO CAB 53/29.
53. 'Ministerial Committee Report on Defence Requirements', para. 15, 31 July 1934, PRO CAB 16/110.
54. Pownall diary, 17 July 1934, Brian Bond (ed.), *Chief of Staff* (London: Leo Cooper, 1972), vol. 1, p. 48.
55. Hobart to Liddell Hart, 24 July 1934, LHCMA, Liddell Hart mss 1/376/7.
56. 'The formation of a mobile division', minute 1, 15 Oct 1934, PRO WO 32/2847.
57. War Office letter 20/Cavalry/831, 8 Dec. 1934, PRO WO 32/2847.
58. 'Handing over notes', section 2, 'Present army policy', LHCMA, Montgomery-Massingberd mss 10/6.
59. DRC 14, 'Introductory', para. 1, PRO CAB 16/109.
60. 'Interim report', DRC 25, PRO CAB 16/112.
61. 'Third report', 21 Nov. 1935, DRC 37; 'Introductory', para. 5, PRO CAB 16/112.
62. 'The future reorganisation of the British Army', 9 Sept. 1935, PRO WO 32/4612.
63. Minutes 1–10, PRO WO 32/4612.
64. 'Future', introduction.

65. 'Report of the Committee on the Lessons of the Great War', 13 Oct. 1932, PRO WO 33/1297.
66. 'Future', part 1, 'Main characteristics of the war 1914–18', paras. 2 and 3, PRO WO 32/4612.
67. Ibid, paras 3 and 4.
68. Ibid, para. 6.
69. Ibid.
70. 'Future', part 1, 'Tendencies between 1918 and 1935', para. 3.
71. Ibid, 'Probable conditions of our entry into a European war and forecast of the type of force required'.
72. Ibid.
73. 'Statement by the Chief of the Imperial General Staff', DRC 7, 9 Jan. 1934, PRO CAB 16/109.
74. 'Future', part 1, 'Forecast of the opening stages of a war with Germany', para. 5, PRO WO 32/4612.
75. Williamson Murray, *The Luftwaffe, 1933–45: Strategy for Defeat* (London: Brassey's, 1996), pp. 19–21.
76. 'Future', part 1, 'Probable conditions of our entry into a European war', para. 8, PRO WO 32/4612.
77. 'Future', part 1, 'Considerations governing the organisation and equipment of the Field Force'.
78. 'Future', part 3, 'General conclusions', para. 1.
79. Defence Policy and Requirements Sub-Committee (DPR) 4th Meeting, 16 Jan. 1936, CAB 16/123.
80. Peden, *British Rearmament*, pp. 124–5.
81. Montgomery-Massingberd's, 'Notes for my successor', LHCMA, Montgomery-Massingberd mss 10/6.
82. 'Treasury Inter-Service Committee, 37th meeting, 7 Oct. 1936 and 40th meeting, 27 Oct. 1936', T 161/1316, PRO.
83. Cabinet minutes, 5 May 1937, PRO CAB 53/29; A. Duff Cooper, *Old Men Forget* (London: Hart-Davis, 1953), p. 206.
84. An indication of Hore-Belisha's vulnerability at this period is the remark by the Tory diarist 'Chips' Channon that if Hore-Belisha failed at the War Office 'we can cart him, for he is not a Conservative'. Quoted in J. Ramsden, *The Age Of Balfour and Baldwin* (London: Longman, 1978), p. 329.
85. A. Danchev, *Alchemist of War: The Life of Basil Liddell Hart* (London: Weidenfeld & Nicolson, 1998), p. 191; Peden, *British Rearmament*, pp. 137–9.
86. Minney, *Private Papers*, pp. 71–6; Bond, *British Military Policy*, p. 255.
87. Minney, *Private Papers*, pp. 71–2.
88. For a more detailed discussion of Hore-Belisha and the Army Council changes, see J. P. Harris, 'Two War Ministers: A Reassessment of Duff Cooper and Hore-Belisha', *War and Society*, vol. 6 (1988), pp. 65–78.
89. Minney, *Private Papers*, p. 69.
90. Bond, *Chief of Staff*, pp. 130–3, 141–3.
91. Author interview with Sir Ronald Adam at his Sussex home in 1978.
92. Bond, *British Military Policy*, pp. 300–1.
93. Hore-Belisha to Chamberlain, 31 Jan. 1938, and reply from Chamberlain's office to Hore-Belisha's private secretary, 2 Feb. 1938, PRO PREM 1/241.
94. 'Talk with Hore-Belisha', LHCMA, Liddell Hart mss 11/HB 1937/57b, 19 Oct. 1937.
95. 'Future', part 1, 'Mobile troops' and 'The infantry division and its supporting units', PRO WO 32/4612.
96. See Harris, *Men, Ideas and Tanks*, pp. 260–3.
97. 'Proceedings of a meeting held in CIGS's room', 23 Dec. 1937, PRO WO 32/4441.
98. Peden, *British Rearmament*, p. 143.
99. Harris, 'British Military Intelligence', pp. 395–417.
100. Gort to Hore-Belisha, 21 Nov. 1938, WO 190/723.
101. Gort to Liddell Hart, 31 Oct. 1937, LHCMA, Liddell Hart mss 1/322/52(a).
102. Bond, *Liddell Hart*, p. 104.
103. 'Outline', LHCMA, Liddell Hart mss 11/1938/89.

104. See CID, 269th meeting, 16 April 1935, item 6, PRO CAB 2/6.
105. Pownall's diary, 14 Feb., 21 Feb. and 4 April 1938, Bond, *Chief of Staff,* vol. 1, pp. 133–5, 141.
106. DRC 7, para. 8, PRO CAB 16/109.
107. This view was articulated most clearly and dramatically by Pownall: 'My view is that support of France is home defence – if France crumbles we fall': Pownall's diary, 13 Jan. 1938, Bond, *Chief of Staff*, vol. 1, p. 129.
108. These valid points are made in French, *Raising Churchill's Army*, pp. 81–121, 164–5.
109. Harris, *Men, Ideas and Tanks*, pp. 237–40; Richard Ogorkiewicz, *Armour* (London: Stevens, 1960), p. 154.
110. French, *Raising Churchill's Army*, pp. 165–6.

12: 'A Particularly Anglo-Saxon Institution': The British General Staff in the Era of Two World Wars

1. National Archives, #2017-223, 'The British Army', n.d. [1920], p. 1. Record Group 165 Box 636.
2. For a summary of seven possible usages of the term 'General Staff', see Dallas D. Irvine, 'The Origin of Capital Staffs', *Journal of Modern History*, vol. 10 (1938), pp. 161–79.
3. John Gooch, *The Plans of War: The General Staff and British Military Strategy c.1900–1916* (London: Routledge & Kegan Paul, 1974), pp. 32–108.
4. John Sweetman, 'Towards a Ministry of Defence: First Faltering Steps, 1890–1923', see Ch. 2 above. See also John Ehrman, *Cabinet Government and War 1890–1940* (Cambridge: Cambridge University Press, 1958), *passim*.
5. N. H. Gibbs, *The Origins of Imperial Defence* (Oxford: Oxford University Press, 1955), p. 9.
6. Roberts to Brodrick, 30 August 1903, quo. David James, *Lord Roberts* (London: Hollis & Carter, 1954), p. 393; Cd.1790, Minutes of Evidence taken before the Royal Commission on the War in South Africa (London: HMSO, 1904), Q. 13 238; Wolseley to the Duke of Cambridge, 1 January 1904, quo. Willoughby Verner, *The Military Life of HRH the Duke of Cambridge* (London: John Murray, 1905), vol. II, p. 426.
7. J. S. Omond, *Parliament and the Army, 1642–1904* (Cambridge: Cambridge University Press, 1933), p. 146.
8. David Steele, 'Lord Salisbury, the "False Religion" of Islam and the Reconquest of the Sudan', in E. M. Spiers (ed.), *Sudan: The Conquest Reappraised* (London: Cass, 1998), p. 16; British Library, Lansdowne to Salisbury, 29 October 1896, Lansdowne mss L (5) 53. I am grateful to Dr Steele for providing me with the latter reference.
9. David Dilks, *Curzon in India*, vol. I: *Achievement* (London: Hart Davis, 1969), p. 218 (the phrase is Lord Curzon's); Spenser Wilkinson, *Thirty-Five Years 1874–1909* (London: Constable, 1933), pp. 182–3.
10. On the constitutional significance of the structure and functioning of the CID, see John P. Mackintosh, 'The Role of the Committee of Imperial Defence before 1911', *English Historical Review*, no. CCIV, July (1962), esp. pp. 494–5; John P. Mackintosh, *The British Cabinet* (London: Stevens, 1962), pp. 263–74.
11. Imperial War Museum, Wilson diary, 31 August 1903, HHW #1/12. See also the entry for 15 June 1904.
12. I. F. W. Beckett (ed.), *The Army and the Curragh Incident, 1914* (London: Army Records Society/The Bodley Head, 1986), pp. 22–3, 276, 285–6.
13. Jan Karl Tanenbaum, *General Maurice Sarrail 1856–1929: The French Army and Left-Wing Politics* (Chapel Hill, NC: University of North Carolina Press, 1974); P. C. F. Bankwitz, *Maxime Weygand and Civil–Military Relations in Modern France* (Cambridge, MA: Harvard University Press, 1967), pp. 38–9.
14. National Archives, #2657-A-215(1)/25302, 'Conversation with Lieut. General Sir Webb Gilman', 11 June 1929; also #2657-A-215(2)/26125, 'Conversation with Lieutenant General Sir Webb Gilman, Master General of the Ordnance', 21 October 1929. Record Group 165, un-numbered box.
15. National Library of Scotland, 'Report on a conference of General Staff Officers at the Staff College, 7th to 10th January 1908, held under the Direction of the Chief of the General

Staff.' Haig mss H/81.

16. National Library of Scotland, 'Report on a conference of General Staff Officers at the Staff College, 18th to 21st January 1909, held under the Direction of the Chief of the General Staff', p. 59. Haig mss H/81.

17. Imperial War Museum, 'Standards of Efficiency Lecture I', 13 November 1907, p. 14; also 'Standards of Efficiency Lecture II', 25 November 1907, p. 9. Wilson mss 3/3/5.

18. Imperial War Museum, Wilson diary, 7 May 1909. Wilson mss HHW #1/18. For an assessment of Wilson's term as commandant, see Brian Bond, *The Victorian Army and the Staff College 1854–1914* (London: Eyre Methuen, 1972), pp. 248–56, 263–70.

19. J. Charteris, *Field Marshal Earl Haig* (London: Cassell, 1929), pp. 55–6.

20. Tim Moreman, 'Lord Kitchener, the General Staff and the Army in India, 1902–14', see Ch. 4 above.

21. J. A. Spender and C. Asquith, *Life of Herbert Henry Asquith, Lord Oxford and Asquith* (London: Hutchinson, 1932), vol. II, p. 192.

22. Public Record Office, Chatfield to Hankey, 17 February 1931. CAB 21/424. Quo. H. G. Welch, 'The Origins and Development of the Chiefs of Staff Sub-Committee of the Committee of Imperial Defence, 1923–1939', PhD, University of London, 1973, p. 115.

23. A. C. Pedley, 'Notes on the Days that are Passed, 1877–1927', n.d., p. 137. War Office Library A.011.1.

24. Imperial War Museum, Interviews between Col. Lawson and Col. Brinsley Fitzgerald, Priv. Sec. to F.M. Sir John French, 22 May 1915. Burnham mss. I am grateful to Professor Keith Jeffery for drawing this remark to my attention.

25. Ian F. W. Beckett, '"Selection by Disparagement": Lord Esher, the General Staff and the Politics of Command, 1904–14', see Ch. 3 above; Cd. 1790, op. cit., Qs. 8911–8915 (Wolseley), 10 183 (Roberts). The only witness of any significance to depart from this shibboleth was Colonel Ian Hamilton, later to command the Dardanelles expedition: ibid., Qs. 13 889–13 902. The general view was shared by Campbell-Bannerman: see Michael Tadman, 'The War Office: A Study of its Development as an Organisational System 1870–1904', PhD, University of London, 1991, pp. 209–10.

26. Gary Sheffield, 'The Australians at Pozières: Command and Control on the Somme, 1916', see Ch. 7 above. On Rawlinson's command style, see Robin Prior and Trevor Wilson, *Command on the Western Front: The Military Career of Sir Henry Rawlinson 1914–18* (London: Blackwell, 1992), *passim*.

27. Public Record Office, 'Co-ordination of the Fighting Services', 28 June 1923. CAB 21/262. Quo. *Welch, Chiefs of Staff Sub-Committee*, p. 50.

28. Public Record Office, COS 6th meeting, 8 January 1924, Appendix: Consideration of Strategic Problems, Note by C.I.G.S. Quo. Brian Bond, *British Military Policy between the Two World Wars* (Oxford: Oxford University Press, 1980), p. 74.

29. National Archives, #2277-A-48/3, 'Visit to the Staff College at Camberley', 20 May 1932. Record Group 165 Box 1111.

30. National Archives, #R17420, 'What the Future Holds No.1 – Field Warfare', 28 February 1925, p.1. Record Group 165 Box 638.

31. Welch, *Chiefs of Staff Sub-Committee*, p. 167.

32. Hew Strachan, 'The British Army, its General Staff and the Continental Commitment 1904–14', see Ch. 5 above.

33. National Library of Scotland, Kitchener to Haig, 28 April 1909. Haig mss H/334/E.

34. Imperial War Museum, Wilson diary, 21 January 1907; 'Opening Remarks', 23 January 1907. Wilson mss HHW #1/16, 3/3/9.

35. Bond, *Staff College*, p. 266.

36. National Archives, #2277-A-63(25)/37153, 'Visit to the Staff College at Camberley', 9 March 1935. Record Group 165 Box 1112.

37. Bond, *Staff College*, p. 254; Field Marshal Wavell, *Generals and Generalship* (London: Times Publishing Co., 1941), p. 8.

38. Imperial War Museum, Nicholson–Wilson correspondence, 29 August–September 1913. Wilson mss 2/70/9-16. See also K. M. Wilson, *The Policy of the Entente: Essays on the Determinants of British Foreign Policy, 1904–1914* (Cambridge: Cambridge University Press, 1985), pp. 130, 180; Zara Steiner, *The Foreign Office and Foreign Policy, 1898–1914* (Cambridge: Cambridge University Press, 1969), p. 124.

39. H. H. R. Bailes, 'The Influence of Continental Examples and Colonial Warfare upon the

Reforms of the Late Victorian Army', PhD, University of London, 1980, *passim*.

40. For example, the 20,000-man 'great' division that was made the basis of the British Expeditionary Force in 1906 was designed to be deployable in India: see John Gooch, *The Prospect of War: Studies in British Defence Policy 1847–1942* (London: Cass, 1981), pp. 108–9.

41. Richard A. Preston, *Canada and 'Imperial Defense'* (Durham, NC: Duke University Press, 1967), pp. 308–9.

42. Matthew S. Seligmann, 'A View from Berlin: Colonel Frederick Trench and the Development of British Perceptions of Aggressive German Intent, 1906–1910', *Journal of Strategic Studies*, vol. 23 no. 2 (2000), pp. 114–47. As Dr Seligmann rightly points out, it is virtually impossible to discern what effect attachés' reports had on the higher councils of the General Staff due to the destruction of the relevant War Office records. Some idea of what may have been lost to historians can be gleaned from the response of the Director-General of Mobilisation and Military Intelligence when questioned about the role of military attachés by the Royal Commission on the South African War: they wrote private letters to the head of their respective geographical sections, Nicholson said, 'and on matters of importance they frequently write to me'. Cd. 1790, op. cit., Q. 385.

43. William Philpott, 'The General Staff and the Paradoxes of Continental War', see Ch. 6 above.

44. Welch, op. cit., p. 33; Bond, *Military Policy*, p. 34.

45. Public Record Office, 30th meeting of COS committee, 27 May 1926. CAB 53/1. Quo. Welch, op. cit., pp. 85, 107.

46. A. J. Trythall, 'J. F. C. Fuller: Staff Officer Extraordinary', see Ch. 9 above.

47. National Archives, #2017-1147/1/33441, 'General Sir Ian Hamilton on the Next War', 14 February 1933. Record Group 165 Box 646.

48. National Archives, #2017-921(17)/24732, 'The Mechanized Force: Statement by Maj. Gen. C. Bonham Carter', 27 March 1929. Record Group 165 Box 643. See also R. H. Larson, *The British Army and the Theory of Armored Warfare, 1918–1940* (Newark: University of Delaware Press, 1984), p. 115.

49. National Archives, #2017-807 (32)/20536, 'War Principles uneffected [sic] by Mechanication [sic] – Statement of Sir George F. Milne, British Chief of Staff', 11 November 1927. Record Group 165 Box 639.

50. National Archives, #2017-807(41)/20944, 'Mechanized Force – A Critical Survey of the recent training operations at Aldershot, published in "The Fighting Forces",' [1928]. Record Group 165, Box 639. The extent of that revolution has only recently been properly appreciated: see David French, *Raising Churchill's Army: The British Army and the War against Germany 1919–1945* (Oxford: Oxford University Press, 2000), esp. pp. 12–32.

51. National Archives, #2017-807(18)/20263, 'Visit to the Chief of the Imperial General Staff', 13 September 1927. Record Group 165 Box 639. Milne appears to have been reiterating themes of an address given to officers of the mechanised force at Tidworth on 8 September: French, *Raising Churchill's Army*, p. 14. (French does not include the observation about Antwerp in his account.)

52. J. P. Harris, 'The British General Staff and the Coming of War, 1933–39', see Ch. 11 above. Imperial War Museum. 'Lecture on Initiative & on Power of Manoeuvre', December 1909. Wilson mss 3/3/15W.

53. National Archives, #2017-1232/1/36900, 'The British Army and Intervention on the Continent', 18 January 1935. Record Group 165 Box 647.

54. National Archives, #2017-1025/34/38431, 'National Defence Policy Pertaining to Army, Navy and Air-General', 17 December 1936. Record Group 165 Box 643.

55. For contradictory views of how well Military Intelligence assessed the German army's doctrine and capabilities up to 1940, see J. P. Harris, 'British Military Intelligence and the Rise of German Mechanized Forces, 1929–1940', *Intelligence and National Security*, vol. 6, no. 2 (1991), pp. 395–417; Tim Harrison Place, 'British Perceptions of the Tactics of the German Army, 1938–40', *Intelligence and National Security*, vol. 9, no. 3 (1991), pp. 495–519.

56. John Ferris, '"Worthy of Some Better Enemy?": The British Estimate of the Imperial Japanese Army 1919–41, and the Fall of Singapore', *Canadian Journal of History*, vol. XVIII, no. 2 (1993), pp. 224–56 (esp. p. 231).

57. Philip Towle, 'The British General Staff and Japan, 1918–41', see Ch. 8 above. See also

Antony Best, 'Constructing an Image: British Intelligence and Whitehall's Perception of Japan, 1931–1939', *Intelligence and National Security*, vol. 11, no. 3 (1996), pp. 403–23. For a rare foray into the world of military attachés, see Edward Roland Sword (ed. Elizabeth Turnbull and Adrzej Suchcitz), *The Diary and Despatches of a Military Attaché in Warsaw 1938–1939* (London: Polish Cultural Foundation, 2001).

58. Imperial War Museum, Gort to R. D. Inskip, 30 August 1938. Gort-Inskip mss no. 37.
59. David French, '"An Extensive Use of Weedkiller": Patterns of Promotion in the Senior Ranks of the British Army, 1919–39', see Ch. 10 above.

Notes on Contributors

Ian F. W. Beckett is Major-General Matthew C. Horner Distinguished Professor of Military Theory at the US Marine Corps University, Quantico, Virginia for 2002–03. He was previously Professor of Modern History at the University of Luton and has also been Visiting Professor of Strategy at the US Naval War College. His publications include *The Great War, 1914–18* (2001).

David French was educated at the University of York and at King's College London, where he was supervised as a doctoral student by Brian Bond. He is Professor of History in the Department of History at University College London. In 2001 his most recent book, *Raising Churchill's Army. The British Army and the War Against Germany, 1919–1945* (2000) was awarded the Templer Medal by the Society for Army Historical Research.

John Gooch is Professor of International History at the University of Leeds. He has been the co-editor of the *Journal of Strategic Studies* since 1978 and is Series Co-editor of the Cass Series on Military History and Policy. His recent publications include *Decisive Campaigns of the Second World War* (1990), *Air Power: Theory and Practice* (1996), and *The Boer War. Direction, Experience and Image* (2000).

Paul Harris is a Senior Lecturer in War Studies at the Royal Military Academy Sandhurst. He read History at King's College London and has a PhD in War Studies from King's College. He is the author of *Amiens to the Armistice* (1998), *Men, Ideas and Tanks: British Military Thought and Armoured Forces* (1995), co-editor of *Armoured Warfare* (1990), and has contributed articles to a large number of books and academic journals.

Brian Holden Reid is Professor of American History and Military Institutions and Head of the Department of War Studies at King's College London. From 1987 to 1997 he was seconded by the Department to the Staff College, Camberley, where he served as Resident Historian, and was the first civilian to serve on the Directing Staff for over a century. He is the author of numerous publications on British and American military history, including *J. F. C. Fuller: Military Thinker* (1987), and *The American Civil War and the Wars of the Industrial Revolution* (1999).

Halik Kochanski is the author of *Sir Garnet Wolseley* (1999). She has been a College Lecturer at University College London and a Visiting Lecturer at King's College London.

Timothy Moreman is a Visiting Fellow in War Studies at King's College London. He was educated at the University of Reading and took a first-class honours degree in history and international relations before going on to complete both an MA and a PhD in War Studies at King's College. He is the author of *The Army in India and the Development of Frontier Warfare, 1849–1947* (1998).

William Philpott worked with Brian Bond as a post-doctoral researcher between 1991 and 1992 on a joint research project at King's College London on British civil–military relations since 1850. After holding teaching posts at North London, Bradford and London Guildhall Universities, he rejoined the War Studies Department at King's College in 2002 as Lecturer in Military History. He is the author of *Anglo-French Relations and Strategy on the Western Front, 1914–18* (1996) and co-editor (with Martin Alexander) of *Anglo-French Defence Relations Between the Wars* (2002).

Gary Sheffield is Senior Lecturer in Defence Studies, King's College London, and Land Warfare Historian on the Higher Command and Staff Course, Joint Services Command and Staff College, Shrivenham. His most recent book is *Forgotten Victory: The First World War – Myth and Reality* (2001).

Hew Strachan is Chichele Professor of the History of War at Oxford University and a Fellow of All Souls. His most recent book is *The First World War, Volume 1: To Arms* (2001).

John Sweetman read Modern History at Brasenose College Oxford and gained his PhD at King's College London. He was formerly the Head of Defence and International Affairs at the Royal Military Academy, Sandhurst, and is currently an Honorary Research Fellow at Keele University.

Philip Towle is Reader in International Relations at the University of Cambridge. His two most recent books are *Enforced Disarmament from the Napoleonic Campaigns to the Gulf War* (1997) and *Democracy and Peacemaking: Negotiations and Debates 1815–1973* (2000).

A. J. Trythall served in the Royal Army Education Corps from 1947 to 1949 and from 1953 to 1984. From 1984 to 1995 he was Managing Director and subsequently Deputy Chairman of Brassey's. In 1969 he took an MA in War Studies with distinction under Brian Bond and has published *'Boney' Fuller: the Intellectual General* (1977).

Index